Japanese Constitutional Revisionism and Civic Activism

Japanese Constitutional Revisionism and Civic Activism

Edited by Helen Hardacre,
Timothy S. George, Keigo Komamura,
and Franziska Seraphim

LEXINGTON BOOKS
Lanham • Boulder • New York • London

Published by Lexington Books
An imprint of The Rowman & Littlefield Publishing Group, Inc.
4501 Forbes Boulevard, Suite 200, Lanham, Maryland 20706
www.rowman.com

6 Tinworth Street, London SE11 5AL, United Kingdom

British Library Cataloguing in Publication Information Available

Library of Congress Cataloging-in-Publication Data

Library of Congress Control Number: 2021932928

ISBN: 978-1-7936-0906-9 (paper)
ISBN: 978-1-7936-0905-2 (electronic)

Contents

PART II: ACTIVISTS FOR AND AGAINST CONSTITUTIONAL REVISION, EDITED BY HELEN HARDACRE

PART III: UNDERSTANDING JAPANESE CONSTITUTIONAL REVISION IN HISTORICAL AND COMPARATIVE PERSPECTIVES, EDITED BY FRANZISKA SERAPHIM

PART IV: HUMAN RIGHTS AND ENVIRONMENTAL ISSUES IMPLICATED IN CONSTITUTIONAL REVISION DEBATES, EDITED BY TIMOTHY S. GEORGE

Acknowledgments

Japanese Constitutional Revisionism and Civic Activism results from joint research conducted by members of the research project on Japanese constitutional revision, sponsored by the Edwin O. Reischauer Institute of Japanese Studies at Harvard University, Keio University's Faculty of Law, and Keio University Global Research Institute over the years 2015 through 2019. The authors and editors are deeply indebted to both institutions for their generous support. In addition to the Reischauer Institute, the Asia Center at Harvard supported an international workshop, as did Oberlin College. The project also received support from the Northeast Asia Council of the Association for Asian Studies.

This volume could not have been completed without the support and participation of numerous colleagues. In addition to the authors whose research appears in this volume, previous workshops and conferences on which this volume builds benefited greatly from participation by colleagues at Harvard and Keio Universities: Theodore Bestor, Mary Brinton, Christina Davis, Shinju Fujihira, Theodore Gilman, Andrew Gordon, Susan Pharr, Mark Ramseyer, Daniel Smith, Karen Thornber, former President of Keio Atsushi Seike, Yuichirō Shimizu, Hideko Sumita, Juro Iwatani, and Junya Nishino. Deepest thanks are due also to the Boston Consulate-General of Japan, former Consul General Rokuichirō Michii, former Consul General Tsutomu Himeno, and Aiko Inoue. We also wish to thank colleagues who have participated in project events over the years: Richard Samuels, Sheila Smith, Thomas Berger, Emer O'Dwyer, Ingu Hwang, Tokujin Matsudaira, Kenneth Mori McElwain, Yasuo Hasebe, Yongwook Ryu, Chaihark Hahm, Kyle Hecht, and Mina Watanabe.

Among Reischauer Institute staff, special thanks go to Stacie Matsumoto, Gavin Whitelaw, Katherine Matsuura, Hannah Perry, Sachie Shishido,

Yukari Swanson, Maya Holden, and Ruiko Connor. In addition to contributing an essay to this volume, Dr. Makiko Ueda has served as the project assistant in charge of data collection and documentation concerning issues of special interest to project advisors. Numerous Harvard graduate students have worked on the project, including Kumiko Igushi, Shi-lin Loh, Adam Lyons, Katrina Moore, Michael Thornton, Eric Swanson, and Benjamin Cox. Graduate students from Keio also contributed greatly to the project, including Masatoshi Kokubo, Jun Mihara, Mai Sugaya, Tomoshi Yoshikawa, Kodai Zukeyama, and Anthony Campana.

The editors particularly wish to thank Alexis Dudden, who serves as an advisor to the project, for her many contributions over the years, including workshop and conference presentations and initial drafting of Appendix entries. Her participation has contributed greatly to the present volume, and the editors are deeply grateful.

Warm thanks also to Eric Kuntzman and Hannah Fisher of Lexington Books for shepherding this volume to publication; to indexer extraordinaire, Dave Prout; and to the Reischauer Institute for funding the indexing.

The Constitution of Japan

We, the Japanese people, acting through our duly elected representatives in the National Diet, determined that we shall secure for ourselves and our posterity the fruits of peaceful cooperation with all nations and the blessings of liberty throughout this land, and resolved that never again shall we be visited with the horrors of war through the action of government, do proclaim that sovereign power resides with the people and do firmly establish this Constitution. Government is a sacred trust of the people, the authority for which is derived from the people, the powers of which are exercised by the representatives of the people, and the benefits of which are enjoyed by the people. This is a universal principle of mankind upon which this Constitution is founded. We reject and revoke all constitutions, laws, ordinances, and rescripts in conflict herewith.

We, the Japanese people, desire peace for all time and are deeply conscious of the high ideals controlling human relationship, and we have determined to preserve our security and existence, trusting in the justice and faith of the peace-loving peoples of the world. We desire to occupy an honored place in an international society striving for the preservation of peace, and the banishment of tyranny and slavery, oppression and intolerance for all time from the earth. We recognize that all peoples of the world have the right to live in peace, free from fear and want.

We believe that no nation is responsible to itself alone, but that laws of political morality are universal; and that obedience to such laws is incumbent upon all nations who would sustain their own sovereignty and justify their sovereign relationship with other nations.

We, the Japanese people, pledge our national honor to accomplish these high ideals and purposes with all our resources.

CHAPTER I. THE EMPEROR

- Article 1. The Emperor shall be the symbol of the State and of the unity of the people, deriving his position from the will of the people with whom resides sovereign power.
- Article 2. The Imperial Throne shall be dynastic and succeeded to in accordance with the Imperial House Law passed by the Diet.
- Article 3. The advice and approval of the Cabinet shall be required for all acts of the Emperor in matters of state, and the Cabinet shall be responsible therefor.
- Article 4. The Emperor shall perform only such acts in matters of state as are provided for in this Constitution and he shall not have powers related to government.
  (2) The Emperor may delegate the performance of his acts in matters of state as may be provided by law.
- Article 5. When, in accordance with the Imperial House Law, a Regency is established, the Regent shall perform his acts in matters of state in the Emperor's name. In this case, paragraph one of the preceding article will be applicable.
- Article 6. The Emperor shall appoint the Prime Minister as designated by the Diet.
  (2) The Emperor shall appoint the Chief Judge of the Supreme Court as designated by the Cabinet.
- Article 7. The Emperor, with the advice and approval of the Cabinet, shall perform the following acts in matters of state on behalf of the people:

  1. Promulgation of amendments of the constitution, laws, cabinet orders and treaties.
  2. Convocation of the Diet.
  3. Dissolution of the House of Representatives.
  4. Proclamation of general election of members of the Diet.
  5. Attestation of the appointment and dismissal of Ministers of State and other officials as provided for by law, and of full powers and credentials of Ambassadors and Ministers.
  6. Attestation of general and special amnesty, commutation of punishment, reprieve, and restoration of rights.
  7. Awarding of honors.
  8. Attestation of instruments of ratification and other diplomatic documents as provided for by law.
  9. Receiving foreign ambassadors and ministers.
  10. Performance of ceremonial functions.

- Article 8. No property can be given to, or received by, the Imperial House, nor can any gifts be made therefrom, without the authorization of the Diet.

CHAPTER II. RENUNCIATION OF WAR

- Article 9. Aspiring sincerely to an international peace based on justice and order, the Japanese people forever renounce war as a sovereign right of the nation and the threat or use of force as means of settling international disputes.
  (2) In order to accomplish the aim of the preceding paragraph, land, sea, and air forces, as well as other war potential, will never be maintained. The right of belligerency of the state will not be recognized.

CHAPTER III. RIGHTS AND DUTIES OF THE PEOPLE

- Article 10. The conditions necessary for being a Japanese national shall be determined by law.
- Article 11. The people shall not be prevented from enjoying any of the fundamental human rights. These fundamental human rights guaranteed to the people by this Constitution shall be conferred upon the people of this and future generations as eternal and inviolate rights.
- Article 12. The freedoms and rights guaranteed to the people by this Constitution shall be maintained by the constant endeavor of the people, who shall refrain from any abuse of these freedoms and rights and shall always be responsible for utilizing them for the public welfare.
- Article 13. All of the people shall be respected as individuals. Their right to life, liberty, and the pursuit of happiness shall, to the extent that it does not interfere with the public welfare, be the supreme consideration in legislation and in other governmental affairs.
- Article 14. All of the people are equal under the law and there shall be no discrimination in political, economic or social relations because of race, creed, sex, social status or family origin.
  (2) Peers and peerage shall not be recognized.
  (3) No privilege shall accompany any award of honor, decoration or any distinction, nor shall any such award be valid beyond the lifetime of the individual who now holds or hereafter may receive it.
- Article 15. The people have the inalienable right to choose their public officials and to dismiss them.

(2) All public officials are servants of the whole community and not of any group thereof.
(3) Universal adult suffrage is guaranteed with regard to the election of public officials.
(4) In all elections, secrecy of the ballot shall not be violated. A voter shall not be answerable, publicly or privately, for the choice he has made.

- Article 16. Every person shall have the right of peaceful petition for the redress of damage, for the removal of public officials, for the enactment, repeal or amendment of laws, ordinances or regulations and for other matters; nor shall any person be in any way discriminated against for sponsoring such a petition.
- Article 17. Every person may sue for redress as provided by law from the State or a public entity, in case he has suffered damage through illegal act of any public official.
- Article 18. No person shall be held in bondage of any kind. Involuntary servitude, except as punishment for crime, is prohibited.
- Article 19. Freedom of thought and conscience shall not be violated.
- Article 20. Freedom of religion is guaranteed to all. No religious organization shall receive any privileges from the State, nor exercise any political authority.
  (2) No person shall be compelled to take part in any religious act, celebration, rite or practice.
  (3) The State and its organs shall refrain from religious education or any other religious activity.
- Article 21. Freedom of assembly and association as well as speech, press and all other forms of expression are guaranteed.
  (2) No censorship shall be maintained, nor shall the secrecy of any means of communication be violated.
- Article 22. Every person shall have freedom to choose and change his residence and to choose his occupation to the extent that it does not interfere with the public welfare.
  (2) Freedom of all persons to move to a foreign country and to divest themselves of their nationality shall be inviolate.
- Article 23. Academic freedom is guaranteed.
- Article 24. Marriage shall be based only on the mutual consent of both sexes and it shall be maintained through mutual cooperation with the equal rights of husband and wife as a basis.
  (2) With regard to choice of spouse, property rights, inheritance, choice of domicile, divorce and other matters pertaining to marriage and the family, laws shall be enacted from the standpoint of individual dignity and the essential equality of the sexes.

- Article 25. All people shall have the right to maintain the minimum standards of wholesome and cultured living.
  (2) In all spheres of life, the State shall use its endeavors for the promotion and extension of social welfare and security, and of public health.
- Article 26. All people shall have the right to receive an equal education correspondent to their ability, as provided by law.
  (2) All people shall be obligated to have all boys and girls under their protection receive ordinary education as provided for by law. Such compulsory education shall be free.
- Article 27. All people shall have the right and the obligation to work.
  (2) Standards for wages, hours, rest and other working conditions shall be fixed by law.
  (3) Children shall not be exploited.
- Article 28. The right of workers to organize and to bargain and act collectively is guaranteed.
- Article 29. The right to own or to hold property is inviolable.
  (2) Property rights shall be defined by law, in conformity with the public welfare.
  (3) Private property may be taken for public use upon just compensation therefor.
- Article 30. The people shall be liable to taxation as provided by law.
- Article 31. No person shall be deprived of life or liberty, nor shall any other criminal penalty be imposed, except according to procedure established by law.
- Article 32. No person shall be denied the right of access to the courts.
- Article 33. No person shall be apprehended except upon warrant issued by a competent judicial officer which specifies the offense with which the person is charged, unless he is apprehended, the offense being committed.
- Article 34. No person shall be arrested or detained without being at once informed of the charges against him or without the immediate privilege of counsel; nor shall he be detained without adequate cause; and upon demand of any person such cause must be immediately shown in open court in his presence and the presence of his counsel.
- Article 35. The right of all persons to be secure in their homes, papers and effects against entries, searches and seizures shall not be impaired except upon warrant issued for adequate cause and particularly describing the place to be searched and things to be seized, or except as provided by Article 33.
  (2) Each search or seizure shall be made upon separate warrant issued by a competent judicial officer.

- Article 36. The infliction of torture by any public officer and cruel punishments are absolutely forbidden.
- Article 37. In all criminal cases the accused shall enjoy the right to a speedy and public trial by an impartial tribunal.
  (2) He shall be permitted full opportunity to examine all witnesses, and he shall have the right of compulsory process for obtaining witnesses on his behalf at public expense.
  (3) At all times the accused shall have the assistance of competent counsel who shall, if the accused is unable to secure the same by his own efforts, be assigned to his use by the State.
- Article 38. No person shall be compelled to testify against himself.
  (2) Confession made under compulsion, torture or threat, or after prolonged arrest or detention shall not be admitted in evidence.
  (3) No person shall be convicted or punished in cases where the only proof against him is his own confession.
- Article 39. No person shall be held criminally liable for an act which was lawful at the time it was committed, or of which he has been acquitted, nor shall he be placed in double jeopardy.
- Article 40. Any person, in case he is acquitted after he has been arrested or detained, may sue the State for redress as provided by law.

CHAPTER IV. THE DIET

- Article 41. The Diet shall be the highest organ of state power, and shall be the sole law-making organ of the State.
- Article 42. The Diet shall consist of two Houses, namely the House of Representatives and the House of Councillors.
- Article 43. Both Houses shall consist of elected members, representative of all the people.
  (2) The number of the members of each House shall be fixed by law.
- Article 44. The qualifications of members of both Houses and their electors shall be fixed by law. However, there shall be no discrimination because of race, creed, sex, social status, family origin, education, property or income.
- Article 45. The term of office of members of the House of Representatives shall be four years. However, the term shall be terminated before the full term is up in case the House of Representatives is dissolved.
- Article 46. The term of office of members of the House of Councillors shall be six years, and election for half the members shall take place every three years.

- Article 47. Electoral districts, method of voting and other matters pertaining to the method of election of members of both Houses shall be fixed by law.
- Article 48. No person shall be permitted to be a member of both Houses simultaneously.
- Article 49. Members of both Houses shall receive appropriate annual payment from the national treasury in accordance with law.
- Article 50. Except in cases provided by law, members of both Houses shall be exempt from apprehension while the Diet is in session, and any members apprehended before the opening of the session shall be freed during the term of the session upon demand of the House.
- Article 51. Members of both Houses shall not be held liable outside the House for speeches, debates or votes cast inside the House.
- Article 52. An ordinary session of the Diet shall be convoked once per year.
- Article 53. The Cabinet may determine to convoke extraordinary sessions of the Diet. When a quarter or more of the total members of either House makes the demand, the Cabinet must determine on such convocation.
- Article 54. When the House of Representatives is dissolved, there must be a general election of members of the House of Representatives within forty (40) days from the date of dissolution, and the Diet must be convoked within thirty (30) days from the date of the election.
  (2) When the House of Representatives is dissolved, the House of Councillors is closed at the same time. However, the Cabinet may in time of national emergency convoke the House of Councillors in emergency session.
  (3) Measures taken at such session as mentioned in the proviso of the preceding paragraph shall be provisional and shall become null and void unless agreed to by the House of Representatives within a period of ten (10) days after the opening of the next session of the Diet.
- Article 55. Each House shall judge disputes related to qualifications of its members. However, in order to deny a seat to any member, it is necessary to pass a resolution by a majority of two-thirds or more of the members present.
- Article 56. Business cannot be transacted in either House unless one-third or more of total membership is present.
  (2) All matters shall be decided, in each House, by a majority of those present, except as elsewhere provided in the Constitution, and in case of a tie, the presiding officer shall decide the issue.
- Article 57. Deliberation in each House shall be public. However, a secret meeting may be held where a majority of two-thirds or more of those members present passes a resolution therefor.

(2) Each House shall keep a record of proceedings. This record shall be published and given general circulation, excepting such parts of proceedings of secret session as may be deemed to require secrecy.
(3) Upon demand of one-fifth or more of the members present, votes of members on any matter shall be recorded in the minutes.

- Article 58. Each House shall select its own president and other officials.
(2) Each House shall establish its rules pertaining to meetings, proceedings and internal discipline, and may punish members for disorderly conduct. However, in order to expel a member, a majority of two-thirds or more of those members present must pass a resolution thereon.
- Article 59. A bill becomes a law on passage by both Houses, except as otherwise provided by the Constitution.
(2) A bill which is passed by the House of Representatives, and upon which the House of Councillors makes a decision different from that of the House of Representatives, becomes a law when passed a second time by the House of Representatives by a majority of two-thirds or more of the members present.
(3) The provision of the preceding paragraph does not preclude the House of Representatives from calling for the meeting of a joint committee of both Houses, provided for by law.
(4) Failure by the House of Councillors to take final action within sixty (60) days after receipt of a bill passed by the House of Representatives, time in recess excepted, may be determined by the House of Representatives to constitute a rejection of the said bill by the House of Councillors.
- Article 60. The budget must first be submitted to the House of Representatives.
(2) Upon consideration of the budget, when the House of Councillors makes a decision different from that of the House of Representatives, and when no agreement can be reached even through a joint committee of both Houses, provided for by law, or in the case of failure by the House of Councillors to take final action within thirty (30) days, the period of recess excluded, after the receipt of the budget passed by the House of Representatives, the decision of the House of Representatives shall be the decision of the Diet.
- Article 61. The second paragraph of the preceding article applies also to the Diet approval required for the conclusion of treaties.
- Article 62. Each House may conduct investigations in relation to government, and may demand the presence and testimony of witnesses, and the production of records.
- Article 63. The Prime Minister and other Ministers of State may, at any time, appear in either House for the purpose of speaking on bills, regardless

of whether they are members of the House or not. They must appear when their presence is required in order to give answers or explanations.

- Article 64. The Diet shall set up an impeachment court from among the members of both Houses for the purpose of trying those judges against whom removal proceedings have been instituted.
  (2) Matters relating to impeachment shall be provided by law.

CHAPTER V. THE CABINET

- Article 65. Executive power shall be vested in the Cabinet.
- Article 66. The Cabinet shall consist of the Prime Minister, who shall be its head, and other Ministers of State, as provided for by law.
  (2) The Prime Minister and other Ministers of State must be civilians.
  (3) The Cabinet, in the exercise of executive power, shall be collectively responsible to the Diet.
- Article 67. The Prime Minister shall be designated from among the members of the Diet by a resolution of the Diet. This designation shall precede all other business.
  (2) If the House of Representatives and the House of Councillors disagree and if no agreement can be reached even through a joint committee of both Houses, provided for by law, or the House of Councillors fails to make designation within ten (10) days, exclusive of the period of recess, after the House of Representatives has made designation, the decision of the House of Representatives shall be the decision of the Diet.
- Article 68. The Prime Minister shall appoint the Ministers of State. However, a majority of their number must be chosen from among the members of the Diet.
  (2) The Prime Minister may remove the Ministers of State as he chooses.
- Article 69. If the House of Representatives passes a non-confidence resolution, or rejects a confidence resolution, the Cabinet shall resign en masse, unless the House of Representatives is dissolved within ten (10) days.
- Article 70. When there is a vacancy in the post of Prime Minister, or upon the first convocation of the Diet after a general election of members of the House of Representatives, the Cabinet shall resign en masse.
- Article 71. In the cases mentioned in the two preceding articles, the Cabinet shall continue its functions until the time when a new Prime Minister is appointed.
- Article 72. The Prime Minister, representing the Cabinet, submits bills, reports on general national affairs and foreign relations to the Diet and exercises control and supervision over various administrative branches.

- Article 73. The Cabinet, in addition to other general administrative functions, shall perform the following functions:

  1. Administer the law faithfully; conduct affairs of state.
  2. Manage foreign affairs.
  3. Conclude treaties. However, it shall obtain prior or, depending on circumstances, subsequent approval of the Diet.
  4. Administer the civil service, in accordance with standards established by law.
  5. Prepare the budget, and present it to the Diet.
  6. Enact cabinet orders in order to execute the provisions of this Constitution and of the law. However, it cannot include penal provisions in such cabinet orders unless authorized by such law.
  7. Decide on general amnesty, special amnesty, commutation of punishment, reprieve, and restoration of rights.

- Article 74. All laws and cabinet orders shall be signed by the competent Minister of State and countersigned by the Prime Minister.
- Article 75. The Ministers of State, during their tenure of office, shall not be subject to legal action without the consent of the Prime Minister. However, the right to take that action is not impaired hereby.

CHAPTER VI. JUDICIARY

- Article 76. The whole judicial power is vested in a Supreme Court and in such inferior courts as are established by law.
  (2) No extraordinary tribunal shall be established, nor shall any organ or agency of the Executive be given final judicial power.
  (3) All judges shall be independent in the exercise of their conscience and shall be bound only by this Constitution and the laws.
- Article 77. The Supreme Court is vested with the rule-making power under which it determines the rules of procedure and of practice, and of matters relating to attorneys, the internal discipline of the courts and the administration of judicial affairs.
  (2) Public procurators shall be subject to the rule-making power of the Supreme Court.
  (3) The Supreme Court may delegate the power to make rules for inferior courts to such courts.
- Article 78. Judges shall not be removed except by public impeachment unless judicially declared mentally or physically incompetent to perform

official duties. No disciplinary action against judges shall be administered by any executive organ or agency.

- Article 79. The Supreme Court shall consist of a Chief Judge and such number of judges as may be determined by law; all such judges excepting the Chief Judge shall be appointed by the Cabinet.
  (2) The appointment of the judges of the Supreme Court shall be reviewed by the people at the first general election of members of the House of Representatives following their appointment, and shall be reviewed again at the first general election of members of the House of Representatives after a lapse of ten (10) years, and in the same manner thereafter.
  (3) In cases mentioned in the foregoing paragraph, when the majority of the voters favors the dismissal of a judge, he shall be dismissed.
  (4) Matters pertaining to review shall be prescribed by law.
  (5) The judges of the Supreme Court shall be retired upon the attainment of the age as fixed by law.
  (6) All such judges shall receive, at regular stated intervals, adequate compensation which shall not be decreased during their terms of office.
- Article 80. The judges of the inferior courts shall be appointed by the Cabinet from a list of persons nominated by the Supreme Court. All such judges shall hold office for a term of ten (10) years with privilege of reappointment, provided that they shall be retired upon the attainment of the age as fixed by law.
  (2) The judges of the inferior courts shall receive, at regular stated intervals, adequate compensation which shall not be decreased during their terms of office.
- Article 81. The Supreme Court is the court of last resort with power to determine the constitutionality of any law, order, regulation or official act.
- Article 82. Trials shall be conducted and judgment declared publicly.
  (2) Where a court unanimously determines publicity to be dangerous to public order or morals, a trial may be conducted privately, but trials of political offenses, offenses involving the press or cases wherein the rights of people as guaranteed in Chapter III of this Constitution are in question shall always be conducted publicly.

CHAPTER VII. FINANCE

- Article 83. The power to administer national finances shall be exercised as the Diet shall determine.
- Article 84. No new taxes shall be imposed or existing ones modified except by law or under such conditions as law may prescribe.

- Article 85. No money shall be expended, nor shall the State obligate itself, except as authorized by the Diet.
- Article 86. The Cabinet shall prepare and submit to the Diet for its consideration and decision a budget for each fiscal year.
- Article 87. In order to provide for unforeseen deficiencies in the budget, a reserve fund may be authorized by the Diet to be expended upon the responsibility of the Cabinet.
  (2) The Cabinet must get subsequent approval of the Diet for all payments from the reserve fund.
- Article 88. All property of the Imperial Household shall belong to the State. All expenses of the Imperial Household shall be appropriated by the Diet in the budget.
- Article 89. No public money or other property shall be expended or appropriated for the use, benefit or maintenance of any religious institution or association, or for any charitable, educational or benevolent enterprises not under the control of public authority.
- Article 90. Final accounts of the expenditures and revenues of the State shall be audited annually by a Board of Audit and submitted by the Cabinet to the Diet, together with the statement of audit, during the fiscal year immediately following the period covered.
  (2) The organization and competency of the Board of Audit shall be determined by law.
- Article 91. At regular intervals and at least annually the Cabinet shall report to the Diet and the people on the state of national finances.

CHAPTER VIII. LOCAL SELF-GOVERNMENT

- Article 92. Regulations concerning organization and operations of local public entities shall be fixed by law in accordance with the principle of local autonomy.
- Article 93. The local public entities shall establish assemblies as their deliberative organs, in accordance with law.
  (2) The chief executive officers of all local public entities, the members of their assemblies, and such other local officials as may be determined by law shall be elected by direct popular vote within their several communities.
- Article 94. Local public entities shall have the right to manage their property, affairs and administration and to enact their own regulations within law.

- Article 95. A special law, applicable only to one local public entity, cannot be enacted by the Diet without the consent of the majority of the voters of the local public entity concerned, obtained in accordance with law.

CHAPTER IX. AMENDMENTS

- Article 96. Amendments to this Constitution shall be initiated by the Diet, through a concurring vote of two-thirds or more of all the members of each House and shall thereupon be submitted to the people for ratification, which shall require the affirmative vote of a majority of all votes cast thereon, at a special referendum or at such election as the Diet shall specify.
  (2) Amendments when so ratified shall immediately be promulgated by the Emperor in the name of the people, as an integral part of this Constitution.

CHAPTER X. SUPREME LAW

- Article 97. The fundamental human rights by this Constitution guaranteed to the people of Japan are fruits of the age-old struggle of man to be free; they have survived the many exacting tests for durability and are conferred upon this and future generations in trust, to be held for all time inviolate.
- Article 98. This Constitution shall be the supreme law of the nation and no law, ordinance, imperial rescript or other act of government, or part thereof, contrary to the provisions hereof, shall have legal force or validity.
  (2) The treaties concluded by Japan and established laws of nations shall be faithfully observed.
- Article 99. The Emperor or the Regent as well as Ministers of State, members of the Diet, judges, and all other public officials have the obligation to respect and uphold this Constitution.

CHAPTER XI. SUPPLEMENTARY PROVISIONS

- Article 100. This Constitution shall be enforced as from the day when the period of six months will have elapsed counting from the day of its promulgation.
  (2) The enactment of laws necessary for the enforcement of this Constitution, the election of members of the House of Councillors and the procedure for the convocation of the Diet and other preparatory procedures

necessary for the enforcement of this Constitution may be executed before the day prescribed in the preceding paragraph.

- Article 101. If the House of Councillors is not constituted before the effective date of this Constitution, the House of Representatives shall function as the Diet until such time as the House of Councillors shall be constituted.
- Article 102. The term of office for half the members of the House of Councillors serving in the first term under this Constitution shall be three years. Members falling under this category shall be determined in accordance with law.
- Article 103. The Ministers of State, members of the House of Representatives, and judges in office on the effective date of this Constitution, and all other public officials who occupy positions corresponding to such positions as are recognized by this Constitution shall not forfeit their positions automatically on account of the enforcement of this Constitution unless otherwise specified by law. When, however, successors are elected or appointed under the provisions of this Constitution, they shall forfeit their positions as a matter of course.

Chronology of Events Related to Constitutional Revision in Japan

February 11, 1889	Promulgation of the Constitution of the Empire of Japan.
February 1946	The Constitution of Japan was drafted by staff of the Allied Occupation of Japan.
	Formation of the Association of Shinto Shrines (*Jinja Honchō*).
November 3, 1946	The Constitution of Japan was promulgated.
May 3, 1947	The Constitution of Japan went into effect.
June 1950	Outbreak of the Korean War.
September 8, 1951	Japan signed the Treaty of Peace with Japan (*San Furanshisuko Kōwa Jōyaku*, together with the U.S.-Japan Security Treaty (*Nichibei Anpo Jōyaku*; effective April 28, 1952).
April 1952	Japan regained full sovereignty; end of the occupation.
July 21, 1952	Passage of the Anti-Subversive Activities Act (*Hakai katsudō bōshi hō*).
July 1, 1954	Formation of the Defense Agency and the Self-Defense Force of Japan.
November 1955	Formation of the Liberal Democratic Party (*Jiyū minshū tō*).
September 1956	Student demonstrations protesting the expansion of the Tachikawa Air Base begin, accompanied by violent clashes with the police.
October 12, 1956	In the "Bloody Sunagawa" incident, some 3,000 protesters clashed with 1,400 armed riot police in Sunagawa Town, near the Tachikawa Air Base.

December 18, 1956	Japan joined the United Nations.
July 8, 1957	A group of students protesting the expansion of the Tachikawa Air Base, near Sunagawa Town, entered the base and erected barriers to prevent aircraft from takeoff or landing. They were arrested on charges of trespassing, marking the beginning of the Sunagawa case.
November 5, 1958	A reported four million persons participated in demonstrations opposing revision of the U.S.-Japan Security Treaty.
December 16, 1959	The Supreme Court, in ruling on the Sunagawa case, declared that it should not pass judgment on the constitutionality of issues of political significance.
January 19, 1960	Signing of the revised Treaty of Mutual Cooperation and Security (the U.S.-Japan Security Treaty) between Japan and the United States of America.
1959–1960	Widespread protests against the U.S.-Japan Security Treaty.
November 17, 1964	Founding of Kōmeitō.
1969	Formation of the parliamentarians' group affiliated with the Association of Shinto Shrines (*Shintō seiji renmei*).
1970	Widespread protests against the the U.S.-Japan Security Treaty.
November 25, 1971	Author Yukio Mishima and a subordinate in his Shield Society committed suicide after failing to provoke the Self-Defense Force to stage a coup d'état and demand constitutional revision.
September 29, 1972	Normalization of Sino-Japanese relations.
October 14, 1972	The Cabinet Legislative Bureau formalized the government's official position to the effect that Japan possesses the right to collective self-defense, but not the right to exercise it.
1973–1984	Otaru Canal Preservation Movement.
1976	Formation of the Society to Answer the War Dead, aiming to re-establish state support for the Yasukuni Shrine.
October 27, 1978	Yasukuni Shrine installed the spirits of Hideki Tōjō and other Class-A war criminals as deities of the shrine.
June 6, 1979	Passage of the Era Name Law (*Gengo hō*).

1981	Founding of the People's Council to Protect Japan (*Nihon o Mamoru Kokumin Kaigi*), the predecessor of Nippon Kaigi.
February 24, 1989	State funeral for Emperor Hirohito.
January 24, 1991	Government decision to contribute funds, but not troops, to the U.S.-led coalition of forces in the first Gulf War.
April 26, 1991–October 1991	Six minesweeper vessels of the Self-Defense Force were deployed to the Persian Gulf.
June 15, 1992	Passage of the Peacekeeping Operations Cooperation Law and the International Emergency Assistance Troop Dispatch Law, allowing for overseas deployment of the Self-Defense Force to participate in United Nations missions for medical and reconstruction support, policing, election monitoring, and other purposes.
August 19, 1992–September 1993	The Self-Defense Force participated in a United Nations Peacekeeping Operation in Cambodia.
1992	Nippon Kaigi issued its "Outline for a New Constitution."
May 1993–January 1995	The Self-Defense Force participation in a United Nations Peacekeeping Operation in Mozambique.
August 6, 1993	Coalition government began, under Prime Minister Morihiro Hosokawa of the Japan New Party.
September–December 1994	Deployment of the Self-Defense Force to assist the United Nations international disaster relief effort in Rwanda.
November 3, 1994	The *Yomiuri* Newspaper issued a draft for a revised constitution.
1994	Revision of the election law, to introduce the "First-Past-the Post" system in the Lower House.
February 1996	Self-Defense Force deployed to the Golan Heights.
January 30, 1997	Formation of the Society for the Making of New History Textbooks (*Atarashii Rekishi Kyōkasho o Tsukuru Kai*).
May 30, 1997	Formation of Nippon Kaigi and its associated group of affiliated parliamentarians (*Nippon Kaigi kokkai giin kondankai*).
November–December 1998	Self-Defense Force deployed to assist the United Nations international disaster relief effort in Honduras.

August 9, 1999	Passage of a law giving official status to the national flag and the national anthem (*Kokki Kokka Hō*).
September–November 1999	Self-Defense Force deployed to assist United Nations international disaster relief effort in Turkey.
October 16, 2000	Publication of the Armitage Report, "The United States and Japan: Advancing Toward a Mature Partnership," calling on Japan to establish emergency laws permitting the exercise of collective self-defense.
December 2001	After a six-hour confrontation off Amami Ōshima with a vessel later determined to be a spy ship belonging to North Korea, the Japanese Coast Guard sank that ship.
2001	Self-Defense Force deployed to assist the United Nations international disaster relief effort in Afghanistan.
February 2002–June 2004	Self-Defense Force deployed to assist the United Nations international disaster relief effort in East Timor.
December 2003–January 2004	Self-Defense Force deployed to assist the United Nations international disaster relief effort in Iran.
February 4, 2004	Dispatch of 9,600 Self-Defense Force troops to Samawa, Iraq, in support of the U.S.-led reconstruction of Iraq.
December 2004–January 2005	Self-Defense Force deployed to assist the United Nations international disaster relief effort in Thailand.
January–March 2005	Self-Defense Force deployed to assist the United Nations international disaster relief effort in Indonesia.
June 2005	The LDP issued a draft of issues to be revised in the constitution, titled "Points of Discussion" (*Ronten seiri*), advocating revision of Article 9 and Article 24, which upholds "the essential equality of the sexes," and also advocating a statement of the duty of the people to support the family.
June 1, 2005	Self-Defense Force dispatched to Indonesia to assist in disaster relief activities.
August 1, 2005	LDP publishes its first draft constitution organized into articles. The draft, referred to as the Mori Draft, deletes Article 9's prohibition on maintaining armaments and provides for the creation of a Self-Defense Army.

December 28, 2005	Self-Defense Force ships dispatched to Thailand's Phuket Island, to assist in disaster relief following a massive tidal wave and earthquake.
2005	Self-Defense Force deployed to assist the United Nations international disaster relief efforts in Indonesia, Russia, and Pakistan.
October 12, 2006	Self-Defense Force dispatched to Pakistan to assist in disaster relief following a massive earthquake.
December 22, 2006	Revision of the Fundamental Law on Education (*Kyōiku kihon hō*).
2006	Self-Defense Force deployed to assist the United Nations international disaster relief effort in Indonesia.
May 14, 2007	The Upper House passes the National Referendum Law governing revisions of the constitution. The legislation holds that a referendum on the issue cannot take place before 2010, and requires the approval of a majority of voters.
January 2008–January 2010	Self-Defense Force deployed to the Indian Ocean to provide water and fuel to U.S. military ships.
February 7, 2008	The Tokyo District Court ordered the Tokyo Metropolitan Government to pay 27.5 million yen in lost wages to thirteen former high school teachers who were denied post-retirement re-employment because they refused to sing the national anthem. The teachers had been reprimanded for disobeying a metropolitan directive of October 2003 that required all teachers to stand and sing the anthem while facing the national flag during official school ceremonies.
October 2009	Self-Defense Force deployed to assist the United Nations international disaster relief effort in Indonesia.
December 10, 2010	Self-immolation of a protester in Tunisia sparked the beginning of the Arab Spring.
2010	Self-Defense Force deployed to assist the United Nations international disaster relief efforts in Haiti and Pakistan.
March 11, 2011	Japan rocked by a triple disaster: the largest earthquake in recorded history, a tidal wave that destroyed large areas of northeastern Japan, and a nuclear meltdown.

July 1, 2011	Opening of the Self-Defense Force Counter-Piracy Facility in Djbouti.
September 2011	The Occupy Wall Street Movement began.
2011	Self-Defense Force deployed to assist the United Nations international disaster relief effort in New Zealand.
April 27, 2012	The LDP issued a full draft for a revised constitution with an accompanying booklet for general readers.
2012	Founding of Association Q (Association to Promote Quotas), to facilitate an increase of female political representatives.
December 2013	Passage of a new law on state secrets, the Act on the Protection of Specially Designated Secrets (*Tokutei Himitsu no Hogo ni kansuru Hōritsu*).
April 2014	Founding of Constitutional Democracy, a group of scholars opposed to constitutional revision as promoted by the Abe administration.
December 15, 2014	Formation of the All-Out Action Committee (*Sōgakari*), opposed to constitutional revision as promoted by the Abe administration.
2014	Formation of the Society for the Creation of a Constitution for Beautiful Japan.
	Sunflower Movement in Taiwan; Umbrella Movement in Hong Kong.
May 3, 2015	Foundation of SEALDs (Students Emergency Action for Liberal Democracy.
June 2015	Formation of the Association of Scholars Opposed to the Security Bills.
July 2015	Foundation of Mothers Against War, a protest group opposed to constitutional revision.
September 17, 2015	Passage of new security legislation, allowing Japan to exercise the right of collective self defense. Massive demonstrations protesting the legislation, involving 60,000 to 100,000 persons ensued, lasting several months and extending across the country.
December 20, 2015	Formation of the Civil Alliance for Peace and Constitutionalism, an alliance of the major groups opposed to constitutional revision.
2015	Formation of the Parliamentarians' Group for Women's Political Participation and Empowerment.

Summer, 2016	SEALDs disbanded.
October 13, 2016	The LDP announced its decision henceforth to treat its 2012 draft for a new constitution as a "historical document," rather than the basis for further inter-party negotiations on constitutional revision.
October 30, 2016	The Women's Active Museum on War and Peace (Tokyo), a feminist group promoting increased Japanese government funding for the former "comfort women" of Korea, received a bomb threat in response to its exhibition of documents relating to the comfort women.
Late 2016	The Candlelight Struggle in South Korea helped lead to the impeachment of President Geun-hye Park in March 2017.
November 2016	Lawsuits challenging the constitutionality of the 2015 security legislation were raised in eleven District Courts.
2016	During this year, the Japan Coast Guard sighted Chinese Coast Guard vessels infringing maritime territory claimed by Japan around the Senkaku Islands (Chinese: Diaoyu Islands) thirty-six times.
January 6, 2017	A Tokyo court ordered suspension of publication of a book about Nippon Kaigi by Osamu Aoki, titled *Nippon Kaigi no Shōtai*, based on a claim of defamation by an individual depicted in the book.
November 3, 2017	Nippon Kaigi announced that it seeks revision of article 24, the clause declaring "the essential equality of the sexes."
May 2018	Passage of the Gender Parity Law (Law for the Promotion of Gender Parity in Politics).
2018	Publication of proposals for a new kind of debate on constitutional revision, "rooted in constitutionalism," by Shiori Yamao in *Rikkenteki Kaiken: Kenpō wo Riberaru ni Kangaeru Nanatsu no Tairon* (Chikuma Shinsho).
April 30, 2019	Abdication of Emperor Akihito.
2020	The corona virus (COVID-19) pandemic began.
September 16, 2020	Shinzō Abe resigned as Prime Minister, succeeded by Yoshihide Suga.

Introduction

Helen Hardacre and Keigo Komamura

RESEARCHING THE DEBATE ON CIVIC ACTIVISM SURROUNDING CONSTITUTIONAL REVISION

This volume stems from joint research undertaken by the Constitutional Revision in Japan Research Project[1] at the Edwin O. Reischauer Institute of Japanese Studies, Harvard University, and the Faculty of Law, Keio University. Following an agreement signed in 2015 and renewed in 2018 with the Keio University Global Research Institute, project leaders decided to adopt a project titled "The 'Constitution' of Postwar Japan" (*Sengo Nihon no 'Katachi'*), adopting the double meaning in English of the word *constitution*, as a nation's basic code of law on the one hand, and on the other, following the *Oxford English Dictionary*, "the way in which anything is constituted or made up; the arrangement or combination of its parts or elements, as determining its nature and character." The project aims to use debate surrounding Japan's basic law code as a springboard for broader investigations of the issues shaping contemporary Japan. The project is co-directed by Komamura Keigo (Keio University, Faculty of Law) and Helen Hardacre (Reischauer Institute, Harvard University). The essays in this volume have been edited by Hardacre, Komamura, Timothy George (University of Rhode Island), and Franziska Seraphim (Boston College).[2] Two conferences were held at Keio, in 2015 and 2016, with a third conference held at Harvard on November 3, 2017, the seventieth anniversary of the promulgation of the Constitution of Japan. An International Workshop was held at Keio in late 2019.

This collection of essays presents fourteen studies of contemporary civic activism in the context of Japanese legal culture as well as in historical and comparative perspective, noting links to other kinds of activism, such as those focused on human rights and protection of the environment. Revisionists in Japan seek, among other things, to enhance the powers of the head of government, and thus their activism should be understood in comparison to South Korean, Taiwanese, and Chinese revisionism, which all share that goal. Analysis of activism concerning constitutional revision in Japan includes identifying its ideological commitments, the legal interpretations that activists adopt or dispute, activists' international connections, and relations with domestic party politics.

While a comprehensive study of all the activist organizations that debate constitutional revision exceeds the scope of any single volume, this collection introduces a wide range of activists and their projects, with a variety of perspectives on the issues. These studies take a broad view of civic activism, including student and labor union activists, public intellectuals, political party members, and the residents of specific communities. Activists' methods vary tremendously, from political demonstrations in public spaces like the area in front of the National Diet Building, with speeches adopting call-and-response chants addressed to huge audiences, to negotiations with legislators; politicians drafting proposals for constitutional revision; organizations collaborating to lobby prefectural, city, and town assemblies; and counter-cultural displays using song, dance, and music, as well as mass meetings in formal settings. Activists differ greatly in their use of media, from such established formats as newsletters, magazines, pamphlets, and books, to hosting websites, producing DVDs, and sponsoring YouTube channels, cable TV outlets, and social media of many kinds.

JAPAN'S DEBATE ON CONSTITUTIONAL REVISION

Formally speaking, the Constitution of Japan (*Nihon Koku Kenpō*, implemented 1947) represents a revision of The Constitution of the Empire of Japan (*Nihon Teikoku Kenpō*, 1889). In fact, however, the postwar constitution was drafted by officials of the American Occupation of Japan in a mere seven days in 1946, at the direction of the Supreme Commander of the Allied Powers, General Douglas MacArthur. MacArthur set aside an indigenous project to amend Japan's constitution, led by Japanese legal scholars, because in his view their revisions did not go far enough. Once the American drafters had done their work and Japanese objections had been negotiated, the Japanese Diet (the Parliament) ratified the document. Many Japanese welcomed the new constitution. Because Japan was still under censorship when the fact of the constitution's foreign authorship became widely known, criticism was muted. After Japan regained sovereignty in 1952, the Liberal Democratic Party (founded 1955) adopted constitutional revision as a goal. Meanwhile, the new constitution's principles of popular sovereignty, human rights, and pacifism gained strong popular support. While conservatives made numerous proposals for revision (Winkler, this volume), they gained so little "traction" that the issue was informally tabooed. While constitutional revision retained great symbolic importance among nationalists, it appeared to be a dead issue as far as the political agenda was concerned until the 1990s.

As long as the generations who had experienced Japan's prewar and wartime regime remained active, constitutional revision remained deeply unpopular, because revisionists appeared to favor a return to the ideals and institutions of the imperial period. Support for preserving the constitution without change remained bedrock solid. As that generation passed into retirement, however, Japan's relations with the United States began to change, resulting in pressure on Japan to revise Article 9, the clause renouncing war:

> ARTICLE 9. (1) Aspiring sincerely to an international peace based on justice and order, the Japanese people forever renounce war as a sovereign right of the nation and the threat or use of force as means of settling international disputes. (2) In order to accomplish the aim of the preceding paragraph, land, sea, and air forces, as well as other war potential, will never be maintained. The right of belligerency of the state will not be recognized.

Specifically, the U.S. pressured Japan to send troops to the First Gulf War of 1990 to 1991. When Japan demurred, citing the restrictions established by Article 9 and sending monetary support instead of troops, it was widely ridiculed. This galling diplomatic humiliation produced new impetus in government to reconsider Article 9. Since that time, Japan's geopolitical situation has further shifted due to the rise of China and continued provocations from a nuclear-armed North Korea. The rapidly evolving situation has made constitutional revision seem an urgent necessity to some and more palatable to others. Meanwhile, younger generations less attached to retaining the constitution unchanged have taken the reins in politics, and changes in the electoral system have greatly enhanced the power of the prime minister and the party secretary-general in candidate selection, making politicians fear reprisals if they should oppose the party platform on constitutional revision.[3]

Since the 1990s, Japan has been debating new proposals to revise Japan's postwar constitution, accompanied by significant political activity and civic engagement. The 1994 publication by the *Yomiuri* newspaper of a draft for a new constitution was a watershed event that broke through foregoing taboos on discussing the issue. The Liberal Democratic Party published a new draft constitution in 2005, issuing a revised version of that draft in 2012. It was so ubiquitously criticized that the party later issued a simple list of four points for revision that constitute its publicly announced agenda at present.[4] LDP prime ministers, especially Abe Shinzō, have loudly proclaimed their intention to pursue constitutional revision. Politicians like Ishiba Shigeru and Yamao Shiori (Kuramochi, this volume), scholars such as Inoue Tatsuo, professor of jurisprudence at Tokyo University, the other political parties, major newspapers, business associations, and a variety of civil society groups have also become involved. Many of them have issued their own drafts for a new constitution.

While proposals to amend Article 9 have received the most discussion, other changes proposed for the constitution itself and for related laws could significantly alter Japan's military defense (the U.S.-Japan Alliance, especially), the status of women, imperial succession (including provisions for female succession to the throne), the educational system, and public corporations (a category which includes non-profit organizations, foundations, social welfare organizations, and religious organizations), and other issues. Because such sweeping legal changes could transform political, diplomatic, economic, social, and religious institutions, constitutional revision carries wide-ranging implications for Japanese society and politics.

THE CONTEMPORARY HISTORY OF CIVIC ACTIVISM REGARDING CONSTITUTIONAL REVISION

Civic activism surrounding constitutional revision has developed in the context of a longer history of Japanese civil society, as shown in Nakano's and Ueda's essays in this volume. The fountainhead of all subsequent civic activism was the Anpo protests of the 1960s and 1970s. The term *Anpo* is the conventional abbreviation used in Japanese to refer to the "Treaty of Mutual Cooperation and Security between the United States and Japan."[5] Signed in 1951 along with the Treaty of San Francisco that officially ended the war, the security treaty permitted U.S. military forces to remain in Japan even after Japan regained sovereignty. When LDP Prime Minister Kishi Nobusuke (1896–1987) proposed to revise the treaty in 1960 to allow the U.S. to maintain permanent military bases in Japan in return for a commitment to defend Japan in the event of an attack, the largest protest movement in postwar Japanese history unfolded. Led by university students, labor union members, and intellectuals opposed to the U.S. bases, violent confrontations with the police in Tokyo and around the military bases, as well as student "occupations" of universities and related protests, roiled Japanese society for several years. Veterans of the Anpo protests, including those who opposed the protesters and supported the government position, later re-emerged in the debates over constitutional revision.

Political activism during the 1970s targeted the war in Vietnam and was largely identified with the Citizen's League for Peace in Vietnam (informally called *Beheiren*), led by novelist and peace activist Oda Makoto (1932–2007). Beheiren served as an umbrella for numerous organizations opposed to the war in Vietnam and to Japan's role as a staging ground for the conflict. Anti-war activism was followed by a period of relative inactivity in the 1980s. Japan fell into a recession at the beginning of the 1990s that continued for more than a decade. Economic woes contributed to student apathy and sapped the left of youthful energy. On the right, the organizations that later amalgamated to form *Nippon Kaigi* ("Japan Conference," the largest umbrella organization of civil society groups favoring constitutional revision; see Ueda, and Hardacre, this volume) galvanized in opposition to those on the left, attracting the support of numerous religious groups and conservative spokespeople. The best-selling celebrity *manga* writer Kobayashi Yoshinori popularized his evolving opinions on a variety of topics, including constitutional revision, sometimes adopting liberal positions, sometimes taking a nationalist stance.

In the 2000s, Nippon Kaigi and other activists on the right gained strength through political lobbying at all levels of government, surpassing their opponents on the left. Nippon Kaigi and its affiliates, especially the Association of Shinto Shrines (*Jinja Honchō*), expanded their activities to every prefecture and succeeded in passing resolutions in favor of constitutional revision in the legislatures of almost every one of them.

The triple disasters of earthquake, tidal wave, and nuclear meltdowns that occurred on March 11, 2011, devastated much of northeastern Japan, leaving it contaminated with radioactivity. The government's promotion of nuclear power was widely criticized, as was the media, which initially downplayed the scale of the disaster. Reflecting the widespread consensus that the government's response was unforgivably incompetent and weak, civil society groups of every description galvanized to help northeastern Japan recover. The ongoing revitalization effort re-energized civic activism on an unprecedented scale, setting the stage for a period of intense activism about constitutional revision. Activism on the left was reignited by opposition to new security legislation passed in July 2015, which removed former restrictions on "collective self-defense" and handed the government new powers to deploy Japan's military forces in coalition with the U.S. (see Soeya, this volume).[6] Whereas foregoing interpretations of Article 9 had strictly limited military deployments to self-defense or peacekeeping operations under the auspices of the United Nations, the new legislation permitted broader use of the military, spelling out situations in which Japan could extend logistical support to the U.S. military even when Japan itself was not under direct threat and in locations as far away as the Middle East. Moreover, the legislation permits the prime minister to act unilaterally, seeking Diet ratification of his decisions only after the fact.

The legislation met strong resistance from opposition parties, and it was greeted by massive protests outside the Diet building and around the country, continuing for months. Demonstrations associated with the student group SEALDs saw crowds numbering from 60,000 to 100,000 people in August 2015. Opponents argued that the new legislation was unconstitutional and violated Article 9. In their view, the government had effectively gutted Article 9, bypassing the formal revision process, thereby denying the people their right to ratify or reject a new constitution. Opponents used social media to attract large numbers of university students and others to repeated public demonstrations across the country. These protests revealed massive opposition to LDP proposals for constitutional revision and represent the most intense civic activism around the issue up to the time of this writing (2020).

THE ORGANIZATION OF THIS VOLUME

The essays are divided into four Parts. Each Part includes "Reflections" authored by the editor of that Part as its final component. Part I, "Activism and Constitutional Politics," edited by Komamura, discusses aspects of the relationship between civic activism and constitutional politics in postwar Japan. The essays by Komamura and Yamamoto take up an early instance of civic activism bearing on the constitution that preceded the Anpo protests and involved a wide spectrum of participants. The Sunagawa case (1959) of the Supreme Court of Japan was a landmark decision in Japan's constitutional and political history, provoking debate around Article 9, and effectively removing the Supreme Court as highest arbiter on constitutional questions. The "Sunagawa struggle" was the first postwar civic movement that drew public attention to the proliferation of nuclear weapons and the connection between that issue and the presence of U.S. military bases on Japanese soil. Komamura clarifies the legal and political implications of the Sunagawa judgment, arguing that the Supreme Court—at least in the text of its decision—affirmed the role of civic activism in debating politically charged constitutional issues such as the U.S. military bases. Yamamoto tries to elicit hitherto unseen implications of the Anpo protests, questioning the conventional understanding of them as an unsullied icon of liberalism. Nakano holds that the Abe government has precipitated a crisis for Japanese democracy, along with a "crisis of representation." He spotlights the roles of media in civic activism, showing how major media outlets, subject to varying degrees of pressure from state regulators, sway public opinion, stimulate activists, and inspire them to create independent media to facilitate communications free of state interference. Nakano also examines the evolving repertoire of protest techniques stemming from the 1960s. He shows how Japanese activists have forged ties with other progressive movements in Hong Kong, Taiwan, and the U.S. Kuramochi discusses revision proposals inside and outside government, focusing on proposals by legislator Yamao Shiori of the Constitutional Democratic Party of Japan (CDPJ, *Rikken minshutō*).[7] Yamao seeks to provoke debate about the constitution based on liberalism, suggesting among other things that the constitution be revised to recognize same-sex marriage, and changing Article 9 to limit the use of Japan's military forces to self-defense. Prior to her initiative, political parties outside the ruling coalition had generally declined to participate in revision discussions, based on their determination to leave the constitution unchanged. From Yamao's perspective, this stance has left CDPJ on the periphery of important arguments on which it should not keep silent. Kuramochi also discusses a movement among journalists, *manga* authors, and researchers seeking a "third way" beyond "for" or "against" positions on constitutional revision.

Part II, "Activists for and against Constitutional Revision," edited by Hardacre, examines activists on all sides of the debate. Makiko Ueda's essay analyzes the discourse of revisionism and its rhetoric of "constitutionalism." Along with "sovereignty," and "sovereign people" (see Komamura, Nakano, and Horikawa this volume), constitutionalism emerges as a key concept structuring the philosophical dimension of the debate. Miura discusses feminists' success in passing the Gender Parity Law,[8] which pressures political parties to nominate an equal number of female and male electoral candidates. Basing themselves on Article 14, guaranteeing equal protection under the law regardless of sex (and other differentiations), Article 24, which proclaims "the essential equality of the sexes," and Article 44, which prohibits discrimination against electors based on sex, feminist activists succeeded in challenging the electoral system so that it more fully embodies these constitutional guarantees. As a result, the proportion of opposition parties' female candidates significantly increased in the Upper House election of 2019, with smaller increases in the LDP and its junior partner Kōmeitō. McLaughlin and Hardacre highlight the importance of religious organizations in constitutional revision activism. McLaughlin addresses the meanings of activism within the Buddhist religious group Sōka Gakkai, which founded the "Clean Government Party" (Kōmeitō) in 1964. Sōka Gakkai is solidly committed to pacifism, based on its leader's position, but since 1993 Kōmeitō has allied with the LDP as its coalition partner. Until recently, Sōka Gakkai members unanimously supported Kōmeitō and performed significant electioneering for the LDP, but as Prime Minister Abe moved with greater determination to change

Article 9, members are becoming increasingly uneasy. They face an irresolvable quandary, striving both to remain influential in government and to be true to their religious convictions, with many expressing pained ambivalence. Hardacre examines Nippon Kaigi, its history, strategies for garnering support for constitutional revision, and its connections with religious organizations, whose members and facilities it uses to promote its agenda, particularly the Association of Shinto Shrines.

Part III, "Understanding Japanese Constitutional Revision in Historical and Comparative Perspectives," edited by Seraphim, takes up the possibilities and significance of comparative research on constitutional revision. It considers how we may best understand the relation between current Japanese revisionism and that occurring elsewhere in East Asia (Chen and Kim), as well as the relation of contemporary Japanese activism to earlier phases of the debate in Japan (Soeya). Chen compares Taiwan's approaches to constitutional revision adopted during the 1990s with strategies seen in Japan in 2015. He finds that in spite of Taiwan's legacy of authoritarian rule, its methods were more democratic than the tactics adopted in Japan. He further compares the role of the U.S. in both cases; in Taiwan the U.S. encouraged constitutional revision, but only within limits that would not provoke China, while in Japan it has favored constitutional revision in order to secure Japanese military cooperation. Sung Ho Kim notes that the leaders of both Japan (Abe Shinzō) and South Korea (Moon Jae-in) are intent on constitutional revision. Yet while South Korea has revised its constitution nine times and Japan has never formally revised, Japan has arguably changed more and Korea less. One striking change was Japan's creation of the Self-Defense Force (Jieitai) in 1954, a de facto military force, without changing Article 9. In other words, the way in which constitutionalism is enacted may change drastically without a formal amendment (Japan), while the nature of constitutionalism may remain largely the same even after multiple amendments (Korea). Both Kim and Soeya note that the Cold War and the Korean War broke out soon after Japan's postwar constitution went into effect, and that it was probably inevitable that changes to the constitution or its interpretation would arise to cope with new and unanticipated circumstances. Soeya's essay compares earlier changes in interpretation of Article 9 that first created the Self-Defense Force and then in 1960 permitted permanent U.S. military bases to exist in Japan, on the one hand, with changes enacted through security legislation affirming collective self-defense in 2015, on the other. He finds that while each prime minister in charge at the time vigorously declared his intention to achieve independence from the U.S. through overturning postwar reforms, each actually ended up deepening Japan's entrenchment within its alliance with the U.S.

Part IV, "Human Rights and Environmental Issues Implicated in Constitutional Revision Debates," edited by Timothy George, examines the repercussions of the constitutional revision debate for related discussions regarding human rights and protection of the environment. This Part addresses the place of these issues in current drafts for a new Japanese constitution, analyzes how local- and national-level civic action are coordinated, and sets the issues of human rights and the environment in the larger context of East Asia. Revisionists frequently point to Article 9 as an instance of victors' justice, a wrongful foreign imposition of "irrational pacifism." Erik Esselstrom counters this view with a study of Japanese war resisters in China during the 1930s who used the language of human rights to craft a vision of postwar pacifism for Japan. Not only a product of postwar reforms, Japanese human rights discourse has roots in the experience of these war resisters who perceived a connection between the agony of the Chinese people under Japanese imperialism and the suffering of the Japanese people under a fascist regime. Horikawa examines a historic preservation movement in Otaru City, Hokkaidō Prefecture seeking to preserve a historic canal, noting a similarity between its activists' style of self-presentation and the student group SEALDs. The examples demonstrate activists' concern to differentiate themselves from the radical protesters of the 1960s, whom people today associate with destructive tactics and internecine violence. Horikawa links progressive activists' rhetoric of preservation and their non-threatening self-presentation style to a shared vision of popular sovereignty stemming from the constitution. Winkler examines the content of forty-four proposals for constitutional revision composed by conservative elites since 1947, emphasizing changes aiming, on the one hand, to alter or decrease constitutionally guaranteed rights, or on the other, to increase the number of constitutionally mandated duties that citizens must fulfill. He identifies a distinctive rhetoric seen in proposals aiming to require new duties, such as respecting the flag and anthem, defending the nation, and preserving Japanese tradition, stemming from a widely held belief among conservative proponents of revision. The belief, seen also in the LDP's original proclamation of its intention to revise the constitution, holds that the occupiers' motive for the 1946 drafting of a new constitution was to destroy the customs, traditions, and spirit of the Japanese people. While this notion is only rarely stated so baldly, it comes through in revisionists' proposals over the last seven decades and is still echoed by pro-revision activists.

NOTES

1. Founded in 2005, the Constitutional Revision in Japan Research Project, sponsored by the Edwin O. Reischauer Institute of Japanese Studies, Harvard University,

pursues research on the contemporary debate about constitutional revision in the longer historical context of constitutionalism in Japan. Identifying relevant digital materials is a major focus for the project. Because information on current activities of individuals and groups involved in the issue is mainly "born digital," the project's website collects and produces digital resources to assist researchers to access the debate.

2. George, Komamura, Seraphim, and Dudden serve as advisors to the Harvard research project; Hardacre is its Director.

3. Arthur Stockwin and Kweku Ampiah, *Rethinking Japan: The Politics of Contested Nationalism* (Lanham, MD: Lexington Books/New Studies in Modern Japan, 2017), 76ff.

4. The four points call for a new constitution to (1) incorporate recognition of the Self-Defense Force into Article 9; (2) enhance the emergency powers of the Cabinet; (3) eliminate "combined districts" (*gōku*) in Upper House elections; and (4) expand the scope of education provided for free.

5. The Japanese title of the document is *Nihonkoku to Amerika gasshūkoku to no aida no sōgō kyōryoku oyobi anzen hoshō jōyaku*. For the text see https://www.mofa.go.jp/mofaj/area/usa/hosho/jyoyaku.html (accessed Feb. 20, 2020); for the English text see https://www.cia.gov/library/readingroom/docs/CIA-RDP07-00469R000100950001-2.pdf (accessed Feb. 20, 2020).

6. In contrast to the right of self-defense, the right to "collective self-defense" (*shūdanteki jiei ken*) includes going to the aid of an ally when the ally has been attacked. In the context, "ally" means the U.S.

7. Yamao moved to the Democratic Party for the People (DPFP, *Kokumin minshutō*) in 2020.

8. Law for the Promotion of Gender Parity in Politics (*Seiji bun'ya ni okeru danjo kyōdō sankaku suishin hō*).

Part I

ACTIVISM AND CONSTITUTIONAL POLITICS

Chapter One

Article 9 Meets Civic Activism

Reflection on the Sunagawa Case

Keigo Komamura

WHY SUNAGAWA MATTERS?

In the spring of 1945, Sunagawa, a village in western Tokyo, was bombed by American B-29 bombers targeting the nearby Tachikawa Airbase. Five years later, American B-29s were busily taking off from the same airbase to bomb Korea.

This is how the story of the Sunagawa struggle begins.[1] Sunagawa was originally a farm village in the suburbs of Tokyo, but in 1922, the Imperial Japanese Army Air Fleet opened a base in the village because of the location adjacent to the Tachikawa railway station. The convenient location made it easy for the army to transport fuel and soldiers to the base. In the 1920s, the air base was actually a dual-use airfield serving both civilian and military flights. Residents in the city seem to have been proud of the association with the air base as Tachikawa advertised itself as the first "*city of the sky*" in Japan.[2] It was in part due to this profile that Sunagawa became the target of airstrikes by B-29s during the final stages of WWII. The bombing was deliberately concentrated on the area surrounding the base.[3] The real target was Tachikawa city itself, and not the Tachikawa air base. As the war ended in 1945, the United States Air Force marched in and took over the Tachikawa air base undamaged.

When the Korean War broke out in 1950, the Tachikawa air base began to play an important role as one of the largest bases in the Far East for operations involving troop carrier units conducting the evacuation and relocation of U.S. civilians and transporting the flood of Allied military personnel and material into the Korean war zone. But the air base had a big problem. It was not suitable for larger aircraft, particularly for the jet fighters that had been newly introduced at that time. Even propeller aircraft struggled because the runway was only around 1,500 m (4,900 ft) long in its effective range. Thus, the U.S. decided to expand the air base for a longer runway, and then, on May 4th, 1955, the Tokyo branch office for the Public Procurement Service (the predecessor of the Defense Facilities Administration Agency) notified the town mayor of Sunagawa, Denzaemon Miyazaki (aka Miyaden-san) of its plan to expand the Tachikawa air base. The following day, it handed over the expropriation plan, indicating an intention to take over 126 farmhouses and 170,000 mi^2 land.[4] Members of the town council and other residents immediately formed an organization to oppose the plans and moved to action. They started protest campaigns against the coming land survey. This was the beginning of the Sunagawa struggle.

The struggle intensified, culminating in the so-called "bloody Sunagawa" (*ryūketsu no Sunagawa*) incident. In September 1956, many college students, union members, farmers, and residents gathered in the village to obstruct the compulsory land survey there. On October 12th, around 3,000 protesters and over 1,400 armed policemen clashed hard, and more than 260 were wounded. The next day, another clash took place, and around 200 were wounded. By the final stage of this uprising, both parties had become utterly exhausted, and they fell silent confronting each other at the border of the air base. While they were at a standstill, someone began singing a song. It was not a song of protest, but a nursery song, *Akatombo* ("red dragonfly"). Both parties joined in singing the song together.[5] On October 14th, facing public outcry over its handling of the "bloody Sunagawa" incident and criticisms of the police as "a cruel mob," the government decided to cancel the land survey.

The tension between the protesters and the police intensified again in 1957 because the Public Procurement Service announced another plan for a land survey. It was quite different from the former one. This time, the survey scheduled was for the land within the air base, not off-base. The lease contracts between the U.S. Air Force and the residents who owned the land within the base had expired, and the residents refused to renew them. Thus, the Air Force sought to seize the land in order to maintain its runway. The land survey was a legal prerequisite for the expropriation of the land. The protesters thus decided to break into the base to prevent the survey from being conducted. In order to do so, they would inevitably commit the crime of trespassing. The land survey was ultimately completed successfully before protesters could enter the base, but in the early morning on July 8th, 1957, radical students and workers intruded into the base and placed obstacles on the runway to prevent aircraft from taking off or landing. Two months later, these protesters were arrested on charges of trespassing. The arrests mark the beginning of the famous criminal case known as the *Sunagawa case.*

The Sunagawa Struggle as a New Civic Activism

The Sunagawa struggle and the Sunagawa case are of crucial importance for postwar Japan in a few respects. The Sunagawa struggle established a basic model for a new type of civic activism.

At the beginning, the team of protesters was formed by the members of the town council of Sunagawa and local farmers there. Soon after, the protest group expanded throughout the City of Tachikawa and neighboring towns. In the process of forming the protest group, not only male leaders, but also their wives and children participated in the activism. At that time, the Japanese Socialist Party (JSP) and its support organization, *Sōhyō* (*Nihon rōdōkumiai sōhyōgikai*: the General Council of Trade Unions of Japan [JCTU]) tried to change its policy and method of activity from an old model to a new one focused on community-based movements in line with the slogan "*kazoku gurumi, chiiki gurumi*" (a movement with all members of one's family and with the whole community).[6] The Sunagawa struggle became the prototypical example of this type of activity. The leadership of the local labor unions successfully mobilized a great number of workers with strong support from the JSP and Sōhyō. College students and public intellectuals like Ikutarō Shimizu, Yoshio Nakano, Tatsuzō Ishikawa, and Kazuo Hirotsu also joined the movement to offer both practical and moral support to protesters. The protests gradually gained nationwide support.[7]

This type of mass movement was unprecedented, but it appears that the mid-1950s saw such mobilizations began to spring up in response to various social issues. For example, the anti-nuclear movements that took place between 1954 and 1955 were ignited by the accident of the *Daigo Fukuryū Maru* fishing boat (Lucky Dragon No. 5), a victim of a U.S. hydrogen bomb test by the U.S. Anti-war movements of this kind were synchronized with the Sunagawa struggle. In what sense were these movements new? As Sasaki-Uemura suggests, "the old paradigm" of violent activism represented by the Japanese Communist Party (JCP) was beginning to be displaced by "an arc of protests that built up over the latter half of 1950s," the era of the Sunagawa struggle.[8] In October of 1951, the JCP declared the armed struggle policy in its manifesto, and in line with this policy, they created their *chūkaku jieitai* ("the core self-defense force") and *sanson kōsakutai* ("the village sappers") in line with Chinese people's front.[9] These radical measures brought about many intrigues and riots. Due to its violent activities, the JCP lost all of its seats in the House of Representatives in the national election of 1951. In response to the JCP's radicalism, the government passed the Anti-Subversive Activities Act (1952). At the 6th National Congress of the Party in July 1955, the JCP abandoned its armed struggle policy and opted to change course, no longer following the model of the Chinese Communist Party (CCP). As the

JCP shrank and worked to rebuild itself, the JSP and Sōhyō brought themselves to the forefront of Japanese politics as national politics came to be defined by the "1955 system." The term refers to the two-party system established in 1955 which saw the dominant LDP (the Liberal Democratic Party: the conservatives) competing against its major rival the JSP (the socialist Left). Under this arrangement, the JSP began to take reformist measures and to mold itself against its rival conservative counterpart.

Thus, while the JCP declined, the JSP and Sōhyō came to lead the new civic protests that developed in the latter half of 1950s. However, the local front of the Sunagawa struggle differed from this party-led activism. The JSP and Sōhyō tried to hold hegemony over the protests in Sunagawa and asked farmers and students there to preclude the JCP's members from joining the protests.[10] The local farmers and residents rejected these instructions from the JSP because they wanted to keep the protest open.

Furthermore, in November 1955, the JSP tried to make a deal with the government to exchange withdrawal of union members for withdrawal of policemen from the front line in Sunagawa. But this negotiation was seen as a betrayal. The result was that farmers had to fight against the police with no help from the members of Sōhyō. In September 1956, Ikutarō Shimizu, a famous public intellectual; Minoru Takano, a past chairman of Sōhyō; and Ichigorō Aoki, a leader of the protest, held a meeting with Morita Minoru, a student leader of the *Zengakuren* (*Zen nihon gakusei jichikai sōrengō*: the National Federation of Students' Self-Government Association). They urged Morita to mobilize students by suggesting that the JSP was about to make a compromise with the government and betray the protesters.[11] The local protesters in Sunagawa actually had a negative view on the student activists from the Zengakuren because they were communist sympathizers and regarded as being too radical. And Shimizu, a star in the intellectual society of the time, had a complicated but deep affection for communism.[12] Immediately after, Morita decided to support the protest and announced that the Zengakuren would mobilize and dispatch 3,000 students to Sunagawa. The student activists were welcomed and stood on the front line in the battlefield to protect the farmers and residents from the riot police. On the one hand, it appears that the form of the Sunagawa struggle was influenced indirectly by the JCP, communism, and the "old paradigm" of violent activism.[13] On the other hand, however, it is certain that the Sunagawa struggle yielded a novel style of civic engagement. While the students took an aggressive strategy against the police, they faithfully abided by Mao Zedong's rule of revolution, "Do no wrong to the farmers," and they did farmwork together with the residents. It would appear that the post-Sunagawa style of civic activism combined elements of the older model of communist political activism with the new model of full community engagement. This model too was eventually succeeded by new forms of civic activism that developed surrounding the 1960s Anpo Struggle.

The Sunagawa Struggle as Constitutional Protection Movement

The Sunagawa struggle was originally fighting for the farmers' land. Farmlands in the village had been repeatedly taken over by the government. It is also true, however, that the struggle was fighting to advocate for a particular interpretation of the constitution as well. One of the former Sunagawa protesters, Kiichi Hoshi, has been working to collect and publish accounts of the struggle, and he accurately points to three issues that tie the protests to public debates about the recently established Constitution of Japan. The 1946 Constitution had been created just nine years prior to the Sunagawa struggle, and debates about the interpretation of this foundational legal framework were one of the major features of the civic activism of the era.[14]

First, the Sunagawa protesters were advocating for the right to local self-government as guaranteed in Chapter 8 of the Constitution of Japan. The expansion of the air base's runway, if realized, would deprive the farmers not just of their lands but also of the right to determine their daily lifestyle by dividing up the main avenue running through the center of their community. The expansion would have violated their right to local autonomy and transformed residential life fundamentally.

Second, the protesters wanted to exercise their right to advocate for their own freedoms and rights in general. The protests could be seen as a civic exercise of the freedoms and rights guaranteed to the residents in the village. Ichigorō Aoki, the local leader of the protest, made this sentiment explicit at an early stage in the struggle: "They can drive a pile into our land but not into our mind."[15]

Third, the protesters wanted to express support for Article 9, the famous and controversial war renunciation clause inscribed in the postwar Constitution of Japan. Some Japanese people (then and now) viewed the expansion of the military base as effectively bringing more warfare to their country, and there were concerns about exacerbating the risk of nuclear war in particular.

In addition to these three issues that appear in Hoshi's accounts, I would also add that there was likely another underlying issue relevant to the constitution, and it is that of state sovereignty. After the end of WWII, many of the Japanese people welcomed the U.S. forces as if they were liberators. But the nationwide proliferation of U.S. military bases and the outbreak of the Korean War rapidly fomented anti-America sentiment among the Japanese. It was through the lens of this rebellious sentiment that people saw a policeman giving a rough kick to a young female protester as she cried for her mother during the bloody clash in 1956.[16] A young policeman who had joined the riot police resigned and committed suicide after his resignation, leaving a final note of regret about the violence perpetrated by the police.[17] All these tragedies fostered a grave doubt in people's minds: "For what reason do we, the Japanese people, have to fight each other over the American air force?"[18] So the Sunagawa struggle, and the 1960 Anpo struggle as well, can be understood in light of a growing nationalistic activism based upon a broad anti-America sentiment. In this sense, many Japanese people shared a growing sense that political activism was connected to the fight for *national independence from the U.S. and the assertion of national sovereignty*.

The Sunagawa Case as the First Close Encounter between Article 9 and Civic Activism

The uprisings and clashes of the struggle finally reached the courts in the form of criminal action of the Sunagawa case. As mentioned, it was on July 8th, 1957, that the protesters broke into the air base. Two months later, seven of them were arrested and charged with trespassing. What made this case exceptional was that the government charged them not with the ordinary crime of trespassing as defined by the general penal code of Japan, but rather with a more serious form of trespassing on the facilities of the stationed U.S. military forces defined by a special law enacted under the U.S.-Japan Security Treaty.

The defendants pleaded against the charges on the grounds that the U.S.-Japan Security Treaty violated Article 9 of the Constitution and that the special law therefore had no legal basis. Thus, the Sunagawa case became a constitutional controversy.

The case became the first opportunity for Article 9 and civic activism to meet together at the bench of the Supreme Court of Japan. Furthermore, as I mention later, the Sunagawa case went on to be retried in 2016, and utilized by a conservative revisionist as a way to justify his ambitions to repeal Article 9. In this sense, this truly landmark case is still alive and hanging over Japan like a ghost. In the following sections, I will focus on the judicial rulings regarding the Sunagawa case and the opinions and remarks made by the judges from the perspective of *constitutional law* (not *politics*) in order to articulate what *legal* professionals at that time thought about the issues of popular sovereignty, civic activism, and other political agendas surrounding Article 9.

THE SUNAGAWA CASE: REDUX

The first instance of the Sunagawa case was tried by the Tokyo District Court. On March 30th, 1959, Chief Judge Akio Date held that the court found the defendants not guilty simply because the U.S. Air Base and the U.S.-Japan Security Treaty violated Article 9 of the Constitution of Japan. Article 9 reads as follows:

> (1) Aspiring sincerely to an international peace based on justice and order, the Japanese people forever renounce war as a sovereign right of the nation and the threat or use of force as means of settling international disputes. (2) In order to accomplish the aim of the preceding paragraph, land, sea, and air forces, as well as other war potential, will never be maintained. The right of belligerency of the state will not be recognized.

In the opinion of the court, Judge Date interpreted Article 9 as demanding the government to not hold "war potential" (all military forces) in paragraph (2) while allowing to have a right to self-defense itself in paragraph (1). It is eminently clear that the U.S. Air Force was a form of war potential, and Date interpreted the stationing of the U.S. forces as the governmental conduct of Japan. Thus, Judge Date concluded that the stationing of the U.S. Air Force was unconstitutional because it violated Article 9.

The Japanese government was shocked by this judgment by the Tokyo District Court (aka *the Date ruling*) because the renewal of the Security Treaty had been scheduled to occur just one year later, January 1960. So the government stepped over the Court of Appeals and jumped onto the final appeal at the Supreme Court of Japan.

Main Holdings

On December 16, 1959, eight months after the Date's ruling and only one month before the renewal of the U.S. Security Treaty, the Supreme Court of Japan reversed the Date ruling on the basis of the so-called "political question doctrine"[19] by which the Court avoids touching constitutional issues. However, the text of the opinion is much more complicated and challenging. For example, here are excerpts from the text of the main holdings of the Sunagawa case.[20]

> Holding 1: "[I]t is only natural for our country, in the exercise of powers inherent in a state, to maintain peace and security, to take whatever measures may be necessary for self-defense, and to preserve its very existence. We, the people of Japan, do not maintain the so-called war potential provided in paragraph 2,

> Article 9 of the Constitution, but we have determined to supplement the shortcomings in our national defense resulting therefrom.

The Court states that our country can take *self-defense measures* as one of the powers inherent to a state. But Article 9 does not allow Japan to maintain *war potential*. So, "we, the people of Japan" need to supplement the shortcomings in our self-defense measures. The Court responds to this supplement.

> Holding 2: "This, however, does not necessarily mean that our recourse is limited to such military security measures as may be undertaken by *an organ of the United Nations, such as the Security Council*, as stated in the original decision. It is needless to say that we are free to choose whatever method or means deemed appropriate to accomplish our objectives in the light of the actual international situation, as long as such measures are for the purpose of preserving the peace and security of our country. Article 9 of the Constitution does not at all prohibit our country from *seeking a guarantee from another country in order to maintain the peace and security of the country*." (emphasis added)

Holding 2 clearly addresses that there are two options which Article 9 allows in order to "supplement the shortcomings" in self-defense measures: in context, these would be for Japan to rely on the Security Council of the United Nations or to seek a guarantee from another country such as the U.S. through the U.S.-Japan Alliance. According to this logic, it would be constitutionally viable to permit the U.S. military force to make arrangements to help Japan rectify any possible security shortcomings that may arise from the renunciation of war. The question arises: Is not the maintenance of a U.S. military force on Japanese soil precisely the kind of war potential that Article 9 explicitly prohibits? The Court replies:

> Holding 3: "[W]hat has been prohibited by this paragraph is the possession of war potential of our own over which we can exercise the right of command and supervision. In final analysis, it means the war potential of our country; and consequently, it may be properly construed that the provision of paragraph 2 does not include foreign armed forces even if they are to be stationed in our country."

As we can see, foreign armed forces such as the U.S. military do not fall under the scope of Article 9 because the Japanese government has no right to command and supervise these forces. In Holdings 1 to 3, as referrred to above, the Court articulates its constitutional interpretations of what measures Article 9 shall allow the government to take. If so, the next step for the Court to proceed to would be applying those constitutional interpretations to the stationing of the U.S. military force. But the Court narrows its frame of the scope of judicial review on these kind of issues.

> Holding 4: "The Security Treaty, . . . , is featured with an extremely high degree of political consideration, having bearing upon the very existence of our country as a sovereign power, and any legal determination as to whether the content of the treaty is constitutional or not is in many respects inseparably related to the high degree of political consideration or discretionary power on the part of the Cabinet which concluded the treaty and on the part of the Diet which approved it. Consequently, as a rule, there is a certain element of incompatibility in the process of judicial determination of its constitutionality by a court of law which has as its mission the exercise of the purely judicial function. Accordingly, *unless the said treaty is obviously unconstitutional and void at a glance*, it falls outside the purview of the power of judicial review granted to the court. It is proper to construe that the question of the determination of its constitutionality should be left primarily to the Cabinet which has the power to conclude treaties and the Diet which has the power to ratify them; and ultimately to the political criticism by the people with whom rests the sovereign power of the nation." (emphasis added)

The Court would not interfere in the constitutional controversy over these highly political issues on the basis of the so-called "political question doctrine." At the same time, however, in this Holding, the Court reserves the possibility of judicial review by noting that it would review issues if there were reason to believe them to be "obviously unconstitutional and void at a glance." That would mean the political question doctrine the Court invoked here is not a typical or original one.The doctrine in its original form[21] would have required that the Court refrain from touching on highly political questions *even if* those questions are obviously unconstitutional.

Along those lines, the Court applied its interpretations of Article 9 to the U.S.-Japan Security Treaty, and finally held that the stationing of the U.S. military force was *not obviously unconstitutional and void at a glance*.

Three Fates of Article 9 (1): Two Options to Take for the Self-Defense Measure

In my understanding, the Sunagawa case determined the three "fates" of Article 9, which would deeply affect the future of defense measures and the peace policy of Japan.

First, the opinion in the Sunagawa case provides two options for the government of Japan to take for its self-defense measures and peace policy. Holding 1 doesn't allow the government to maintain war potential and therefore admits some gaps or shortcomings in the defense measure of our country. In order to make up for these gaps, the Court offers an interpretation of Article 9 in Holding 2 that permits the government not only to rely on the Security Council of the United Nations but also to seek more security assurances from another country like the U.S. As many historians recognize, Japan shared a sentiment to go forwards and walk along with the United Nations for rebuilding the country (so-called UN centrism) at least during the early stages of the process of making the current Constitution of Japan.[22] Actually the preamble of the Constitution of Japan states, "We, the Japanese people, . . . are deeply conscious of *the high ideals controlling human relationship*, and we have determined to preserve our security and existence, trusting in the justice and faith of *the peace-loving people of the world*" (emphasis added). In his ruling at the first instance of the Sunagawa case, Judge Date also indicated this orientation towards the UN by relying on this section of the preamble, and he suggested that the stationing of the U.S. military forces in Japan would be not unconstitutional if the UN gave Japan an order to station such forces. Nonetheless, the Supreme Court places those different measures as parallel options without offering any particular reason. This could be because the Court was seeking to erase Judge Date's view because the Court intended to justify the U.S.-Japan Alliance.[23] This is the first fate of Article 9.

Three Fates of Article 9 (2): Normative Instability

In Holding 4, the Court invokes the political question not in the pure and original form, because it reserves the power of judicial review over the issue when and if the issue is "obviously unconstitutional and void at a glance." If the political question doctrine had been invoked in the pure form, the Court could have completed the case by just saying that the constitutionality of the Security Treaty was highly political (it is highly political indeed) and that it shall be a political question. Then, the Court would not have needed to make Holdings 1 through 3. However, the Court needed its interpretation of Article 9 in those Holdings because the Court wanted to reserve the power of review to ask whether or not the Security Treaty is "obviously unconstitutional and void at a glance." Important things follow from here: if the Security Treaty is taken to be a political question beyond the Court's review, then other issues, including the existence of *Jieitai* (the Self-Defense Force of Japan), the national security laws, and measures for the right to individual/collective self-defense, could similarly be declared political questions beyond the Court's review as well, and then these questions could be subjected to judicial review should they be found "obviously unconstitutional and void at a glance" by the Court. This means that, even if it is a limited review, the legal status of political questions related to national security or international affairs may become unstable. More importantly, this situation also means that the normative force of Article 9 will also become unstable. This instability that surrounds legal issues involving Article 9 is what I shall refer to as fate 2.

Three Fates of Article 9 (3): Political Criticism by the Sovereign People

The third fate of Article 9 is about people's sovereignty. To clarify this issue, it would be appropriate here to introduce the story of a famous political figure's misunderstanding of the meaning of the Sunagawa ruling. On June 11th, 2014, in the middle of the nationwide debate about introducing the right to collective self-defense the government had never acknowledged for a long time, at the Constitutional Review Committee in the House of Representatives, Mr. Masahiko Kōmura, the then Vice President of the LDP, stated the following: Holding 4 of the Sunagawa case made it clear that unless the political question was obviously unconstitutional and void at a glance, it fell outside the scope of judicial review and should be left to the hands of the political branches, the National Diet and the Cabinet. So, political questions could be entirely entrusted to the political branches, not to the hands of constitutional law scholars.[24]

Kōmura is incorrect. As we can see in the end of the last paragraph of Holding 4, the Court said, "The question of the determination of its constitutionality should be left *primarily* to the Cabinet which has the power to conclude treaties and the Diet which has the power to ratify them; and *ultimately to the political criticism by the people with whom rests the sovereign power of the nation*" (emphasis added). He ignores, either intentionally or unintentionally, these parts in the holding.

This text in the opinion of the Sunagawa case may express the Court's expectations regarding civic activism. To solve the constitutional controversy over highly political questions like those relating to international affairs and national security, the Court primarily leaves these issues up to the political branches: the Cabinet and the Diet. However, the Court leaves them ultimately to the criticism of the people themselves, whose civic activism is assumed to have bearing on such political questions. The Sunagawa case is a landmark decision through which the Court provided *the crossroads where Article 9 and civic activism encounter each other*. The court acknowledges the connection between these two during the early days of the postwar period.

This line of thought raises key questions: What does "*political criticism*" mean? Who are "*the people with whom rests the sovereign power of the nation*"? What kind of legal implications for civic activism should we draw from the case? In the following, I will explore this main topic for this essay.

ANIMOSITY: IN THE CASE OF CHIEF JUSTICE KŌTARŌ TANAKA

"The political criticism by the people with whom rests the sovereign power of the nation" is a mysterious text (hereinafter shortend as "*the political criticism by the sovereign people*"). Which Justice inserted this phrase into the dictum, and why, is unknown, because the process of deliberation in the panel of the Justices is not disclosed.[25] But one thing appears certain. This phrase was not welcome from the perspective of the Justice who presided over the Court in the Sunagawa case. The judge in question is Chief Justice Kōtarō Tanaka.

Kōtarō Tanaka was a giant in the world of legal experts in Japan. In 1946, Tanaka signed on the Constitution of Japan as the Minister of Education. He became a member of the House of Councillors in 1947. In 1950, Tanaka was appointed Chief Justice of the Supreme Court, and, from 1961 to 1970, he was a judge of the International Court of Justice. In his youth, he was non-denominational, but later in life he converted to Catholicism. It appears that Catholic doctrine inspired him to think seriously about the significance of the law and the state. And, of course, Tanaka was a passionate anti-communist.

The Motion to Remove C.J. from His Bench

As the Chief Justice, Tanaka presided over the Sunagawa case. Unusually, however, during the trial of Sunagawa case, the defendants filed a motion to challenge C.J. Tanaka in order to put him out of the trial. The reasons were as follows.

First, C.J. Tanaka issued New Year statements in the *Journal of the Judiciary* in 1951/1952. In the statements, as an anti-communist, Tanaka repeatedly emphasized the historical mission of human beings to fight against "red imperialism." The text in his statement suggested that he seemed to strongly believe in the U.S.-Japan alliance as an anti-communist front in the Far East. For the defendants of the Sunagawa case, it was obviously unfair for the C.J. who made his attitude very clear for the U.S.-Japan alliance to review the constitutionality of the Security Treaty and the stationed troops. The defendants said the trial would be a biased one.

Second, his remarks in the interview with *Yomiuri* newspaper in June 1959, just six months before the Sunagawa case ruled, were very controversial too. His remarks read:

> Experts on international law and constitutional law are expressing their opinions in various ways. It is said that we should not listen to these *noises* because it is a pending action. But I do not think so. I would like to welcome academic research and willingly use them because these opinions are not *so called social noises*. Social sensations admire a judicial opinion when it is comfortable one. But when it is uncomfortable for them they tend to use force and campaigns to obstruct it. I am disappointed at this. (emphasis added)

Chief Justice Tanaka arguably regards the protest in Sunagawa and even civic activism in general as "social noises." And when he says, "When it is uncomfortable for them they tend to use force and campaigns to obstruct it," it appears as if the trespassing by the Sunagawa protesters may have been in his mind. Thus, it seems that, based on his public statements, he was inclined against the defendants in this case. So the defendants claimed that C.J. Tanaka was so biased that he tended to think of the defendants as guilty and was thus ineligible to preside over the Sunagawa case. But, by July 1st, 1959, the motion to challenge was denied by the Supreme Court itself because C.J. Tanaka was simply sharing his "impressions" about social phenomena.[26]

Whose Sovereignty Comes First?: The Chief Justice as "an Informant"

About five decades later, another problem with respect to C.J. Tanaka's conduct relating to the Sunagawa case was discovered.

In 2008, an independent expert on international affairs, Mr. Shōji Niihara accidentally found the Sunagawa-case-related documents at the National Archives, Washington, DC. His discovery started an investigation of confidential documents exchanged between Douglas MacArthur II, the then ambassador to Japan, and the U.S. government with respect to the Sunagawa case, about how to deal with the Date ruling. By virtue of efforts of a journalist, Mr. Yasushi Suenami, and a professor of jurisprudence, Ms. Reiko Reiko, using the Freedom of Information Act, the National Archives finally disclosed the diplomatic documents, confidential letters, and a telegram. Those documents revealed and suggested the alleged facts that people at the U.S. Embassy and Chief Justice Tanaka met several times, and Tanaka told them the trial schedule and expected divergence of opinions of the S.Ct. Justices, expected conclusion, his effort to shorten trial time, and so on.[27] The Sunagawa case survivors and lawyers brought a lawsuit in order to demand a retrial of the Sunagawa case to nullify the 1959 decision on the grounds that it was made in violation of the constitutional principle of the independence of the judiciary and fair trials.

On March 8th, 2016, the Tokyo District Court dismissed these motions.[28] The decision held that while the court recognized it was undesirable for the judge to meet the party of the case he presided over, Tanaka's remarks did just refer to general or procedural matters or the remarks were just his general prospects on the trial.

C.J. Tanaka's remarks and conduct were problematic in light of the constitution when the opinion in the Sunagawa case promised that the constitutionality of highly political questions shall be left "ultimately to the political criticism by the sovereign people." C.J. Tanaka betrayed this promise. He did not take the people's voice seriously, suggesting that the voices of the Sunagawa protesters were just noises. One could conclude that he did not respect the sovereign power of his fellow citizens. Instead, Tanaka respected the sovereign power of a foreign country, the United States. If that is the case, then Tanaka may have committed a double betrayal of the S.Ct opinion in the Sunagawa case.

POLITICAL CRITICISM BY THE SOVEREIGN PEOPLE: ITS NORMATIVE RELEVANCE

In any event, the phrase "ultimately to the political criticism by the sovereign people," against which C.J. Tanaka had a complicated feeling or even animosity, was inscribed in the opinion of the Sunagawa case. From constitutional concern, it is very important for Japan to have had an opportunity in the final year of 1950s where Article 9 and civic activism based on "the political criticism by the sovereign people" came to meet together at the stage of a landmark case. The next analysis is to consider if we are able to assign some positive meaning to the concept of "the political criticism by the sovereign people." I am sure that we can assign the concept not only positive meaning but also even *normative* force or relevance. In order to clarify this, it would be helpful to introduce the case opinions written by two judges.

Judge Kishi

In the Sunagawa case of 1959, the Supreme Court of Japan provided an unclear constitutional judgment and reversed the original decision, the Date ruling. Then the Court finally remanded the case back to the court of the first instance, the Tokyo District Court, for further consideration of the defendants' crimes.

The presiding judge at the remanded Sunagawa case was Judge Seiichi Kishi. The defendants claimed that their conduct should be justified because they so deeply believed that it was unconstitutional for the government to permit the stationing of the U.S. Air Force at Sunagawa that their conduct was based on the motive to protect constitutional law. In the decision on March 27th, 1961,[29] Judge Kishi rejected this claim. However, he referred to the constitutional meaning of political criticism by the sovereign people by citing the text of the opinion of the 1959 Sunagawa case. First, Judge Kishi acknowledged that the military base issues had been dividing the national debate on how to interpret Article 9 and stated that the courts should not make any decision on political controversies but focus on legal judgment because of their genuinely judicial mission and function. The courts should not endorse either side and have to maintain their neutral position on political question like this. And he continued:

> As the Supreme Court ruling on the Sunagawa case suggested, these highly political issues should be left ultimately to the political criticism by the people with whom rests the sovereign power of the nation. And the contested debate on the issues will continue and won't stop in the future. However, [omitted] no one can be a prophet who tells what the best policy for the international peace will come to be, *so in a democratic state, it is people's freedom to have a passion for the world peace, to criticize policies of the time, and to put it into further action in various ways*. The more genuine, faithful or constructive the criticism and debate are, the more significant they become. (emphasis added)

The fact that Judge Kishi uses the word "criticism" three times in the paragraph above suggests that he makes much account of civic activism. Importantly, he tries to draw "people's freedom" to criticize policies and freedom to take "further action" from the Sunagawa case by citing the meaningful term, "the political criticism by the sovereign people." In Judge Kishi's understanding, this term allows the people to exercise "people's freedom" in various ways as long as the debate on the political question is continued. This is a sort of normative force which he confers to the term.

Consequently, however, Judge Kishi didn't fully use this normative force. Judge Kishi stated that even if people have freedom to criticize policies and take further action, those activities should be limited within the legal order, and this arrangement can be applied to civic movement. So he suggested that the "people's freedom" never justify criminal culpability of civic activity beyond legal limitations. In the next step of assessment or sentencing, however, Judge Kishi provided his view as follows:

> Japanese People have long had a keen interest in and casted doubt on the issue of constitutionality of the stationed troops. But now, this constitutional puzzle was solved by the Sunagawa decision at last in which the Supreme Court

upheld its constitutionality and this interpretation has been generally announced to the people.

From this view, Judge Kishi concluded that he sees no necessity to punish the defendants severely. For that reason, he simply fined the defendants for trespassing.

Judge Kishi's opinion is important for my interests because it helps us to consider the normative implications of the phrase "the political criticism by the sovereign people." Implications may be as follows. One: Judge Kishi made it clear that to criticize policies and to take further actions for this purpose was to be considered as a component of the people's freedom. Two: People cannot help but take radical actions like trespassing on the U.S. airbase when a pressing political question is left unresolved and a topic of debate. I imagine that Kishi thought the government should share responsibility for the people's radical actions.

Judge Kishi became a Supreme Court Justice ten years after this ruling.

Judge Tomikawa

One decade from 1959, the Sunagawa case was suddenly revived at a local court in western Japan in a way that appeared to vest the strongest legal significance in the phrase "the political criticism by the sovereign people."

In July 1968, around fifty students and activists intruded into a railroad track at the Japan National Railways station in Kure city, Hiroshima prefecture, and blocked trains transporting weapons of the U.S. military forces. These actions delayed the train to Kokura station by around ten minutes. The case went to the Hiroshima District Court. On May 29th, 1970, Judge Hideaki Tomikawa (who was the presiding judge on the bench) wrote the opinion to this criminal case.[30]

In this opinion, Judge Tomikawa interpreted the phrase "the political criticism by the sovereign people" as seen in the Sunagawa case and considered the important implication of this phrase.

> When the grand bench of the Supreme Court was about to review the constitutionality on the stationed U.S. military forces in the Sunagawa case, it held ". . . [omitted] . . . [I]t is proper to construe that the question of the determination of its constitutionality should be left primarily to the Cabinet which has the power to conclude treaties and the Diet which has the power to ratify them; and ultimately to *the political criticism by the people with whom rests the sovereign power of the nation*." This holding means to leave the ultimate judgment on whether the issue be constitutional or not to *the national referendum for constitutional revision* provided in Article 96 of the Constituion of Japan. If not so, the political criticism by the people in the opinion comes down to be that of the

> national election for the Diet members. But the election system is designed just to select the representatives, being subject to various views and policies and complicated local interests, not to give the people a chance to make a decision on the specific agenda or issues. (emphasis added)

Summarizing the passage above, Judge Tomikawa states, "The point of the holding of the Sunagawa case lies in that the people who have the sovereign power will be able to retain the invariance of the constitution as the basic law of the nation by making an explicit judgement by themselves, in other words, by the national referendum for constitutional revision regarding highly political questions like the security treaty." And he continues:

> If so, since the final judgment on constitutionality of the former national security treaty as well as the new one is still open and there is a considerable possibility to be held unconstitutional and void in the future, the current circumstances could be compared to a case in which the people of Japan are in an undecided situation, as if it were during election campaign. Thus, in the process of making a final judgement, it is right for the defendants, as the people who retain sovereignty, to express their opinions and spread them.

In contrast with Judge Kishi, who thinks the Sunagawa ruling solved the constitutional puzzle by upholding the security treaty not "obviously unconstitutional and void at a glance," Judge Tomikawa finds that the puzzle is still unsolved and national referendum for constitutional revision by the sovereign people shall be the only way to solve it. His point lies in that until the puzzle is finally solved, the people have the *right* to express their views and take action for the debate on the political question. But he doesn't stop here:

> Under the present circumstances of crisis entailing the possible annihilation of human being by nuclear war, it is quite natural for the defendants, who are residents of Hiroshima, the first victims of atomic bombing on the planet, to persist in protesting the perceived unconstitutionality of the new security treaty and for them to protest against the transportation of weapons by the Japan National Railway following the administrative agreement based upon the treaty given that they believe that the U.S. military forces bring about "the horrors of war through the action of government" (preamble of the Constitution of Japan) . . . [omitted]. . . . And it would rather even amount to a *duty* for the sovereign peoole to do that because Article 11 provides that '[t]he freedoms and rights guaranteed to the people by this Constitution shall be maintained by the constant endeavor of the people.'" (emphasis added)

For Judge Tomikawa, engaging in civic activism shall be not just right but also duty for the people until constitutional revision clearly resolves doubts about the constitutionality of the political question. Thus, he concluded that the motive of the defendants was legitimate and the actions they took did not go far beyond the social allowance. He found the defendants not guilty.

Judge Tomikawa's decision is really a rare example in which a judge gives clear normative force to the meaning of the phrase "ultimately to the political criticism by the people" and applies it to the judgment of a real criminal case. The normative implications of Judge Tomikawa's interpretation deserve consideration. One: Constitutional revision is the only way to solve a doubt as to whether the political question is constitutional or not. That would be a faithful interpretation of the phrase, "the political criticism by the people with whom rests the sovereign power of the nation." Two: Deliberation at the national election will never be substituted for debate at constitutional revision because people cannot focus on the specific constitutional issues during the regular election campaign. Three: Until constitutional revision is done, it is a right, even a duty, for the people to engage in civic activism for the debate whether the political question is constitutional or not. Four: The motive of the defendants should be legitimate as long as they exercise these rights and duties.

Nine years after this case, Judge Tomikawa committed suicide in the hospital in Chiba prefecture on October 14th, 1979. He was a judge at the Kanazawa branch of the Nagoya High Court at the time.

CONCLUSION: CIVIC ACTIVISM AND LEGACY OF THE SUNAGAWA CASE[31]

As we have seen, the phrase of "the political criticism by the people with whom rests the sovereign power of the nation" in the Sunagawa case is full of rich and profound implications from the perspective of constitutional law. This composite prism was inscribed into the text of the opinion of the Court by the Justices in spite of the negative sentiment of C.J. Tanaka, who presided over the Sunagawa case. Efforts made by Judge Kishi and Judge Tomikawa would have tried to give normative meaning to this prism and break it down into legal doctrines for criminal cases. By way of conclusion, I will explore how "the political criticism by the sovereign people" shall work for solving the political questions a little bit further.

In my view, "the people" have three different statuses or faces as they appear in the text of the Constitution of Japan. There are the *sovereign people* (a short form of "the people with whom rests the sovereign power of the nation"), the *voters*, and the *citizens.*[32] Corresponding to those three statuses, there may be three different registers of meaning implied in the phrase "the political criticism by the people." As a heuristic, I make provide Table 1.1 below and show that these three registers can be compared to three "games,"

Table 1.1. Political Criticism by the Sovereign People

Player	*Constitutional basis*	*Game*
Mode 1 Sovereign People	Article 96	National Referendum for Constitutional Revision
Mode 2 Voters	Article 15	Voting, Running for Election
Mode 3 Citizens	Article 21	Protest, Assembly, Demonstration, Public Speech, etc.

with the three "players" corresponding to the three statuses of the people as they appear in the three constitutional basis.

In the first place, "the people" is, of course, the sovereign people (Mode 1). The people in Mode 1 will most typically appear as the sovereign people when they express their will at the national referendum for the proposal draft of constitutional revision prescribed in Article 96 of the Constitution of Japan.[33] In Mode 2, the people appear as voters (or the electorate). Voters express their will at the elections prescribed in Article 15[34] by voting. And in Mode 3, the people take various actions as citizens such as protest, assembly, demonstration, public speech, symbolic speech, and so on.[35] Additionally, the Constitution of Japan respects the people in all three Modes *as individuals*.[36]

As Judge Tomikawa's interpretation of the phrase "the political criticism by the sovereign people" suggested, the constitutional controversy over the political questions shall be completely and finally solved only by the national referendum for constitutional revision. So I guess Mode 1 exactly corresponds to what Justices at the Sunagawa case imagined when in the opinion of the Court they used the phrases "*ultimately to*" or "the people with whom rests *the sovereign power.*" Voting in Mode 2 may also be seen as a sort of exercise of the sovereign power of the people, and even protest or civic movement in Mode 3 can be fueled by responsibility of the people who retain the sovereign power. However, those two forms of exercise of the sovereign power are indirect at the most. The referendum for changing the highest code of the nation is the most direct one. Mode 1 is a conduct of the people worthy of the name of "sovereign."

Some scholars argue that, under certain conditions, constitutional changes would take place even when those changes occurred outside an official revision of the constitution. For example, Bruce Ackerman, one of the prominent American constitutional law professors, distinguishes "higher lawmaking" or "constitutional politics" from normal politics.[37] This dualist democracy theory sees constitutional transformation without complying with the formal process of amendment that would occur when political leaders put grave controversies over constitutional crises on the national agenda, and "We, the People" awake from sleep and accept dramatically exceptional policies or legislations even through the regular process of lawmaking or election under great deliberations and mass mobilizations among the nation.[38]

I do not fully agree with Ackerman's view as a general theory of constitutional transformation.[39] At least the Sunagawa case takes a different way. The opinion of the Sunagawa case uses the words "the political *criticism*," not the political *judgment* or *decision* by the sovereign people. This suggests that the Supreme Court of Japan would take into account the process of decision-making as well as the decision itself. In order to reach the final solution for constitutional controversy over the political question, it would be essential for the people to participate in robust deliberation in an appropriate agenda-setting which enables them to focus on the specific issues to be solved. As Judge Tomikawa articulated, the regular election campaign will not offer a single promise in order to solve a specific constitutional issue. Candidates and parties deliberately make their campaign promises obscure or complicated to avoid being specific. The regular process of legislation cannot satisfy "the political criticism by the sovereign people" requirement because the people participate in the legislative process only indirectly. Proponents of Ackerman's theory might argue that the moment of higher lawmaking is different because, even during the regular election campaign or the regular legislative process, the people and political leaders could set the specific constitutional agenda, and the agenda would accelerate extraordinary mass mobilization to bring about a landslide victory for the candidates or parties who promise constitutional change. I do not necessarily deny those things happen. But, if so, why do not the people revise the constitution? If they insist on or believe in a grave change in the people's mind, the formal revision of constitution would have taken place. Informal revision certifies that a grave change among the people is just a fiction or a fake.

Here again, the main part of Holding 4 in the Sunagawa case reads ". . . the determination of its constitutionality should be left primarily to the Cabinet . . . and the Diet . . . ; and ultimately to the political criticism by the people with whom rests the sovereign power of the nation." This phenomenal moment would be actualized only when the people themselves do "the political criticism" in a robust way, outside the Cabinet and the Diet, and continue it until the constitutional controversies are ultimately solved by the revision in the national referendum. Until the final decision on the political questions is made, or in order to stop the final decision-making, the people would be responsible to engage themselves in protest, uprising, assembly, demonsration, or mass mobilization. Of course, criminal action might be brought to these kinds of uprisings. But, as we have seen, Judge Kishi and Judge Tomikawa tried to rescue the defendants from severe punishments because these activities are rights for the people as citizens and they might even be counted as the duties of the people as the sovereign. In this way, the Sunagawa case connects the political questions including Article 9 issues with civic activism.

Mr. Kōmura and Chief Justice Tanaka suggested that the political questions should be left in the hands of the political elites. I think this is wrong. For Japanese society to engage with political questions, the constitution calls for citizen participation in civic activism.

NOTES

1. Kenji Hasegawa, "The Lost Half-Decade Revived and Reconfigured: Sunagawa, 1956," *Journal of the International Student Center, Yokohama National University* 16 (March 2009), 117. Hasegawa's description is based upon Makiko Itō, Keizō Uchida, and Akira Nakajima. *Sunagawachō kassenroku* (Tokyo: Gendaisha, 1957), 21. I just modified some parts of the original text of Hasegawa's article.

2. Masao Miyaoka, *Sunagawa tōsō no kiroku* (Tokyo: Sanitsu shobō, 1970), 32. See also, Masataka Yamaura, "'Sora no miyako' kioku wo tsunagu: Tachikawa (1)," *Asahi Shinbun Digital*, May 9th, 2019, http://www.asahi.com/area/tokyo/articles /MTW20190509131520001.html.

3. Miyaoka, *Sunagawa tōsō no kiroku*, 36.

4. Kiichi Hoshi ed., *Sunagawa tōsō 50 nen sorezore no omoi* (Tokyo: Keyaki shuppan, 2005), 2.

5. Hiroshi Kojima, "'Muteikō' de jimoto no shinrai wo e, kokumin no habahiroi shiji mo eta," in Hoshi ed., *Sunagawa tōsō 50 nen*, 66–67.

6. Eiji Oguma, *Shakai wo kaeruniwa* (Tokyo: Kōdansha, 2012), 107.

7. Kojima, "Muteikō," 65. Kojima recalled those days and stated that when student protesters asked for donations near Yurakuchō station (a famous and busy railway station in the center of Tokyo) wearing bloodstained shirts, they could easily make around ¥300,000 just one night. Ibid. ¥300,000 in 1955 was worth around ¥1,800,000 in today's value of currency (around $16,500).

8. Wesley Sasaki-Uemura, *Organizing the Spontaneous: Citizen Protest in Postwar Japan* (Honolulu: University of Hawai'i Press, 2001), 2–3, 5.

9. Taisuke Ara, *Shinsayoku towa nan dattanoka* (Tokyo: Gentōsha, 2008), 34.

10. Miyaoka, *Sunagawa tōsō no kiroku*, 126–127.

11. Minoru Morita, "Zengakuren wo shiki–Zensen wa 'hikiuke masu,'" in Hoshi Kiichi ed., *Sunagawa tōsō 50 nen*, 53. Hasegawa, "The Lost Half-Decade," 125.

12. His following remarks imply that he saw the JCP as "salt on the earth." "I like to repeat it over again. To understand and love people's life is salt to give life to all kind of thoughts. I have a lot of criticism of and dissatisfaction with the JCP who believes in communism. At the same time, however, it is still true that the JCP contains the salt [on the earth] so much." Ikutarō Shimizu, *Watashi no shakai kan* (Tokyo: Kadokawa, 1954), 180. See also Yō Takeuchi, *Shimizu Ikutarō no haken to bōkyaku* (Tokyo: Chuōkōron shinsha, 2018), 235.

13. As Kenji Hasegawa suggests in his brilliant article, "the 1956 Zengakuren protests in Sunagawa was a crucial event that revived and reconfigured the 'failed' student movement of the early 1950s, establishing a pattern of protest that was inherited in the more well-known 1960 Anpo protests." Hasegawa, "The Lost Half-Decade," 118.

14. Hoshi ed., *Sunagawa tōsō 50 nen*, 2–3.

15. Hoshi ed., *Sunagawa tōsō 50 nen*, 2.

16. Miyaoka, *Sunagawa tōsō no kiroku*, 118.

17. Hiroshi Ido, a young policeman from the Tokyo Metropolitan Police Department, committed suicide at a hotel in Kamakura city on October 21st, 1956, at the age of 26. In his suicide note, Ido confessed, "My view of life has been changed since the Sunagawa struggle. I deeply apologize for having taken the measure like that." Hoshi ed., *Sunagawa tōsō 50 nen*, 84.

18. Miyaoka, *Sunagawa tōsō no kiroku*, 118; Hoshi ed., *Sunagawa tōsō 50 nen*, 84.

19. Political question doctrine is a case law which has been traditionally recognized by the United States Supreme Court. The doctrine can be summarized as follows: "Federal courts will refuse to hear a case if they find that it presents a political question. This doctrine refers to the idea that an issue is so politically charged that federal courts, which are typically viewed as the apolitical branch of government, should not hear the issue" (https://www.law.cornell.edu/wex/political_question_doctrine).

20. The *Sunagawa* case (case number: 1959 [A] 710) (*Keishū* Vol. 13, no. 13, 3225 [Sup. Ct. Grand Bench. December 16th, 1959]). As for the English translation of the original text of the Sunagawa case, see the website of the Supreme Court of Japan (http://www.courts.go.jp/app/hanrei_en/detail?id=13). I modified some parts of the original translation.

21. In *Jones v. United States*, 137 U.S. 201, 212 (1890), the U.S. Supreme Court states, "Who is the sovereign, de jure or de facto, of a territory is not a judicial, but is a political, question, the determination of which by the legislative and executive departments of any government *conclusively binds the judges*, as well as all other officers, citizens, and subjects of that government" (emphasis added).

22. As well known, at very early stage of making the Constitution of Japan, General Douglas MacArthur, the Supreme Commander for the Allied Powers (SCAP) stated in the MacArthur Note (Feb. 3rd, 1946) as follows:

"War as a sovereign right of the nation is abolished. Japan renounces it as an instrumentality for settling its disputes and even for preserving its own security. It relies upon *the higher ideals which are now stirring the world* for its defense and its protection. No Japanese army, navy, or air force will ever be authorized and no rights of belligerency will ever be conferred upon any Japanese force" (emphasis added).

As this text suggested, a possible interpretation of the motive to establish Article 9 is reliance and trust upon "*the higher ideals which are now stirring the world*"—this is a reference to the United Nations and its Charters. These motives of UN centrism (also referred to as "world federalism") seem to have been shared by Prime Minster Shigeru Yoshida and Minister Tokujirō Kanamori as well. For the details, see Shōichi Koseki, "*Heiwa kokka" Nippon no saikentō* (Tokyo: Iwanami shoten, 2013), 36–42. As for the relationship between Article 9 and an ideal of the world federation, see

Naoyuki Hayashi, "The Sovereign State and World Federalism-UN Centrism in Post-War Japan," *Ritstumeikan bungaku* 637 (March 2014), 1424–1427.

23. See, e.g., Takeo Sogawa, "Sunagawa jiken jōkokushin hanketsu no ronri to sono hihan," *Hanrei jihō*, no. 211 (February 1960), 8.

24. https://www.jimin.jp/activity/colum/127966.html.

25. As Tatsuhiko Yamamoto suggests, it seems to have been Justice Toshio Irie who made an effort to introduce this phrase into the text of the opinion of the Sunagawa ruling. See Tatsuhiko Yamamoto, "Amerika ni okeru 'jinmin shuken' ron to kenpō hendō," *Kenpō mondai* (*Constitutional Law Review*) (2017), 57–58.

26. The decision to the petition for challenge case (case number: 1959 [Su] 189) (*Keishu* 13, no. 7 [Sup. Ct. Grand Bench. July 1st, 1959]), 1001.

27. Reiko Fukawa and Shōji Niihara, *Sunagawa jiken to Tanaka saikōsai chōkan* (Tokyo: Nihon hyōronsha, 2013).

28. The Sunagawa case (the first instance of the retrial) (case number: 2014 (Ta) 12) (*Hanrei jihō*, no. 2364, P. 6 (Tokyo District Court. March 8th, 2016).

29. The remanded Sunagawa case (case number: 1960 [Toku Wa] 6) (*Hanrei jihō*, no. 255, P. 7 [Tokyo District Court. March 27th, 1961]).

30. The blocking weapon transportation case (case number: 1968 [Wa] 124) (*Hanrei jihō*, no. 595, P. 43 [Kure branch of Hiroshima District Court. May 29th, 1970]).

31. A basic idea of this part of my article was presented at the conference titled "Debating Japan's Constitution: On the Street, In Parliament, and In the Region" (November 3rd, 2017. Edwin O. Reischauer Institute of Japanese Studies, Harvard University).

32. Tatsuhiko Yamamoto offers a different classification of the sovereign people. Constitutional Constitutent (Lv.1), Constitutional Amending Power (Lv.2), Voters (Lv.3) (Yamamoto, "Amerika," 58–59). Lv.2 and Lv. 3 are equivalent to Mode 1 and Mode 2 in my classification. My classification lacks the category of Lv.1 in Yamamoto's because I just classify the statuses of the sovereign people *in the Constitution of Japan* as a positive law. In general understanding, constitutional constituent (constitutional-making power) is a hypothetical agent assumed to exist outside the space of positive law with the Almighty power to establish the system of law unless natural law confines it. Since any agent can become constitutional constituent—not only the sovereign people but also rebel, foreign country, invader, extraterrestrial life, and so on—it would be inappropriate to confer this "status" on the sovereign people inside the space of constitutional law.

33. Article 96§1 of the Constitution of Japan reads, "Amendments to this Constitution shall be initiated by the Diet, through a concurring vote of two-thirds or more of all the members of each House and shall thereupon be submitted to the people for ratification, which shall require the affirmative vote of a majority of all votes cast thereupon, at a special referendum or at such election as the Diet shall specify."

34. Article 15§1 reads, "The people have the inalienable right to choose their public officials and to dismiss them."

35. Article 21§1 provides various forms for civic activism. It reads, "Freedom of assembly and association as well as speech, press and all other forms of expression are guaranteed."

36. Article 13 states, "All of the people shall be respected as individuals." However, it may differ among the three Modes how they shall be respected as individuals.

37. Bruce A. Ackerman, *We the People: Foundations* (Cambridge, MA: Harvard University Press, 1991).

38. Tatsuhiko Yamamoto seems to introduce Ackerman's theory and apply it to constitutional politics in Japan under certain conditions. I will return this issue in "Reflections on Part I," in this volume.

39. As for my comment on Ackerman's theory, see Keigo Komamura and Satoshi Machidori eds., *"Kenpōkaisei" no hikaku seijigaku* (Tokyo: Kōbundō, 2016), 474–475. In the U.S., there are various criticisms on Ackerman's theory. See, e.g., Michael J. Klarman, "Constitutional Fact/Constitutional Fiction: A Critique of Bruce Ackerman's Theory of Constitutional Moments," *Stanford Law Review* 44, no. 3 (February 1992) and Frederick Schauer, "Deliberating About Deliberation," *Michigan Law Review* 90, no. 6 (May 1992).

REFERENCES

Ackerman, Bruce A. *We the People: Foundations*. Cambridge, MA: Harvard University Press, 1991.

Ara, Taisuke. *Shinsayoku towa nan dattanoka* (What Was the New Left?). Tokyo: Gentōsha, 2008.

Fukawa, Reiko, and Shōji Niihara. *Sunagawa jiken to Tanaka saikōsai chōkan* (The Sunagawa case and Chief Justice Tanaka). Tokyo: Nihon hyōronsha, 2013.

Hasegawa, Kenji. "The Lost Half-Decade Revived and Reconfigured: Sunagawa, 1956." *Journal of the International Student Center, Yokohama National University* 16 (March 2009): 117–134.

Hayashi, Naoyuki. "The Sovereign State and World Federalism-UN Centrism in Post-War Japan." *Ritstumeikan bungaku* 637 (March 2014): 1413–1427.

Hoshi, Kiichi ed. *Sunagawa tōsō 50 nen sorezore no omoi* (The Sunagawa Struggle 50 Years After: Various Memoirs). Tokyo: Keyaki shuppan, 2005.

Itō, Makio, Keizō Uchida, and Akira Nakajima. *Sunagawachō kassenroku* (A Chronicle of the Battle of Sunagawa Town). Tokyo: Gendaisha, 1957.

Klarman, Michael J. "Constitutional Fact/Constitutional Fiction: A Critique of Bruce Ackerman's Theory of Constitutional Moments." *Stanford Law Review* 44, no. 3 (February 1992): 759–797.

Kojima, Hiroshi. "'Muteikō' de jimoto no shinrai wo e, kokumin no habahiroi shiji mo eta" (interview). In Kiichi Hoshi ed., *Sunagawa tōsō 50 nen sorezore no omoi* (The Sunagawa Struggle 50 Years After: Various Memoirs). Tokyo: Keyaki shuppan, 2005.

Komamura, Keigo and Satoshi Machidori eds. *"Kenpōkaisei" no hikaku seijigaku* (Comparative Political Science on "Constitutional Revision"). Tokyo: Kōbundō, 2016.

Koseki, Shōichi. *"Heiwa kokka" Nippon no saikentō* (Reconsideraration of Japan as "Pacifist State"). Tokyo: Iwanami shoten, 2013.

Miyaoka, Masao. *Sunagawa tōsō no kiroku* (A Document of the Sunagawa Struggle). Tokyo: Sanitsu shobō, 1970.

Morita, Minoru. "Zengakuren wo shiki–Zensen wa 'hikiuke masu'" (interview).In Hoshi ed., *Sunagawa tōsō 50 nen sorezore no omoi* (The Sunagawa Struggle 50 Years After: Various Memoirs). Tokyo: Keyaki shuppan, 2005.

Oguma, Eiji. *Shakai wo kaeruniwa* (How to Change Society). Tokyo: Kōdansha, 2012.

Sasaki-Uemura, Wesley. *Organizing the Spontaneous: Citizen Protest in Postwar Japan*. Honolulu: University of Hawai'i Press, 2001.

Shimizu, Ikutarō. *Watashi no shakai kan* (My View on Society). Tokyo: Kadokawa, 1954.

Schauer, Frederick. "Deliberating About Deliberation." *Michigan Law Review* 90, no. 6 (May 1992): 1187–1202.

Sogawa, Takeo. "Sunagawa jiken jōkokushin hanketsu no ronri to sono hihan." *Hanrei jihō*, no. 211 (February 1960): 6–9.

Takeuchi, Yō. *Shimizu Ikutarō no haken to bōkyaku* (Hegemony and Oblivion of Shimizu Ikutarō). Tokyo: Chuōkōron shinsha, 2018.

Yamamoto, Tatsuhiko. "Amerika ni okeru 'jinmin shuken' ron to kenpō hendō (The Theory of 'Popular Sovereignty' in the U.S. and Constitutional Change)," *Kenpō mondai* (*Constitutional Law Review*) 28 (2017): 45–60.

Yamaura, Masataka. 2019. "'Sora no miyako' kioku wo tsunagu: Tachikawa (1) (To Preserve Memories of 'City of Sky': Tachikawa [1]), " *Asahi Shinbun Digital*, May 9th, 2019, http://www.asahi.com/area/tokyo/articles/MTW20190509131520001 .html.

Chapter Two

Crisis of Constitutional Democracy and the New Civic Activism in Japan

From SEALDs to Civil Alliance

Koichi Nakano

This chapter provides an analysis of the growing crisis of constitutional democracy in the post–Cold War era and the emergence of a new civic activism that arose to counter the erosion of government accountability. In particular, it shall focus on the events and political developments that followed the nuclear power accident in March 2011 and the return of Shinzō Abe's Liberal Democratic Party (LDP) to power in December 2012 that exposed the failure of Japan's system of representation—in terms of both electoral representation of the popular will and the media representation of truth and reality. The security legislation in 2015 that lifted the constitutional ban on the exercise of collective self-defense without a formal revision of the constitution gave birth to large-scale protests by SEALDs (Students Emergency Action for Liberal Democracy) and other civic groups, which then moved on to form the Civil Alliance for Peace and Constitutionalism (Civil Alliance or Shimin Rengō in short) in an attempt to restore balance to the party system by boosting the electoral prospects of the constitutionalist opposition parties.

THE NEOLIBERAL TURN OF PARTY POLITICS IN THE POST–COLD WAR ERA

From the late 1980s to the mid-1990s, as the Cold War was coming to an end, a fundamental shift occurred in Japan's party system and in its relationship with civil society through the reform of the so-called "medium-size constituency" electoral system (single non-transferable vote system in multi-member constituencies) that had served as the basis for the 1955 system—one-party dominance of the LDP, characterized by a gradual de-ideologization of its position as it prioritized electoral success over policy consistency. "Political

Reform" became an unassailable cause of the time that eventually coalesced around the establishment of the two-party system through the introduction of the "small constituency electoral system" (single member constituencies, also known as the first-past-the-post [FPTP] system).

The professed goal of the pro-reform politicians and the media was to rid Japan of its tendencies to seek consensus and avoid controversial but much-needed neoliberal reforms by remodeling its political system into a British-style, decisive single-party government noted for the centralization of power around the executive branch—a type of political system known as the "Westminster model" that is based on a two-party system with regular alternations in power.

This new vision of a majoritarian, winner-takes-all democracy was very much in line with "another theory of democracy" that was put forth by the Harvard economist, Joseph A. Schumpeter.[1] Having dismissed as unrealistic the proposition of the classical theory of democracy that the people hold a "definite and rational opinion about every individual question" and that they entrust the elected representatives to carry out that opinion, Schumpeter proposed limiting the role of the people to the selection of the political leadership, which would then do the deciding on behalf of the people.

According to Schumpeter's alternative theory of democracy, "the democratic method is that institutional arrangement for arriving at political decisions in which individuals acquire the power to decide by means of a competitive struggle for the people's vote."[2] In other words, just as firms compete against each other for customers by offering goods and services, the people are to be courted by the political parties that offer candidates and policy promises in the electoral marketplace, as it were.

According to the classical theory of democracy, the sovereign people are the active subjects of the democratic process, who take part in collective deliberation for the decision-making of the polity, but in the Schumpeterian doctrine, they become passive objects in the parties' competition for votes and consumers of the government services offered and promised. All they need to do is to choose either of the two larger parties as the government and let them govern.

The spread of neoliberalism is commonly discussed in relation to the socioeconomic changes that result from the norms and policies of small government, privatization, deregulation, and individual self-responsibility, but precisely in order to make the single-minded pursuit of these policies possible, the political system too had to first undergo neoliberal reforms that brought about a top-down, corporate model of governance. In Japan in the 1990s, it was argued that the corruption and stagnation that characterized the 1955 system, which was excessively consensus oriented, showed that it needed to be reformed into a bold, reformist political system with the introduction of the FPTP system. Only then could "customer satisfaction" with politics be improved. As a result, the electoral law was revised in 1994 to introduce the FPTP system in the Lower House, and the new electoral system was used for the first time in 1996.

The devastating impact of the FPTP system was seen for the first time in Japan at the time of the postal privatization election in 2005. In that snap election that Prime Minister Jun'ichirō Koizumi called as a virtual referendum on his plan for the privatization of postal services, the pro-privatization candidates backed by the LDP and its coalition partner Kōmeitō received 49% of the votes cast, while 51% of the votes went to the anti-privatization candidates from various opposition parties. Therefore, if this had actually been a referendum, Koizumi would have lost, but thanks to the magic of the FPTP system, the LDP and Kōmeitō combined won 75% of the single-member district seats.

Similarly, a disproportional number of seats delivered by the workings of the FPTP system was behind the landslide victory that propelled the Democratic Party of Japan (DPJ) to power in 2009. And even though Japanese democracy seemed to have made a significant step forward with the historic change of government, the people soon realized that in the new neoliberal model of democracy, their role was now reduced to, at best, selecting the party that forms the government, and particularly in the absence of a functioning opposition that holds the government accountable and offers an alternative to the people, they were at the mercy of unaccountable politicians on both sides of the aisle.

It bears emphasizing that such fundamental transformation in the relationship between the people and the political parties was also accompanied by a rightward shift of the party system. Throughout the era of the 1955 system and up until 1993, the center-left opposition led by the Japan Socialist Party (JSP) consistently held about a third of the seats in the Diet. As the New Frontier Party, and later the DPJ, replaced the JSP as the main opposition party, the relative weight of the center-left voices in party politics sharply declined in the decades that followed, with the JSP and the Japan Communist Party (JCP) combined occupying less than 5% of the Diet seats, as the two-party system was manufactured by the FPTP system. This has contributed to the growing number of abstentions by alienated voters, while also creating a gap between the persistent presence of center-left opinions among the general public on the one hand and the increasing dominance of right-leaning voices in the Diet on the other.

The failure of the representative system became apparent on a large scale for the first time in the aftermath of the nuclear power accident that was caused by the Great East Japan Earthquake and Tsunami on March 11th, 2011.

NEW CIVIC ACTIVISM SINCE 2011

Needless to say, civic activism was not unknown in Japan in the earlier postwar decades. The Anpo protests against the revision of the U.S.-Japan Security Treaty in 1960 and 1970, and indeed the student protests throughout the 1960s and into the 1970s, have been widely reported and studied in the past. However, since the conservatives succeeded in keeping power and in turning mainstream public opinion against the student sects that increasingly showed radical and violent tendencies as they became isolated, demonstrations and protests on campuses and on the streets receded very rapidly from the mid-1970s onwards. Once highly politicized and engaged, Japanese popular culture, particularly youth culture, came to be known for its consumerist orientation and political apathy.

It is against this historical backdrop that an era of new civic activism was ushered in in the immediate aftermath of the triple disasters of earthquake, tsunami, and nuclear power accident of 2011. The nuclear power accident in Fukushima in particular exposed the failure of the representative system in Japan in the eyes of its citizens in two very important ways: the failure of representative democracy and the failure of media representation.

Japanese society experienced a marked return of demonstrations and protests as a growing number of concerned and worried citizens, many of whom until then lacked knowledge and interest in politics, took to the streets of Tokyo and other cities. Faced with a situation in which they could no longer trust the politicians who were supposed to be their elected representatives to truly represent their views and priorities, and in which they could no longer believe that the mass media were conveying to them the true magnitude of the nuclear disaster and its health risks, or reporting on their concerns and anger, a growing number of citizens decided to take matters into their own hands by reasserting their long neglected rights and duties as the "sovereign people" and by calling on others to do the same through demonstrations and through the active use of social media; in other words, by becoming themselves the media.

In an often-quoted speech at an anti-nuclear demonstration in Shinjuku on September 11th, 2011, the renowned philosopher and literary critic, Kōjin Karatani made the following points:[3]

> I have been taking part in anti-nuclear demonstrations since April. I was here in this rally in front of Shinjuku Station on June 11th.
>
> Since I started going to demonstrations, I have received lots of questions about demonstrations. Almost all of them are negative questions, for instance, questions like "Can you change society by having demonstrations?" To this, I answer as follows. We can certainly change society by having demonstrations.

> This is because, by having demonstrations, Japanese society changes to a society in which people demonstrate.
>
> Think about it. Until March this year, there were almost no demonstrations in Japan except in Okinawa. Now, demonstrations are being organized all over Japan. In that sense, Japanese society has changed a little . . .
>
> To demonstrate is a right of the sovereign people. We may even say that if we cannot demonstrate the people are not sovereign . . .
>
> Then, why are there so few demonstrations in Japan? Why are they considered to be an odd thing? It is because we did not gain popular sovereignty with our own power, through our own struggle. The Japanese gained popular sovereignty in the postwar. That was, however, due to the war defeat; in effect, thanks to the occupation forces. It was not won by our own doing, but given us by someone else. So, what can we do to make it our own? We should demonstrate.
>
> Another question I receive is "Aren't there other means than demonstrations?" Certainly, there are other means than demonstrations. There are elections, to begin with. There are also other means. Demonstrations, however, are fundamental. As long as there are demonstrations, other means are also effective. If there are no demonstrations, they won't function. It will all be the same as before.

Karatani touched upon a couple of key features that marked the new civic activism that began at this time with the anti-nuclear protests and that were to continue to develop in relation to a variety of different issues, including the opposition against the security legislation in 2015. The most important of them is that the new civic activism since 2011 in Japan has taken the form of a "movement of the sovereign people," and as such served as a foundation for, rather than being hostile to, renewed civic involvement in electoral politics. I shall develop these points in more detail later.

Not even a month after Karatani made the above speech in Shinjuku, Sidney Tarrow, the influential scholar of social movements, noted about the Occupy Wall Street movement, which was growing very rapidly into a U.S.-wide, and indeed, global phenomenon, that it was a movement of a completely new type.[4] Tarrow argued that, unlike the Tea Party movement or even the civil rights movement that were created to serve specific constituencies and their interests and policies, Occupy Wall Street was a "we are here" movement—a movement which demanded through its presence, "Recognize us!"

Michael Hardt and Antonio Negri similarly echoed Tarrow's point when they noted that the Occupy Wall Street protests took inspiration from the other encampment movements of the previous year, including the encampments in central squares in Spain that called for "real democracy now" against the perceived "failure of representation."[5] Just as Hardt and Negri argued that Occupy Wall Street was as much an expression of indignation against corporate greed as it was a protest against the failure of political representation, the anti-nuclear protests in Japan were not only against the electricity giant, TEPCO, that ran the nuclear power plant in Fukushima, but also against the political collusion that promoted nuclear power, caused the widespread radioactive contamination, and covered up the magnitude of the accident in the first place.

In the sense that the Japanese protesters, like their Spanish or American counterparts, aspired for democratic renewal, they similarly sought to start a "democratic constituent process" (in the words of Hardt and Negri) bottom up by asserting their identity and their presence as the sovereign people by claiming a symbolic public space right in front of the Prime Minister's Office.

The civic activism that was renewed by the anti-nuclear protests was not simply an attempt to counter the failure of representative democracy, but also a reaction against the failure of media representation at the same time. Much has been made about the role played by the social media in the organization and mobilization for contemporary civic activism globally, and in Japan, too, the social media, Twitter in particular, came to be an important tool for the activists. For instance, a group called TwitNoNukes organized some of the earliest protests against nuclear power in 2011 using Twitter as its main tool for disseminating information about their demonstrations, and they have since been a member of the Metropolitan Coalition Against Nukes, known even today for its weekly Friday protest in front of the Prime Minister's Office.

The reliance on social media, as well as the demonstrations themselves, were reflections of the general distrust and alienation from the mass media. The labor studies professor Mitsuko Uenishi, who came to be known by the wider public through her opposition to labor reform bills, has since June 2018 started a unique form of "demonstration" called National Diet Public Screening "with the aim of making the real state of 'the representative body of the Japanese people' accessible and transparent to the public by showing actual Diet deliberations on the street"—essentially because "when we have a chance to see or read about the Diet deliberations through the mass media, it is already reduced into short pieces of information that no doubt reflect the reporter's own interests and agenda as well."[6]

Uenishi enunciated effective criticisms against the introduction of discretionary work systems in Japan that were widely feared to give a legal cover allowing businesses not to pay for overtime work and to aggravate the problems of overwork as a result. Just like Occupy Wall Street, and just like the opposition to nuclear power, the opposition to discretionary work represented popular anger against corporate greed and unequal distribution of risks and insecurity in the global capitalist economy, but it was also a fight against the distortions of the systems of political and media representation that gave license to the collusion of the unaccountable elites in politics, business, and the media in the first place.

In a brief essay on the remembrance of the victims of the disasters that started on March 11, 2011, Uenishi recounted the reasons why she started to take part in street protests, citing Karatani's speech above:[7] "Media reports suddenly felt oppressive after the explosions in the Fukushima Daiichi Nuclear Power Plant. I was in Tokyo searching for information about what would happen to the nuclear power plant and whether it was all right to continue with daily life, but I felt that there was a strong power of suppression that shut up what needed to be told."

It was only after she started her "National Diet Public Screening" actions in public spaces in front of Shinbashi and Shinjuku stations that Uenishi came to fully understand Karatani's words.[8]

> Without getting a permit for road usage, we became ourselves the media and communicated what we thought should be communicated. The repetition of that practice itself was to be the "constant endeavor"[9] that defends the freedom of expression in the public space. We can at any time, without any permission from anyone, engage in expressive activities on the street, state our opinions, and become the subjects that change politics. We not only feel dissatisfaction with politics and the media, but we can also be the subjects that bring about change to the situation ourselves.
>
> This is a realization that I came to acquire through the accumulation of practices. It is only through the birth of sovereign people like that that society changes at last on the basis of a firm foundation. In retrospect, I feel that Karatani had the insight to see through to this already in the chaotic situation that we were in in 2011.

SOME COMPARATIVE OBSERVATIONS IN THE WORLD HISTORICAL CONTEXT

As we seek to understand the renewed civic activism in Japan since 2011, it is important to place it in the wider global context. The protests that were sparked by a case of self-immolation in Tunisia in December 2010 quickly led to a massive wave of demonstrations that came to be known as the Arab Spring in early 2011. This, in turn, influenced the spread of encampment movements in southern Europe, including Spain. By autumn, the Occupy Wall Street movement quickly captured worldwide attention. The impact of the Occupy movement on SEALDs, as we shall note later, cannot be ignored.

East Asia, too, experienced its own share of civic activism, with the Sunflower movement in Taiwan in spring 2014 and Umbrella movement in Hong

Kong in autumn of the same year. SEALDs, again, had had exchanges with the youth leaders in these groups. As a result of the Candlelight Struggle in winter 2016–2017, South Korean citizens succeeded in impeaching President Park Geun-hye, and these developments continue to serve as a source of inspiration for many, particularly among the older civic activists of the postwar baby-boom generation.

Needless to say, the exact causes and backgrounds of the protests vary from society to society, but they broadly share a common opposition to the global spread of unaccountable, corporate oligarchies in post–Cold War contexts. In that respect, from the anti-austerity protests in Europe and Occupy Wall Street to the Candlelight Struggle and the civic activism in Japan since 2011, the demonstrations can be said to represent a grassroots reaction against what Colin Crouch called "post-democracy."[10]

As societies move toward a "post-democratic" model, "while elections certainly exist and can change governments, public electoral debate is a tightly controlled spectacle, managed by rival teams of professionals expert in the techniques of persuasion, and considering a small range of issues selected by those teams. The mass of citizens plays a passive, quiescent, even apathetic part, responding only to the signals given them. Behind the spectacle of the electoral game, politics is really shaped in private by interaction between elected governments and elites that overwhelmingly represent business interests."[11]

Therefore, we may be able to identify several common, comparative traits among these worldwide protests since the 2010s.

First, one can point to the direct connections between such direct actions as street protests and encampment movements, on the one hand, and electoral politics, on the other. Even though it is commonplace to conceptualize direct democracy (e.g. demonstrations) and indirect democracy (i.e., elections) as being in tension, if not in confrontation or contradiction, with each other, these direct actions invariably led to attempts to change the party-political dynamics through the elections. For instance, the Spanish protesters gave birth to Podemos, while those in Taiwan established the New Power Party, and in Hong Kong several prominent leaders of the pro-democracy protests, including Nathan Law of Demosisto, won seats in the Legislative Council. It is also well known that the veterans of Occupy Wall Street animated the Bernie Sanders campaign in 2016, and needless to say, Moon Jae-in's election to the presidency in 2017 was predicated on the Candlelight Struggle that ousted his predecessor. In the Japanese case, the various protest groups against the security legislation of 2015 went on to establish the Civil Alliance in order to promote the collaboration of the opposition parties known as "the opposition parties' joint struggle" (Yatō Kyoto).

Secondly, the centrality of media strategy was common in all these movements. The problem was understood to be as much the failure of political representation of the popular will as the failure of media representation of reality. In other words, post-democracy and post-truth needed to be combated simultaneously. Much of the established, organized media were regarded as unreliable at best by the protesters, if not as an integral part of the collusion of the ruling elites. This has motivated the protesters to make the most of social media, internet-based media, freelance journalism, and also at times appeals to foreign media (particularly in East Asian cases). These were not only used to disseminate information and mobilize people in themselves, but also as a means to draw the attention of the mainstream media so that they would have to report on the protests too.

The third salient feature of the global protests of the 2010s was that the protesters identified themselves as a "majority" movement. It was significant that the slogan "We are the 99%" became nearly synonymous with the Occupy movement, as it underlines the difference from the anti-capitalism of the old that tended to show a more specific focus on the plight of the working class. At the same time this was, of course, a reflection of the huge concentration of capital and power in the hands of the few that has severely undermined the economic security of even the middle class in today's global capitalism. The rise of corporate oligarchs resulted in the concentration of power in the hands of the few as well, so these movements identified themselves as movements of the sovereign people as a whole rather than of a specific segment or class within it.

In addition to these globally common characteristics, however, one may also detect some significant regional and country variations.

Generally, in East Asia, issues of the rule of law and constitutionalism appear to be more central than in Europe or the U.S., where economic issues that have to do with anti-austerity or anti-globalization have often been predominant. This is not to argue that the growing disparities that neoliberal globalization brought about have been ignored in East Asia, but they certainly seem to have taken a back seat to protests against the concerns with legality, constitutionality, and governance overall.

One may point to the persistence of authoritarian legality in East Asia, where the legacies of a hegemonic brand of conservatism tended to endure even after the liberalization and democratization of the political systems since the final phase of the Cold War. In such a political context, neoliberalism was often seen as a reformist ideology that challenged and exposed elite collusion. In contrast, more competitive party systems with regular alternation in power were common in Western Europe and the U.S., but the major parties often shared the blame for having introduced neoliberal policies that widened the gap between the rich and the poor. In consequence, a certain level of social support for the neoliberal reformist norms persisted in East Asia, while a wholesale criticism of the unaccountable political systems was often expressed in Western Europe and the U.S. through the rejection of neoliberal globalization. Needless to say, even though economic disparities grew across the board, East Asia as a region was more of a winner of the post–Cold War globalization of the economy, while relative decline was the common experience in the West.

As we focus on the characteristics of Japanese civic activism today in particular, we should point to the fact that it has exhibited a remedial, and perhaps, in a sense, even "conservative," nature rather than being revolutionary or reformist in orientation. Of course, the protesters uphold and advocate progressive political views, but because the movements emerged in response to the perceived failure of representation, which has, in turn, come to endanger the principles of constitutionalism and the rule of law, the general focus of the movements has inevitably been to defend postwar democracy and the constitution that served as its foundation, and not so much to advocate further change or progress. This observation is obviously linked to the fact that the direct action of the citizens was understood to complement and contribute to the rebuilding of indirect (elective) democracy, and not to be in confrontation with it.

In the Japanese case, the anti-security legislation movements of 2015 that coalesced into the Civil Alliance did not even seek to set up a new political party of their own, but instead opted to back the existing opposition parties and encourage them to join forces—in contrast to the protest movements in other countries that we mentioned above. This moderate, remedial orientation also stands in contrast to the far more radical and confrontational tendencies that the Anpo protest and the student protests of the 1950s to the 1970s showed in relation to parliamentary democracy and the political parties in Japan then.

ANTI-SECURITY LEGISLATION PROTESTS OF 2015

It is no exaggeration to say that the party system quite literally collapsed in the December 2012 Lower House election that put Abe back in power. The DPJ imploded prior to the election itself, and as a result of its division, the DPJ's share of the votes out of all eligible voters in the FPTP plummeted to 13% from the 32.2% it had gained when it had won power in 2009 (to 9.3% from 28.7% in the proportional segment of the election). As a result of the devastating effect of the first-past-the-post system, the DPJ seats in the

Lower House (combining both the PR seats and the FPTP seats) went down from 308 in 2009 to 57 in 2012 (out of a total of 480 seats). This meant that the largest opposition party, the DPJ, was now in control of a mere 11.9% of the seats in the Lower House. In addition, the Japan Restoration Party (JRP), which was led by the former LDP right-winger Shintarō Ishihara, was now breathing down the neck of the DPJ with as many as 54 seats. Another right-wing party, Your Party, which was also led by yet another former member of the LDP, Yoshimi Watanabe, increased its presence by more than doubling its seats to 18.

The LDP won by a landslide, gaining 294 seats, and together with its coalition partner Kōmeitō's 31 seats, the governing parties secured more than a two-thirds majority of the Lower House. This crushing victory for the LDP, and for the Right more broadly, took place in spite of the fact that the LDP's share of the votes out of all eligible voters in the FPTP portion of the election actually dropped to 24.7% in 2012 from 26.3% in 2009 when it was soundly defeated by the DPJ (to 16% in 2012 from 18.1% in 2009 in the PR part). With a divided opposition, a depressed turnout (the lowest on record until then, at a mere 59.3%), and the magic of the FPTP system, the LDP share of the seats in the Lower House jumped to 61.3% from 24.8% in 2009, even though the party actually received fewer votes than when it suffered the historical rout in the previous election. In fact, the LDP under Abe has since continued to win subsequent Lower House elections in 2014 and in 2017, but it has not been able to get back to the level of votes that it won when it was defeated in 2009. In other words, the LDP can and does continue to triumph without getting even its previous level of support, as long as the opposition parties remain divided and the turnout low—all thanks to the bias inherent in the FPTP system.

In other words, in order to restore some checks and balances to the party system and rebuild parliamentary democracy, it was imperative for the civic activism in Japan to promote opposition collaboration and also to bring back voters to the polling booths. So long as the opposition remained divided, the Abe government did not face any effective checks and balances from the party system, and what made matters worse, in the absence of a significant partisan brake in the Diet, it proceeded to override other institutional, and even constitutional, constraints in the wider political system. Thus, the Abe government passed the highly contested state secrets law in December 2013, and changed the official government interpretation of the constitution to allow for the lifting of the ban on collective self-defense in spite of the fact that the text of Article 9 remains unchanged since 1947. In doing these things, Abe broke with long-standing conventions that ensured that certain key parts of the public sphere were off limits for direct partisan intervention by placing his political appointees as the heads of the Bank of Japan (central bank), NHK (public broadcaster), and the Cabinet Legislation Bureau.

Such a marked authoritarian turn by a prime minister known for his nationalist and revisionist convictions alarmed the peace activists of the old school. The leftist peace movement has suffered from multiple fissures, most notably between those who are close to the Japan Communist Party (JCP), sometimes called Yoyogi-leaning (as the JCP headquarters are located in Yoyogi) and those who are not, the non-Yoyogi group. Ken Takada, a prominent leader of the non-partisan peace movement acknowledged that "the division and rivalry between 'Yoyogi' and 'non-Yoyogi'" had to be overcome on the side of the civil society as well.[12] As a result of such deep-seated animosity, at the time of elections, civic movements either campaigned for the different parties that they supported, or refrained from any involvement so as not to be caught in between the rival campaigns. Thus, the divisions among the opposition parties were mirrored in the divisions in the civil society as well.

When Abe called a snap election in December 2014, the outcome was nearly identical to that of the Lower House election two years earlier, as the opposition parties remained divided—another "landslide" victory for the LDP-Kōmeitō coalition, even though the ruling parties' votes continued to stagnate below the level of their defeat in 2009. In fact, this author, together with a couple of other scholars from Constitutional Democracy, including the political scientist Jirō Yamaguchi, met with the leaders of the JCP and asked them to collaborate with the DPJ to unify candidates in the single member districts prior to the election, but the conditions for such an electoral pact did not exist in either of the two parties at the time. As a result, the opposition parties fielded multiple candidates in the single member districts against the LDP-Kōmeitō joint candidates and lost in most of them by splitting their votes, to the advantage of the ruling coalition.

Constitutional Democracy is a group of liberal-leaning constitutional law scholars, political scientists, and other scholars that was established in April 2014 in response to Abe's professed intention to push through the revision of the government interpretation of the constitution to allow for the lifting of the ban on collective self-defense. Its core members included such prominent constitutional law scholars as the late Yasuhiro Okudaira, Yōichi Higuchi, Setsu Kobayashi, Yasuo Hasebe, and Kenji Ishikawa, among others.

On December 15th, 2014, the day after the election, however, an important development that would provide the foundation for opposition collaboration took place with the establishment of the All-Out Action Committee, commonly abbreviated as Sōgakari. Sōgakari consisted of the pacifist groups and labor unions that support the DPJ as well as the JCP, and also the non-partisan movements. In view of the long-standing rivalry and even animosity between the different strands of leftist movements, the emergence of Sōgakari was truly groundbreaking. Each time Sōgakari organized protests and rallies, it invited the parliamentarians and leaders of the rival opposition parties to address the protesters. As they took the podium, they were, in turn, urged by the crowd to collaborate with each other in the Diet and the elections. Thus, Sōgakari provided an important basis for the eventual realization of the opposition collaboration.

Equally significant was the official founding of SEALDs on May 3rd, 2015, as the Abe government was poised to submit the security bills that would provide the legal basis for the exercise of collective self-defense to the Diet. SEALDs was to organize protests in front of the Diet throughout summer 2015 until the ultimate passage of the bills on September 19th. Sōgakari's weekly protests were on Thursdays, whereas SEALDs's were on Fridays, though as the protests intensified in the final stage of the legislative process and became daily, the two groups coordinated with each other by dividing and sharing the time and areas for the protests.

SEALDs was a student protest group whose core members hailed from another movement by the name of SASPL (Students Against Secret Protection Law), which protested against the state secrets law that was enacted by Abe in December 2013.[13] In fact, in the run-up to the Lower House election in December 2014, SASPL members were already using the banner "Students Emergency Action for Liberal Democracy" as they launched a YouTube video campaign to get young people to vote, and to vote strategically. These students, the most famous of whom was Aki Okuda, were generally university students in the Tokyo area, but in contrast to student activism of the earlier postwar decades did not necessarily belong to the same university or organize per university as a unit. There were, however, regional SEALDs groups, including SEALDs KANSAI, which was founded on the same day as SEALDs itself, among others. In July, a group of high school students who took part in the SEALDs protests began their own movement that was called TSOWL (Teen Students Opposed to the War Law).

SEALDs also inspired another key protest group, Mothers Against War (commonly known as Mama no Kai), which is the brainchild of a young mother and University of Kyoto graduate student, Minako Saigō, and which began its activism in July 2015. Saigō called for anyone (not necessarily just mothers) who supported the slogan "Let Nobody's Child Be Killed" to join her, and also to set up their own affiliated groups. Very quickly, prefectural and local Mothers Against War groups sprang up nationwide.

SEALDs protests were eventually joined by the academics who gathered around the Association of Scholars Opposed to the Security-Related Bills (commonly known as Gakusha no Kai) that was established in June 2015 by

Manabu Satō, a renowned professor emeritus of education of the University of Tokyo. The membership of the Association of Scholars overlapped to a degree with those of Constitutional Democracy (including this author), but there were some important differences as well. The former drew scholars from broader fields of studies, and included such prominent figures as Seigo Hirowatari, a former president of the Science Council of Japan, Toshihide Masukawa, a Nobel laureate (theoretical physics), and Chizuko Ueno, a famed feminist sociologist. The Association of Scholars is generally more leftist in its tendencies, whereas Constitutional Democracy is liberal in its orientation. It was also more focused on street protests, and it spawned a nationwide network as Satō called for the setting-up of university-level voluntary associations.

Both Mothers Against War and the Association of Scholars collaborated closely with both Sōgakari and SEALDs by co-hosting protests and dispatching speakers at their respective rallies, and vice versa. Constitutional Democracy was arguably the most bookish of the groups, but it, too, sent speakers to the rallies and protest events, and in the final week of the Diet deliberation right before the Abe government rammed through the bills, it held a protest of its own in front of the Diet. A loose but important alliance of the various groups formed over time during the summer months of the protests.

What is remarkable, and indeed different from the Anpo protests of the 1960s, is the fact that both Sōgakari and SEALDs had their eyes set on impacting party politics by forcing the opposition parties to collaborate with each other by bringing together as far as possible large and diverse segments of the civil society in their direct actions. Already at the time of its founding, SEALDs "set its goals as the prospective double elections of both houses of the Diet in 2016, and on rallying the liberal forces in society around the themes of constitutionalism, national security, and social security."[14]

In its June 27th, 2015, protest in front of Shibuya Station, SEALDs called for the parliamentarians from the opposition parties to join them for the first time. At that time, a parliamentarian from the right-wing JRP (and former member of the DPJ) took part in the protest, and was subsequently disciplined by the party leadership for having taken action together with the leaders of the JCP. The incident served as a trigger for the split of the JRP, and the more liberal elements ended up joining the DPJ to form the Democratic Party (DP). Thus, the enhanced civic involvement in politics and its demand for opposition collaboration served as a catalyst for party system change from fairly early on.

While SEALDs shared the same goal as Sōgakari of blocking the passage of the security bills and of rebuilding the opposition parties by demanding their collaboration, and to those ends, liaised and coordinated their movements, its very existence was also an indication of the youths' desire to create a movement that was different from the "old school." This is, of course, not surprising, considering their generational differences. Many in Sōgakari were of the baby-boom generation, who either continued or came back to civic activism from their earlier experience in the student protests in the 1960s. The central members of SEALDs were initiated to civic activism in the aftermath of the triple disasters of the earthquake, tsunami, and nuclear power accident of March 2011, and most recently in the protests against the state secrets law of 2013, and they felt the need to create their own movement that would be more appealing to youths like themselves.

In contrast to the leftist and collectivist subculture of the civic activism of the older generation, SEALDs exhibited a marked liberal and individualist orientation. The core members of SEALDs read books and debated together, but they had little in common with the Marxist subculture of Japanese student movements of the past. In fact, the disconnect is such that one even hesitates to call SEALDs a student movement, as the term evokes associations that are entirely different. Indeed, SEALDs sought to avoid having a political subculture altogether, and made a point of "normalizing" civic activism in a society in which taking part in demonstrations and protests had become something of a taboo, as Karatani pointed out.

SEALDs put an enormous emphasis on reaching out to those who were either uninterested or disaffected with politics and went to great lengths to make their movement both media-friendly and self-mediatized at the same time by being fashion-conscious and telegenic and by effective use of social media, particularly Twitter. The video imagery as well as the sound of the protests was designed to be cool and hip. Combined with the use of slogans and chants in English, SEALDs protests looked like a page from a fashion or music magazine, and indeed, it eventually also ended up having an impact on popular culture in contemporary Japan. SEALDs members studied and experimented with marketing techniques in an attempt to reach out to as many people as possible in a world that is saturated by consumerist messages, and they were successful to the point that some in the "old school" Left criticized them for selling out to global capitalism.

SEALDs, however, was undeterred as it was not seeking to hold a hegemonic position in the civic protest, nor was it trying to be the vanguard party that led the masses. It became the catalyst for one of the largest protest movements in Japanese history by providing a platform for citizens, youths, and opposition politicians to come together to express their anger at Abe's attacks on their basic values of constitutionalism, democracy, and pacifism. The adapted a new style of "call and response" protest from the Occupy movement—"tell me what democracy looks like," "this is what democracy looks like"—that contrasted sharply with a more traditional "*schprechchor*" that consists of the protesters chanting the same slogans as the leaders repeatedly. The protest sites felt more like a forum for discussions and dialogues. The opposition politicians and leaders who were invited to come to the demonstrations were not only given an opportunity to address the protesters. The occasions were equally for them to hear what the protesters had to say, since, as they waited their turn to speak, ordinary citizens and students got the microphone to make speeches as well.

Indeed, the "protests" were as much a site for protesting against the security legislation and the Abe government as they were for cheering, and in fact, changing the opposition politicians as the sovereign people gathered around the Diet in an attempt to defend and rebuild the broken system of representation. As the government rammed the bills through the Diet and as the outnumbered opposition sought to resist and delay the inevitable, the protesters chanted, "Hang in there, opposition!" "Fight together, opposition!" and even cheered individual politicians who were seeking to filibuster—and their voice was heard inside the Diet by the struggling politicians.

After a moment of silence that was as pregnant with despair as it was with anger when the bills were forced through the Upper House in the early hours of September 19th, 2015, the gathered people immediately shouted, "Let's go vote." The passage of the security bills did not end civic engagement, as the focus shifted immediately to the election.

CIVIL ALLIANCE AND OPPOSITION COLLABORATION

On December 20th, 2015, representatives from the five major civil society groups that opposed the security legislation, namely, Sōgakari, SEALDs, Mothers Against War, Constitutional Democracy, and the Association of Scholars Opposed to the Security-Related Bills, established the Civil Alliance for Peace and Constitutionalism. As we have noted above, both Sōgakari and SEALDs have direct roots in the opposition parties' failure to mount a serious challenge against the Abe government in the December 2014 Lower House election, and Constitutional Democracy members, too, unsuccessfully lobbied for an electoral pact between opposition parties in the same election. Thus, it was logical for these groups to come together in order to pressure the opposition parties to collaborate with each other so that they could defeat the Abe government and eventually revoke the unconstitutional security legislation.

A notable precedent of such a citizens' alliance in Japan was the Citizen's League for Peace in Vietnam that was active between the mid-1960s and the mid-1970s, and was more commonly known as Beheiren. In addition, the word "citizen" (*shimin*) came increasingly to have the connotation of urban, well-educated middle class (including housewives), ironically, as the civic movements grew in number and scope from the 1980s, and they were usually differentiated from student movements or labor movements. In fact, in part because of the bourgeois tendency of the citizen concept, and in part because of the vanguard party identity of the JCP that was supposed to lead mass movements, the civic movements and the JCP were also often at odds with each other.

What the new civic activism has done is to give a new life to the concept of the citizen. As the various groups coalesced to form the Civil Alliance, it came to express the solidarity of workers, students, mothers, scholars, lawyers, and other people from all walks of life that together represented the sovereign people.

The initial main target for the Civil Alliance was to unify opposition candidates in the 32 single member districts that were to be contested in July 2016 in the Upper House election. The Upper House election consists of a proportional segment and a prefecture-based segment, and the latter was further divided between single member districts and multiple member districts that range between two and six members, depending on the population of the prefectures. On the one hand, the opposition parties had little chance of winning any of the 32 single member districts if they each contested these seats separately and split the opposition votes against the unified candidates backed by the ruling LPD and Kōmeito. As a matter of fact, in the Upper House election in 2013, the LDP won 29 of the then 31 single member districts. It was thus obvious that some electoral pact was indispensable for the opposition parties to have any chance at all. On the other hand, in the proportional segment and in the multiple member districts, the opposition parties must field their own candidates separately, and that fact complicated matters since in one and the same election, the opposition parties had to simultaneously collaborate with and compete against each other.

Concretely, the Civil Alliance insisted that the opposition parties collaborate with each other in the single-member districts with the goals of (1) abolishing the security legislation, (2) restoring constitutionalism (and rescinding the Cabinet decision that lifted the ban on collective self-defense), and (3) pursuing a set of policies centered around the ideal of defending individual dignity. The Civil Alliance formed a network of civil society associations all over the country that shared the same vision and goals and that were active on the prefecture/constituency level.

On February 19th, 2016, exactly five months after the forced passage of the security legislation, the leaders of the five opposition parties, the DPJ, the JCP, the JRP, the Social Democratic Party (SDP), and Seikatsu (Livelihood)

Party concluded an agreement on the following four points: (1) to set the abolition of security legislation and the rescinding of the Cabinet decision that lifted the ban on collective self-defense as a common goal, (2) to put an end to the Abe government, (3) to deprive the ruling parties and their collaborators of a majority in national elections, and (4) to cooperate as much as possible in the Diet as well as in the national elections.

Furthermore, on June 7th, 2016, the Civil Alliance formed a 19-point policy agreement with these constitutionalist opposition parties. As the unification of opposition candidates was gradually realized in all of the 32 single member districts, the Civil Alliance signed policy agreements with each of the unified candidates as well. The activities of the Civil Alliance not only sought to change politics through elections, but also to change elections themselves through active and innovative engagement of young people and other citizens in the campaigns.

In the end, the Civil Alliance–backed joint-opposition candidates won 11 of the 32 single member districts, which was no small achievement, considering the fact that opposition had only been able to win two out of 31 three years earlier, as the single member districts were all located in the depopulated, rural areas where the LDP had a particular advantage. The constitutionalist opposition parties managed to win back a little more than a third of all of the seats up for election, though because the ruling parties retained well over two-thirds of the seats that were not up for election in 2016, the parties in favor of constitutional revision went over the crucial two-thirds majority in the Upper House as well.

Moreover, the opposition collaboration strategy of the Civil Alliance was further tested when Abe called a snap election for the Lower House in October 2017. The right-leaning leader of the DP, Seiji Maehara, decided to join forces with the conservative Governor of Tokyo, Yuriko Koike, to form a new Party of Hope. At the last minute, the liberal wing of the DP, led by Yukio Edano, defected and launched the Constitutional Democratic Party of Japan (CDPJ), and against all odds, managed to come ahead of the Party of Hope to be the largest opposition party. The founding of the CDPJ—a little more than two weeks before the day of the election no less—would not have been possible without the prior engagement of the Civil Alliance and the opposition collaboration that it promoted. It is no exaggeration to say that Maehara and Koike took the funds and the organizations that the DP had with them, so a brand-new party had to be made from scratch.

The left wing of the Rengō-affiliated trade unions that had been a central pillar of Sōgakari provided much of the emergency help in personnel with the electoral campaign experience, in spite of the fact that the right-leaning unions that belonged to the same national center supported the Party of Hope.

At the same time, even though SEALDs disbanded (as planned) in summer 2016, many of its core members came to the rescue of the nascent CDPJ and played a crucial role in the formulation and implementation of its successful campaign strategy. Indeed, under the extraordinary circumstances, Edano and other CDPJ candidates were unusually dependent on whatever help they could get, and the ex-SEALDs members were given a rare opportunity to design the CDPJ campaign. In a virtuous cycle that was reminiscent of SEALDs's media strategy, the CDPJ Twitter account created a remarkable buzz in a short period, drawing the attention of the mass media in turn, which then led to the mobilization of increasingly large crowds at its outdoor campaign rallies as the voting day approached.

Another factor that was essential for the successful launching of the CDPJ was cooperation from the JCP. In the face of a critical situation that could have led to the demise of a liberal voice in party politics, the JCP made the unilateral decision to pull out all candidates in the single-member constituencies contested by former DP members who did not join the Party of Hope in order to avoid splitting the liberal Left vote. This decision had the effect of encouraging some of the wavering ex-DP incumbents to stand as independents or under the CDPJ banner, and did indeed allow many of them to get re-elected. The JCP would not have made such a decision were it not resolutely committed to the opposition collaboration strategy, since this did actually cost it votes and seats. The CDPJ and the JCP did not directly form a pact, and it was the Civil Alliance that bridged the two parties as well as the SDP by exchanging the same policy agreement with each of them.

The breakup of the DP resulted in the further fragmentation of the opposition camp, however, and exposed a fundamental weakness of the opposition collaboration strategy of the Civil Alliance that essentially consisted of "recycling" the existing opposition parties, even though it was clear that the DPJ/DP parliamentarians (particularly at the leadership level) were generally much more to the right of the political spectrum than were the citizens. In fact, one may even say that it was a remarkable accomplishment of civil society pressure that the DPJ as a whole opposed the security legislation in 2015, and it was only a question of time until some of these parliamentarians followed their more right-wing personal convictions.

In the event, the Party of Hope ended in failure, and its members sought to reposition themselves by reorganizing themselves yet again as a new Democratic Party for the People (DPP) in May 2018, while some of the more liberal members drifted towards the CDPJ and those who were decidedly conservative left to drift toward the LDP. The Civil Alliance persevered in attempting to rebuild the opposition collaboration by bringing the DPP back into its fold, and it succeeded in doing so by November 2018.

When the Upper House election took place in July 2019, the Civil Alliance signed a 13-point policy agreement with the constitutionalist opposition parties, namely, the CDPJ, DPP, JCP, SDP, and a small parliamentary group of senior former DP members. These opposition parties unified their candidates in all of the 32 single-member districts, and won 10 of them. Moreover, even though the depressed turnout dropped below the symbolic 50% mark, the constitutionalist opposition parties succeeded in depriving the Abe government and its allies of the two-thirds majority that Abe needed for the revision of the constitution.

At the time of writing, the Abe government appears adrift with no sense of direction, without concrete or realistic prospects for the revision of the constitution. The CDPJ and the DPP agreed to form a joint parliamentary group on the basis of the 13-point policy agreement that the Civil Alliance brokered, and they were having further dialogues aimed at joining their forces more fully. With an eye on the upcoming Lower House election, which would take place at some point before autumn 2021, the Civil Alliance is preparing for further developing policy agreements with the constitutionalist opposition parties.

NOTES

1. Joseph A. Schumpeter, *Capitalism, Socialism and Democracy* (third ed.) (New York: Harper & Brothers, 2008).
2. Schumpeter, *Capitalism, Socialism and Democracy*, 269.
3. Kōjin Karatani, "Speech at the 9.11. Stop Nuclear Power Demo" (2011) (http://associations.jp/archives/437).
4. Sidney Tarrow, "Why Occupy Wall Street Is Not the Tea Party of the Left: The United States' Long History of Protest." *Foreign Affairs* (October 10, 2011) (https://www.foreignaffairs.com/articles/north-america/2011-10-10/why-occupy-wall-street-not-tea-party-left).
5. Michael Hardt and Antonio Negri, "The Fight for 'Real Democracy' at the Heart of Occupy Wall Street: The Encampment in Lower Manhattan Speaks to a Failure of Representation." *Foreign Affairs* (October 11, 2011) (https://www.foreignaffairs.com/articles/north-america/2011-10-11/fight-real-democracy-heart-occupy-wall-street).
6. https://w.atwiki.jp/kokkai_publicviewing/pages/41.html (Last retrieved on October 23, 2019.)
7. Mitsuko Uenishi, "Engraving 3.11. in Our Heart" (2019) (https://tanemaki.iwanami.co.jp/posts/2024).
8. Uenishi, "Engraving 3.11. in Our Heart."
9. Article 12 of the Constitution of Japan states, "The freedoms and rights guaranteed to the people by this Constitution shall be maintained by the constant endeavor

of the people, who shall refrain from any abuse of these freedoms and rights and shall always be responsible for utilizing them for the public welfare."

10. Colin Crouch, *Post-Democracy* (Cambridge: Polity Press, 2004).
11. Crouch, *Post-Democracy*, 4.
12. Ken Takada, *2015 Anpo, Sōgakari Kōdō* (Tokyo: Nashinokisha, 2017), 122.
13. David H. Slater, O'Day, Robin, Uno, Satsuki, Kindstrand, Love, and Takano, Chiharu. "SEALDs (Students Emergency Action for Liberal Democracy): Research Note on Contemporary Youth Politics in Japan." *The Asia-Pacific Journal* 13, issue 37, no. 1 (September 14, 2015) (https://apjjf.org/-David_H_-Slater/4375).
14. Aki Okuda, *Kaeru* (Tokyo: Kawade Shobō Shinsha, 2016), 159.

REFERENCES

Crouch, Colin. *Post-Democracy*. Cambridge: Polity Press, 2004.

Hardt, Michael, and Negri, Antonio. "The Fight for 'Real Democracy' at the Heart of Occupy Wall Street: The Encampment in Lower Manhattan Speaks to a Failure of Representation." *Foreign Affairs* (October 11, 2011) (https://www.foreignaffairs.com/articles/north-america/2011-10-11/fight-real-democracy-heart-occupy-wall-street).

Karatani, Kōjin. "Speech at the 9.11. Stop Nuclear Power Demo." (2011) (http://associations.jp/archives/437).

Okuda, Aki. *Kaeru.* Tokyo: Kawade Shobō Shinsha, 2016.

Schumpeter, Joseph A. *Capitalism, Socialism and Democracy* (third edition). New York: Harper & Brothers, 2008.

Slater, David H., O'Day, Robin, Uno, Satsuki, Kindstrand, Love, and Takano, Chiharu. "SEALDs (Students Emergency Action for Liberal Democracy): Research Note on Contemporary Youth Politics in Japan." *The Asia-Pacific Journal* 13, issue 37, no. 1 (September 14, 2015) (https://apjjf.org/-David_H_-Slater/4375).

Takada, Ken. *2015 Anpo, Sōgakari Kōdō*. Tokyo: Nashinokisha, 2017.

Tarrow, Sidney. "Why Occupy Wall Street Is Not the Tea Party of the Left: The United States' Long History of Protest." *Foreign Affairs* (October 10, 2011) (https://www.foreignaffairs.com/articles/north-america/2011-10-10/why-occupy-wall-street-not-tea-party-left).

Uenishi, Mitsuko. "Engraving 3.11. in Our Heart" (2019) (https://tanemaki.iwanami.co.jp/posts/2024).

Chapter Three

Popular Sovereignty, Social Movements, and Money

The Political Process in 1960 and 2014 Surrounding National Security

Tatsuhiko Yamamoto

THE *TŌCHI-KŌI RON* AS THE PRINCIPLE OF POPULAR SOVEREIGNTY

In 1959, the Japanese Supreme Court decided a historically infamous case, the Sunawaga case,[1] and adopted the *Tōchi-Kōi Ron*, which might be called the "political question doctrine," in English.

The main issue was whether the permission granted by the Japanese Government for the presence of U.S. troops violated Article 9, Paragraph 2 of the Constitution, which prohibits the government from having armed forces. Although this could be considered a legal question, the Court refrained from deciding the case, saying that questions about highly political actions, *tōchi kōi*, should "be left to the political judgement of the people of the nation, with whom sovereignty lies."

There is a difference between the *Tōchi Kōi Ron* in Japan and the political question doctrine in the U.S. The latter involves the principle of separation of powers, or the institutional competence of each branch.[2] On the other hand, in Japan, the *Tōchi Kōi Ron* involves the principle of popular sovereignty.[3] If we read the doctrine in that light, it constitutionally requires political forces, if they wish to change the political regime dramatically, to inform the people of the importance of such a change, propose their own ideas, and give the people an opportunity to make careful and conscious decisions on the transformation.[4]

From this perspective, what happened in 2014 was problematic. As is well known, in July 2014 the Abe Cabinet made an important decision changing the previous interpretation of Article 9 in order to allow Japan the right to collective self-defense. Even though the Cabinet dissolved the House of Representatives on November 21, four months after the Cabinet decision, and held a general election in December, the ruling Liberal Democratic Party (LDP) intentionally downplayed national security issues at the time of this election and focused on economic issues instead. The Prime Minister called the dissolution the "Abenomics Dissolution" and called this an election for a good economy. By doing so, the LDP tried to turn people's eyes away from a highly political question, and the people seemed to lose their opportunity to decide on the question. In addition, national security legislation based on the Cabinet decision was passed in September 2015, but no national election, which could have been an opportunity to consult the people on the issue, was held then.

A similar alienation of the sovereign people occurred in 1960 when Prime Minister Kishi, grandfather of Shinzō Abe, revised the Security Treaty between the United States and Japan. Here I shall give an overview of the political situation of 1960 to clarify the difference between Kishi in 1960 and his grandson Abe in 2014, and I will focus on civic activism and constitutional politics. I will conclude that civic activism has been quite vulnerable to money, and that constitutional politics have been influenced or manipulated by the *zaikai* (the financial world), and probably also by the U.S. government.

NOBUSUKE KISHI, SOCIAL ACTIVISM, AND THE FINANCIAL WORLD

Illusionary Victory

Kishi is said to have won a victory in 1960. This is because he consistently advocated for the independence of Japan and the establishment of an independent constitution, after being held in Sugamo Prison as an accused war criminal and returning to public life, and achieved his primary goal of revising the Security Treaty between the U.S. and Japan and the U.S.-Japan Status of Forces Agreement. As is well known, Kishi "believed that the peace treaty [concluded by Shigeru Yoshida] disgraced the Japanese people, that the Security Treaty should be revised to a more autonomous one, and that as the revision requires rearmament, the constitution should also be revised."[5]

As will be described later, "frustration of various kinds pervading Japanese society during the Occupation" was "pent up" in this era.[6] Part of this "accumulated resentment and suffering"[7] was directed at the revision of the Security Treaty sought by Kishi, leading to the campaign against the Japan-U.S. Security Treaty in 1960, in which *Zengakuren* (the All-Japan Federation of Students' Self-Governing Associations) played a central role. *Zengakuren* was formed in 1948 under the guidance of the Communist Party not for political reasons but due to an economic issue, increases in university tuition. In short, "*Zengakuren* was formed as a result of the sensitive reaction and resistance of economically challenged students to the economic problem of increases in tuition fees."[8] However, the federation strengthened its political character through participation in anti–atomic and anti–hydrogen bomb movements and the Sunagawa Struggle, i.e., the protest movement against the expansion of U.S. military bases that led to the Sunagawa case discussed above. In particular, the "perfect springboard"[9] for their participation in the campaign against the Security Treaty was the movement against the revision of the Police Duties Execution Act after the fall of 1958. Kishi's proposed amendment of the Police Duties Execution Act, which came to light as negotiations began between Japan and the United States for revision of the Security Treaty, was the exact opposite of the revision. If the purpose of treaty revision was to address "diplomatic issues for complete independence," the revision of the Police Duties Execution Act to reinforce the authority of police officers for security enforcement after the termination of the occupation was to address "domestic issues required for complete independence."[10] Kishi frankly stated that revision of the Police Duties Execution Act was "aimed at wiping out the side effects of post-war occupation policy to create a truly independent system in Japan."[11]

The opposition forces, including *Zengakuren*, saw this as an attempt to prevent and control what the authorities considered political crimes, and organized in response. For example, the number of participants in a demonstration on November 5, 1958, "reached about four million, including those in labor union strikes and work meetings."[12] Social movements linked to the internal struggles of the Socialist Party and other opposition parties served as precursors to the movement against revision of the Security Treaty by forcing the proposed amendment of the Police Duties Execution Act to be withdrawn. This success, and cases such as the forced entry of demonstrators (1,200 members of labor unions and *Zengakuren*) into the Diet to oppose the Reparations Agreement with Vietnam being rammed through the House of Representatives in November 1959, intensified the campaign against the Security Treaty in 1960.

However, as noted, the Kishi Administration is said to have won a comeback victory in 1960 after failing to amend the Police Duties Execution Act. This is because Kishi achieved the revision of the Security Treaty, his long-cherished wish. Nevertheless, it was not an easy victory. The Kishi Administration, established in February 1957, signed an agreement with U.S. Ambassador Douglas MacArthur II in August 1958 to fully revise the Security Treaty. On January 19, 1960, a new treaty and a new agreement were signed in Washington. At that time, Kishi and President Eisenhower reached an important agreement. They agreed that Eisenhower would visit Japan for two days from June 19 in exchange for a visit by the Crown Prince and Princess to the U.S. to commemorate the 100th anniversary of the friendship between Japan and the U.S. Kishi was determined that the new treaty must be approved by the Diet and ratified by the Cabinet before Eisenhower's June 19 visit to Japan, which would be the first by a sitting U.S. president.[13] According to Article 61 of the Constitution, a treaty, like a budget, is automatically approved by the Diet if the House of Councillors does not make a decision within 30 days after it is passed by the House of Representatives. To have it approved by June 19, therefore, the revision had to be passed by the House of Representatives on May 19 at the latest. As a result, May 19 became a critical date for the Kishi Administration as well as for the forces opposing revision, including labor unions, the General Council of Trade Unions of Japan, and *Zengakuren*.

The opposition forces tried to prevent the House of Representatives from passing the amendment by May 19 by organizing both peaceful and violent demonstrations. They demanded the resignation of the Kishi Cabinet and the dissolution of the House of Representatives. In the end, however, the LDP discussed and passed the bill on its own from midnight on the 19th to dawn on the 20th, and the session was extended for the approval of the new treaty by the House of Representatives as well as automatic approval in the House of Councillors. After this steamrolling on May 19, protests to prevent the final ratification by the Kishi Cabinet (demanding the resignation of the Kishi Cabinet and the dissolution of the House of Representatives) intensified. On May 26, waves of demonstrations surrounded the Diet (540,000 participants according to the National Police Agency), and the largest postwar nationwide protest was held by 5.4 million people (450,000 people according to the Public Security Intelligence Agency) on June 4. On June 10, Press Secretary James Hagerty, who came to Japan to make arrangements for President Eisenhower's visit, was placed under siege at Haneda Airport (he escaped to the U.S. Embassy by helicopter), while on June 15 the confrontation between the police and mainstream members of *Zengakuren* who forced their way into the Diet resulted in the death of Michiko Kanba, a student of the University of Tokyo. The next day, Kishi held an extraordinary Cabinet meeting and postponed (in effect canceled) President Eisenhower's visit to Japan, with which he had been obsessed, in consideration of the safety of the President and the Emperor, who had been scheduled to meet him. Nevertheless, the new treaty was automatically approved on June 19 and ratified by the Kishi Cabinet.

Defeat in Reality

Because Kishi finally achieved the long-awaited revision of the Security Treaty in 1960 despite intense resistance, he seems to have won a victory. But did he? A careful examination of the political process in 1960 suggests that he was defeated.

Dissolution

The Kishi Administration was established in February 1957, three years before the revision of the Security Treaty. In May of 1958, a general election of the House of Representatives was held, and Kishi's LDP won an absolute majority. Negotiations for the full revision of the Security Treaty began in August of that year, but the revision had not been an issue in the election. According to his memoir, to an interviewer's question as to whether he thought that treaty revision was still a long way off, and that it was too early to seek popular judgment in this election, Kishi answered "yes."[14] In other words, in the general election held two years before the revision of the Security Treaty, Kishi avoided discussing the matter. However, he did not mean to avoid judgment by "the people of the nation as the sovereign" on this "highly political" issue. In fact, after the signing of the new treaty on January 19, 1960, in Washington, Kishi planned to hold a snap general election. "After signing the new treaty, I thought I should appeal to the country," said Kishi.[15] Kishi repeatedly mentions this in his memoir, and elsewhere he also stated, "I think the House of Representatives should have been dissolved immediately after the signing [of the new treaty]," "I wanted to explain the difference between the [old] Security Treaty and the new one, and demonstrate how noble and profitable the new treaty is for Japan in the general election. I was confident of winning."[16] He also said, "I was unable to sleep at that time (when Eisenhower's visit to Japan was canceled), and [. . .] when I gave up on the dissolution (after the new treaty was signed),"[17] which indicates that he was highly motivated to dissolve the Diet after the treaty was signed. Interestingly, Kishi had the same idea as the forces opposing the revision, including the Socialist Party, in that a snap general election should be held before the Diet approval.

If a general election had been held, Kishi might have lost. Nevertheless, his obsession with holding a snap general election despite that possibility seems to have been largely due to his political beliefs. To quote Kishi, "I do not compromise on my basic political position. I always make sure my political position is clear. Since this allows the public to decide which side to take, I cannot leave fundamental problems unclear or avoid them."[18] Kishi added, "As the Japanese people are extremely indifferent to security issues and lack much awareness of them, I had the intention of debating to let the people decide."[19]

This idea is close to the constitutional transformation theory elaborated by Bruce Ackerman, a professor of constitutional law, which requires informing the public of issues and seeking the people's deliberate judgment through active discussions with opposition forces. Therefore, if the snap election had been held as desired by Kishi, and the LDP had won an overwhelming victory, the anti-Kishi forces within the LDP and the opposition forces would have been suppressed, and procedures such as the steamrolling would not have been necessary, while the constitutional legitimacy of the revision of the Security Treaty would have been enhanced.

However, the dissolution did not take place after the signing of the new treaty, as a result of strong opposition by three anti-mainstream LDP factions (the Ikeda, Miki-Matsumura, and Ishibashi factions) to Kishi's idea of dissolution. (Ikeda was serving as Minister of International Trade and Industry in the Kishi Cabinet at that time. However, he attended meetings of the three anti-mainstream factions to hold Kishi in check.) Kishi himself said that the LDP was "unable to dissolve [the Diet] due to special circumstances within the party,"[20] and stressed the fact that the idea of snap general election both Kishi and those opposing the revision of the treaty desired was crushed by the opposition of the LDP. This abandonment of dissolution intensified the movement against Kishi and the revision of the Security Treaty, eventually leading to his resignation before achieving his goal.

From this perspective, Kishi seems to have lost against the anti-Kishi forces in the Liberal Democratic Party, as he had to give up the dissolution after the signing of the new treaty.

Resignation

Kishi resigned on June 23, 1960, four days after the new treaty was automatically approved and ratified. It may be more appropriate to say that he was "forced" to resign, as he had not intended to do so. In fact, he wanted to remain in office to fulfill another long-held desire, the amendment of the Constitution. In an interview, Kishi replied "yes" when asked by a reporter if he wished to carry out constitutional revision after the revision of the Security Treaty.[21] Immediately after the meeting with President Eisenhower and the signing of the new treaty, he also said, "I do not plan to resign with the revision of the Treaty as my triumph. The new treaty is not a goal but a start."[22] Clearly, his retirement at this time (the Ikeda Cabinet was established on July 19) was earlier than Kishi wanted.

So why was he compelled to resign at this point before he had the chance to achieve his goal?

As described earlier, the new treaty was railroaded through the House of Representatives on May 19, but the Kawano and the Miki-Matsumura factions held meetings the next day expressing their anti-Kishi position. On the 21st, the Ikeda faction held a meeting, in which the majority advocated a change in the political situation. Meetings were held between Kishi and Ikeda on the 25th, and between Kishi and Miki on June 2. Kishi seemed to be unwilling to attend these meetings and is said to have done so only at the insistence of Ikeda, and some pointed out that these meetings were realized with strong recommendations from Ikeda and financial circles.[23] At the meeting between Kishi and Miki, Miki handed Kishi a document requesting the resignation of the prime minister with the approval of the new treaty (a similar document was also prepared by Vice President Banboku Ōno, and was said to have been drafted by three anti-mainstream factions within the LDP and part of the Socialist Party).[24] Under such pressure from the party, Kishi finally announced his resignation on June 23. The aforementioned sensational Kanba Incident took place on June 15 before the announcement of his resignation, and Ikeda proposed responding in force to "mobilize police officers to crack down on the mob." Furthermore, he is said to have astonished others in justifying such hard-line measures, saying, "It was a conspiracy of the Communist International. Use the Self-Defense Forces and mobilize the police from all over the country."[25] According to Yasuhiro Nakasone, who was to became the 71st Prime Minister of Japan (1982), perhaps Ikeda promoted the Anti-Kishi movement by making Kishi take such a hard-line measure to "remove him from the Cabinet."[26] If one believes the remark made by Nakasone, it suggests that Kishi's enemies were inside his Cabinet.

Based on all of this evidence, the resignation of Kishi seems to have been a result of his defeat by opposition forces within the LDP. However, it may not be as simple as that. To understand what defeated Kishi, it is necessary to identify the reality of the opposition forces. It is important to consider who succeeded Kishi, who was supporting that successor, and what political beliefs he had. The first question is easy to answer: It was Hayato Ikeda. One answer to the question "Who was supporting Ikeda?" would be the "business world." Nakasone describes Ikeda as follows: "He [Ikeda] was from the Tax Bureau [of the Ministry of Finance] and had been recognized by the mainstream of the business world for dealing with property taxes," so he "had gained solid support from the leadership of the business world."[27] According to Nakasone, Ikeda "had a hand" in the business world.[28] If it was Ikeda who prompted the resignation of Kishi,[29] Kishi may seem to have lost to the business world through Ikeda. In fact, Nakasone pointed out the strong influence of business at that time, describing "the time of the Ikeda Cabinet in particular" as a period of "unity between the government and business."[30]

Along with the business world, the U.S. government is believed to have instigated both the resignation of Kishi and the establishment of the Ikeda Cabinet. According to *Altered States: The United States and Japan since the Occupation*, by Michael Schaller, a historian specializing in U.S. diplomatic history, U.S. National Security Council meetings were held on May 31 and June 8 after the steamrolling, in which the director of the CIA said, "What is desirable for Japan is that Kishi resigns and, if possible, he is replaced by [Shigeru] Yoshida."[31] Schaller also pointed out that "the CIA used its financial influence on the Liberal Democratic Party to quickly replace Kishi with a more moderate Conservative politician."[32] On June 20, U.S. Ambassador MacArthur and Shigeru Yoshida held a meeting, in which Yoshida stated that "Ikeda or Satō is desirable." On the 21st, just before Kishi's announcement of his resignation on the 23rd, Ikeda informed MacArthur that he would succeed Kishi, and MacArthur also "described Ikeda as a faithful supporter of the cooperation between Japan and the U.S. and the best candidate to replace Kishi."[33]

Based on the above, financial circles and the U.S. government seem to have driven Kishi, who tried to stay in power after the revision of the treaty in order to amend the Constitution, into resignation. What the new Ikeda Cabinet intended to achieve on their behalf was best represented by the general election of the House of Representatives held on November 20, 1960. (The dissolution took place on October 24.) In this election, which should have been held earlier from the perspective of Kishi and those opposing treaty revision, the Ikeda Cabinet presented the Income Doubling Plan as its slogan. The LDP airbrushed the problems of constitutional reform and security issues out of this election. In other words, Ikeda removed those "highly political" questions from the contested ground of the election and focused on economic problems, just as Kishi's grandson, Shinzō Abe, did in the general election of December 2014. This strategy worked, and the LDP made gains in the November election (going from 287 seats to 296 seats, or from 61.45% to 63.38%).

In short, Ikeda's goal was to end the "political period" or the "constitutional period" and welcome the "economic growth period."[34] This was not irrelevant to the fact that the Income Doubling Plan approved by the Ikeda Cabinet strongly promoted the science and mathematics education fields by, for example, greatly increasing the number of students in science and engineering.[35] Humanities students in law and literature schools tend to show a strong interest in politics and the Constitution, which was seen as possibly destabilizing society and hindering economic development. In contrast, students in science and engineering were seen as immersing themselves in politically neutral scientific and technological research, and being relatively indifferent to politics and debates over the Constitution. Ikeda, who enjoyed "a world composed of numbers,"[36] promoted science and mathematics education to make those interested in politics and the Constitution appear eccentric and make it difficult for the people of the nation as the sovereign to establish a period of constitutional politics. It goes without saying that this promotion of science and mathematics education advanced science and technology and become a driving force for economic growth. As is well known, the economy grew rapidly in the 1960s.

Keeping the people away from the Constitution and directing their attention toward the economy was convenient for the business community and the U.S. government, which supported the new Ikeda Cabinet. It has been pointed out that "Japan in the 1960s, shaken by security issues, had another problem in its relationship with the U.S., which was considered a more important issue for the Government and the financial community."[37] This was the issue of trade liberalization. Dwelling on security issues was not in the best interest of financial circles or the United States. The business world may have also perceived the political beliefs of Kishi as a risk to economic development. As described earlier, Kishi believed in uncompromising and confrontational political tactics, and stated that the opposition parties "need to have a spirit of assuming the reins of government and to be prepared to do so."[38] During this period when the Socialist Party still had significant support, he insisted on a two-party system.[39] Through this confrontational posture, he showed a kind of respect for his opponents. For example, he thought that the lower court decision of the Sunagawa case (the Date case, 1959) that found the U.S. military presence unconstitutional "had some points worth paying attention to in considering the argument for the unconstitutionality of the matter."[40] Likewise, with regard to the mass movement against the Police Duties Execution Act, he "did not think the mass movement itself was a problematic situation."[41] As his words quoted earlier, "I cannot leave fundamental problems unclear or avoid them"[42] indicate, Kishi believed strongly in the importance of debating the opposition forces.[43] For the business world, this confrontational political stance made it difficult to concentrate the energy of the people on economic development and thus needed to be avoided. For rapid economic growth, a "prosperous business culture"[44] which requires a "harmonizing cabinet"[45] is more important than a political culture.

In addition, Kishi's political stance against the United States could pose a risk to the U.S. government. In the revision of the Security Treaty, Kishi's original idea was to establish a substantive bilateral treaty based on an equal relationship between Japan and the United States. He criticized Shigeru Yoshida's stance as "favoring the United States,"[46] and wished Japan to be independent from the U.S. to some extent.[47] It is well known that Ikeda followed the stance of Shigeru Yoshida and took a pro-American attitude.

It is clear, therefore, that, Kishi may have won revision of the Security Treaty, but he seems to have been defeated in many important ways involving the history of the Japanese Constitution. A careful examination of what happened in 1960 suggests that what Kishi was really fighting against was not the movement against the revision of the treaty in which *Zengakuren* participated. Kishi and the movement against revision were in agreement in that, as described earlier, both desired a snap general election after the signing of the new treaty. They both believed that the people of the nation, as sovereign, should be given the opportunity to make political decisions on "highly political" questions. Although their standpoints were completely opposite, they both had strong beliefs about constitutional issues. If the snap general election had been held at the appropriate time after the signing of the new treaty, and if Kishi had remained in power and proceeded with the amendment of the Constitution,[48] Japan would have, despite its struggles, produced citizens[49] aware of their role as sovereign, and mature social movements. This supposition suggests that they may both have been defeated by elite pragmatism[50] based on economic rationality and Japan's relationship with the United States.

The next section will focus on the political movements of the people, including student organizations, to identify their characteristics and what they fought against.

ZENGAKUREN, SOCIAL ACTIVISM, AND THE BUSINESS WORLD

The Political Movement of the People

As mentioned above, this section will discuss the year 1960 focusing on the movement for the revision of the Security Treaty.

First of all, it is necessary to discuss whether it is appropriate to refer to this as a "mass movement." Was the number of participants in the movement large enough to use the term "mass?" In a poll conducted by the Cabinet Office in late July 1959, fifteen percent were in favor of the revision while ten percent were against it.[51] The results of other newspaper polls are as follows (tables 3.1–3.4). [52]

Table 3.1.

Q: What do you think about the current Security Treaty?

Answer	*Percentage*
It does not have to be changed	12.5%
It should be amended immediately	7.2%
It should be amended but it does not have to be now	20.6%
It should be abrogated immediately	6.4%
It should be abrogated at some point in the future	13.0%
Indifferent	11.4%
Not sure	24.8%
Other	4.1%

Source: A poll conducted by *Mainichi Shimbun* in mid-August 1959 (*Mainichi Shimbun*, August 26, 1959)

Table 3.2.

Q: What do you think about the new treaty?	
Answer	*Percentage*
Good	21.6%
Bad	36.0%
Indifferent	15.3%
Not sure	26.5%
No answer	0.6%

Source: A poll conducted by *Mainichi Shimbun* in mid-March of 1960 (*Mainichi Shimbun*, April 4, 1960)

Table 3.3.

Q: The new treaty will not take effect unless approved by the Diet. Do you think it should be approved?	
Answer	*Percentage*
Should be approved	15.8%
Should not be approved	27.9%
Approval is inevitable	18.8%
Not sure	31.4%
Other	6.1%

Source: A poll conducted by *Mainichi Shimbun* in mid-March of 1960 (*Mainichi Shimbun*, April 4, 1960)

Table 3.4.

Q: Do you want the Diet to approve the Security Treaty?	
Answer	*Percentage*
Yes	21%
No	28%
No opinion / not sure	51%

Source: A poll conducted by *Yomiuri Shimbun* in early March 1960 (*Yomiuri Shimbun*, April 3, 1960)

The above results indicate that those against revision of the treaty did not account for the majority of the population. In fact, the opposition seems to be in the minority when passive responses such as "Not sure" are taken into consideration. Kishi said, "If you only look at what is happening outside the Diet, it looks as if a coup or revolution is about to take place in Japan. However, in Kōrakuen [stadium] located three kilometers away, a baseball game is being held and tens of thousands of people are watching it. In Ginza, located two kilometers away, young people are strolling around as always. I realized that after all, the silent majority was in favor of me, that only those manipulated were against me. For this reason, the case of Syngman Rhee is essentially different from Japan's security issues."[53] In short, unlike the South Korean social movement that forced President Syngman Rhee to resign (April 26, 1960), "Japan's movement against the revision of the Security Treaty was . . . never a national opposition movement."[54] Kishi's remarks need to be analyzed critically, but these poll results indicate that they did not miss the point completely.[55] As Kishi pointed out, if many people were living their lives mainly as consumers in 1960, it is debatable whether or not the "people of the nation as the sovereign" who would make a final decision on "highly political" issues were present in Japan at that time.

An Imagined Movement

Sports Festival

Social movements always begin with a minority, and it is important not to place too much emphasis on popular opinion polls, but to understand the significance of movements from a longer-term perspective. However, even from this perspective, one can identify the fictitious nature of the movement against the revision of the Security Treaty in 1960, or at least its limitations, based on the following two points.

The first is the motivation for the movement against revision. For example, Susumu Nishibe, a member of the Executive Committee (Vice Chairman) of *Zengakuren* at that time, who later became a University of Tokyo professor, called this movement a "spree"[56] and stated: "In general, the campaign against the Japan-U.S. Security Treaty in 1960 was not a struggle against the Treaty. Most of the participants including a large part of the leadership were ignorant and even indifferent about exactly what the new treaty would bring to international politics and military affairs. The campaign was a kind of theatre of ideas that revealed the contradictions in postwar trends."[57] At the same time, Shin Satō described the opposition movement by *Zengakuren* as "similar to a sports festival."[58] What mattered, he said, was the "bodily sensation" felt through the "movement," and that the physical sensation made the participants forget "which faction the demonstrations had originally been situated in or what they were protesting against."[59] He also pointed out that "the young people who supported *Zengakuren*" were "disgusted by the attitude of trying to give a noble meaning to their actions, including their constitutional rights."[60] This kind of criticism is consistent with Nakasone's opinion that the campaign in 1960 occurred because of "repressed nationalism since the occupation" and to "relieve frustration."[61] Also, Keiichi Matsushita mentioned that the opposition activities by the General Council of Trade Unions and labor unions were carried out on a per diem basis, pointing out that "there was a daily allowance of around ¥300 for mobilization (equivalent to about ¥2000 now), so when they ran through the budget, the mobilization itself lost its momentum."[62] It seems that not every participant in the movement against the revision of the Security Treaty had a clear opinion regarding constitutional issues. Many young people participated in the movement as a sports festival, and many adults as a business operation.

However, as Nishibe and Satō pointed out, some of the participants understood the constitutional implications or the highly political nature of the issue. In addition, Shōzō Fujita pointed out the possibility that the "steamrolling" by the LDP on May 19, 1960, could change the nature of social movements in postwar Japan. According to Fujita, social movements prior to May 19 were resistance movements carried out to reject a return to the wartime state and "to settle wartime grudges."[63] However, this form of resistance movement is "a retaliation for being offended, and problematic behaviors tend to be forgotten quickly,"[64] as they are different from "addressing the problem itself and making the other party take responsibility for their action that caused the problem."[65] This type of "vengeful" movement, which dovetails with Nakasone's description of the campaign against the Security Treaty as a "method of relieving frustration" accumulated after Japan's defeat in World War II,[66] is a politically empty movement, in line with the postwar emphasis on private lives and consumption. However, on May 19, when the people who used to see the Constitution as a mere means to rationalize their desires saw that "the ruler who imposed the Constitution . . . turned out not to be bound by the Constitution at all," they began to consider this as a "mental stimulus" and develop a social movement backed by "political passion," not "retaliation."[67]

"The End of Money" and the Business World

As discussed above, the movement against the revision of the treaty in 1960 was certainly not a movement in which the majority of the population participated, but a nihilistic movement in which "most"[68] participants did not understand the constitutional or political implications. However, as pointed out by many, including Fujita,[69] it had the potential to develop into a mature social movement by the people of the nation as the sovereign. Nevertheless, the second limitation of this movement—the plural layers of actors as well as its financial vulnerability—seems to have destroyed such potential.

As is well known, the movement against the revision was organized by multiple entities including the General Council of Trade Unions, the Socialist Party, labor unions, *Zengakuren*, and the Communist Party. *Zengakuren* was under the leadership of the Communist Party at first, but they entered into an adversarial relationship in 1960. (By the summer of 1958, the mainstream anti-Communist faction inside *Zengakuren* had already begun to overpower the Communist faction.) They began to differ greatly on the reason for opposing the revision of the Treaty. The Communist Party "opposed the revision of the Security Treaty in order to prevent Japan from becoming even more dependent on the United States."[70] In other words, they positioned their movement as an anti-U.S. struggle for independence. In contrast, *Zengakuren* was "opposed to becoming independent from the United States through the revision of Treaty and moving towards Japan developing its own militarism."[71] The two sides were therefore 180 degrees apart in their stance towards the United States. The Communist Party was anti-American, and *Zengakuren* was pro-American.

This difference became visible in the Hagerty Incident. The *Zengakuren* mainstream did not position the campaign against the Security Treaty as an anti-U.S. struggle, so they did not see much importance in the secretary's visit to Japan. The demonstrators who surrounded Hagerty mainly consisted of Communist Party anti-U.S. forces. Subsequently, "after the Communist Party went ahead of *Zengakuren* in the Hagerty Incident, the federation charged into the Diet on June 15."[72] The adversarial relationship of the forces against the revision of the treaty, therefore, seems to have been the driving force of the Hagerty Incident and June 15.

Ideological differences were also reflected in financial support. As is commonly known, Seigen Tanaka, chairman of the Central Committee of the prewar Communist Party and a businessperson after the war, was the one who provided *Zengakuren* with financial support in 1960. The federation needed funds for transportation to demonstrations and to bail out those charged or detained during demonstrations. Therefore, Yoshinobu Yoshihara, Director of Finance at the Secretariat of *Zengakuren*, Kentarō Karoji, the chairman of the federation, and the executives Hiroshi Kojima and Kōichirō Shinohara got in touch with Tanaka to request financial support.[73] The members of Zengakuren "did not know what Seigen was thinking or doing at that time," but he certainly knew about them.[74] As he was "profoundly disgusted by the Communist Party," he "plotted to hinder the advancement of the Communist Party" by providing the *Zengakuren* mainstream with financial support.[75] Especially important is the following testimony of Shinohara, the former executive of *Zengakuren*:

> At that time, business leaders created a secret group, and (Hiroki) Imazato (CEO of NSK Ltd.) and others disapproved of Kishi and aimed to overthrow him. This is why the *anti-Kishi* trend became a powerful force. . . . [T]hose people used the campaign to overthrow Kishi. *Seigen Tanaka played a part in it.* He allied with financiers and worked with Imazato and Sōhei Nakayama (President of

> Industrial Bank of Japan). It seems that young business leaders at that time felt the urgent need to remove Kishi from power (emphasis by the author).[76]

This testimony by Shinohara highlights the strange and complex relationship between Kishi, the business world (including Hayato Ikeda), and *Zengakuren*. As described earlier, Kishi lost the battle against the business world. However, this deprived the nation of the opportunity for a snap general election and the amendment of the Constitution. This defeat also meant the defeat of politics (democracy) by economy (money).[77] The above testimony of Shinohara alludes to the fact that *Zengakuren* experienced a similar defeat due to its involvement with Seigen Tanaka as a result of its ideological difference with the Communist Party. Shinohara made the following comment:

> Actually, the business leaders ended up using our [Zengakuren's] idea of "opposing an independent [from the United States] militaristic nation." Ikeda and the LDP began to focus on the economy based on this idea of moving away from Japan's own militarism for a while as it was strongly opposed by the people. . . . Thus, in a sense, what we had said came true. "Kishi was the official winner, but Zengakuren was the one who really won."[78]

But did *Zengakuren* really win? Perhaps the federation ended up serving as a tool of the business community to overthrow Kishi by relying for its activities on funds obtained through Tanaka's connection with financiers. Perhaps, after its funds were controlled by the business world, including Seigen Tanaka, the federation's mentality was distorted by the power of money.[79] As described earlier, many expected the emergence of citizenhood through the movement organized by students in 1960. For instance, the sociologist Ikutarō Shimizu, admiring the purity of their "selflessness,"[80] stated that "students were different from workers who were paid to participate in demonstrations. They were different from members of organizations who earned a living and gained access to promotion through the movement. No matter what they did, they did not gain anything. They were not paid, honored, or promoted. Despite, or because of the fact that they did not gain anything, they had nothing to lose and moved straight toward their goals."[81] Also, political scientist Kan'ichi Fukuda expected the campaign against the Security Treaty, in which people other than members of political parties participated, to spontaneously produce active citizens who were responsible for national decisions and would be integrated under the Constitution of Japan for the first time in Japan, where there had been up to then only people adhering to the existing sense of community and the status of "subjects."[82] However, the student movement did not develop in the direction expected by Shimizu and Fukuda after 1960. This may have been due to the loss of its purity as a result of its deep involvement with the business world, which caused it to tilt sharply toward partisan and political purposes, that is, the narrow-minded personal and situational goals of overthrowing Kishi and defeating the Communist Party. If, for example, (a part of) the *Zengakuren* mainstream advocated a pure political movement independent of existing political parties at least for a certain period, the loss of purity due to the power of money seems to represent its defeat. Indeed, the The Bund (Communist alliance) forming the *Zengakuren* mainstream after the campaign against the Security Treaty split and dismantled.

Needless to say, it was not only big business that undermined the development of civic movements. The Supreme Court led by Chief Justice Kōtarō Tanaka also had a negative impact on the potential development of civic movements. Immediately after the establishment of the Ikeda Cabinet on July 20, the Supreme Court rendered a decision that appeared to celebrate the drama of this regime change, which was the transition from the political period to the economic growth period. It was a decision in the case of the Tokyo Public Safety Ordinance.[83] This case involved the constitutionality of the regulations on demonstrations under the Public Safety Ordinance. The Supreme Court acknowledged the constitutionality of the regulations by characterizing a political demonstration as dangerous activity ignited by "crowd psychology," declaring:

> Unlike forms of expression such as speech and publication, the expression of ideas by collective behavior is characterized by being supported by the power of a collective entity consisting of many people, that is, a kind of underlying physical power. Such potential forces are of a nature that can be very easily mobilized according to a plan or by sudden internal or external stimuli, or crowd manipulation. In this case, even calm groups can sometimes get caught in a wave of excitement. Based on the law of crowd psychology and facts, it is obvious that they can become mobs in an instant and trample on law and order by virtue of their own strength, creating a situation that neither police force nor the leader of the collective entity can control in extreme cases.

This is how the legitimacy of political movements as forms of expression was denied by the judiciary in the summer of 1960.[84]

CONCLUSION

This essay has argued that Kishi's orthodox political approach and the campaign against the Japan-U.S. Security Treaty in 1960 represented by the activities of *Zengakuren* could have created an opportunity for the people of

Japan as consumers to become citizens, or "the people of the nation as the sovereign," and thus that the political question doctrine that allows people to make decisions on "highly political" questions such as security issues could have been applied, but the Ikeda Cabinet with its Income Doubling Plan supported by the business community, as well as U.S. policy toward Japan based on similar ideas, deprived Japan of such possibilities in 1960. However, I do not intend to criticize this result from today's perspective, because economic development was also an inevitable demand in 1960, and Japan's rapid economic growth could only have been achieved by marginalizing politics and the Constitution. What is important now that the economy has developed is how to evaluate and overcome this postwar regime formed by the events of 1960.

From that perspective, the political process of 2014 seems problematic. Shinzō Abe is often compared with his grandfather, Kishi. However, in the general election for the House of Representatives held in December 2014 after the July 2014 Cabinet decision to substantially accept the right to collective self-defense, Abe focused on his economic policy, "Abenomics," and downplayed security issues. This shift of his focus to economic issues resembled the political tactics adopted by the forces against Kishi, including Ikeda in 1960, rather than the political style of Abe's grandfather, Kishi, who encouraged "the public to debate the matter [security issues] and make up their minds about self-defense.[85] In a sense, Abe imitated the method used to overthrow his grandfather. Also, while he did not seek the people's deliberate political judgment on the Cabinet decision, military legislation was passed based on the Cabinet decision in September 2015. (The next general election of the House of Representatives was held in October 2017, and the issue of the Security Treaty had become a past problem by then.[86])

From the above perspective, Shinzō Abe, whose earnest desire is to amend the Constitution, seems to be still living in the "economic period" initiated by the Ikeda Cabinet. Lingering in this period may have been justifiable in 1960, but that may not be the case today. Continuing to lie about the legitimacy of the military legislation in a manner not conforming to the political question doctrine[87] means keeping the people as primarily "consumers" under a private-life-first policy. This will delay the arrival of the "constitutional period" and hinder the long-awaited amendment of the Constitution.

NOTES

1. "The Judgment of the Grand Bench by the Supreme Court of Japan on December 24, 1959," *Keishu*, vol. 13, 3225.

2. See Tara Leigh Grove,"The Lost History of the Political Question Doctrine," *New York University Law Review* 90 (2015): 1908, 1952–57.

3. See Tatsuhiko Yamamoto, "Popular Sovereignty and Acts of Government," *Hōgaku Seminar*, No. 729 (2015): 50; and Tatsuhiko Yamamoto, "The Principle of Popular Sovereignty and Constitutional Changes in the United States," *Kenpō Mondai*, No. 28 (2017): 45. For a view by Toshio Irie, who was a Supreme Court Justice at the time of the Sunagawa case, see Toshio Irie, "Acts of Government," *Kōhō Kenkyū*, No. 13, 90.

4. For a similar argument, see the trilogy *We the People* (*Foundations* [1991], *Transformations* [1998], and *The Civil Rights Revolution* [2014]). (According to his theory, the deliberative judgment of the sovereign people in the exceptional *period of constitutional politics*, as in the period of the New Deal, has the same significance as the establishment of a constitution.)

5. Yoshihiko Yoshino, "Financial Policy in the Era of Ikeda Finance Minister in the Kishi Cabinet," in Takafusa Nakamura and Masayasu Miyazaki, eds. *The Nobusuke Kishi Administration and Economic Growth* (Tōyō Keizai Inc., 2003), 94.

6. Tomonori Morikawa, ed. *Security Treaty in 1960: Testimony of Six People*, (Dōjidaisha, 2005), 286 (actual statement of Morita).

7. Ibid.

8. Ibid., 279.

9. Yoshihisa Hara, ed. *Testimony of Nobusuke Kishi* (Chūō Kōron Shinsha, 2014), 208.

10. Ibid., 207.

11. Ibid., 231–232 (statement of Kishi).

12. Ibid., 208.

13. Yasuhiro Nakasone, then minister who later served as prime minister, said, "There was no need for the approval and ratification by the Diet to be scheduled on the day of Eisenhower's visit to Japan." Yasuhiro Nakasone, *All Sentient Beings*, (Bungei Shunju, 1996), 201.

14. Hara, op. cit., 216.

15. Ibid., 253.

16. Ibid., 302.

17. Ibid., 393.

18. Ibid., 224. Kishi also said, "Given the situation of Japan at the time, my idea was that someone should let the people face and consider seriously the essence of problems." Ibid., 240.

19. Ibid., 229.

20. Ibid., 304.

21. Ibid., 301.

22. Ibid., 301.

23. Ibid., 357.

24. Ibid., 370.

25. Nakasone, op. cit., 210.

26. Ibid., 210.

27. Ibid., 211.

28. Ibid.

29. Hara, op. cit., 329.

30. Nakasone, op. cit., 211.

31. Schaller, Michael (Translated by Yōichi Ichikawa), *Altered States: The United States and Japan since the Occupation*, (Sōshisha, 2004), 272.

32. Ibid., 279. Schaller also stated: "In order to promote stability, the CIA decided to offer financial support to a 'moderate' molecule amongst the LDP that seemed to be able to better meet the Japanese voters' demand for progressive domestic policy." Ibid.

33. Ibid., 280.

34. Satō Shin, *The Reality of the 1960s* (Minerva Publishing, 2011), 48.

35. Sayaka Oki, *Why Were Humanities and Sciences Separated?* (Seikaisha, 2018), 108.

36. Satō, op. cit., 49 (quote from Masaya Itō, *Hayato Ikeda and His Era* [The Asahi Shimbun Company, 1985]).

37. Shingo Hayashi and Tomoyasu Kuzuoka, *Choice of the Japanese: Postwar History of General Elections* (Heibonsha, 2007), 83.

38. Hara, op. cit., 213 (statement of Kishi).

39. Ibid., 214.

40. Ibid., 252 (statement of Kishi).

41. Ibid., 238 (statement of Kishi).

42. Ibid., 224 (statement of Kishi).

43. This seems to contradict the forced passage of the bill under the Kishi Administration. With respect to this, Kishi explained that the forced passage was not "desirable," and that "one should not resort to an aggressive method and force his opinions on those opposing his ideas," but he would have no choice but to do so in order to maintain the parliamentary government if the opposition parties boycotted a session. Ibid., 237.

44. Susumu Nishibe, *Security Treaty in 1960* (Bungei Shunju, 2018), 21.

45. Nakasone, op. cit., 210.

46. Hara, op. cit., 278.

47. Ukeru Magozaki, *The Identity of Postwar History* (Sōgensha, 2012), p. 206. However, there is no doubt that Kishi had ambiguous feelings about the United States. For example, his obsession with Eisenhower's visit to Japan on June 19, 1960, and the ratification of the new treaty by this date was due to his strong awareness of the presence of the United States.

48. Sakamoto pointed out that Kishi succeeded in the revision of the Security Treaty, but this very success "prevented him from fulfilling his other desire, the amendment of the Constitution."

49. Oguma explains the discussion of Kan'ichi Fukuda as: "The word 'citizen' represents the state of simultaneous emergence of self-reliance and solidarity during the campaign against the Japan-U.S. Security Treaty." Oguma, op. cit., 524–525.

50. Tatsuhiko Yamamoto, "Constitutional Change without Sovereignty: Identity of the Constitutional Order of Japan," *Ronkyu Jurist*, No. 25 (2018): 151–160, describes the process of formation of the Japanese constitutional order based on the antagonism between elite pragmatism and popular fundamentalism. See Satoshi Yokodaidō et al., "[Discussion] For Whom and What Is the 'Constitutional Code?,'"

Hōritsu Jiho 90, No. 12 (2018): 92–99, for a comprehensive examination of "elite pragmatism" from constitutional, political, and historical perspectives.

51. Rokurō Hidaka, ed. *May 19* (Iwanami Shoten, 1960), 34–35 (a summary of each poll).

52. Ibid.

53. Hara, op. cit., 328–329 (statement of Kishi).

54. Ibid., 328.

55. Takumi Satō, a leading expert on public opinion research, pointed out that Kishi's concept of public opinion focuses on "unrepresented public opinions" and "corresponds to the one-person-one-vote principle of the general election system." See Takumi Satō, *Popular Sentiments and Public Opinion* (Shinchōsha, 2008), 163. For the dual nature of Kishi in relation to democracy (his characteristics as a defender and a destroyer of democracy), see Satoshi Yokodaidō, "Campaign against the Japan-U.S. Security Treaty in 1960 and Democracy," in Keigo Komamura and Shunya Yoshimi, ed., *The Postwar History of Japanese Constitutional Politics: Another Reflection on Postwar Japan* (Hōritsubunkasya, 2020), 112–114.

56. Nishibe, op. cit., 11.

57. Ibid., 15–16.

58. Satō, op. cit., 12.

59. Ibid., 13.

60. Ibid., 33.

61. Nakasone, op. cit., 202.

62. Keiichi Matsushita, *The Issues and Politics of the Late Shōwa Period* (Bokutakusha, 1988), 131.

63. Hidaka, op. cit., 17 (written by Fujita).

64. Ibid.

65. Ibid.

66. Nakasone, op. cit., 286. According to Shunya Yoshimi, "the 1950s was an era in which the people were hungry for festivals." Shunya Yoshimi, "Empress Michiko and Michiko Kanba," in Akira Kurihara, ed., *People's Mental History, Vol. 3: Security Treaty in 1960* (Iwanami Shoten, 2015), 17.

67. Ibid., 15, 19.

68. Nisibe, op. cit., 11.

69. For example, Kan'ichi Fukuda, "Possibility of Japanese Democracy," *Sekai*, August 1960 issue, 58; Takeshi Ishida et al., "Current Political Situation," *Sekai*, August 1960 issue, 237 (Yoshikazu Sakamoto).

70. Morikawa, op. cit., 285–286 (actual testimony of Morita).

71. Ibid., 233 (testimony of Kōichirō Shinohara).

72. Ibid., 286 (testimony of Morita).

73. Ibid., 50–51 (testimony of Hiromi Kojima), pp. 226–227 (testimony of Morita).

74. Ibid., 232 (testimony of Shinohara).

75. Ibid., 232.

76. Morikawa, op. cit., 232 (testimony of Morita).

77. For the use of the term "democracy" in this part, see Satō, op. cit., 163. In the meantime, Nishibe stated that "the prosperous business culture that began with the

rapid economic growth disinfected not only the conflicted feelings toward the U.S. but also magic words such as 'peace,' 'humanism,' 'democracy,' and 'progressivism.'" Nishibe, op. cit., 21.

78. Morikawa, op. cit., 233–234 (testimony of Shinohara).

79. Shingen Tanaka also played the role of creating alternatives for those who left Zengakuren. In fact, Karoji and Higashihara joined Tanaka's affiliated company, while Shinohara joined a private company (Kōyō Unyū) through Tanaka. Ibid., 244 (testimony of Shinohara).

80. Oguma, op. cit., 530–531.

81. Shimizu Ikutarō (Reiko Shimizu, ed.) *Ikutarō Shimizu Collection 14: Fragments of My Life* (Kodansha, 1993), 78.

82. See Kan'ichi Fukuda, "Possibility of Japanese Democracy," *Sekai*, August 1960 issue, 55–56. See also Akai Oi, "The Problems of Postwar East Asia and Endogenous 'Formation of the National' by Kan'ichi Fukuda," *Interdisciplinary Social Sciences*, No. 20 (2010): 3.

83. "The Judgment of the Grand Bench by the Supreme Court of Japan on July 20, 1960," *Keishu* 40, No. 9, 1243.

84. For the Supreme Court's generosity in meetings within the facility and intolerant attitude toward collective activities in the street, see Tatsuhiko Yamamoto, "Speech in a Cage: Closeness of Public Facilities/Openness of the Street," in Akio Nakabayashi and Tatsuhiko Yamamoto, *Context of Constitutional Court Cases* (Nihon Hyōronsha, 2019), 274 and below.

85. Hara, op. cit., 229 (statement of Kishi).

86. The House of Counsillors election was held on July 2013 and July 2016. In the former, the Security Treaty was not an issue, while in the latter, the issue was brought up by opposition parties, but the ruling parties focused on economic policies.

87. Kishi stated that it was important to make his political position clear, and that "he cannot leave fundamental problems unclear to avoid them." Hara, op. cit., 224 (statement of Kishi).

REFERENCES

Fukuda, Kan'ichi. "Possibility of Japanese Democracy." *Sekai*, (August 1960): 55–56, 58.

Grove, Tara L. "The Lost History of the Political Question Doctrine." *New York University Law Review* 90. (2015): 1908, 1952–57.

Hara, Yoshihisa, ed. *Testimony of Nobusuke Kishi*. Tokyo: Chūō Kōron Shinsha, 2014.

Hayashi, Shingo and Kuzuoka, Tomoyasu. *Choice of the Japanese: Postwar History of General Elections*. Tokyo: Heibonsha, 2007.

Hidaka, Rokurō, ed. *May 19*. Tokyo: Iwanami Shoten, 1960.

Ikutarō, Shimizu. *Ikutarō Shimizu Collection 14: Fragments of My Life*. Edited by Shimizu, Reiko. Tokyo: Kodansha, 1993.

Irie, Toshio. "Acts of Government." *Kōhō Kenkyū*, No. 13. (1955): 90.

Ishida, Takeshi. "Current Political Situation." *Sekai* (August 1960): 237.

Magozaki, Ukeru. *The Identity of Postwar History*. Tokyo: Sōgensha, 2012.

Matsushita, Keiichi. *The Issues and Politics of the Late Shōwa Period*. Tokyo: Bokutakusha, 1988.

Morikawa, Tomonori, ed. *Security Treaty in 1960: Testimony of Six People*. Tokyo: Dōjidaisha, 2005.

Nakamura, Takafusa and Miyazaki, Masayasu, eds. *The Nobusuke Kishi Administration and Economic Growth*. Tokyo: Tōyō: Keizai Inc., 2003.

Nakasone, Yasuhiro. *All Sentient Beings*. Tokyo: Bungei Shunju, 1996.

Nishibe, Susumu. *Security Treaty in 1960*. Tokyo: Bungei Shunju, 2018.

Oguma, Eiji. *"Democracy" and "Patriotism": Nationalism and the Public Sphere in Postwar Japan*. Tokyo: Shinyosha, 2002.

Oi, Akai. "The Problems of Postwar East Asia and Endogenous 'Formation of the National' by Fukuda, Kan'ichi." *Interdisciplinary Social Sciences*, No. 20 (2010): 3 and below.

Oki, Sayaka. *Why Were Humanities and Sciences Separated?* Tokyo: Seikaisha, 2018.

Satō, Shin. *The Reality of the 1960s*. Tokyo: Minerva Publishing, 2011.

Satō, Takumi. *Popular Sentiments and Public Opinion*. Tokyo: Shinchōsha, 2008.

Schaller, Michael. *Altered States: The United States and Japan since the Occupation.* Translated by Ichikawa, Yōichi. Tokyo: Sōshisha, 2004.

Yamamoto, Tatsuhiko "Constitutional Change without Sovereignty: Identity of the Constitutional Order of Japan." *Ronkyu Jurist*, No. 25 (2018): 148.

Yamamoto, Tatsuhiko. "Popular Sovereignty and Acts of Government." *Hōgaku Seminar*, No. 729. (2015): 50.

Yamamoto, Tatsuhiko. "Speech in a Cage: Closeness of Public Facilities/Openness of the Street." In *Context of Constitutional Court Cases*. Tokyo: Nihon Hyōronsha, 2019.

Yamamoto, Tatsuhiko. "The Principle of Popular Sovereignty and Constitutional Changes in the United States." *Kenpō Mondai*, No. 28. (2017): 45.

Yokodaidō, Satoshi et al. "[Discussion] For Whom and What Is the 'Constitutional Code?,'" *Hōritsu Jiho* 90, No. 12 (2018): 92–99.

Yokodaidō, Satoshi. "Campaign against the Japan-U.S. Security Treaty in 1960 and Democracy." In *The Postwar History of Japanese Constitutional Politics: Another Reflection on Postwar Japan*, ed. Keigo Komamura and Shunya Yoshimi, 93. Kyoto: Hōritsubunkasya, 2020.

Yoshimi, Shunya. "Empress Michiko and Michiko Kanba." Edited by Akira, Kurihara. *People's Mental History, Vol. 3: Security Treaty in 1960*. Tokyo: Iwanami Shoten, 2015.

Chapter Four

"Constitutional Revision" Inside and Outside the National Diet

Rintaro Kuramochi

"Do we really have the time to be asking things like who's better than who or what happened to someone's work? Now is the time for us to come together as one."

—Kenji Miyazawa, "*Seitoshokun ni yoseru*" ["To My Students"].[1]

INTRODUCTION

This[2] chapter will examine statements within and without the Diet regarding constitutional revision from political parties, Diet representatives, legal scholars, lawyers, journalists, and civic activists. I show how action (or inaction) with regard to these statements has (or has not) led to developments in Japan's constitutional revision debate.

The statements of these figures show us not only their individual views on law and politics, but also that Japanese people each have their own unique take on the meaning of "democracy" and "constitutionalism." How has postwar society come to debate (or not debate) the Constitution of Japan? Have their methods of debate been appropriate? What issues might they have deliberately not discussed, and why? Is this a pathological state unique to Japanese society? Or is this an advantage in which Japanese should take pride? Over the more than seventy years of the postwar period, what has been the nature of Japanese constitutional debate?

Debating the constitution is often reduced to oversimplified, meaningless labels of "constitutional revisionists" versus "constitutional protectionists." These identities then mix with Japan's "conservative/liberal" and "right-wing/left-wing" political spectrum in complex ways. The resulting spectrum is thus exceedingly political and factionalized. Because these debates are tinged with particular ideologies, it is difficult to encourage debate among analysts or specialists, let alone citizens. What causes these trends?

Unless one opposes all debate over the constitution, the question is how to have free and fruitful debate. This chapter shows how the obstacles to such debate on the constitution are related to feelings of entrapment and apathy in Japanese society.

Debate about constitutional revision is currently stagnated. While the people seek nonpartisan debate about constitutional revision from Diet members —a goal one might assume Diet members share—debate over revision is at a standstill due to Diet members' partisanship. Moreover, the Diet's Committee on the Constitution, established to discuss the constitution, has not created a procedural environment conducive to extensive debate. Civic activism has also contributed to this obstructive partisanship, further hindering debate over revision. Ultimately, civic activism focuses on elections and supporting parties. It therefore hinders nonpartisan debate over constitutional revision.

Debate over the constitutional revision should not be determined by the political moment, or solely by each party's stance. Rather, Diet members should discuss these issues with open minds as "representatives of all Japanese citizens." For them to do so, procedural and substantive systems for such discussions must be arranged. I use the constitution as a lens through which to examine the interstices between politics and law as well as between theory and practice, because I want to encourage enlightening debate over constitutional revision.

I therefore see current conditions for constitutional debate as unfavorable. At the same time, the obstacles to debate that I have mentioned, and their relationship to skewed civic activism, represent problems that are also at the root of other current societal issues plaguing Japan. This twofold nature of Japan's current condition is highly undesirable.

This chapter offers suggestions for breaking the current stalemate and for the form such a breakthrough would ideally take, but immediate movement toward this ideal is unlikely. Nevertheless, as a legal professional invited to contribute to this book, I hope to further the debate over constitutional revision and civic activism, something to which I have long devoted myself.

CONSTITUTIONAL REVISION SEEN FROM THE DIET AFTER THE JULY 2019 HOUSE OF COUNCILLORS ELECTION

Media Catch Phrases Hinder Debate

With the July 2019 House of Councillors' election, a change of four seats disrupted the *kaiken seiryoku* (the two-thirds of both houses needed to initiate debate over constitutional revision). However, expressions such as "*sanbun no ni*" (two-thirds) and "*kaiken seiryoku*," referring to the proportion of seats held by the ruling party and its coalition partners, were originally just catch-phrases made up by the mass media. The balance of power in the Diet tends to be determined by these "coalitions," but it is not simple to measure the significance of the number of seats held by Kōmeitō (one party in the ruling coalition), which is half-hearted about constitutional revision, or the Democratic Party for the People (an opposition party), which is more flexible regarding revision. A closer examination of items proposed for revision would no doubt suggest a multiparty consensus where a majority of the Diet would agree to revise certain clauses. It is therefore almost meaningless to count the number of seats after an election and measure whether the two-thirds mark has been reached, yet media outlets still summarized election results this way in 2016. The more they do this, the more they entrench the fictitious logic of "ruling party versus opposition party" where each Diet member is strictly sworn to follow party lines. By dividing constitutional debate along partisan lines, the media's emphasis on this ratio politicizes what should be a non-partisan issue.

The politics sections of major media outlets have recently been reduced, and now include reporters who follow only mainstream politicians, and only the party or politicians they are assigned to. This has meant little coverage of the essence of constitutional debate. Of course the media would play a key role at the time of a national referendum to decide on amending the constitution. Their obstruction of debate over constitutional revision via irresponsible reporting has carried a heavy price.

WHAT WAS THE REAL MEANING OF CONSTITUTIONAL REVISION FOR PRIME MINISTER ABE?

On May 3, 2017, Prime Minister Abe suggested keeping the first and second clauses of Article 9 and simply adding the Self-Defense Forces (SDF) into the text, a proposal that I will refer to as the "Abe Proposal."[3] Abe argued that merely adding mention of the SDF would end the debate over its constitutionality, which has plagued the SDF since its founding. Abe asserted that this was a minor addition, and leaving Articles 9.1 and 9.2 untouched meant nothing would be substantially changed. However, as long as Article 9.2 is unchanged, the constitutionality of the SDF will be questioned because of the clause's renunciation of all war potential. Moreover, given the wording of the Abe Proposal, the SDF would be rebranded as a "necessary method for self defense," enabling it to go beyond limited collective self-defense and resort to "full-spec" collective self-defense. Therefore, the Abe Proposal not only fails to accomplish the prime minister's original objective for revision (ending the debate over the SDF's constitutionality), but the scope of the right to self-defense exercised by the SDF would be unrestrained and subject to administrative interpretation (i.e., "nothing will change" is a lie). The proposal is poorly written, and would do no good but a great deal of harm.[4]

The LDP approved this proposal along with three others in March 2018, making this the official party constitutional revision proposal.[5] However, as discussed later, the Committee on the Constitution is dysfunctional. Further, due to the opposition parties insisting that the National Referendum Law be amended before any debate over constitutional revision, the debate carried over to 2020. Even though the Abe Proposal was pushed aggressively in 2017, there has been no progress whatsoever toward revision.

The newly inaugurated cabinet and LDP personnel changes of September 11, 2019, brought a change in the LDP Constitutional Reform Promotion Headquarters. The aggressive Hakubun Shimomura was replaced as chair by his predecessor, the mild Hosoda Hiroyuki. Furthermore, Abe remarked that constitutional revision would be directed by the party's policy chief, who is currently former Minister of Foreign Affairs Fumio Kishida, a contender to succeed Abe as prime minister. Kishida also heads the Kōchikai, an LDP faction with a rather liberal stance on constitutional revision. If he is to have a chance to succeed Abe, Kishida cannot ignore Abe's wishes. Constitutional revision may become a loyalty test in the post-Abe race.

Constitutional revision may be no more than a tool Abe used to control intra-party politics and ingratiate himself with active supporters of revision. The media did not report any efforts on Abe's part to persuade Kōmeitō to form a coalition with the LDP (in stark contrast to the 2015 National Security Omnibus Bill, where the LDP persuaded Kōmeitō to support the law's allowance of collective self-defense in certain situations).

WHAT IS THE REAL MEANING OF "CONSTITUTION" FOR OPPOSITION PARTIES?

In response to the tactics of the LDP and the Abe administration, the opposition parties established a united front demanding "no constitutional revision under the Abe administration." Reiwa Shinsengumi—a new party formed after the 2019 House of Councillors' election, single-handedly carrying the hopes of left-wing liberals—and the Communist Party jointly demanded "protection of Article 9 as is" (*kyūjō goken*). The ruling and opposition parties alike are merely using constitutional revision as a means to control internal party politics or to sway their supporters. Therefore the debate over revision seems unlikely to become more meaningful. Even looking beyond Abe, none of the opposition parties has offered counter-proposals. If their mantra is simply no revision under the Abe administration, this implies that they would participate in debates over revising the constitution once Abe is out of office. Therefore, unless the opposition parties present their opinions about the constitution, it is unclear how voters can determine whether they deserve to control the government. I will delve further into the contradiction between the platform of the top opposition party, the Constitutional Democratic Party, pledging to "proactively conduct debate about the constitution based on constitutionalism" and the party's actual rejection of any such debate.[6]

FINAL DIET SESSION OF 2019 (EXTRAORDINARY SESSION) AND CONSTITUTIONAL REVISION

Debate Makes a "Traitor"? Debate Is "Uncomfortable"?

Who Should Debate the Constitution?

On November 7, 2019, free discussion was held for the first time in two years in the House Committee on the Constitution. While the two-year gap is odd by itself, the session made clear the warped perspectives about debating the constitution that the current ruling and opposition parties hold.

First, let us consider an exchange between Constitutional Democratic Party (CDP) member Shiori Yamao and CDP leader Yukio Edano following Yamao's comments at the House Committee on the Constitution meeting of November 7, 2019.[7]

Yamao supports "constitutional revision debate rooted in constitutionalism."[8] There is no coalition backing this yet, but this comprehensive approach would check the power of government while maximizing individual liberties. In particular, Yamao's proposal revises Article 9 to bring individual self-defense within the limits of Japan's nonaggressive defense policy and formally defines the SDF as war potential, establish a Constitutional Court, and legalize same-sex marriage. During the committee meeting, Yamao called upon other Diet members to discuss revisions to the National Referendum Law and consider what constitutional provisions need revision:

> We should discuss the restrictions on commercials about revision and other procedural matters while also concretely discussing the constitutional provisions to be revised. This discussion should start with every member present freely expressing their views on the constitution, not as mouthpieces for their party or proxies for their constituents, but as representatives of all Japanese citizens.

We should make sure that there is a chance for all people to know what their representatives think are the major points currently at issue regarding our constitution. Lastly, I believe the only forum for discussing these issues is this very Committee on the Constitution.[9]

In response, CDP leader Yukio Edano expressed his "discomfort" with Yamao's statement at a press conference the same day.[10] Edano stated that Yamao's remark went against the CDP platform and that "arrangements for Diet debate are a matter for the Diet Affairs Committee, not up for debate by the masses. The meaning of the CDP policy platform is clear."

It is curious that a party named "constitutional" expresses "discomfort" about "deliberation." The CDP platform clearly calls for debate. The "CDP policy platform" that Edano mentioned in his comment is "*Kenpō ni kansuru kangaekata*" (How we think about the constitution) a document that clearly expresses the party's constitutional values and attitude toward revision:

We do not believe that the Japanese Constitution should not be revised at all. If proposed revisions to not only the constitution but also all relevant legislation are necessary for the people, and limit the power of the government while expanding the rights of the people, then our party will actively discuss and consider such changes. Rather than the binary presented by "constitutional protectionists" and "constitutional revisionists," our fundamental stance is to have a constitutional debate rooted in constitutionalism.[11]

What differs between the CDP platform and Yamao's remarks is Edano's concern only for what his constituents—who are hesitant about constitution revision—will think; this short-sightedness has resulted in Edano distorting his party's platform to the point of obscurity.

During the next meeting of the Committee on the Constitution on November 14, 2019, Yamao clarified her earlier remarks:

Diet members . . . are simply acting as politicians and by doing only that can make a living. The people have it hard—they work to make a living, they manage their households, and they are being told by politicians to take more of an interest in politics. Given that, we as politicians should at least debate, spread the word about what we discuss, take time to convert our talking points into options for the people to choose, and earnestly explain the pros and cons of those options. Then we can say: "let us know what you think. Let's think about these issues together." Let's find answers that will make the people say "I see what you're saying!" Let's do that work right here and now, is what I am trying to say. . . . By "let's debate freely," I mean don't be restricted by anyone or anything. Taking pride in and expressing your own point of view is important. . . . If everyone is focused on their own party, it's going to be difficult to provide the people with the discussion they want, which is a debate that isn't just constitutional protectionism versus constitutional revision.[12]

The exchange between Yamao and Edano encapsulates questions this chapter addresses about debates inside and outside the Diet: Should constitutional scholars be the ones to debate the constitution? Lawyers? Diet members? Or should it be all of us, the people? Who should decide the key issues to be debated? Lastly, what role should the people have as participants, since they are the final decision-makers? Should we believe per the "three-tier structure" theory of the people presented in Komamura's chapter that the people are democratic players even though they may make foolish decisions that they will have to reconsider, or continue to build upon?[13] Or should decisions be made by the elites or political "pros," according to the rules of the closed political world, rather than the fallible people?

The LDP advocates constitutional revision with the duplicitous argument that it doesn't matter what changes—they just want to revise the constitution, even at the cost of the meaning of revision itself. On the other hand, the top opposition party has sworn to "never for all eternity draft a constitutional revision" and categorically refuses to discuss revision.[14] At the same time, before considering whether revision will happen or not, thanks to factional and other political reasons that have stalled debate and led parties to cling to unilateral arguments, we should remember that the constitution must apply to all situations in today's society. However, this deadlock undermines any possible debate on what does and does not need to be updated in the constitution. People who are not enslaved to ideology or party politics, but seek a fruitful debate on these issues, will be pushed aside by this meaningless and harsh antagonism.

A majority of voters identify as "independent." In a December 9, 2019, NHK poll on party support, the greatest support went not to the LDP (36.1%) or the CDP (5.5%), but rather "no party preference in particular" (41.4%), a fact that is closely related to the current debate environment. (The number of people answering "no party preference in particular" has in fact been increasing.) Yamao's opinion about debates over revision has brought attention to the empty debate in the Diet caused by radical antagonism. Yamao expresses the commonsense opinion that Diet members who have the right to initiate debate on constitutional revision should not be subservient to their party or constituents but should discuss their individual responsibilities and philosophies regarding the constitution. This opinion is most likely to strike a chord with the majority of people, too caught up in their day-to-day lives to pay attention to politics. Yamao is confident that most people will understand if the issues are explained to them. The very concept of explaining so that someone will understand such technical issues is an essential requirement of democracy.

In party politics that fail to reflect the reasonable ideas of quotidian civil society, commonsense opinions like Yamao's are rare. Since the CDP was established, its popular support has dropped from 15% to 5%. This remaining 5% are the "loyal customers" to whom the CDP devotes its efforts. The CDP is losing touch with the average person and has abandoned constitutionalism and democracy as core values, hence this loss of support. Yet the true losers in this environment offering no alternative to the current ruling party are the Japanese people themselves.

Pressure and Neglect

Having presented the exchange between Yamao and Edano, I will now introduce two other episodes involving the Committee on the Constitution and debate over revision.

i) The leader of the Democratic Party for the People, Yūichirō Tamaki appeared on an internet program called "Bunkajin Hōsōkyoku" on July 25, 2019. He declared his desire to discuss constitutional revision in the Diet, calling on Prime Minister Abe to hold a conference of the leaders of all parties.[15] Tamaki said that he had "been reborn" and remarked that "it is our responsibility as a party to encourage debate about constitutional revision and make that point to the prime minister. After deciding what our stance is as a party, all party leaders should discuss this issue among themselves."[16] Left-wing supporters reluctant to debate constitutional revision under the Abe administration erupted with criticism of the party leader. When people commented about Tamaki's statement online, they attached the hashtag "*#uragirimoro ni wa shi o*" (lit. "#deathtotraitors"). For a time the hashtag was a top trending word online.

This response to Tamaki's comments gets to the heart of the issues plaguing constitutional debate. If a Diet member directly attacks an individual's character or says something insensitive about bioethics or human dignity, that Diet member will be strictly censured. However, Tamaki's comments simply encourage more proactive discussion of constitutional matters. They may leave room for political misunderstandings, but throwing the word "death" at him over the internet is reminiscent of the mob applauding beheadings at the guillotine in the name of "freedom, equality, and brotherly love." Such responses simply cannot be called liberal.

This episode highlights how most people who are interested in politics and consider themselves liberal believe that their views or ways of being politically active are the only correct ones; anyone going against those views must be condemned. The liberal ideals of "strength in diversity" and "protecting the rights of others to protect one's own rights" are quickly forgotten. These liberals seek only self-purification and self-righteousness. Liberal groups around the world are degenerating due to this self-righteousness.[17]

ii) During meetings of the House Committee on the Constitution in the 2019 extraordinary Diet session, baffling infighting occurred within the LDP. At the center of this episode was Diet member Shigeru Ishiba, formerly LDP chief secretary and Minister of Defense. Ishiba has recently been the only leading LDP figure in the so-called "Abe Dynasty" willing to seriously criticize Prime Minister Abe. Ishiba lost to Abe twice, in the 2012 and 2018 LDP party leader elections. Due to these intra-party politics, not only Ishiba but all Diet members from his faction within the LDP were removed as candidates for ministerial positions within the Abe administration. He was in a way internally purged by the LDP.

Despite this, Ishiba maintained the lead as the preferred next prime minister, ahead of Abe and other prominent bureaucrats, in public opinion polls as recent as December 2019.[18] This support is no doubt the sole threat to the "unopposed Abe" in the eyes of senior LDP members and the Abe administration.

Ishiba is known for his defense policy experience, as the Minister of Defense and as an authoritative figure on national security and military policies. He frequently comments on Article 9, arguing for removing Article 9.2 and giving the SDF the status of national army.[19] Many label this proposal the "Article 9.2 Removal Plan" or the "Ishiba Proposal."

Ishiba's proposals differ fundamentally from the "Abe Addition" method of leaving Articles 9.1 and 9.2 as is and adding a clause defining the SDF as "war potential." Ishiba's revisions aim to free Japan from the restrictions of the postwar world regime.

Ishiba has expressed his clear opposition to Abe's plan: "I cannot possibly agree with [Abe's] method as long as there is no answer regarding how these revisions will conform to the second clause [of Article 9]."[20] Ishiba claims that his draft reflects mainstream opinion in the LDP.[21] These differences produced sharp conflict between Abe and Ishiba.

During the 2019 extraordinary Diet session, Ishiba also served as a member of the House Committee on the Constitution. Every time Ishiba attended a committee meeting, he placed his nameplate face up to request an opportunity to speak. Many other Diet members were called on to speak, but Ishiba was never given the floor, and this continued to the point of absurdity. Ultimately, the 2019 extraordinary Diet session ended without him ever getting the chance to speak in committee. Ishiba commented on the unprecedented situation by questioning the state of democracy in Japan: "I was not called on even once. What does this say about Japan, a supposedly democratic nation?"[22]

In this way, the ruling and opposition parties manage the Committee on the Constitution to serve their parties' interests. Each party's inconsistent, emotion-based self-interest, ulterior motives, and assumptions about the ideas of others dictate how committees work. This does not foster an environment where Diet members are able to conduct sincere and essential debate about revision. The committee chairperson supports the administration by abusing the right to recognize committee members and suppressing opinions inconvenient for the ruling party.

In the Yamao and Ishiba episodes, we see similar tactics from both ruling and opposition parties. This silencing is a result of the Diet's internal state, the state of affairs in each party, and the parties' blind allegiance to narrow-minded voices. The attack on Tamaki is an extreme example of political purification by a section of his own support base (which might be called the "noisy minority"). This "noisy minority" outside the Diet tried to remove someone whose opinion differed from theirs by "shouting" in a radical way. The fact that liberals who tout the core values of diversity and freedom of speech were the ones guilty of stifling Tamaki's freedom of speech shows how liberal, left-wing voters—self-proclaimed supporters of the opposition parties—are actually laying the groundwork for their own demise. To borrow from Voltaire, this is where they should say, "I disapprove of what you say, but I will defend your right to say it." Instead, these factions say, "It is only natural for we who disapprove of your views to limit your right to speak them." This illustrates the current weakened state of Japan's left-wing liberals.

There is merit in having a variety of ways to show people the flaws in Abe's proposal and prevent the initiation of the amendment process. Tamaki (like Yamao) argues that by debating Abe over the constitution, the flaws and inconsistencies of his proposal will come to light. Yamao expresses her critiques of the Abe Proposal both in and outside of the Diet.[23] If the objective is to increase the number of people who are unconditionally opposed to the Abe Proposal, then every Diet member should help the people to understand it. In opposition to this goal, certain fundamentalist voters who only accept a particular way of debating, and parties that feed on that fundamentalism, are slowly eliminating the diversity of discussion methods.

Civic activism has now lost the spirit of acting for a particular goal. Instead, civic activists act only for activism's sake. Their movements are losing their unifying force. Left-wing liberal, civic activism since Abe's rise to prime minister has rapidly devolved, especially since it has not reflected the breadth of constitutional issues. By maintaining an extremely limited type of civic activism, the activists are reducing their impact, abandoning through their words and deeds the essential liberal values of diversity, inclusion, patience, and tolerance. Instead, they have adopted intolerance, impulsive responses, and restriction of free and diverse speech and opinion. Naturally, the numbers of supporters and the power of the parties who depend on such groups and such activism are diminishing.

As noted, the mass media (specifically their politics bureaus), political parties, and civic activists tied closely with these parties are obstacles to debates on the constitution within and without the Diet. Next, I will turn to the views of figures in and outside the Diet regarding constitutional debate. A bird's-eye perspective will illuminate the views of the Japanese people concerning debating the constitution.

"NOW ISN'T THE TIME FOR CONSTITUTIONALISM": THE LEFT AND RIGHT OF JAPAN'S CURRENT POLITICAL PLAYING FIELD

We have examined arguments regarding constitutional revision within and outside the Diet by looking at the big picture. Here I will introduce a newspaper article touching upon the relationship between activities inside the Diet (party politics and politicians) and outside the Diet (civic activists and others).

On September 22, 2019, *Tokyo Shimbun* published an article titled "Now Isn't the Time for Constitutionalism" (*Rikkenshugi dokoro ja nai*). It is not an interview of a constitutional destructionist or a government opponent. The title is a quote from the leader of the Reiwa Shinseigumi party, Tarō Yamamoto, who caused a stir in the July 2019 House of Councillors election. Yamamoto directs attention away from the core principles of constitutionalism toward more practical matters: "While the argument for politics based on constitutionalism is important, now is not the time for constitutionalism. What kind of policies are needed to make people's difficult lives a bit more comfortable—we need to be talking about that sort of thing in more detail." Yamamoto's statement would be met with strong opposition—especially from liberals—in a state touting itself as a constitutional democracy. However in Japan, people—in particular leftist activists—unanimously displayed agreement with this statement through likes and shares on Facebook. These reactions highlight a contradiction within the Japanese conception of constitutionalism. Moreover, Yamamoto's statement is the key to understanding constitutional revision and civic activism in Japan today.

As Shirō Sakaiya of Tokyo Metropolitan University notes, in the immediate postwar years, many people agreed that Article 9 should be revised and Japan should have a national army.[24] Sakaiya argues that assertions such as "the Japanese people overwhelmingly supported Article 9 at the time of the post-war constitution's creation" and "throughout the period of high economic growth, the portion of the Japanese electorate that favored constitutional revision was on the decline" are myths. Before the outbreak of the Korean War, Japan was forced to create the National Police Reserve (*keisatsu yobitai*) and National Safety Force (*hoantai*). The Self-Defense Forces clearly contradict the prohibition of "war potential" in Article 9.2 of the constitution, but Prime Minister Yoshida chose the less politically costly option and revised the constitution via interpretation. Without codifying their existence as constitutional, the Self-Defense Forces were accepted as a fait accompli.

At the beginning of the 1950s Ichirō Hatoyama and Nobusuke Kishi regained their civil rights and conservative factions were restored to power. Nevertheless, conservatives were divided over revising both the Public Office Election Law and the constitution, resulting in a loss of seats to the Socialist Party and other factions and therefore of the two-thirds legislative control needed to start constitutional debate.

On the other hand, the Liberal Democratic Party, which included constitutional revision in its platform, eventually set the issue aside in order to retain power (with even Yasuhiro Nakasone going along). Yet as a nod to their base, the LDP's consistent support for constitutional revision has persisted up to Prime Minister Abe. As the Cold War headed toward detente, even the United States, which had great influence on Japan, came to think that as long as Japan served as an "economic honor student," then all was fine. The calls for a militarized Japan faded, as did the pressure on Article 9.

In other words, among three groups—citizens, politicians, and the United States—a consensus formed: as long as Article 9 did not interfere with national defense, administrative control, people's livelihoods, or national interest, then it remained useful. This amounted to ignoring Article 9. Sakaiya points out that, while under rapid economic growth the people's desire to revise Article 9 waned, the fact that the overwhelming majority of people had expressed support for Japan having a national army in the immediate postwar years means that this "was not because the people saw Article 9 as a sacred text that should not be revised" but rather "Article 9 had clearly become a 'legal principle that did not interfere with the national defense' so the people decided to allow the clause to remain as is."[25]

As evidence, Sakaiya notes that public opinion has consistently been equally divided over writing the SDF into Article 9. Despite such almost even poll results, there has not been a large-scale movement in favor of writing the SDF into the constitution. This is similar to the overwhelming consensus in favor of keeping the Imperial household system and allowing for a female emperor and matrilineal succession to the imperial throne, without a movement to actualize these ideals. The Japanese people will support something as long as it doesn't affect their everyday life, but this does not equate to truly supporting it in the conventional sense.

Table 4.1. The Stances of Parties and Representatives of National Diet on the Constitution

Majority and Minority Parties	*Party Names*	
The Majority Parties	Liberal Democratic Party	**Proactive** about constitutional revision
	Komeito	**Passive** about constitutional revision
The Minority Parties	Constitutional Democratic Party	**Opposed to debating** the Constitution under the Abe administration
	Democratic Party for the People	Believes that constitutional revision **should be discussed**
	Japan Innovation Party	**Proactive** about constitutional revision
	Communist Party	Constitutional Protectionism **(Opposed to constitutional revision)**
	Reiwa Shinsengumi	Constitutional Protectionism (while they believe that politics based on constitutionalism are important, **now is not the time** for these talks)
	Party to Protect the People from NHK	**Will do anything** that will work in their favor politically

CIVIC ACTIVISM CAUGHT UP IN LEFT/RIGHT PARTISAN POLITICS OVER CONSTITUTIONALISM AND COUNTER-DEMOCRACY

So far I have focused on divisions within the Diet over debating constitutional revision, which result from partisanship converging with elections. I will now discuss constitutional revision and civic activism outside the Diet. As outlined earlier, debate over constitutional revision inside and outside of the Diet has become infected with partisanship.

Ever since its formation, the LDP has claimed to be "conservative." Yet in the Abe era, it no longer had even a hint of such conservatism. The LDP puts Japan's relationship with the U.S. before all else and has become indifferent to the rule of law and to constitutionalism.

One of the civic activist groups that has a close relationship with the Abe administration is Nippon Kaigi. Many consider the group conservative and right-wing, but it does not criticize the Abe administration's submission to the U.S. Instead, it focuses on denying equal rights for the LGBT community and on the need for a patrilineal, male emperor. Nippon Kaigi touts these values as "traditional," but they simply highlight its yearning for the Meiji period (1868–1912), which was hardly "traditional Japan." Their views are tainted with structures of eras past—such as the Meiji family law that lacked any concept of human rights. Due to their excessive adherence to formalism, they ironically endanger the continuation of Japan's imperial system, which unequivocally exists as one of Japan's time-honored traditions.

Junior Chamber International Japan (JC) has collaborated with Nippon Kaigi to create a support base for constitutional revision through nationwide activities. These citizens' groups with close ties to the administration are also forming alliances with politicians (e.g., the Nippon Kaigi Diet Member Caucus). Around nine out of ten of their alliances are with LDP Diet members, and nearly all of the ministers in Abe's cabinet are members.

Naturally, the Abe administration, and the LDP at large, must align with Nippon Kaigi on many issues: moral education, the active appointment of female managers, refusing equal rights for LGBT individuals, and strong support for the male/patrilineal Imperial system, to name a few. The best-known activity of Nippon Kaigi is their "Ten Million Signature Campaign for Constitutional Revision." This provided indispensable support for the Abe Proposal. However, Nippon Kaigi calls for an amended Article 9.2 and overall constitutional revision to strengthen Japan's autonomy. Nevertheless, they expressed their support when Abe presented his proposal in 2017. Their support for the Abe Proposal is the reason why it is difficult to see them as a truly "conservative" group. The interdependent relationship among Nippon Kaigi, the Abe administration, and the LDP should be critically examined, following the partisan context of these groups' common decline to the point where their one goal is to achieve constitutional revision even if it means changing just one letter of the constitution.

On the other hand, there are other opposition parties and left-leaning liberal civic activist groups besides the Civil Alliance for Peace and Constitutionalism (*Shiminrengō*). Constitutional Democracy Japan, a group of constitutional scholars, lawyers, sociologists, and journalists, arose when Abe attempted to revise Article 96 of the constitution to more easily initiate the amendment process. *Kokumin Anpō Hōseikon* (Citizens' National Security Legislation Caucus) opposes the *Anpō Hōseikon* (National Security Legislation Caucus), a group that served as the theoretical backbone for Abe's change in Article 9's interpretation for the sake of the 2015 National Security Legislation.[26]

But these groups have not gone beyond "Anti-Abe politics." While *Shiminrengō* places undue focus on changing the party in power, they aim to restrict political parties through their "*Shiminrengō* Manifesto for Policies Under a United Opposition Party of the CDP and Four Other Opposition Parties" ("Manifesto"), similar to the way they threw the hashtag "death to traitors" at Tamaki. In this way, they are chipping away at traits that define liberal ideology (i.e., diversity and open-mindedness), thus promoting an undeserving united opposition party.

The members of Constitutional Democracy Japan and *Kokumin Anpō Hōseikon* consistently express disapproval of any proposal for constitutional revision from the liberal side of the table. They pressure CDP members not to make statements about revision. The words from these idealless, unholy alliances and groups seeking homogeneity without debate unfortunately will not attract those who have "no party preference in particular."

Intentionally or not, the opposition parties also give disproportionate attention to a few civic activists, groups they treat as "loyal customers." The opposition parties then become unable to separate themselves from these left-wing civic activist movements, effectively subjugating themselves to them. The opposition parties do not truly aim to replace the party in power. They merely do what is necessary to win reelection, which perhaps explains this interdependent relationship. However, that begs the question of whether it is acceptable to perpetuate this unfortunate situation offering the people no reasonable alternative to the current leadership.

Civic activist groups that are close to the opposition parties (i.e., *Shiminrengō* and Constitutional Democracy Japan) conceal their constitutional protectionist values under the umbrella of constitutionalism. They are predominantly constitutional protectionist coalitions and tie the opposition parties down with these ideas. This forces the opposition parties to resist debating constitutional revision in the Diet.

Several types of new civic activism have been sparked by frustration with the current civic activism on the Left and the Right. On the Right, manga artist Yoshinori Kobayashi has a reputation as a conservative critic for his consistent calls for a more autonomous Japan. That puts him in the category of conservative, right-wing critics along with Susumu Nishibe. In the past, Kobayashi has opined about issues ranging from the HIV-tainted blood scandal and the Aum Shinrikyo incidents to textbook controversies. His opinions on Japan's "masochistic" view of postwar history have been expressed in a number of provocative works such as *Sensōron* (*On War*). His political manga series *Gōmanism Sengen* (*Gōsen* for short) grapples with Japan's traditions and place in East Asia through volumes such as *Tennōron* (*On the Emperor*), *Okinawaron* (*On Okinawa*), and *Ianfu* (*Comfort Women*). Kobayashi also holds a symposium every two months called Gōsen Dōjō. It has attempted to foster a culture of public debate and organizes itself as a *dōjō* to battle it out via discussion, becoming a national political movement. Gōsen Dōjō has three objectives: 1) realization of a stable system for imperial succession allowing for female emperors and matrilineal succession, and the establishment of female-headed branch families in the imperial family; 2) constitutional revision rooted in constitutionalism and centered on autonomy, with limited government; and 3) raising the status of women in society. The symposium has "pupils" called "*montei*" across all forty-seven prefectures. They help run events and spread information about Gōsen Dōjō recruiting others. I have taken part in this symposium as an "instructor" and a regular panelist. The February 9, 2020, Gōsen Dōjō where I presented the content of this chapter under the title "The 'Disease' of Elections and Partisanship that Japan's Civic Activism Has Devolved To" was broadcast to thirteen live public viewing locations in addition to the main venue in Tokyo holding several hundred people. Through these public viewings, Gōsen Dōjō has attracted active participation all over the country. The *montei* in each region include working women, which sets this movement apart from others.

As a contrast, I will introduce an example of opposition party/liberal civic activism by supporters of the top opposition party the CDP, or by independent voters. The opposition parties and the civic activists supporting them pointedly refuse to discuss the constitution. They fear that debating the constitution would be misconstrued as entering the same debate ring as Abe and thus being exploited by those supporting revision. However, this stance, and the CDP's promise to "never draft a constitutional revision for all eternity" have denied Japanese citizens opportunities to understand the issues surrounding the Abe Proposal. As a result, some citizens who fear that these negative attitudes only help the Abe Proposal decided to make their own forum for discussion. They created the event series "*Kokuminteki Giron Shiyō*" ("Let's Have a Discussion with the People").

This series demonstrates profound knowledge about the debate over revision, where a politician with his or her own unique view on revision is invited to engage in debate with attendees in an open café setting. Past guests include Ishiba, Yamao, and Tamaki as well as other leading politicians ranging widely from CDP leader Yukio Edano, former Minister of Defense Gen Nakatani (LDP), and former LDP Constitutional Reform Promotion HQ chairperson Hakubun Shimomura, who has extremely close ties with Nippon Kaigi, to Communist Party member Akira Koike.

Kokuminteki Giron Shiyō does not invite people to listen to the views of these politicians just because those views align with their own, which distinguishes it from other political events. Events that Constitutional Democracy Japan and the *Shiminrengō* hold typically feature only speakers who are "Anti-Abe" or "Anti-LDP," so that participants can leave feeling satisfied with their own opinions.

Unlike those feel-good political gatherings, *Kokuminteki Giron Shiyō* welcomes younger people and people who have never been to these sorts of events. With the motto of "there are no winners in debate," and with titles and backgrounds set aside, participants have civil discussions with ruling and opposition party. The politicians earnestly answer participants' questions. At times, participants' questions evince their worries, but the series enjoys a high level of attendee satisfaction and has become well known through word of mouth. Major newspapers have also recently reported on these events in special features.

What sets this type of civic activism apart from other efforts is that Gōsen Dōjō and *Kokuminteki Giron Shiyō* serve to counter movements tied to elections and partisanship.

In response to the rise of Trump and Sanders, some in U.S. politics sought a third party or a candidate within the current two-party system who appealed strongly to independent voters. However, the current political system only compounds these third-party candidate voters' frustrations about their votes being used by the party in power. Japan is no exception to this trend. Three politicians discussed earlier demonstrate the potential to break the mold in Japan: Shigeru Ishiba (LDP), Shiori Yamao (CDP), and Yūichirō Tamaki (Democratic Party for the People). Ishiba, the sole LDP member willing to publicly air criticism about Abe, along with Tamaki and Yamao, younger political leaders belonging to opposition parties that tend to avoid debate over constitutional revision or grand design for policy, but who themselves proactively and flexibly approach these issues, make up this third political "pole." The new types of civic activism on both sides naturally have close connections with these three. Counter-democracy by nature should exist together with and complement the system of representative democracy. They must provide each other with pluralist and democratic legitimacy as well as create a relationship where both systems offer a wealth of options, resulting in a democratic decision-making process. These new types of civic activism may be the start of a desirable trend where key figures in the system of representative democracy share sources of pluralist and democratic legitimacy.

Finally, a third type of civic activism that differs from these discussion events yet still addresses the existing system of representative democracy focuses on national or local referendums. Led by journalist Hajime Imai and legal philosopher Tatsuo Inoue, this movement focuses on referendums as a praiseworthy feature of direct democracy. While these two are liberal-minded in terms of politics, they take care not to fall into the dichotomy of "revisionist/protectionist" with regard to the constitution. They are vocal in criticizing both the government for asserting the constitutionality of the SDF and the scholars who have justified this interpretation, and they encourage debate on Article 9. By placing greater importance on the national referendum, these two express their disagreement with the left-wing, liberal view that the political elite should decide the political and legal agenda on behalf of the fallible Japanese people.

It is difficult to know whether these three examples of civic activism have yet affected society as a sort of counter-democracy. Yet they do not simply publicize people's frustrations about the current political situation, but aim to sublimate them. Moreover, this type of activism fosters an optimistic belief in the ability of every citizen. I welcome the efforts of these groups to critique the current system, unmotivated by profit, as vital for the revival of constitutionalism and democracy.

Table 4.2. The Battle Outside of the National Diet

Anti U.S.-made-constitution revisionist	*Nippon Kaigi and other organizations supporting the Abe administration*
Independence/Isolationist Constitutional Revision	Yoshinori Kobayashi (Manga-ka)
New Article 9 Doctrine	Kazuhiro Soda (Film director) Kenji Isezaki (Tokyo University of Foreign Studies [International Law])
Constitutionalist Constitutional Revision Debate	Rintaro Kuramochi (Lawyer)
Article 9 Deletion	Tatsuo Inoue (The University of Tokyo [Jurisprudence])
National Referendum Promotion Group	Hajime Imai (Journalist)

GOING FORWARD: STRUCTURAL OBSTACLES TO CONSTITUTIONAL REVISION

Given these conditions, there is little chance for Diet progress on constitutional debate. Although Ishiba portrays himself as a respectable, conventional LDP member, his criticism of the Abe Dynasty has led to the near silencing of his voice within the party. Meanwhile, the opposition parties remain inflexibly opposed to any revisions. Neither Yamao's constitutional revision rooted in constitutionalism nor Tamaki's proposal, revisions proposed from within their own ranks, has budged the other factions.

Groups outside the Diet push Abe's views, and traditional conservative groups promote constitutional revision. Nevertheless, the more traditional conservative groups all share undertones of criticism vis-à-vis the Abe Proposal, presenting a problem for the conservative factions.

If the goal is national autonomy, these traditional groups should be leading the crusade against the Abe Proposal, which further entrenches the postwar order. We can hope that these groups will support constitutional revision that will bring real change and speak out against Abe's desire to revise the constitution purely in order to revise it. Revising the constitution simply for revision's sake would spell suicide for traditional conservatives, given their philosophy up to now. Only Yoshinori Kobayashi is arguing for revision based on traditional, conservative principles. He criticizes both the Left and the Right and is in turn criticized by both sides.

To attack debate is to reject democracy. Groups outside the Diet need not be constrained by concern for the two-thirds majority required to initiate debate. Not discussing the constitution is becoming a voluntary restraint by overpolitical citizens—in short, the death of democracy.

Nevertheless, a united front of Ishiba, Yamao, and Tamaki would have a considerable support base by demonstrating common ground on which conservatives and liberals can compromise. Their collaboration would not stimulate debate within the Diet, but we should watch for developments that might come from their joining forces.[27]

Given the current state of debate, the majority of Diet members, and citizens outside of the Diet, are not very interested in the constitution. A sort of "constitutional nihilism" obtains instead; people often say, "The provisions of the constitution don't really affect my everyday life" or "As long as the constitution doesn't disturb the status quo, discrepancies between constitutional provisions and reality are okay." Supported by this nihilism, what has been protected (what hasn't been changed) is the constitution. I hope readers will consider whether these circumstances are acceptable.[28]

It is disappointing that we cannot hope for extensive debate over constitutional revision. Yet I have also outlined how democracy, both from above (i.e., those in government) and below (i.e., civic activism), is controlled by elections and the partisanship they foster. These conditions hamper discussion of the constitution, a document that requires nonpartisan debate. Democracy must be divorced from elections and partisanship if only in this one instance. That experiment might happen when movements discussed earlier grow in scale, since they show a potential for counter-democracy. Also, the ideal outcome of the reciprocal, complementary dynamism between counter-democracy and conventional democratic elections would be to elect Diet members who are receptive to this interplay.

However, this process may take 20, 30, or perhaps even 50 years. Only the steady growth of such movements has the potential to fundamentally change democracy in Japan. If this fails, we will have surrendered to the temptations of heroism, clinging to a democracy as stable as a house of cards.

The counter-movements I have described are still small, but there are bound to be more of them. This type of civic activism works to counter the current electoral system and structures of representative democracy, and serves as a beacon of hope.

THE PAST AND FUTURE OF THE CONSTITUTION: THE MYTH OF A COLLAPSED JAPAN

My arguments intersect in several ways with Komamura's essay: 1) While the constitution enshrined the immediate postwar values adopted by the UN, the Supreme Court's Sunagawa Decision gave the U.S. armed forces on American bases in Japan equal weight with those values. 2) By giving the U.S. an equal status to those UN values, Article 9 provided legal justification for the exercise of collective self-defense per the United States' demands. 3) If Article 9 depended on the UN being the center of the postwar world order, then in the current situation where the UN has become relatively weak, Article 9's legitimacy should be reconsidered. 4) Japan's national security, centered on Article 9 and the U.S. armed forces, is ultimately a question for the Japanese people, whether in 1950 or in the 2015 National Security Legislation. 5) Nevertheless, the people as three-tiered "sovereigns" feel no sense of inconvenience or strong interest about these issues. (They chose Prime Minister Abe and he chose to allow collective self-defense.) The relationship between the current text of Article 9 and the SDF (which now can invoke the right of collective self-defense) unquestionably enjoys democratic legitimacy. Moreover, while constitutionalism may have the power to check democracy, those "sovereigns" believe that "now isn't the time for constitutionalism." As such, the ticking time bomb embedded in Article 9 via the Sunagawa Decision's allusion to the contextual meaning of that constitutional provision has ended in failure.

Since the court avoided a decision on matters of governance, it caused a mismatch between their legal reasoning and the initial response function included in Article 9. The mismatch has remained, and the issues surrounding Article 9 have simply been handed off from the courts to other parties. The people should rebuke this attitude of the courts, the institution that ought to be the final protector of constitutionalism.

Who is tasked with resolving these issues? The three-tiered "individuals" defined by Komamura. The embodiment (representative) of the state for these "individuals" are the Diet members (the courts also have some responsibility, yet considering their status as undemocratic and passive, I will leave them aside). Under Article 96, "a concurring vote of two-thirds or more of all members of each House" is needed to initiate the constitutional amendment process, so Diet members have the right to initiate the amendment process as representatives of the people.

But the people have their own lives to worry about, so society entrusts professionals with exclusive rights and responsibilities. Surgeries are left to doctors, and for legal issues people seek a legal professional's advice. A firefighter runs to extinguish a fire. An architect—not an amateur—designs a house and a carpenter builds it. The people may want to keep an eye on those running the government twenty-four hours a day, but they do not have the time, so the mass media watches them on their behalf and conveys the news.

What about politics? With the exception of scandals, a politician's identity lies in election success, not policy achievements. What they do in the Diet has little bearing on whether they win reelection. The concept of failing at their work in the Diet has virtually disappeared. The only failure that exists is losing an election.

Further, because their work has no direct link to election success, Diet members' work is elections themselves. They are professionals at elections. Thus, when the Diet is in session, there are no professionals doing the policy work that only politicians can do. There are "career politicians," but no professional politicians. These people claim that there are "things that should be left for the people to decide" or that they "want to bring the people's voice to the Diet," but they pass the buck to a fictional "people" and abandon their responsibility to debate as politicians. "Popular will," "the will of the people," "the seat of politics," "highest organ of state power"—these phrases have lost all meaning, and Japan has become a nation where election victories are the sole source of legitimacy for politicians. The ruling and opposition parties use these meaningless phrases in their position talks according to what is opportune for the Right or Left. The people are then forced to go along with the politicians' hollow statement that "Japan is a democratic state." The people who are forced to go along with this comprise the "constituents" that support the charade, whereas the remaining people will lose interest in the drama. And in fact there are more independent voters than supporters of the "unopposed" LDP.

The constitution and debate over revision are casualties of the disease plaguing society. It may be unnecessary to refer to the concept of a "representative" in this case, but if the representative were synonymous with the people, then no representative would be needed. The role of a "legal representative" is certainly not simply to aggregate the opinions of a heterogeneous people.

Therefore the judgment entrusted to the people by the Sunagawa Decision and the responsibility to provide basic information and arguments so the people as sovereigns may decide matters lie with Diet members. This function for Diet members is also apparent from their exclusive right to initiate the constitutional amendment process and their designation as representatives for all of the people. It is crucial that Diet members perform this role, since only they can. There must also be a break from conventional civic activism by extreme political groups on the right and the left. Unless someone frees the inside and outside of the Diet from elections as their point of connection and installs new pipelines for democracy, civil society will only weaken further.

Other countries implement a range of methods when discussing constitutional revision. During the Thatcher administration, the United Kingdom saw the rise of Charter 88, which supported the creation of a written constitution to restrict the executive branch.[29] Europe and America often create think tanks on the left or the right. Constitutional scholars in South Korea actively push for constitutional revisions. Japan has yet to construct a framework for these discussions outside of the Diet.

Industry groups exist to lobby for private benefits, but Japan lacks intermediary groups bringing together political policies and other ideas. And these industry groups also are ultimately only involved with elections. Due to their co-dependent relationship with Diet members concerned only with winning elections, broader policy issues come second.

Some civic activism exists merely to "purify" policies and ideas within factions. However, such attempts by liberal civic activist groups in particular have not expanded their share of the pie, because they are also tied too closely to elections. Some method must be found to link those inside and outside the Diet and legitimize this connection.

To do this, it is essential not to assume that one's own view or method is the only correct one. All involved must remember that one of the core tenets of the liberal project created by the complementary relationship between democracy and constitutionalism is the limits of human infallibility.

In the beginning of this chapter, I quoted a Kenji Miyazawa poem in which he speaks to his students. In the school of postwar democracy that is Japan, we the students are still far from graduating. Regarding constitutionalism, we are probably not even in the lower grades of elementary school. With the shift from the drama of the Shōwa era to the cold Heisei era lacking political policies, not just the constitution, but the systems supporting the Imperial Family, social security, finance, the economy, taxes, work environment, education, and the cultivation of legal professionals will not last. Those in charge of these systems bury their heads in the sand. Patchwork jobs in all of these fields have brought us to the brink of collapse. Trusting someone else to handle a task, and trusting the infrastructure created by corporations and the bureaucracy, have encouraged hopelessness and apathy toward politics and helped conceal the rotting pillars of Japanese society. Constitutional issues are the most extreme example of this rot. We will reach a point of no return, at which the core values sustaining Japanese society will crumble.

In the words of Miyazawa, we do not "have the time to be asking things like who's better than who or what happened to someone's work." Miyazawa closes his poem with the following lines:[30]

> Ah, now don't you
> Feel that clear wind blowing this way
> From each of your magnificent futures?

We must promote civic activism as the clear wind blowing this way from the futures of the apathetic Japanese people—not the rigid, traditional civic activism tied to political parties. We must stress not the differences between ourselves and others but the commonalities we share.

"Now is the time for us to come together as one."

NOTES

1. Kenji Miyazawa, "*Seitoshokun ni yoseru* [To My Students]," *Asahi Hyōron*, April 1946.

2. This chapter was originally a Japanese article translated by Allejah Franco. His help with translation was indispensable for my contribution to this project. Unless noted otherwise, this chapter and all translations herein are his.

3. Refer to Tetsuo Itō's article "'*Sanbun no Ni*': *Kakutokugo no Kaiken Senryaku* [Two-Thirds: Strategies for Constitutional Revision Once We Get the Numbers]," in the September 2016 edition of *Ashita e no Sentaku* [The Choice for Tomorrow].

Moreover, the Japan Policy Institute where Tetsuo Itō serves as director is a think tank with ties to Nippon Kaigi, the core special interest group supporting the Abe administration. Itō also acts as a standing director (policy director) for Nippon Kaigi. For more about the origins and current details about Nippon Kaigi, see the Japan Policy Institute's homepage at http://www.seisaku-center.net/ and Tamotsu Sugano, *Nippon Kaigi no Kenkyū* [Research on Nippon Kaigi] (Tokyo: Fusōsha, 2016).

4. For more about some of the issues with Abe's proposed constitutional revisions, see Rintarō Kuramochi, "*Abe Kaiken de wa Abe Kaiken no Mokuteki wa Tassei Dekinai? Jieitai Meiki no Jiko Mujun* [The Abe Proposal Can't Fulfill Its Own Goal?: The Self-Contradiction of Writing in the Self-Defense Forces]," *Asahi Shimbun Ronza*, March 6, 2018, https://webronza.asahi.com/politics/articles/2018030200004.html; and "'*Abe Kaiken' no Hontō no Mondai to wa: Abe Kaiken wa Soshi Shitai kedo Rikkenteki kaikenron ni wa Hihanteki na Hitotachi e (Shita)* [The Real Problem with the Abe Proposal: To the People Who Want to Stop the Abe Proposal but Are Critical of Constitutional Revision Rooted in Constitutionalism (Part 2)]," *Asahi Shimbun Ronza*, October 19, 2018, https://webronza.asahi.com/politics/articles/2018101500004.html.

5. Liberal Democratic Constitutional Reform Promotion Headquarters, "*Kenpō ni kansuru Giron no Jōkyō ni tsuite* [Concerning the State of Constitutional Debate]," March 26, 2018, https://jimin.jp-east-2.storage.api.nifcloud.com/pdf/constitution/news/20180326_01.pdf.

6. Constitutional Democratic Party, "*Kenpō ni kansuru Kangaekata: Rikkenteki Kenpō Giron* [Our Thoughts on the Constitution: Debating the Constitution with Constitutionalism]," July 19, 2018, https://archive2017.cdp-japan.jp/policy/constitution.

7. Shiori Yamao, *Rikkenteki Kaiken: Kenpō o Riberaru ni Kangaeru Nanatsu no Tairon* [Constitutional Revision Rooted in Constitutionalism: Seven Tête-à-Têtes Thinking about the Constitution Liberally] (Tokyo: Chikuma Shinsho, 2018). In her book, Representative Yamao offers her idea of "constitutional revision rooted in

constitutionalism" as a liberal constitutional revision that limits the government. As a member of an opposition party, Yamao's proposal marks her as a rare type of Diet member. CDP leader Yukio Edano, who has expressed his "discomfort" regarding Yamao's proposal, released his own draft revision for Article 9 in 2013. See Yukio Edano, "*Kenpō Kyūjō—Watashi nara Kou Kaeru: Kaiken Shian Happyō* [This Is How I Would Change Article 9 of the Japanese Constitution: Yukio Edano's Own Constitution Revision Proposal]," *Bungeishunjū*, October 2013.

8. For more on arguments about constitutional revision rooted in constitutionalism, see also Rintarō Kuramochi, "*Kenpō no Hōyōryoku yo Futatabi: Dare mo ga Toujisha no Rikkenteki Kaikenron* [Tolerance within the Constitution Again: Everyone Has a Stake in Constitutional Debate Rooted in Constitutionalism], *Asahi Shimbun Ronza*, January 12, 2018, https://webronza.asahi.com/politics/articles/2017122600003.html; Yoshinori Kobayashi et al., *Gōsen (Kenpō) Dōjō I: Shiro Obi* [Gosen (Constitution) Dojo I: White Belt] (Tokyo: Mainichi Shimbun Publishing: 2018); and Yoshinori Kobayashi et al., *Zokkoku no Kyūjō: Gōsen (Kenpō) Dōjō II, Kuro Obi* [Dependency of Article 9: Gosen (Constitution) Dojo II, Black Belt] (Tokyo: Mainichi Shimbun Publishing, 2018). *Zokkoku no Kyūjō: Gōsen (Kenpō) Dōjō II, Kuro Obi* introduces some statements Edano made in May of 2018 where he acknowledged that with "Yamao's theory [of constitutional revision rooted in constitutionalism], discussion will go smoother" (79). Edano also notes that he himself believes in Yamao's theory of constitutional revision rooted in constitutionalism: "When it comes to discourse regarding the constitution, I as the CDP leader have to give preference to matters of political discourse. Yamao then does a lot of the more difficult work that I can't do. . . . I want everyone here to understand that everything that she is saying about the constitution is almost identical to what I am saying" (85, 87).

9. *Shūgiin Kenpō Chōsakai* [House of Representatives Committee on the Constitution], "*Dai-nihyaku Kokkai Kenpō Chōsakai Dai-nigō* [200th National Diet Session, House of Representatives Committee on the Constitution Meeting Minutes, Session 2]," November 7, 2019, http://www.shugiin.go.jp/internet/itdb_kaigiroku.nsf/html/kaigiroku/025020020191107002.htm.

10. "*Ritsumin Edano Daihyō, Kenpōshin de no Yamao shi no Hatsugen ni Fukaikan* [CDP Leader Edano Expresses Discomfort with Yamao's Statement in Committee on the Constitution]," *Sankei Shimbun* Digital, November 7, 2019, https://www.sankei.com/politics/news/191107/plt1911070028-n1.html.

11. Constitutional Democratic Party, "*Kenpō ni kansuru Kangaekata: Rikkenteki Kenpō Giron* [Our Thoughts on the Constitution: Debating the Constitution with Constitutionalism]," July 19, 2018, https://archive2017.cdp-japan.jp/policy/constitution.

12. *Shūgiin Kenpō Chōsakai* [House of Representatives Committee on the Constitution], "*Dai-nihyaku Kokkai Kenpō Chōsakai Dai-sangō* [200th National Diet Session, House of Representatives Committee on the Constitution Meeting Minutes, Session 3]," November 14, 2019, http://www.shugiin.go.jp/internet/itdb_kaigiroku.nsf/html/kaigiroku/025020020191114003.htm.

13. See Keigo Komamura's chapter in this book and his article "*Kyūjō no Mitsu no Unmei to wa* [The Three Fates of Article Nine]," *Asahi Shimbun Ronza*, November 22, 2017, https://webronza.asahi.com/politics/articles/2017111900001.html. Kom-

amura posits that the "sovereigns" to whom the Japanese Supreme Court delegates the final decision over the dynamic state of Article 9 of the Japanese Constitution can be construed as having a multi-tiered identity where said "sovereigns" act as "sovereigns," "voters," and "the people."

14. This statement comes from the CDP Constitutional Research Committee chairperson Ikuo Yamahana, in charge of the party's position on the constitution. See "*Ritsumin Yamahana-shi 'Mazu CM Kisei Giron o': Kaiken-an, Miraieigō Dasazu Kakutō Kenpō Sekininsha ni Kiku* [CDP Member Yamahana "Discussing Commercial Limitations Comes First": No Proposal of Constitutional Revision For All Eternity, Talking to Each Party's Person in Charge of Constitutional Matters]," *Nikkei Shimbun*, August 15, 2019, https://www.nikkei.com/article/DGKKZO48563430U9A810C1PP8000/.

15. During his time to ask questions as party leader during the plenary session of the Diet in October 2018, Tamaki presented his "Constitutional Revision Rooted in Peace" Plan. See Democratic Party For the People, "*[Shūin Honkaigi] Tamaki Yūichirō Daihyō, 'Nichibei Chii Kyōtei no Kaitei' tō ni tsuite Abe Sōri ni Daihyō Shitsumon* [(House of Representatives Plenary Session) Party Leader Yūichirō Tamaki Questions Prime Minister Abe about Revising U.S.-Japan Status of Forces Agreement]," October 29, 2018, https://www.dpfp.or.jp/article/200730?fbclid=IwAR3VSr9FFQeKR4jGm2xKF7BtM8KwTwFSk2bwHO7mjgpRRkH74FX-B7y3gWU. Also, Tamaki has referred to the Swiss Constitution in his writings and has borrowed the idea of rights for consumer safety for his own constitutional revision proposal. See Yūichirō Tamaki, *Reiwa Nippon Kaizōron* [A Theory of Remodeling Reiwa Japan] (Tokyo: Mainichi Shimbun Publishing, 2019). While I have mentioned this already, opposition party members offering their own versions for constitutional revision in the Diet of present-day Japan is quite rare.

16. "*Tamaki Kokuminminshu Daihyō 'Abe Shusō to Kaidan wo': Kaiken Rongi ni Maemuki* [Democratic Party for the People Leader Tamaki 'Let's Talk Prime Minister Abe': Positive Outlook on Debating Constitutional Revision]," *Jiji Dot Com News*, July 25, 2019, https://www.jiji.com/jc/article?k=2019072501307&g=pol.

17. For sources that indicate how problematic this liberal phenomenon is, see Mark Lilla, *The Once and Future Liberal: After Identity Politics*, trans. Dai Natsume (Tokyo: Hayakawa Shobō, 2018); and Cass Sunstein, *#Republic: Divided Democracy in the Age of Social Media*, trans. Naomi Itō (Tokyo: Keiso Shobo Publishing, 2018).

18. For results of polls of businesses, see "*Jikishushō Kōho, Ishiba Shiji ga Abe Shushō o Nuite Yakushin: Nihon Kigyō e no Chōsa de* [Ishiba Rapidly Overtakes Abe as Candidate for Next Prime Minister: Results from a Survey for Japanese Companies]," *Newsweek Japan*, December 6, 2019, https://www.newsweekjapan.jp/stories/business/2019/12/post-13556.php.

19. Shigeru Ishiba, "*Korekara no Seiji Kadai: Kenpō Kaisei, Kita-Chōsen, Kyōiku o Megutte* [Political Issues to Consider: Constitutional Revision, North Korea, and Education]," *Gekkan Sekai to Nihon*, July 2017. See also Shigeru Ishiba's policy compilation *Ishiba Shigeru to Suigetsu-kai no Nihon Sōsei* [Shigeru Ishiba and Suigetsu-kai's Revitalization of Japan] (Tokyo: Shinkōsha, 2018).

20. See note 17.

21. Liberal Democratic Party, "*Nihonkoku Kenpōkaisei Sōan* [Draft Revisions to the Constitution of Japan]," Liberal Democratic Constitutional Reform Promotion Headquarters, April 27, 2012, https://jimin.jp-east-2.storage.api.nifcloud.com/pdf/news/policy/130250_1.pdf.

22. "*Ishiba-shi, Tsukue Tataite Fuman Arawa: Tamaki-shi ga Hatsugen Motomeru mo. . . Shūin Kenpō Shinsakai* [Ishiba Makes Dissatisfaction Known by Hitting Desk: Even if Tamaki Asks for a Chance so Ishiba May Speak . . . House of Representatives Committee on the Constitution]," *Mainichi Shimbun*, November 28, 2019, https://mainichi.jp/articles/20191128/k00/00m/010/226000c.

23. See note 8.

24. Shirō Sakaiya, *Kenpō to Yoron: Sengo Nihonjin wa Kenpō to Dou Mukiattekitanoka* [The Constitution and Public Opinion: How Have the Post-War Japanese People Faced the Constitution Up to Now?] (Tokyo: Chikuma Shobō, 2017).

In a 1950 public opinion poll, the Asahi Shimbun asked respondents, "Some people say that Japan should make their own army. Do you agree or disagree with this statement?" However, the newspaper also printed a definition that distinguished this "army" from the existing National Police Force at the time: "'Army' refers to a group that will protect Japan from being invaded and is different from the National Police Reserve and the Coast Guard." Even with this qualification to the definition of "army," 54% of respondents agreed with establishing an army, greatly overtaking the mere 28% against having an army. Given the current state of public opinion, results like this should shock present-day Japan.

25. Shirō Sakaiya, "*Kyūjō e no 'Mu' Ishiki Susumu: Jūyōsa Fuyasu Yoron Chōsa no Shitsu* [A Progressing "Un"-Consciousness about Article 9: Quality of Public Opinions that Raise Significance]," *Journalism*, February 2019.

26. Constitutional Democracy Japan (Tumblr), https://constitutionaldemocracy japan.tumblr.com/setsuritsushyushi.

27. As of December 2019, CDP leader Edano has been calling out to the Democratic Party for the People among other opposition parties to coalesce into a bigger opposition party. As it stands, the CDP and Democratic Party for the People have already entered talks about joining forces. Many experts say that there is a high possibility that the merger may happen. However, since Democratic Party for the People leader Tamaki has the rare ability to reach even the apathetic voters, if they were to form one party with the CDP who vow to not produce draft constitutional revisions for all eternity, the potential damage to fulfilling and enriching debate will be inestimably great. Given those risks, Tamaki should not give in to the swaying of party approval ratings but instead seriously consider not joining the CDP for the sake of reviving the opposition parties in the distant future.

28. When I talked with Ari Hatsuzawa—a photographer that went to report on the resistance movement happening in Hong Kong over the 2019 Fugitive Offenders bill—he shared the following reflection comparing China and Japan: "Japan is like China now. Whenever I go to interview Chinese people about Hong Kong, many of them note that 'The Chinese Constitution may be a dead letter, but as long as you don't criticize the government, there is no freer place on earth. I just don't get why the people in Hong Kong are demanding for that much freedom.' In Japan, we have

the imperial system and the LDP, and as long as you don't criticize the administration, then it's like who cares about the constitution?" (November 12, 2019).

29. Along with politicians and researchers, symphony conductor Simon Rattle is a member of Charter 88. Rattle conducted the Berlin Philharmonic for sixteen years, and was so vocal about Brexit that at the encore for the outdoor concert Waldbühne, before conducting "Pomp and Circumstance" by the British composer Edward Elgar, he said: "Here's to hoping that the U.K. does not leave the E.U." In this way, Rattle is the epitome of a liberal patriot.

30. Kenji Miyazawa, "*Seitoshokun ni yoseru* [To My Students]," *Asahi Hyōron*, April 1946.

REFERENCES

Ackerman, Bruce and James S. Fishkin. *Deliberation Day*. Translated by Norikazu Kawagishi, Masashi Yazawa, and Yutaka Aoyama. Tokyo: Waseda University Press, 2015.

Ashibe, Nobuyoshi and Kazuyuki Takahashi. *Kenpō Dai Nanaban* [The Japanese Constitution: Version Seven]. Tokyo: Iwanami Shoten, 2019.

Constitutional Democratic Party. "*Kenpō ni kansuru Kangaekata: Rikkenteki Kenpō Giron* [Our Thoughts on the Constitution: Debating the Constitution with Constitutionalism]." July 19, 2018. https://archive2017.cdp-japan.jp/policy/constitution.

Democratic Party For the People. "*[Shūin Honkaigi] Tamaki Yūichirō Daihyō, 'Nichibei Chii Kyōtei no Kaitei' tō ni tsuite Abe Sōri ni Daihyō Shitsumon* [(House of Representatives Plenary Session) Party Leader Yūichirō Tamaki Questions Prime Minister Abe about Revising U.S.-Japan Status of Forces Agreement]." October 29, 2018. https://www.dpfp.or.jp/article/200730?fbclid=IwAR3VSr9FFQeKR4jGm2xKF7BtM8KwTwFSk2bwHO7mjgpRRkH74FX-B7y3gWU.

Edano, Yukio. "*Kenpō Kyūjō—Watashi nara Kou Kaeru: Kaiken Shian Happyō* [This Is How I Would Change Article 9 of the Japanese Constitution: Yukio Edano's Own Constitution Revision Proposal]." *Bungeishunjū*. October 2013.

Higuchi, Yōichi, Kenji Ishikawa, Tsunemasa Arikawa, Jōji Shishido and Sōta Kimura. *Kenpō o Gakumon Suru* [Studying the Japanese Constitution]. Tokyo: Yūhikaku Publishing, 2019.

Imai, Hajime and the Committee for the Production and Spread of *Kokumin Tōhyō no Subete* [Everything About National Referendum]. *Kokumin Tōhyō no Subete* [Everything About National Referendum]. Tokyo: Yūbunsha, 2017.

Ishiba, Shigeru. *Ishiba Shigeru to Suigetsu-kai no Nihon Sōsei* [Shigeru Ishiba and Suigetsu-kai's Revitalization of Japan]. Tokyo: Shinkōsha, 2018.

Ishiba, Shigeru. "*Korekara no Seiji Kadai: Kenpō Kaisei, Kita-Chōsen, Kyōiku o Megutte* [Political Issues to Consider: Constitutional Revision, North Korea, and Education]." *Gekkan Sekai to Nihon*. July 2017.

"*Ishiba-shi, Tsukue Tataite Fuman Arawa: Tamaki-shi ga Hatsugen Motomeru mo . . . Shūin Kenpō Shinsakai* [Ishiba Makes Dissatisfaction Known by Hitting Desk: Even if Tamaki Asks for a Chance so Ishiba May Speak . . . House of

Representatives Committee on the Constitution].” *Mainichi Shimbun*. November 28, 2019. https://mainichi.jp/articles/20191128/k00/00m/010/226000c.

Itō, Tetsuo. “‘*Sanbun no Ni*’: *Kakutokugo no Kaiken Senryaku* [Two-Thirds: Strategies for Constitutional Revision Once We Get the Numbers].” *Ashita e no Sentaku* [The Choice for Tomorrow]. September 2016.

Iwasaki, Masahiro. *Seitō Shisutemu* [Party System]. Tokyo: Nihon Keizai Hyōronsha, 2020.

“*Jikishushō Kōho, Ishiba Shiji ga Abe Shushō o Nuite Yakushin: Nihon Kigyō e no Chōsa de* [Ishiba Rapidly Overtakes Abe as Candidate for Next Prime Minister: Results from a Survey for Japanese Companies].” *Newsweek Japan*. December 6, 2019. https://www.newsweekjapan.jp/stories/business/2019/12/post-13556.php.

Kanamori, Tokujirō. *Kenpō Yuigon, Kenpō Zuisō, Kenpō Uraomote, Watashi no Rirekisho* [Constitution as Will, Reflections Upon the Constitution, Both Sides of the Constitution, My Resume]. Edited by Katsutoshi Takami. Tokyo: Jigakusha, 2013.

Kobayashi, Yoshinori, Tatsuo Inoue, Shiori Yamao, Keigo Komamura, and Masahiro Sogabe. *Gōsen (Kenpō) Dōjō I: Shiro Obi* [Gosen (Constitution) Dojo I: White Belt]. Tokyo: Mainichi Shimbun Publishing, 2018.

Kobayashi, Yoshinori, Tatsuo Inoue, Shiori Yamao, Yukio Edano, Kenji Isezaki, Hajime Yamamoto, Takeshi Inoue. *Zokkoku no Kyūjō: Gōsen (Kenpō) Dōjō II, Kuro Obi* [Dependency of Article 9: Gosen (Constitution) Dojo II, Black Belt]. Tokyo: Mainichi Shimbun Publishing, 2018.

Komamura, Keigo. “*Kyūjō no Mitsu no Unmei to wa* [The Three Fates of Article Nine].” *Asahi Shimbun Ronza*. November 22, 2017. https://webronza.asahi.com/politics/articles/2017111900001.html.

Komamura, Keigo, Satoshi Machidori, Yasushi Kondō, Kensuke Ueda, Hiroshi Okayama, Norikazu Kawagishi, Tōru Yoshida, Shigeru Minamino, Masaki Kondō, Kōichi Akasaka, Takeshi Itō, Hajime Tajika, Yūki Asaba, Noriko Kokubun, Kazuhiro Takii, and Yūichi Nishimura. *“Kenpō Kaisei” no Hikaku Seijigaku* [Comparative Political Studies of “Constitutional Revision”]. Edited by Keigo Komamura and Satoshi Machidori. Tokyo: Kōbundō, 2016.

Kuramochi, Rintarō. “*Abe Kaiken de wa Abe Kaiken no Mokuteki wa Tassei Dekinai? Jieitai Meiki no Jiko Mujun* [The Abe Proposal Can’t Fulfill Its Own Goal?: The Self-Contradiction of Writing in the Self-Defense Forces].” *Asahi Shimbun Ronza*. March 6, 2018. https://webronza.asahi.com/politics/articles/2018030200004.html.

Kuramochi, Rintarō. “*‘Abe Kaiken’ no Hontō no Mondai to wa: Abe Kaiken wa Soshi Shitai kedo Rikkenteki kaikenron ni wa Hihanteki na Hitotachi e (Shita)* [The Real Problem with the Abe Proposal: To the People Who Want to Stop the Abe Proposal But Are Critical of Constitutional Revision Rooted in Constitutionalism (Part 2)].” *Asahi Shimbun Ronza*. October 19, 2018. https://webronza.asahi.com/politics/articles/2018101500004.html.

Kuramochi, Rintarō. “*Kenpō no Hōyōryoku yo Futatabi: Dare mo ga Toujisha no Rikkenteki Kaikenron* [Tolerance within the Constitution Again: Everyone Has a Stake in Constitutional Debate Rooted in Constitutionalism].” *Asahi Shimbun Ronza*. January 12, 2018. https://webronza.asahi.com/politics/articles/2017122600003.html.

Liberal Democratic Constitutional Reform Promotion Headquarters. "*Kenpō ni kansuru Giron no Jōkyō ni tsuite* [Concerning the State of Constitutional Debate]." March 26, 2018. https://jimin.jp-east-2.storage.api.nifcloud.com/pdf/constitution/news/20180326_01.pdf.

Liberal Democratic Party. "*Nihonkoku Kenpōkaisei Sōan* [Draft Revisions to the Constitution of Japan]." Liberal Democratic Constitutional Reform Promotion Headquarters. April 27, 2012. https://jimin.jp-east-2.storage.api.nifcloud.com/pdf/news/policy/130250_1.pdf.

Lilla, Mark. *The Once and Future Liberal: After Identity Politics*. Translated by Dai Natsume. Commentary by Keigō Komamura. Tokyo: Hayakawa Shobō, 2018.

Miyazawa, Kenji. "*Seitoshokun ni yoseru* [To My Students]." *Asahi Hyōron*. April 1946.

Mizushima, Jirō, Mitsuo Koga, Takako Imai, Shōgo Noda, Kanji Tokura, Takeshi Itō, Yuko Sakuuchi, Akira Taguchi, Yohei Nakayama, Takayuki Nishiyama, and Kōji Nakakita. *Popyurizumu toiu Chōsen: Kiro ni Tatsu Gendai Demokurashī* [The Populist Challenge to Democracy: Europe, the U.S. and Japan]. Edited by Jirō Mizushima. Tokyo: Iwanami Shoten, 2020.

"*Ritsumin Edano Daihyō, Kenpōshin de no Yamao shi no Hatsugen ni Fukaikan* [CDP Leader Edano Expresses Discomfort with Yamao's Statement in Committee on the Constitution]." *Sankei Shimbun* Digital. November 7, 2019. https://www.sankei.com/politics/news/191107/plt1911070028-n1.html.

"*Ritsumin Yamahana-shi 'Mazu CM Kisei Giron o': Kaiken-an, Miraieigō Dasazu Kakutō Kenpō Sekininsha ni Kiku* [CDP Member Yamahana 'Discussing Commercial Limitations Comes First': No Proposal of Constitutional Revision For All Eternity, Talking to Each Party's Person in Charge of Constitutional Matters]." *Nikkei Shimbun*. August 15, 2019. https://www.nikkei.com/article/DGKKZO48563430U9A810C1PP8000/.

Sakaiya, Shirō. *Kenpō to Yoron: Sengo Nihonjin wa Kenpō to Dou Mukiattekitanoka* [The Constitution and Public Opinion: How Have the Post-War Japanese People Faced the Constitution Up to Now?]. Tokyo: Chikuma Shobō, 2017.

Sakaiya, Shirō. "*Kyūjō e no 'Mu' Ishiki Susumu: Jūyōsa Fuyasu Yoron Chōsa no Shitsu* [A Progressing 'Un'-Consciousness about Article 9: Quality of Public Opinions that Raise Significance]." *Journalism*. February 2019.

Shugiin Kenpō Chōsakai [House of Representatives Committee on the Constitution]. "*Dai-nihyaku Kokkai Kenpō Chōsakai Dai-nigō* [200th National Diet Session, House of Representatives Committee on the Constitution Meeting Minutes, Session 2.]" November 7, 2019. http://www.shugiin.go.jp/internet/itdb_kaigiroku.nsf/html/kaigiroku/025020020191107002.htm.

Shugiin Kenpō Chōsakai [House of Representatives Committee on the Constitution]. "*Dai-nihyaku Kokkai Kenpō Chōsakai Dai-sangō* [200th National Diet Session, House of Representatives Committee on the Constitution Meeting Minutes, Session 3." November 14, 2019. http://www.shugiin.go.jp/internet/itdb_kaigiroku.nsf/html/kaigiroku/025020020191114003.htm.

Sugano, Tamotsu. *Nippon Kaigi no Kenkyū* [Research on Nippon Kaigi]. Tokyo: Fusōsha, 2016.

Sunstein, Cass. *#Republic: Divided Democracy in the Age of Social Media*. Translated by Naomi Itō. Tokyo: Keiso Shobō Publishing, 2018.

"*Tamaki Kokuminminshu Daihyō 'Abe Shusō to Kaidan wo': Kaiken Rongi ni Maemuki* [Democratic Party for the People Leader Tamaki 'Let's Talk Prime Minister Abe': Positive Outlook on Debating Constitutional Revision]." *Jiji Dot Com News*. July 25, 2019. https://www.jiji.com/jc/article?k=2019072501307&g=pol.

Tamaki, Yūichirō. *Reiwa Nippon Kaizōron* [A Theory of Remodeling Reiwa Japan]. Tokyo: Mainichi Shimbun Publishing, 2019.

Taniguchi, Masaki and Jōji Shishido. *Dejitaru Demokurashī ga Yattekuru: AI ga Watashi-tachi no Shakai o Kaerundattara, Seiji mo Sonomamatte Wakeniwaikanainjanai?* [Here Comes Digital Democracy: If AI Is Going to Change Our Society, Then Politics Can't Stay the Same, Right?]. Tokyo: Chūōkōron-Shinsha, 2020.

Tsujimura, Miyoko. *Hikaku Kenpō Shinban* [Comparative Constitutional Law (New Version)]. Tokyo: Iwanami Shoten, 2011.

Watanabe, Masahito. *Amerika Seiji no Kabe: Rieki to Rinen no Hazama de* [The Wall of American Politics: At the Interstice Between Profit and Principle]. Tokyo: Iwanami Shoten, 2016.

Watase, Yūya. *Naze, Seijuku Shita Minshushugi wa Bundan o Umidasunoka?: Amerika kara Sekai ni Kakusan Suru Kakusa to Bundan no Kōzu* [This Is Why Mature Democracy Creates Social Divisions]. Tokyo: Subarusha, 2019.

Yamao, Shiori, *Rikkenteki Kaiken: Kenpō o Riberaru ni Kangaeru Nanatsu no Tairon* [Constitutional Revision Rooted in Constitutionalism: Seven Tête-à-Têtes Thinking about the Constitution Liberally]. Tokyo: Chikuma Shinsho, 2018.

Chapter Five

Reflections on Part I

Keigo Komamura

"Say nothing, just make something."[1]

This proverb describes the spirit of the Japanese craftsman (*Shokunin katagi*). The proverb may seem to contain a truth about the character of the Japanese people. But it is a stereotype, after all. Essays in Part 1 and Part 2 provide various stories of civic activism in Japan which prove the Japanese people are not necessarily obedient and passive but active and sometimes even riotous. In those essays we see a variety of protests and movements, such as the Sunagawa struggle of the latter half of the 1950s (Komamura, Yamamoto), the Anpo struggle of 1960 (Yamamoto), the anti-Vietnam war movement by the Citizen's League for Peace in Vietnam between the mid-1960s and the mid-1970s (Nakano), the anti-nuclear protests after the Fukushima nuclear power plant accident of 2011 (Nakano), the anti-security legislation protests of 2015 (Nakano), enlightenment activities and political lobbying led by religious groups such as Sōka Gakkai (McLaughlin) and the Association of Shinto Shrines (*Jinja Honchō*) (Hardacre), a conservative movement by Nippon Kaigi (Hardacre, Ueda), women's engagement with politics (Miura), a new civic activism led by SEALD's, the Citizen's League, and other groups (Nakano, Ueda), new activism in cyberspace (Ueda), and more.

These activities and movements, of course, happened after the end of World War II. However, these events are by no means peculiar to postwar Japan. There has been a tradition of civic activism and democratic movements since the Meiji period. Constitutional democracy was introduced when Japan established the first modern parliamentary system in Asia in 1889. The *Jiyū minken undō* (Freedom and People's Rights Movement) from 1874 to 1890 greatly affected its establishment.[2] Of course, "democracy" under the Meiji Constitution of 1889 was limited because the parliamentary system coexisted with the Emperor. Despite these limits on the constitutional structure, there were occasions when movements for democratization such as Taishō democracy[3] from 1910 to 1920 arose. Even the Potsdam Declaration of 1945 by which the Allied Powers called for the surrender of Japan recognized this historical development of democracy in Japan. The 10th clause of the Declaration reads:

> The Japanese Government shall remove all obstacles to *the revival and strengthening of democratic tendencies* among the Japanese people. Freedom of speech, of religion, and of thought, as well as respect for the fundamental human rights shall be established.[4] (emphasis added)

It demanded that Japan revive and strengthen democratic tendencies that had once existed, while promising to "establish" guarantees for fundamental human rights that had never existed.

The Constitution of Japan of 1946 established the Diet and limited the role of the Emperor, not the parliament, and released the winds of civic activism through guaranteeing more complete freedom of speech, freedom of assembly, and freedom of religion. Two civic movements in the early period of postwar Japan are important. The Anti-Nuclear Weapons Movement between 1954 and 1955 was actually ignited by an appeal by a housewife living in Tokyo's Suginami Ward, and rapidly expanded its scale to obtain thirty million supporters by the time of the first world conference against nuclear weapons in Hiroshima in 1955. The Sunagawa struggle of the latter half of the 1950s was begun by local farmers in a small village of a rural part of Tokyo, when the residents there asked the city of Tokyo to return their farmlands, which had been taken over for expansion of a U.S. airbase.

Both these civic movements related to Article 9 of the Constitution of Japan. The Sunagawa struggle, in particular, set the national agenda on whether the U.S.-Japan Security Treaty unconstitutionally violated Article 9. The struggle brought about a landmark decision of the Supreme Court of Japan, the Sunagawa ruling of 1959, whose details I referred to in chapter 1 of this volume. After a decade passed, civic activism and Article 9 encountered each other. As I articulated in my essay, the Sunagawa case provided a normative connection between civic activism and constitutional law by holding that constitutional doubt of highly political questions would be ultimately solved through "the political criticism by the people with whom rests the sovereign power of the nation" (hereinafter shortened as "the political criticism by the sovereign people").

* * *

Yamamoto and I interpret this phrase, "the political criticism by the sovereign people," in different ways. I try to draw normative implications from the phrase: (a) in order to make "political criticism" possible, it needs a special agenda-setting to focus on a specific constitutional issue; (b) if so, it would be the best and only solution to highly political questions that national referendum for constitutional revision and civic activism come together. Yamamoto goes a different way. He interprets the phrase as a more flexible one when he shows considerable concern with Yale law professor Bruce Ackerman's formula of constitutional change without a formal amendment. He tries to apply Ackerman's formula to the monumental activism of the postwar Japan, the 1960 Anpo struggle, to verify whether or not the political debate engaged by the people during this struggle led to constitutional change outside the formal process of revision. If a truly critical commitment by the sovereign people occurred during the struggle and then the sovereign people accepted Prime Minister Kishi's proposal for renewal of the U.S.-Japan Security Treaty, Article 9 was informally changed. In other words, he examines if a great event which is properly termed "the political criticism by the sovereign people" happened or not. Following his detailed consideration, Yamamoto comes to a negative conclusion.

I welcome his conclusion that informal revision of the constitution never happened during the Anpo struggle because I don't share the Yamamoto/Ackerman formula itself. In my essay, I distinguish between the sovereign people as *constitutional amending power* and the sovereign people as *voters*. But Yamamoto places an intermediate between these two, "more voter/less amending power," who can revise constitution without resort to formal process of amendment. His project is really challenging. However, I have one question. If higher lawmaking through mass mobilization takes place, why ever is a formal revision not actualized? Does mass mobilization leading to constitutional transformation truly happen? My view on this issue is like this: no formal constitutional revision through the national referendum, no transformative lawmaking. I believe that Yamamoto and Ackerman's view paradoxically underestimates the potential of the sovereign people. They seem to spoil the sovereign people.[5]

Besides that, by and large, Yamamoto's analysis of civic activism during the Anpo struggle is fascinating. He seems to think that activism in the Anpo struggle protesting against the politics of the Kishi administration was politics too. Therefore, civic activism also had to deal with factional disputes and internal division, had to engage in political negotiation, and needed money, in the same ways that Prime Minster Kishi had to deal with the same things with the LDP and opposition parties. Sometimes the Anpo struggle is idealized too much by the liberal camp, who would like to recall its legacy as a sweet memory. Yamamoto successfully demythologizes the over-idealized image of the Anpo struggle. Furthermore, his observation is helpful when we consider how to revitalize civic activism today. In order to make civic activism work, it needs to be more politics-conscious. I will come back to this topic later with Nakano's essay.

Additionally, Yamamoto seems to be doubtful that the Anpo protests were truly critiques of the existing system. In his essay, he inclines to sympathize with views regarding the movement as "a fiction" or "sports festival." I think to understand these views in context, since they might be an overreaction against or an over-demythologizing of the legacy of the Anpo struggle. One undeniable fact is that the Anpo struggle was the biggest protest in postwar Japan. If this struggle were "a fiction," what protest could ever be a real protest at all? One of the reasons Yamamoto tends to understand the Anpo struggle as "a fiction" or "sports festival" may lie in his standard for evaluating civic activism. Yamamoto refers to the "purity" of the protests which Shimizu Ikutarō, an intellectual giant at that time, once found in student activists during the Anpo struggle. Yamamoto argues that the loss of purity made student activists much more political in their movement. Although he finds "politics" in the character of civic activism, Yamamoto evaluates it by the standard of "purity."

* * *

Nakano's essay shows us a gleam of hope for civic activism.

New civic activism has emerged since the great earthquake of 2011 followed by the devastating incident at the Fukushima nuclear power plant. Nakano draws a different picture of new civic activism from Yamamoto's. He also identifies some common/different traits of the current, new civic activism in Japan in comparison with activism in other countries. For Nakano, this new civic activism arose to counter the erosion of constitutional democracy, in particular, two major failures exposed by the return of Shinzō Abe to power in 2012, the failure of representative democracy in terms of electoral representation of the popular will, and the failure of media representation of truth and reality.

First, new civic activism has taken the form of a "movement of the sovereign people" serving as a foundation for, rather than being hostile to, renewed civic involvement in electoral politics in order to make up for the failure of representative democracy. In other countries, civic protesters have tried to change the system of party politics by direct actions such as establishing a new party, or winning seats in the legislature. In Japan, new civic activists did not seek to establish a new political party of their own, but instead opted to establish a political platform, Civil Alliance, into which several civic organizations coalesced and through which they backed the existing opposition parties and promoted opposition collaboration. These remarkable traits of the new civic activism are quite different from the form of former movements such as the Sunagawa struggle and the Anpo struggle. In the Sunagawa struggle, the Japan Socialist Party (JSP) and its supporting labor unions substantially engaged themselves in protests. In the Anpo struggle, the protesters had no desire to channel the movement into electoral politics, but rather denied the parliamentary system itself. More important, in both cases, they were literally struggles. During the struggle, they were active and sometimes even riotous or violent, but they did not set up a continuing platform after the struggle ceased.

Second, developments in communication technology and popular culture have changed the media strategy and style of civil movements. New civic activism no longer totally relies upon the existing mass media, but instead makes its activity both media friendly and self-mediatized by its effective use of social media such as Twitter and by being fashion-conscious and telegenic.

* * *

Nakano's view on new civic activism paints a picture of the near future not just for civic movements but also for the political system in Japan. He concludes that "in order to restore some checks and balances to the party system and rebuild parliamentary democracy, it was imperative for the civic activism in Japan to promote opposition collaboration and also to bring back voters to the polling booths."

However, it is not an easy project to restore the party system and rebuild parliamentary democracy under the current circumstances in Japan. From his unique experiences as a legal advisor to Diet members and as an organizer for various civic meetings, Kuramochi describes dysfunctions of the debates on constitutional issues in the Diet and inside the LDP and the opposition parties, and points out the problem of external forces silencing the voices of Diet members. He gives us a pessimistic diagnosis: many members of the Diet seem to be enslaved by voices of a faceless "noisy minority" who hold extreme opinions, and then these Diet members are unable to play their expected roles as national representatives. Of course, I think Kuramochi still believes in the possibility of connecting the party politics system and the dynamics of civic activism, however, his ambivalence seems to be widely shared. We seem to be at a critical turning point in our civic life, in terms of whether we be able to build or rebuild healthy and well-functioning links between politics and civic activism, as suggested both by Nakano's positive description and Kuramochi's negative description of the current situation.

* * *

Reforming or strengthening civic activism to have a good linkage to politics will be a difficult project. For this purpose, we need to develop a new channel for party politics and mediatize ourselves in new ways (Nakano), to face up to internal politics and financing issues for civic movements (Yamamoto), and to emancipate ourselves from being enslaved by a narrow-minded "noisy minority" (Kuramochi).

Related to these strategies for the future of civic activism, Columbia history professor Mark Lilla states:

> If the steady advance of a radicalized Republican Party, over many years and in every branch and at every level of government, should teach liberals anything, it is the absolute priority of winning elections today. Given the Republicans' rage for destruction, it is the *only way* to guarantee that newly won protections for African-Americans, other minorities, women, and gay Americans remain in place. Workshops and university seminars will not do it. Online mobilizing and flash mobs will not do it. Protesting, acting up, and acting out will not do it. The age of movement politics is over, at least for now. We need no more marches. We need more mayors. And governors, and state legislators, and members of Congress.[6] (emphasis in the original)

I partially share Lilla's view. At the same time, however, I believe that we also need to reexamine the primary meaning of conventional measures of activism such as assemblies, demonstrations, protests, marches, and so on. UC Berkeley philosophy professor Judith Butler once argued as follows:

> Indeed, we have to rethink the speech act in order to understand what is made and what is done by certain kinds of bodily enactments: the bodies assembled 'say' we are not disposable, even if they stand silently.[7]
>
> And even when they are not speaking or do not present a set of negotiable demands, the call for justice is being enacted: the bodies assembled "say" "we are not disposable," whether or not they are using words at the moment; what they say, as it were, is "we are still here, persisting, demanding greater justice, a release from precarity, a possibility of a livable life."[8]

In his essay, Nakano cites Sidney Tarrow's argument and refers to a movement of a completely new type, the Occupy Wall Street movement, which is a "we are here" or "recognize us" movement. Butler and Tarrow share the same view on this just-assembling type of movement. The presence of the bodies assembled speechlessly says, "We are still here," or "We are not disposable," even it specifies no particular social issues.

Gathering also provides a special moment for citizens. The late Makoto Oda, a famous civic activist in Japan who organized the Citizen's League for Peace in Vietnam, once said, "What makes marching in civic movements unique is that participants do not exchange their business cards."[9] No matter what position or status you may have, you are treated as completely equal when you are in the assembly. One of the critical problems still remaining for the future is how to transmit a new mode of civic activism (e.g., power of silent presence, etc.) to the deliberative dynamics of "the political criticism by the sovereign people."

NOTES

1. Takeo Funabiki, *"Nihonjin ron" saikō* ("Discourses on the Japanese People" Redux) (Tokyo: Kōdansha, 2010), 186–188.
2. Daikichi Irokawa, *Jiyū minken* (Tokyo: Iwanami shoten, 1981). Yūsaku Matsuzawa, *Jiyū minken undō* (Tokyo: Iwanami shoten, 2016).
3. Ryūichi Narita, *Taishō demokurashī* (Tokyo: Iwanami shoten, 2007).
4. See the website of the National Diet Library of Japan: https://www.ndl.go.jp/constitution/e/etc/c06.html.
5. Of course, this doesn't necessarily mean that a national referendum for constitutional revision would automatically bring about "the political criticism by the sovereign people." Reading Kuramochi's essay on what is going on in the current debate on constitutional revision inside the Diet of Japan, in LDP, and in the opposition parties, we really cannot say there is robust and rich deliberation which leads to "the political criticism by the sovereign people." We should put an end to this "rough-and-ready work" for constitutional revision and then launch ourselves on robust and rich deliberation. That is what the Sunagawa ruling normatively requests of us in the name of "the political criticism by the sovereign people."
6. Mark Lilla, *The Once and Future Liberal: After Identity Politics* (New York: HarperCollins, 2017), 110–111.
7. Judith Butler, *Notes toward a Performative Theory of Assembly* (Cambridge, MA: Harvard University Press, 2015), 18.
8. Butler, *Notes toward a Performative Theory of Assembly*, 25.
9. Makoto Oda, *Chūryū no fukkō* (Tokyo: Nihon hōsō shuppan kyōkai, 2007), 139–140.

REFERENCES

Butler, Judith. *Notes toward a Performative Theory of Assembly*. Cambridge, MA: Harvard University Press, 2015.

Funabiki, Takeo. *"Nihonjin ron" saikō* ("Discourses on the Japanese People" Redux). Tokyo: Kōdansha, 2010.

Irokawa, Daikichi. *Jiyū minken* (Liberty and People's Rights). Tokyo: Iwanami shoten, 1981.

Lilla, Mark. *The Once and Future Liberal: After Identity Politics*. New York: HarperCollins, 2017.

Matsuzawa, Yūsaku. *Jiyū minken undo* (The Movement for Liberty and People's Rights). Tokyo: Iwanami shoten, 2016.

Narita, Ryūichi. *Taishō demokurashī* (Taishō Democracy). Tokyo: Iwanami shoten, 2007

Oda, Makoto. *Chūryū no fukkō* (Restoration of the Middle Class). Tokyo: Nihon hōsō shuppan kyōkai, 2007.

Part II

ACTIVISTS FOR AND AGAINST CONSTITUTIONAL REVISION

Chapter Six

New Civic Activism and Constitutional Discussion

Streets, Shrines, and Cyberspace

Makiko Ueda

In the 2010s, Japanese civic activism entered a new phase. Taking place in streets, local shrines, and cyberspace, the civic energy of the pro- and anti-constitutional revision movements fiercely grew, involving groups such as intellectuals and political independents who had generally shied away from activism since the 1960 Anpo protest. The most significant fundamental trait of this "new civic activism," having a loose network without strong leadership or coherent ideology, helped attract a wide range of civic participation. Divergent definitions of "constitutionalism" in the civic and political spheres show that Japanese democracy had become increasingly pluralistic. However, new civic activism must still work alongside traditional civic organizations, such as political parties, unions, and other civil society organizations. Additionally, new civic activism uses the internet as a medium to communicate quickly and effectively, but cyberspace often serves to polarize discourse and is not free from the influence of commercial and political power. As the 2019 House of Councillors election showed, political movements with charismatic leaders also appealed to socially neglected communities via the internet, pulling supporters from some new civic activist groups. In addition to these challenges, these activist groups face a difficult dilemma: how to maintain their original grassroots mission and spontaneity as they grow.

INTRODUCTION

The scale of Japanese constitutional activism during the post-2012 Abe administration has come close to that seen during the 1950s and 1960s. However, Japanese civic activism has gradually developed into a new stage in the decades since the Anpo protest of 1960. The main source of civic activism has moved from universities and union halls to open public spaces, including public streets, local shrines, and the internet. Likewise, the way of organizing civic activism shifted from a top-down, leader-driven approach to one based on loose networks of individuals with similar mindsets. Despite this shift, this new form of civic activism has not replaced traditional notions of organization; in fact, it often restores and works with traditional civic forms (Youngs 2019).[1]

During the Anpo protest of 1960, the movement's ideological leaders were academic professionals labeled "progressive intellectuals." They advocated "disarmed neutrality" and opposed the Kishi administration's attempts to revise the U.S.-Japan Security Treaty. After these protests, many intellectuals left student activism (which reached another peak in 1970) and went back to their own scholarship. The anti–Vietnam War movement led by the Beheiren group (see below) in the 1970s was a milestone in opening civic activism to the wider population. Counter-culture performers in the 1980s and 1990s displayed civic activism in parks and streets.[2] In opposition, motivated by a passion to take the civic space from "liberals" and/or "the left wing," radical conservatives built their own grassroots movements throughout Japan. For example, starting from Nagasaki University in the 1960s, predecessors of the Nippon Kaigi group propelled their movement to national influence. During the 1970s, they successfully involved a broad range of people, including religious, business, and culture figures. In the late 1970s, conservative opinion leaders started appearing in newly founded magazines from major publishers. The "right-left" battle became a form of entertainment on TV shows throughout the 1990s. In the 2000s, the "right wing" gathered momentum in a new open space, the internet, overwhelming liberal intellectuals.

In the 2010s, both liberal and conservative sides came into the next phase of civic activism. A student group, the Students Emergency Action for Liberal Democracy (SEALDs), successfully brought academic professionals and traditional organizations to participate in protesting the 2015 security bills. Succeeding the legacies of counter-culture performers in the 1980s and 1990s, SEALDs conducted demonstrations in public areas. This association also led an election campaign in opposition to the government party, the Liberal Democratic Party (LDP), in the 2016 House of Councillors election. On the radical conservative side, Nippon Kaigi and its affiliated groups have deepened their relationship with the LDP. Nippon Kaigi has spread its network through local assemblies and Shinto shrines. Shrines are not solely religious sites, but also open cultural spaces for many Japanese people to make wishes at the beginning of a new year, have summer festivals, and gather with local community members.

This new, bottom-up civic activism has mobilized a wide range of participants, but the dispersed nature of communication means those participants often participate with heterogeneous ideologies and ideas. The definition and use of the term "constitutionalism" expresses this duality, as well as modern constitutional discussion in Japanese civic activism. For both pro- and anti-constitutional revision activists, "constitutionalism" is an undeniable assumption, but their interpretations of the term itself differ significantly. The range of meaning imparted to the idea of constitutionalism by civic activists illustrates the pluralistic character of Japanese democracy.

Social media also played a significant role in the evolution of Japanese activism in the 2010s, as it did in the Arab Spring movement of 2010 and the Umbrella Revolution in Hong Kong in 2014. Digital activism has the potential not only to involve many people, but also to make the middle ground hard to discern, resulting in a polarized online discourse space. Internet Communication Technology (ICT) is deeply and intricately connected to commercial markets and power. Even civic activism that originally started as spontaneous dissent could be subsumed and exploited via ICT's commercial nature and usage of astroturfing by large entities.

COUNTER-ACTIVISM: FROM UNIVERSITIES AND UNION HALLS TO PARKS AND STREETS

Throughout the anti-security bills movement, one of the most influential practitioners of new civic activism was SEALDs. They weren't "well-organized," didn't have official membership like traditional civil society organizations, and, in fact, didn't even have a consistent ideology. However, SEALDs was composed of a generation of activists who grew up with digital technology all around them. They organized and mobilized via social media and demonstrated in public. Their flexibility and ease-of-access created a solidarity between new and older styles of civic activism. Student protests drew in university professors in addition to politicians, celebrities, and various civil society groups, such as labor unions and women's groups, encouraging public intellectuals to come back to the civic activism scene.

From its inception, SEALDs took an approach of focusing on a single issue (disapproval of the security bills), expecting to dissolve after the issue was resolved. SEALDs' predecessor group, SASPL (Students Against Secret Protection Law), was founded in December 2013 to protest the bill for the Act on the Protection of Specially Designated Secrets accepted in the Diet (SASPL 2014).[3] SASPL dissolved on December 10, 2014, the day the law went into effect. SEALDs launched in May 2015, opposing the government-supported security bills that would allow Japan to exercise its collective right of self-defense. They dissolved in August 2016 after conducting a campaign to support the opposition parties in the 2016 House of Councillors election; the security bills were accepted in the Diet in September 2015.

SEALDs succeeded legacies from past groups such as Beheiren (Citizen's League for Peace in Vietnam), an anti–Vietnam War group which was active from 1965 to 1974. Founders of both SEALDs and Beheiren were drawn to a form of direct democracy practiced in ancient Athens (Takahashi and SEALDs 2015, 127–139). Beheiren did not have a clear membership system, and it focused on a single issue: protesting the Vietnam War. Rejecting top-down supervision from political parties, like the communist/socialist parties of the time, Beheiren was associated with Ordinary People's Voices (Koe Naki Koe no Kai), a politically independent citizen's group (Sugawara 2008). However, peace-activist and writer Makoto Oda and well-known scholars like Shunsuke Tsurumi played significant roles in guiding the movement. Along with other scholars, they had participated in the Anpo protest in 1960.

1980s and 1990s counter-culture influenced SEALDs' style of organizing festivals. The economies of the '80s and '90s produced commercial mass culture under a competitive, laissez-faire economy pushed by the Nakasone administration (1982–1987) and the Hashimoto administration (1996–1998). Not everyone enjoyed economic growth in Japan during these neoliberal reforms. Skeptics created counter-culture, publicly questioning inequalities in domestic and global contexts at group events. Socialist parties, labor unions, and academic intellectuals lost the influence in civic activism that they had held in the 1960s. Young unemployed people, non-full-time workers and minimum-wage foreign workers suffered grievances under Japanese capitalism but didn't belong to traditional civil society organizations such as unions. "Progressive Intellectuals" continued applying modern scientific approaches associated with socialism, including traditional Marxism, and became "tame" and "harmless" at depoliticized universities, even becoming the "establishment" in academia (Mōri 2009, 124–126). This mirrored the collapse of the Soviet socialist bloc as the Cold War ended. The presence of top-down "enlightenment" from intellectuals became much less influential in the 1990s, resulting in less counter-cultural energy coming from universities.

During the 1990s, both counter-cultural performers and political protesters held events in public streets and parks, such as Yoyogi Park. In Yoyogi Park, organizers assembled protests for people to show their discontentment, and performers set up stages to play music and hold block parties (Mōri 2009, 143–148). By playing hip-hop music, SEALDs inherited the DIY musical performance style from the counter-culture movement of the '80s and '90s. SEALDs's student protesters designed handmade T-shirts, made rhyming "call and response" interactions between leaders and participants, and made speeches with their own words, without relying on theoretical arguments from intellectuals. One of the most pervasive SEALDs "call and response" interactions was "Minshushugi-tte nanda? (What is democracy?)" and "Koreda! (This is democracy!)," meaning that the demonstration itself expressed democracy. Their demonstrations attracted and involved people who just happened to be present, in public, as impromptu counter-culture music parties did in the 1990s.

SEALDs's style of activism spread throughout Japan. Inspired by SEALDs, many different groups were founded. However, the groups were formally separate from SEALDs, sometimes holding very different or original ideas. Applying SEALDs's style, other local groups were spontaneously launched by college students, such as SEALDs KANSAI, SEALDs TOHOKU, SEALDs RYUKYU, and SEALDs TOKAI. The impact went beyond college students, and encouraged mothers, high-schoolers, and others as well; groups such as Mothers against Wars, TSOWL (for teenagers), MIDDLEs (people in their 40s–60s), and OLDs (people over 65) were founded. MIDDLEs and OLDs assembled on a street in Sugamo in Tokyo which is known as a mecca for older people. Though SEALDs didn't have official leaders to supervise and organize its expanded movement, its model was influential, including with otherwise traditional activist groups.

Aiming to coordinate all opposition parties to vote against the Abe administration in the July 2016 election of the House of Councillors, Shimin Rengō (Civil Alliance for Peace and Constitutionalism) was founded in December 2015. Four opposition parties, including the Democratic Party (DP), Japanese Communist Party (JCP), and Social Democratic Party of Japan (SDPJ), coordinated to support one candidate in each district to give the best chance of winning seats from the governmental parties. SEALDs supported Shimin Rengō along with other antiwar/anti-constitutional-revision citizens' groups, including the Association of Scholars Opposed to the Security-Related Laws. In the election, the pro-constitutional-revision parties gained a two-thirds majority, which is required to submit a constitutional proposal in the Diet.[4] However, it was significant that college students and academic intellectuals worked together again in civic activism; their estranged relationship was healed in public and on the internet, and they worked as equals.

RADICAL CONSERVATIVE MOVEMENT: FROM UNIVERSITIES TO LOCAL SHRINES

The most influential faction and engine of the "radical conservative" movement that led the push for constitutional revision was Nippon Kaigi. Nippon Kaigi, founded in 1997, contains elements of new civic activism; it lacks a comprehensive ideology and clearly centralized leadership. Comprised of various ideological factions and affiliated organizations, Nippon Kaigi has multiple internal ideological and leadership lines, which has led some to describe Nippon Kaigi's aims as enigmatic. Both before and after Nippon Kaigi's creation, organizers of the group worked with like-minded organizations to focus on various conservative issues. For example, Nippon Kaigi currently works with the Society to Answer the War Dead (Eirei ni Kotaeru Kai, founded in 1976) to demand that cabinet members pay tribute at Yasukuni Shrine. In the 1960s, the future founders of the two groups tried and failed to reinstate public funding for Yasukuni Shrine. Nippon Kaigi's secretary-general, Yūzō Kabashima, is also the chair of the Japan Youth Council (Nihon Seinen Kyōgikai), an alumni group of conservative student activists that pushed for passage of the Era Name Law (*Gengō hō*) in 1979. The first chair of the Society to Answer the War Dead, Kazuto Ishida, also played an important role in passing the Era Name Law. Nippon Kaigi has worked with the Society to Celebrate the Founding of Japan (Nippon no Kenkoku o Iwau Kai, created in the mid-1980s) to demand that the government resume sponsoring events to celebrate National Foundation Day (*Kenkoku Kinen no Hi*). Other issues on which radical conservatives around Nippon Kaigi collaborated with other groups include: textbook reform (working with the Society to Create New Textbooks, Atarashii Kyōkasho o Tsukuru Kai, founded in 1996); revision of the Fundamental Law on Education (*Kyōiku kihon hō*) (working with the Society Demanding a New Fundamental Law on Education, Atarashii Kyōiku Kihonhō o Motomeru Kai, founded in 2000); lobbying for a holiday to commemorate the Meiji era (working with the Society for the Creation of a Meiji Era Holiday, Meiji no Hi Suishin Kyōgikai, founded in 2011); and lobbying for constitutional revision (working with the Society for the Creation of a Constitution for Beautiful Japan, Utsukushii Nippon no Kenpō o Tsukuru Kokumin no Kai, founded in 2014).

Nippon Kaigi has roots in two main ideologies: "Minzoku-ha" (ethno-movement) and "Minshu Shakaitō" (Democratic Socialist Party/DSP, a right-wing socialist party). The phrase "Minzoku-ha" was coined in the late 1950s to remove the image of "uyoku (the right/far-right)" from its movement; "uyoku" reminded people of ultranationalist activism associated with violent Yakuza gangs (Fujiu 2017, 10, 43). Nagasaki University students Yūzō Kabashima (future secretary-general of Nippon Kaigi) and Andō Iwao (a future leader in the religious group Seichō no Ie) successfully took over leadership of the student association of Nagasaki University from left-leaning student groups such as Zen Nihon Gakusei Jichikai Sōrengō (Zengakuren).[5] The "anti-Zengakuren" group grew into a nation-wide organization with an alumni group by 1970. Both Kabashima and Andō were adherents of a then-rising religion, Seichō no Ie. Founded in 1930, the religious group and its approach of combining existing religions, such as Shintō, Buddhism, Christianity, Islam and Judaism, with philosophy and sciences like psychology steadily became more popular throughout the twentieth century.

Forming a united front with right-leaning socialists from the Democratic Socialist Party labor group, the "anti-Zengakuren" movement had a more general ambition, "abolition of the Yalta/Potsdam (YP) System," during the 1970s.[6] They called for the revision of the constitution, arguing that Japan's national status as determined in Yalta and Potsdam had been determined by the U.S. and other winners of World War II, rather than Japan itself. They questioned why Japan should defer to these other nations so extensively, relying exclusively on the U.S. for security. Opposing communism and favoring rearmament, the DSP allied with conservative groups (predecessors of the future LDP) in the Diet from the late 1940s to the mid-1950s. One of the DSP's founders and leaders, Suehiro Nishio, aimed to realize socialism through bottom-up civic activism without the supervision of elites (Nishio 1951); a DSP icon, Tadae Takubo, became Nippon Kaigi's chairperson in 2015. Mobilizing intellectuals, politicians and religious dignitaries, the first big milestone in the goal of "abolition of Yalta/Potsdam System," the passage of the Era Name Law (1979), was achieved. Those in favor of this legislation accumulated resolutions for it in local assemblies in 46 prefectures, culminating in its approval in the Diet in 1979.[7] Based on this achievement, Nihon o Mamoru Kokumin Kaigi was launched in 1981. Merging with a conservative religious group, they founded Nippon Kaigi in 1997.

Although Nippon Kaigi has a membership system, its leadership is not vertically structured, and it is not clear who represents the group. However, it is more clear which other groups work with Nippon Kaigi. For example, Jinja Honchō, the biggest association of Shintō shrines, co-organizes events with Nippon Kaigi. Various religious groups associated with Shintō, Buddhism and different new religions work with Nippon Kaigi as well (Hardacre 2017). United against a mutual enemy of "progressives" rather than by a coherent ideology, they continued expanding. Some Nippon Kaigi members identify themselves as "patriots" and abhor being called "nationalists" or "conservatives" (Fujiu 2017, 120). Nippon Kaigi has local branches in Japan and Brazil. Female members founded a women's group, and lawmakers compose an multi-party parliamentary group in the Diet and local assemblies. But these groups are not hierarchically organized. Many LDP lawmakers belong to the Nippon Kaigi's parliamentary group, but some criticize parts of its platform. Seiko Noda and other female members have criticized Nippon Kaigi for its patriarchal ideas.[8] Current chairperson Tadae Takubo disagreed with reports saying he's controlling Nippon Kaigi—according to him, he only allows

Nippon Kaigi to use his name.[9] Yoshiko Sakurai, a well-known journalist and co-director of a pro-constitutional revision group, Utsukushii Nippon no Kenpo o Tsukuru Kokumin no Kai, which Nippon Kaigi links to on its official website, denied a connection with Nippon Kaigi in her speech at the Foreign Correspondents' Club of Japan in 2018.[10] Also, in 2019, Nippon Kaigi officially stated that some of their frequent collaborators, including Sakurai, don't represent Nippon Kaigi, after the collaborators were interviewed regarding the comfort women issue.[11]

As with SEALDs, Nippon Kaigi shows elements of new civic activism: a loose, decentralized network and a focus on a single, critical issue. They also have centers in the public sphere, where pedestrians can encounter Nippon Kaigi's activism. Since the 2000s, local shrines have become the bases of Nippon Kaigi's civic activism to the open public, for example, by collecting signatures for a petition calling for constitutional revision.[12] Local Nation-Protecting Shrines (*Gokoku Jinja*), shrines dedicated to the war dead, organize events to mourn national heroes and clean the shrines. Associated with regional Nippon Kaigi branches, local shrines also provide programs of seminars about modern history, encouraging local and national patriotism. Nippon Kaigi's rise has come about through radical conservative grassroots activism, buoyed by local shrines and religious affiliations.

POLITICAL DEBATE IN MASS CULTURE

In the 1970s, the detente of the Cold War widened the platform of political discussion, making space for conservative opinion leaders with academic backgrounds, such as Tsuneari Fukuda, Jun Etō, and Kanji Nishio. *Shokun!*, a conservative opinion magazine, was first published by major publisher Bungei Shunjū in 1969. Several conservative magazines followed, such as *Seiron* (1973) and *Voice* (1977). According to his autobiography, Shinzō Abe started reading conservative opinion magazines in the 1970s, when he was a college student at Seikei University. He says these magazines were "stimulative" and "fresh" for him because they provided different perspectives from the then-mainstream, progressive intellectuals (Abe 2006, 24–25). Broadly, conservative opinion leaders claimed that the constitution was imposed on Japan by the U.S. and criticized the way that schools were teaching Japanese modern history, excessively emphasizing prewar Japan as an "absolute evil" and a fascist invader of Asia.

In 1995, well-known manga artist Yoshinori Kobayashi restarted his political cartoon series called *Gōmanism Sengen* (Haughtiness or Insolence Manifesto) in the news magazine *SAPIO*.[13] This new material became very popular. He regularly appeared in a debate show, *Asa Made Nama Terebi!* (All-Night TV, or *Asanama* for short), as a "conservative" panelist. Kobayashi highlighted the idealism that Japan had in World War II, aiming to liberate Asian countries from Western imperialism, and questioned the truth of the Nanjing Massacre and stories of comfort women. In 2007, 31-year-old part-time worker and blogger Tomohiro Akagi published an essay entitled "I want to slap Masao Maruyama" (*Maruyama Masao o Hippatakitai*) in the journal *Ronza*. Akagi expressed his frustration as a member of the "lost generation," children of Japan's baby-boom generation. Members of this large, competitive generation were subjected to fiercely competitive school entrance examinations and job markets. During the 2000s, the Koizumi government's neoliberal reforms produced many young non-full-time employees, such as part-time employees and temporary workers. Akagi wrote that aggressive, nationalistic messages on the internet soothed the hurt self-esteem of these non-full-time workers. According to Akagi, they hope that a war (as a metaphor) could come and destroy the status quo and those with vested interests in exploiting their generation (Akagi 2007). The essay title referred to an episode in the life of an elite young scholar at Tokyo Imperial University during World War II, Masao Maruyama, who was sent to the front lines of the war and was slapped by a higher-ranking, less-educated soldier. Maruyama went on to become a leading political science intellectual of postwar Japan. Using nationalistic rhetoric, Kobayashi and Akagi challenged progressive intellectuals and gained popularity via a mass media landscape that was broadly open to political debates in the 1990s and 2000s.

"CONSTITUTIONALISM"

In constitutional discussion in the 2010s, "constitutionalism" became a contested political term. Fundamentally, "constitutionalism" is the idea that the government should be legally limited in its power.[14] "Modern constitutionalism" is defined as governance based on constitutions composed of the principles of "protection of human rights" and "separation of power" (Komamura 2014, chap. 1). In September 2015, at Yoyogi Park, Chizuko Ueno, a feminist sociologist and pioneer of women's studies, gave a speech at an anti–security bills demonstration. In the speech, she stated that the "fight" against the security bills unleashed "constitutionalism" from the world of academia to the public (Ueno 2016). Throughout the postwar period, except for highly technical discussion in the field of constitutional study, the term "constitutionalism" had rarely been used. The constitutional debate was ideologically polarized by disputes about rearmament, derived from Japan's "war renunciation" determined in Article 9, as well as capitalist/socialist economic disputes (Higuchi 2005, 223–224). Civic activism in the 2010s finally started establishing a theoretical discourse incorporating the fundamental concept of "constitutionalism."

Students in SEALDs had reinforced their activism with fundamental concepts such as "democracy" and "constitutionalism" since they founded their predecessor group, SASPL.[15] The question that they faced was how to legitimize their demonstration in a democratic context. For example, two of the main founders, Aki Okuda and Yoshimasa Ushida, both criticized the Abe administration for going against "democracy," based on their interest in the direct democracy practiced in ancient Greece. But they had different ideas about the meaning of "constitutionalism" (Takahashi and SEALDs 2015, Part II). While Okuda emphasized the tension between "constitutionalism" and "democracy," Ushida recognized the interdependency between the two concepts. Okuda pointed out the elitism of "constitutionalism." Mentioning the concept of "general will" coined by Jean-Jacques Rousseau, Okuda expressed his interest in involving as many people as possible in discourse and letting them spontaneously make decisions that could be widely acceptable. For him, it is important for people to be able to say "no" to directions that have been decided by a majority. In contrast, Ushida regards "constitutionalism" as a fundamental and absolute assumption of "democracy," determining the principal rules and values of society, including moral norms.

In 2017, momentum against the Abe administration triggered by the anti–security bills movement in 2016 led to the creation of a new political party named after "constitutionalism," the Constitutional Democratic Party of Japan (CDP). CDP leader Yukio Edano identifies himself with "liberal conservatism"; as a liberal, he is opposed to paternalism, but as a conservative, he rejects radicalism and socialism and instead looks for gradual social improvement.[16] In 2018, CDP lawmaker Shiori Yamao proposed "constitutionalistic constitutional revision" (*rikkenteki kaiken*), constitutional revision in a "liberal" direction (Yamao 2018). Yamao suggests amending Article 24 to legalize same-sex marriage and Article 9 to limit the usage of the SDF (Self-Defense Forces) to the sphere of "exclusively defense-oriented policy" (*senshu bōei*), reducing Japan's collective defense right. The CDP officially stood for an even ratio of men and women in the Diet in addition to legalization of same-sex marriage ahead of the House of Councillors election in 2019, broadening the meaning of "constitutionalism" into the liberal domain.

Throughout the protest against the security bills in 2015, "constitutionalism" became a rallying cry for those who opposed constitutional revision under the Abe administration. The term was used by those who criticized the government for ignoring the universal values that they believed the postwar constitution determined: popular sovereignty, basic human rights, and pacifism. Yasuo Hasebe, a constitutional scholar who played a central role in anti–security bill activism in 2015, described two concepts pertaining to "constitutionalism." First, "constitutionalism" as a minimum definition is the idea that government can be limited in its power. Second, what he termed "positive constitutionalism" is the principle that people's private lives and thoughts shouldn't be interfered with by the government and that the constitution can determine norms to manage general welfare. Accordingly, the government shouldn't change the constitution and potentially undermine general welfare.[17] He criticizes the LDP's 2012 constitutional draft for giving the government too much power over people's private lives, including family affairs. In contrast, the LDP claimed that it aimed to restore traditional families and communities which had been damaged by modern, postwar individualism.[18]

The Abe administration has expressed different views on its vision for the constitution. In a Diet session on February 3rd, 2014, Prime Minister Abe indicated that the constitution is supposed to describe an ideal future of Japan, rather than limiting its purview to governmental power today. Abe argued that limitations on government power had become less necessary in the modern period, as political power had shifted away from monarchs and to the people, and political systems changed from monarchies to democracies.[19] This remark roused criticism against Abe for ignoring the idea that "constitutionalism" had become even more important, to limit government power. Such limits under democracy aim to prevent dictators with unchecked political power, like former absolute monarchs, from being created.[20]

In the Nippon Kaigi circle of influence, discourse is similar to the "overcoming-modernity" movement of the 1940s that challenged Western modernity. However, they recognize that constitutional proposals won't be accepted in contemporary Japan if they deny the universal values which Japanese people have enjoyed since the end of World War II. They intend to revive "traditional values," which they believe were destroyed by the Occupation imposition of a postwar constitution written by foreigners. In 2016, Nippon Kaigi published a constitutional proposal, finalizing a first edition originally released in 1993. In the proposal, Nippon Kaigi describes "constitutionalism" as "politics based on people's will, derived from the Meiji period."[21] In May 2016, Nippon Kaigi spokesman Osamu Nishi, a professor at Komazawa University, described the "constitutionalism" referred to by the anti-Abe administration movement as "populist constitutionalism" that regards the government as hostile.[22] Nishi said that the exercising of the right of collective self-defense contributes to securing Japan and its people, which should be a core tenet of "constitutionalism."

In November 2016, the members of the Commission on the Constitution of the House of Representatives discussed the definition of "constitutionalism."[23] While opposition parties criticized the LDP's 2012 constitutional draft and reinterpretation of Article 9 in 2015, the LDP claimed that the constitution's purpose is not simply to limit governmental power and criticize the opposition parties for halting constitutional discussion with impractical arguments.[24] LDP members repeatedly emphasized that the LDP doesn't intend to undermine universal values, such as popular sovereignty, basic human rights, and pacifism. One of the LDP commission members, Kenji Yamada, argued that it would be "constitutional" to amend Article 9 to codify the status of the SDF, which, according to him, is accepted by 98 percent of the Japanese people. This discussion revealed how difficult it is to make a common definition of "constitutionalism" in political space, and how commonly the term has been co-opted for partisan politics.

INTERNET COMMUNICATION TECHNOLOGY (ICT) AS NEW PUBLIC OPEN SPACE

New civic activism exhibits traits of being decentralized and leaderless, and the rise of social media has exacerbated this trend. It has become cheaper and easier to access the internet over the last 20 years; approximately 80% of Japanese households had a smartphone according to one 2018 study.[25] YouTube released a Japanese language system in 2007. Twitter and Facebook became available in Japanese in 2008 and were widespread in Japan by 2009. Connecting people beyond physical space, ICT successfully involves a wide range of people, including "slacktivists," who can participate in civic activism by simply "liking" content on Facebook, Twitter, and YouTube. At present, the internet is a vast, open space for citizens.

SEALDs used ICT effectively. SEALDs used LINE, a free communication and social media app, to organize their events and group (Takahashi and SEALDs 2015, chap. 1). The app suited their loose networking style; they were able to communicate with anyone who was interested in their demonstrations. Throughout the group's decision-making process, it was not clear who was responsible for which ideas. Their demonstration planning started with a user's message saying, "There seems to be a protest," worded to avoid culpability. After various users roughly approved a plan in their LINE group conversation, the group released information and slogans for a demonstration. One of SEALDs's most famous slogans, "*Hontō ni tomeru*" (We will definitely stop it), was created on LINE in this way. SEALDs's slogans spread quickly on Twitter with hashtags as well. Accounts associated with anti–Abe administration groups used hashtags concerning other liberal issues as well: "#Abe seiji o yurusanai (we don't accept Abe politics)," "#Sensō hōan hantai (against war bills)," "#Datsu genpatsu (oppose nuclear power plants)," and "#Okinawa (Okinawa bases)."

In contrast to the younger demographics constituting SEALDs, many founders of the main conservative groups in Japan are from older generations. But conservatives also recognize the importance of social media in today's civic activism. Though Nippon Kaigi officially announced that the group did not have a Facebook or Twitter account in August 2018, it does have an official YouTube channel, which has 8,000 subscribers as of February 2021. Also, a radical conservative television channel and video-sharing website, Japanese Culture Channel Sakura, joined YouTube in 2008. This channel names Nippon Kaigi spokespeople as supporters, including Yūzō Kabashima and Tadae Takubo, and has approximately 521,000 subscribers as of February 2021. On Twitter, radical conservative users created hashtags like "#Kenpō kaisei (constitutional revision)," "#Anpō hōsei (security bills)," "#Rachi higaisha zen'in dakkan (recapture of abduction victims from North Korea)," "#Kinkyū jitai jōkō (emergency clause)" and "#Saigai (disaster)." Highlighting threats against the Japanese people, they support the LDP's 2012 constitutional draft. Proponents on both sides of the constitutional revision debate used "#Rikken shugi (constitutionalism)" in different contexts.

While ICT allowed a broad group of people to get involved in digital activism, it has polarized and ideologized civic space. Given the brevity of social media, complex issues are boiled down into simple topics of debate. Although the results of public opinion polls have shown that the majority of Japanese people are moderate and have practical opinions regarding specific constitutional issues, this middle ground isn't easily visible when the discourse simply focuses on whether to revise the constitution or not (Sakaiya 2017). For example, Japanese liberal internationalism that seeks to contribute to human security via United Nations' peace keeping operations has sometimes been conflated with traditional conservative nationalism, reminding some that the Empire of Japan pursued regional hegemony via military action (Soeya 2015). Social media doesn't accurately reflect real voices of voters, and some users raise the influence of their voice by using multiple accounts (Yamaguchi 2018). Search engines and recommendation systems reinforce users' worldviews by automatically suggesting to them sources with similar worldviews based on their search and post history, creating a "filter bubble" (Pariser 2011). Generally, language on social media tends to be radical and extreme to gain "views." The decline of existing media and the rise of social media make it easier for misinformation to spread. Digital technology emerged as a battlefield potentially undermining national security, as international hackers can create fake accounts purporting to represent local news organizations on social media in other countries, aiming to intervene in their domestic politics (Tufekci 2018). Paradoxically, this shows that the rapid diffusion of information on social media requires traditional media and the government to verify information and control digital platforms.

CONCLUSION

The conceptual debate over "constitutionalism" was a dominant topic in the 2016 election of the House of Councillors, though it had become less of a focus by the 2019 election of the same house. Though the pro-constitutional revision parties did not attain a two-thirds majority in the 2019 election, the previously dominant liberal intellectual approach to the constitution was challenged by a new group. Sometimes regarded as a "liberal-populist" party, a new political party, Reiwa Shinsengumi, arose in a "riot" of people who believed they have been marginalized by Japanese capitalism and democracy.[26] The party's charismatic leader, Tarō Yamamoto, strategically spread his vision and message in the streets and on the internet. Yamamoto argues that politics in the digital era should be constantly appealing to viewers, competing with the flood of compelling, interesting content on the internet.[27] As of February 2021, Yamamoto's YouTube channel had approximately 66,800 subscribers. He uses direct language to recognize the socially vulnerable without using the academic discourse relied upon by scholars and students. Reiwa Shinsengumi attracted people seeking social change; the liberal alliance led by Shimin Rengō and the CDPJ attempted to appeal to this group as well. Yamamoto uses a simple message to spotlight single individuals left behind, including people struggling with poverty or non-permanent employment, who used to devote themselves to radical conservatism. Reiwa Shinsengumi opposes the LDP's 2012 draft of the constitution, arguing that it ignores individuals and gives the government too much power.[28] In the 2019 election, Reiwa Shinsengumi supported a variety of social minority and activist candidates, whose focuses included issues such as sexuality, the environment, the U.S. bases in Okinawa, and those abducted by North Korea. They succeeded in sending two candidates with severe disabilities to the Diet, requiring the Diet building to adhere to the principle of universal design in a symbolic and visible change to the status quo.

The emergence of Reiwa Shinsengumi unveiled weak points of new forms of civic activism. Spontaneous, bottom-up civic activism had erupted in open, public spaces, such as public streets, local shrines, and the internet. New civic activism questioned the parliamentary system, but civic activism still needs to connect local sentiments to the Diet by mobilizing traditional organizations such as political parties and voting constituencies. While new civic activism involves a broad range of participants, it hasn't replaced traditional civil society organizations—rather, it has reinforced them. This leads new civic activism back to an innate dilemma: hierarchicalization and centralization of power undermining the original spontaneity and autonomy of the movement.

NOTES

1. For a comprehensive study of new civic activism, see Richard Youngs, *Civic Activism Unleashed: New Hope or False Dawn for Democracy?* (New York: Oxford University Press, 2019).

2. Yoshitaka Mōri delineates the development of counter-cultural movements from the 1980s to the 2000s in Japan in *Sutorīto no shisō: tenkanki toshite no 1990 nendai* (Tokyo: NHK Bukkusu, 2009).

3. See SASPL official website, "Our History," https://saspl1210.wixsite.com/students-against-spl/our-history, accessed August 30, 2019.

4. In the general election of the House of Representatives in 2017, the pro-constitutional revision parties kept their two-thirds majority.

5. On the "anti-Zengakuren" student movement started at Nagasaki University, see Akira Fujiu, *Dokyumento Nippon Kaigi* (Tokyo: Chikuma shobō, 2017) and Tamotsu Sugano, *Nippon Kaigi no kenkyū* (Tokyo: Fusōsha, 2016).

6. Akira Fujiu, "Nippon Kaigi to kyōtō suru rōdō sensen wa dō tsukurareta no ka: Ikiteita Minshatō hoshu undō o orugusuru," *Web Roza*, May 5, 2019, https://webronza.asahi.com/national/articles/2019042700002.html, accessed August 30, 2019.

7. Nippon Kaigi official website, "Kokumin undō no ayumi," http://www.nipponkaigi.org/activity/ayumi, accessed August 30, 2019.

8. AERA dot. "Kokkai giin 'joshikai' Nippon Kaigi wa danjo kyōdō sankaku ni hantai?" February 1, 2018, https://dot.asahi.com/wa/2018013000019.html, accessed August 30, 2019.

9. Tadae Takubo (via Nippon Kaigi official website), "Nippon Kaigi e no hihan hōdō o tadasu," March 15, 2017, https://www.nipponkaigi.org/opinion/archives/8392, accessed August 30, 2019.

10. Yoshiko Sakurai (via Foreign Correspondents' Club of Japan official website), "The Legal Fight over Reporting of Comfort Women," (video), November 16, 2018, http://www.fccj.or.jp/news-and-views/club-news-multimedia/1874-yoshiko-sakurai-the-legal-fight-over-reporting-of-comfort-women.html, accessed August 30, 2019.

11. Nippon Kaigi official website, "Dokyumentarī eiga 'Shusenjō' ni tsuite," April 19, 2019, http://www.nipponkaigi.org/opinion/archives/11659, accessed August 30, 2019. Nippon Kaigi published a statement on a documentary film dealing with the comfort women issue, *Shusenjo: The Main Battleground of Comfort Women Issue* (2019).

12. Tokyotō Jinjachō official website, "Kenpo kaisei o suishin suru sengen," October 14, 2015, http://www.tokyo-jinjacho.or.jp/kenpou/, accessed August 30, 2019.

13. James Shields, "Revisioning a Japanese Spiritual Recovery through Manga: Yasukuni and the Aesthetics and Ideology of Yoshinori Kobayashi's 'Gomanism,'" *The Asia-Pacific Journal: Japan Focus*, November 22, 2013, https://apjjf.org/2013/11/47/James-Shields/4031/article.html, accessed February 16, 2010.

14. From *Stanford Encyclopedia of Philosophy*, https://plato.stanford.edu/entries/constitutionalism/, accessed August 30, 2019.

15. SASPL official website, "12/09/10," December 9, 10, 2014, https://saspl1210.wixsite.com/students-against-spl/single-post/2015/02/10/120910, accessed August 30, 2019.

16. AERA dot. "Riberaru hoshu o jinin suru Edano Yukio ga akasu hontō no 'shiteki kenpo kaiken'an' to wa?" December 27, 2017, https://dot.asahi.com/wa/2017122600007.html?page=1, accessed August 30, 2019. For a conceptual study on "liberal conservatism," see Takeshi Nakajima, *"Riberaru hoshu" sengen* (Tokyo: Shinchōsha, 2015).

17. Demokura TV, "Yamaguchi, Jirō no muhon kaigi: episode #1," (video), February 21, 2016, https://dmcr.tv/mypage/dmcr_spc.php?prog=muhon (hhps://www.youtube.com/watch?v=9fe-QvPIY4k), accessed August 30, 2019.

18. Liberal Democratic Constitutional Reform Promotion Headquarters official website, "Kenpō kaisei-tte naani? April 2015, http://constitution.jimin.jp/document/pamphlet/, accessed August 30, 2019.

19. House of Representatives, Commission on the Budget, (video), February 3, 2014, http://www.shugiintv.go.jp/jp/index.php?ex=VL&deli_id=43434&media_type=, accessed August 30, 2019.

20. Video News, "Rikkenshugi o hitei suru shushō ga 'kenpō o kaishaku suru no wa watashi da,'" (video), February 15, 2014, https://www.videonews.com/commentary/20140215-02/, accessed August 30, 2019.

21. Nippon Kaigi official website, "Nippon Kaigi no 'shinkenpō no taikō' ni tsuite," November 11, 2016, https://www.nipponkaigi.org/opinion/archives/8502, accessed August 30, 2019.

22. Osamu Nishi (via Sankei News), "Yōkai ga Nihon o haikai shiteiru rikkenshugi to iu yōkaiga," May 2, 2016, https://www.sankei.com/smp/column/news/160502/clm1605020005-s1.html, accessed August 30, 2019.

23. Sankei News, "Shūin kenpo shinsakai rikkenshugi meguri 6 kaiha ga giron mo heikōsen," November 24, 2016, https://www.sankei.com/politics/news/161124/plt1611240017-n1.html, accessed August 30, 2019.

24. The attendees' remarks are available on the website of the Commission on the Constitution of the House of Representatives, http://www.shugiin.go.jp/internet/itdb_kenpou.nsf/html/kenpou/192-11-17.htm, accessed August 30, 2019.

25. Ministry of Internal Affairs and Communications. *Jōhō tsūshin hakusho*. 2019, http://www.soumu.go.jp/johotsusintokei/whitepaper/ja/r01/pdf/index.html, accessed August 30, 2019.

26. Ayumi Yasutomi official website, "Uchigawa kara mita Reiwa Shinsengumi," July 24, 2019, https://anmintei.net/a/688, accessed August 30, 2019.

27. Atsushi Manabe, "Reiwa Shinsengumi no sokojikara o popurizumu hihan dake de wa miyamaru 'shin no riyū,'" *Gendai Bijinesu*, July 28, 2019, https://gendai.ismedia.jp/articles/-/66127, Accessed August 30, 2019. The original Shinsengumi, literally, "newly selected group," was a special police force formed in 1863 to protect shogunal officials during a period of violence and assassinations surrounding the opening of the country to diplomatic relations with Western powers. Not restricted to the samurai class, members included farmers and others outside elite warrior groups. Members were strictly bound by a code of loyalty, vowing that every man would fight to the death if their leader were killed in battle. The Shinsengumi became a trope of popular culture productions, featuring dazzling swordplay and romanticized images of the warrior. *Reiwa* is the era name for the reign of Emperor Naruhito, beginning in 2019 and continuing to the present.

28. Reiwa Shinsengumi official website, *Kenpo-tte nani? Vol. 2*, November 2017, http://www.taro-yamamoto.jp/wp-content/uploads/2017/12/part2_1p_1212.pdf, accessed August 31, 2019.

REFERENCES

Abe, Shinzō. *Utsukushii kuni e*. Tokyo: Bungei shunjū, 2006.

Akagi, Tomohiro. "Maruyama Masao o hippatakitai: 31 sai furītā kibō wa sensō." *Ronza* 140 (2007): 53–59.

Fujiu, Akira. *Dokyumento Nippon Kaigi*. Tokyo: Chikuma shobō, 2017.

Fujiu, Akira. "Nippon Kaigi to kyōtō suru rōdō sensen wa dō tsukurarete kita ka." *Web Ronza*, nos. 1–5, May–June 2019.

Hardacre, Helen. "Political Realignment Among Japan's Religions." *Council on Foreign Relations,* May 15, 2017.

Higuchi, Yōichi. "Rikkenshugi no nihonteki tenkai." *Sengo minshushugi*, edited by Masanori Nakamura, Akira Amakawa, Kŏn-ch'a Yun and Takeshi Igarashi. Tokyo: Iwanami shoten, 2005.

Komamura, Keigo. *Presuteppu kenpō*. Tokyo: Kōbundō, 2014.

Mōri, Yoshitaka. *Sutorīto no shisō: tenkanki toshite no 1990 nendai*. Tokyo: NHK Bukkusu, 2009.

Nishio, Suehiro. *Taishū to tomo ni: watashi no hansei no kiroku*. Tokyo: Sekaisha, 1951.

Pariser, Eli. *The Filter Bubble: What the Internet Is Hiding from You*. New York: Penguin Press, 2011.

Sakaiya, Shirō. *Kenpō to yōron*. Tokyo: Chikuma shobō, 2017.

Soeya, Yoshihide. "The Evolution of Japan's Public Diplomacy: Haunted by Its Past History." *Understanding Public Diplomacy in East Asia: Middle Powers in a Troubled Region*, edited by Jan Melissen and Yul Sohn. New York: Palgrave Macmillan, 2015.

Sugawara, Kazuko. "'Koe naki koe no kai' no shisō to kōdō: sengo shimin undō no genten o saguru." *Niigata kokusai jōhō daigaku jōhō bunka gakubu kiyō* 11 (2008): 41–57.

Takahashi, Gen'ichirō and SEALDs. *Minshushugi-tte nanda?* Tokyo: Kawade Shobō shinsha, 2015.

Tufekci, Zeynep. "How Social Media Took Us from Tahrir Square to Donald Trump." *MIT Technology Review*, August 14, 2018.

Ueno, Chizuko. "Minshushugi wa imaya kokkai no soto ni arimasu." *Genpatsu o tomeru sensō o tomeru: watashitachi no kin'yō kōdō zenkoku no samazamana akushon Ajia no shimin undō hando bukku*, edited by Satoshi Kamata, Takashi Hirose, Masumi Kowata, Setsuko Kuroda, Tampoposha and Saikadō Soshi Zenkoku Nettowāku. Tokyo: Nashinokisha, 2016.

Yamaguchi, Shin'ichi. *Enjō to kuchikomi no keizaigaku*. Tokyo: Asahi shimbun shuppan, 2018.

Yamao, Shiori. *Rikkenteki kaiken: kenpo o riberaru ni kangaeru 7-tsu no tairon.* Tokyo: Chikuma shobō, 2018.

Youngs, Richard. *Civic Activism Unleashed: New Hope or False Dawn for Democracy?* New York: Oxford University Press, 2019.

Chapter Seven

Reviving Constitutional Democracy

Gender Parity and Women's Engagement with Politics

Mari Miura

Article 14 of the Constitution of Japan stipulates, "All of the people are equal under the law and there shall be no discrimination in political, economic or social relations because of race, creed, sex, social status or family origin," and Article 24 stipulates, "Laws shall be enacted from the standpoint of individual dignity and the essential equality of the sexes." Despite these provisions, the underrepresentation of women in politics has been an enduring problem in Japan. Regarding representative democracy, Article 43 states, "Both Houses shall consist of elected members, representative of all the people," and Article 44 more specifically states, "The qualifications of members of both Houses and their electors shall be fixed by law. However, there shall be no discrimination because of race, creed, sex, social status, family origin, education, property or income." These constitutional rights are, nevertheless, not fully realized yet—women constitute only 10.1 percent of the Lower House and 22.9 percent of the Upper House as of September 2019.

To achieve gender-balanced representation, gender quotas are often introduced around the world, which contributes to an increase in the number of women legislators. The Japanese women's movement had long called for the introduction of quotas, which eventually led to the passage of the Gender Parity Law in 2018.[1] It aims to contribute to the development of parity democracy, but it does not obligate the political parties to implement quotas. An obstacle to introducing binding legal quotas in Japan is related to the constitutionality of quotas. The lack of a clear argument for the constitutionality of quotas among constitutional scholars precluded the introduction of legal quotas. Why was the Gender Parity Law then enacted? Is there any possibility for Japan to enforce compulsory quotas in the future? How effective can the Gender Parity Law be without teeth? Finally, how do women engage with the legislative process of the Gender Parity Law, and how do they use it?

This chapter explores the civic activism that aimed to revive constitutional democracy from the angle of women's representation. More precisely, I argue that important changes occurred in four dimensions—the women's movement, political elites, normative discourse, and transnational feminism, which explains the successful adoption of the Gender Parity Law. This chapter first presents the status of women in politics and political situations under which quotas were *not* introduced in Japan. The second section then discusses the content of the Gender Parity Law and constitutional discussions surrounding quotas. The third section examines the legislative process of the Gender Parity Law, exploring women's engagement with politics. Finally, the fourth section discusses the impact of the Gender Parity Law on the consolidated local elections in April 2019 and the Upper House election in July 2019.

CALLING FOR QUOTAS

The persistent underrepresentation of women and the lack of political will to remedy this situation characterize the status of Japanese women in politics. According to the Inter-Parliamentary Union (IPU), Japan's international ranking in Women in National Parliaments is 164 among 193 countries as of September 2019.[2] Women constitute merely 10.1 percent of the total seats in the Lower House and 22.9 percent in the Upper House. The world average in this regard is 24.6 percent and 24.3 percent, respectively.

The literature on women and politics has pointed out that the "selectors" of candidates within political parties bear the primary responsibility for fielding fewer women candidates.[3] Selectors are predominantly men, and they usually recruit candidates from their homosocial networks. Not only are women excluded from such male-dominant political circles, but they also often lack resources to run for office, such as money, time, family support, and connections, making them appear less electable in the eyes of the selectors. Traditional gender socialization also suppresses women's ambition for politics, leading to a constant undersupply of female aspirants.[4] In other words, women are less likely to possess the appropriate "qualification" for office, which in turn prevents them from running. Gender norms shape such formal and informal selection criteria, thereby constituting institutional discrimination against women (Lovenduski 2005, Kenny 2013).

While these structural factors explain the overrepresentation of men across the world, including in Japan, the extremely low number of female Members of Parliament (MPs) in Japan can be accounted for by the lack of partisan competition and the electoral system. Power alternation provides a chance for newcomers, including women, to enter politics. The quasi-permanent dominance of the Liberal Democratic Party (LDP) simply limits the opening of such windows of opportunity. Moreover, the LDP almost automatically endorses incumbents, which lowers the turnover among LDP candidates. Generally, due to their deeper commitment to gender equality and their strategic decision to mobilize women voters, the progressive parties field more women candidates than the conservative parties do. If a nonnegligible portion of women voters shifts from conservative to progressive parties, the conservative parties will eventually be compelled to recruit more women to retrieve the lost votes. This dynamism is often called "contagion theory" (Matland and Studlar 1996). Thus, the partisan competition between the parties is contributing toward increasing women's representation. However, such conditions did not exist in Japan except for a brief period after 1989 when the Japan Socialist Party (JSP) won the Upper House election owing to the leadership of Takako Doi and the election of women candidates called "Madonnas," whom she recruited outside of the labor unions. The JSP's victory put pressure on the LDP, leading to the election and appointment of more women. However, the decline of the JSP in the 1990s precluded this contagious effect from taking root.

In 2009, women's share in the Lower House reached a record high of 11.3 percent because the Democratic Party of Japan (DPJ), with 13.9 percent of women candidates, won the election. However, the DPJ government did not last long enough to yield further support from the Left. In 2012, the LDP, with 8.0 percent female candidates, returned to power, and women's share in elected offices dropped to 7.9 percent. The three successive victories of the LDP in the Lower House elections in 2012, 2014, and 2017 halted the momentum of women's political participation.

While the lack of political competition explains the overall under-representation of women, the gap between the Lower House and the Upper House in this regard should be attributed to the difference in the electoral systems followed by the two houses. It is well known among political scientists that the larger the district magnitude is, the more conducive is it for women's representation (Norris 2004; Krook 2018). In other words, the first-past-the-post system, or single-member districts, are not women-friendly because selectors must find the single most electable candidate in each district, and not many women possess the required attributes. Political parties might pay attention to candidate diversity in the party lists of proportional representation (PR) systems, but in single-member districts, they end up fielding candidates with similar profiles, such as middle-aged healthy men with some political background, including members of local assemblies, bureaucrats, staffers of MPs, or members of political dynasties.

Japan's mixed-member majoritarian system used in the Lower House is weighted in favor of the first-past-the-post system due to the dual-listed candidacy system. In contrast, the Upper House combines a national open-list PR tier and a prefectural-level tier using the single non-transferable vote system (the district magnitude varies from one to six depending on the population). The heavier weight of the first-past-the-post system in the Lower House represents considerable obstacles for women.

THE NON-ADOPTION OF QUOTAS

Quotas are effective tools to break the perpetuation of male-dominant candidate recruitments. A total of 130 countries have already introduced quotas in national and/or local elections. The introduction of effective quotas can rectify cultural and institutional biases against women. Why does Japan not introduce quotas? Krook (2009a) categorized the scholarship on the adoption of gender quotas into four patterns: a strong women's movement, the calculations of the political elites, connections between quotas and reigning political norms, and international organizations and transnational networks. By referring to her categorization, Miura (2014a) argues that strong pressures or favorable conditions did not exist in all four dimensions in Japan. To understand why the Gender Parity Law was then adopted, it is meaningful to survey the reasons for the non-adoption of quotas.

First, the non-adoption of quotas is attributed to a weak women's movement in Japan (Gaunder 2015). Most of the women's organizations are single-issue oriented and small-scale. Some of them, such as the Alliance of Feminist Representatives (AFER) or Pekin JAC (Beijing Japan Accountability Caucus) in the 1990s, called for quotas, but their voices remained marginal. The birth of the Association to Promote Quotas (Association Q) in 2012 fundamentally changed the landscape of the women's movement. I will discuss the role of Association Q in the legislative process of the Gender Parity Law in more detail later.

Second, the strategic decision of elites was largely missing. Japanese political elites did not perceive strategic advantages in adopting quotas, partly because party competition has been weak, and partly because there was no serious opposition to the non-adoption of quotas.[5] As the women's movement remained marginal, political elites did not see the necessity even to engage in an empty gesture to show commitment to women's rights.

Third, international pressure and transnational information-sharing, conducive to stimulating national quota debates, did not have a strong impact on policymaking in Japan. The Japanese government does not fully embrace the recommendations issued by the Committee on the Elimination of All Forms of Discrimination Against Women or the United Nations Human Rights

Committee. Women's organizations developed transnational networks but lacked the leverage to turn international norms into domestic laws because they had difficulty finding allies within the ruling parties.

Lastly, the literature on quota adoption points out the connection between quota provisions and the reigning political norms. Miura (2014a) investigated the quota debates at the Diet in the 1990s and the 2000s and revealed that there were several competing arguments supporting the increase in women's representation. Some parliamentarians emphasized that women embrace different perspectives than men do, suggesting that the increase in female representatives would bring about a "qualitative change" in politics. However, many female parliamentarians mentioned the importance of meritocracy and rejected quotas out of fear that quotas might allow unqualified candidates to win. Overall, sustained debate on quotas did not materialize, given that most parliamentarians questioned the constitutionality of legally binding quotas.

These factors, taken together, explain the non-adoption of quotas in Japan. The passage of the Gender Parity Law appears even more puzzling because Japan's political and social environments are not conducive to the enactment of special measures to increase female representatives. The following sections will unravel the political process of the legislation of this law.

DRAFTING THE GENDER PARITY LAW

The Gender Parity Law was passed unanimously in the Diet in 2018.[6] It is significant that a law that addresses the problem of gender imbalance in politics was indeed enacted. What does the Gender Parity Law stipulate, and why was a binding quota not adopted?

The Gender Parity Law aims to secure opportunities for both men and women to take up public office and participate in decision-making, thereby contributing to the development of democracy in which men and women co-participate. It stipulates as a basic principle that political parties, while their freedom of political activities is secured, should aim at parity in the number of male and female candidates in national and local elections. In particular, it requires political parties to endeavor to take necessary measures, including setting a numerical target, to reflect the basic principles of the law. Taken together, the Gender Parity Law promotes a parity democracy in which equal participation of men and women in decision-making is considered as a basic democratic principle and encourages political parties to adopt quotas, although the actual wording of the law says "numerical targets." The all-partisan Parliamentarians' Group for Women's Political Participation and Empowerment formed in 2015 with the initiative of MP Masahiro

Nakagawa (DPJ), prepared the law. It took them three years to pass the law, but it achieved the maximum of what it could have, given that the LDP, which was not so enthusiastic about quotas, was in the majority in the Diet.

CONSTITUTIONAL DEBATES

The parliamentarians' group was indeed aiming originally at legislating a quota law. However, they gave up on this idea and prioritized the legislation of a principle law instead, because they received the advice from the Legislative Bureau of the House of Representatives that a quota law might be unconstitutional. The Legislative Bureau was concerned about the possibility that quotas would violate the freedom of association. Political parties have the freedom to recruit and nominate their candidates. Moreover, Article 14 of the Constitution of Japan stipulates that people should not be discriminated against based on sex. Legal quotas were considered to be infringing upon men's freedom to run for office, which was seen as discrimination against men. This view resonated with the mainstream opinions of constitutional law scholars. The Legislative Bureau did not find any publications of constitutional scholars that strongly supported the constitutionality of legal quotas. In the spring of 2015, the quota issue was not yet a hot topic and academic discussions as to the constitutionality of quotas were not forthcoming.

In Japan as well as other countries, quotas are usually considered to be discriminatory against men. France amended its constitution to introduce the Parity Law because the introduction of quotas was ruled unconstitutional in the late 1990s. The UK revised the Sex Discrimination (Election Candidates) Act of 2002 so that the use of all-women shortlists by the Labour Party would not infringe upon the law. If quotas are ruled unconstitutional, a constitutional amendment is then necessary to implement positive actions. However, such a progressive amendment is unthinkable in the Japanese political context. All the pro-amendment political forces are conservatives, and the progressive camp has been put in a defensive position.

Moreover, the timing of the discussion was not conducive for pushing forward a bill that might contain a hint of unconstitutionality. In April 2015, the parliamentary group created a working team to draft the bill, and I was appointed as an academic advisor to the working team. It held a weekly meeting until July 2015, which coincided with a rise in protests against the Security Laws proposed by the Abe government. In June 2015, a public hearing of the constitutional committee of the Lower House was conducted with three invited constitutional law scholars, during which Nakagawa, the president of the parliamentarians' group, asked them about the constitutionality of the

Security Laws. Much to the surprise of the LDP, all the testimony of the constitutional law scholars, including the one the LDP had invited, Professor Yasuo Hasebe, proclaimed the Security Laws unconstitutional. This became a turning point for civic activism against the Security Laws and the Abe administration. Since Nakagawa was the one who asked this critical question at the public hearing, there was no way for the parliamentarians' group to draft a bill that could be challenged as unconstitutional.

THE SAME NUMBER, GENDER BALANCE, OR PARITY IN NUMBER

Under the leadership of Nakagawa, the parliamentary group decided to draft a principle bill that would stipulate the basic principle as well as the amendment bill of the Public Offices Election Law to facilitate parties' voluntary implementation of quotas. I thought that if the legal quota was impossible, the principle of "gender parity" should be stipulated and, thus, made this proposal. Japanese government documents often used the term "women's quota," but I thought quotas should be introduced for both sexes. Setting a quota for men would undercut the argument that quotas are discriminatory against men. Moreover, the problem should be conceptualized as men's overrepresentation as much as women's underrepresentation. Lastly, the idea of parity democracy should underline the logic of increasing women's representation. Equal representation of men and women should be considered a basic democratic principle, implying that the parity in candidacy should be the norm. The working team of the parliamentary group welcomed the idea, probably because the idea of 50–50 was instinctively acceptable. However, the problem was how to translate the word "parity" into Japanese. I proposed the principle of gender proportionality (*seibetsu hirei*). I preferred to use the term "gender" (*seibetsu*) instead of "men and women" to not leave out sexual minorities. The term *seibetsu* usually means sex rather than gender, but there is no other equivalent term with Chinese characters in Japanese. Proportionality comes from the terminology used in Taiwan. Quotas are usually translated into "*wariate*" or "*waku*" in Japanese, but "proportionality" has more flexibility, allowing for 40–60 percent representation. The working team decided to use the term "the principle of gender proportionality" in the Public Offices Election Law. For the principle law, the Legislative Bureau drafted the actual wording and used "the same number" of men and women. Parity was then translated into exactly "the same number" (*dōsū*).

None of the parliamentary group imagined that such wording could later delay the legislation. The principle law seemed uncontroversial, and much discussion was dedicated to the actual design of quotas by amending the Public Offices Election Law. However, once the LDP began to examine the principle law within the party, conservatives found that the phrase "the same number" was too strong and instead proposed the term "balance" (*kinkō*). Gender balance in English sounds close to gender parity, but it is completely different in the context of Japanese labor law. The term "balanced treatment" (*kinkōtaigū*) differs from "equal treatment" (*kintōtaigū*) between regular and part-time workers, as it allows for "discrimination based on rational grounds." Therefore, when the LDP proposed the term "balance," many MPs of the opposition parties considered it to mean something much lesser than "the same number." Indeed, "balance" sounded as if 30 percent was enough. If it were a binding quota, opposition parties could have accepted the 30 percent level given that women comprised only 10 percent of the Lower House. However, as a principle law, they did not accept any such compromise.

There is another term in Japanese meaning equality, *byōdō.* The Constitution stipulates the *byōdō* of men and women and is the term that the women's movement always prefers to use. However, it has been difficult to use the term due to the LDP's resistance. When the Equal Employment Opportunity Law was enacted in 1985,[7] women's organizations had demanded that the term *byōdō* be included in the name of the law. However, the government used the term *kintō* instead, implying that *kintō* means something slightly less than *byōdō.* Practically, there is not much difference between *byōdō* and *kintō.* It is more of a symbolic difference. When the clash between "the same number" and "balance" did not go anywhere, Kōmeitō took the initiative to forge a consensus, thereby proposing the term *kintō.* Eventually, the opposition parties accepted this compromise. The parliamentarians' group re-phrased it as "equality in number" or "parity in number" (*kazu no kintō)* instead of just "equality," which strengthened the meaning of 50–50. In addition to the transformation from "the same number" to "equality in number," the ruling parties replaced the phrase that parties "are obligated to aim at" (*mezasa nakereba naranai*) with "should aim at" (*mezasu mono to suru*). It is again a symbolic amendment; however, the revision revealed the LDP's unwillingness to use any strong wording.

Interestingly, in the deliberative process of the Gender Parity Law at the Cabinet Committee of the Lower House, Ms. Kimie Hatano (Japan Communist Party) was allowed to make a statement before the vote; she stated that all the parties confirmed that the term "equality in number" is legally the same as the term "the same number." Her statement was officially recorded in the Diet minutes. The ruling parties won when it came to the actual *wording* of the law, whereas the opposition parties did not make a compromise on the actual *meaning* of its legal implications.

ENACTING THE GENDER PARITY LAW

What accounts for the enactment of the Gender Parity Law in light of the non-adoption of quotas discussed above? What factors have changed and allowed the adoption of the Gender Parity Law? I argue that important changes occurred in the four dimensions—women's movements, calculations of the political elites, normative discourse, and transnational feminism—which explains the successful adoption of the non-binding parity principle.

Reviving the Quota Movement

The revitalization of the quota movement was the key to the enactment of the law. Women's organizations had long demanded the adoption of quotas, but these organizations nonetheless remain a marginal voice. The formulation of the Third Basic Plan for Gender Equality in 2010 under the DPJ government triggered the revitalization of the quota movement. The Basic Plan is scheduled to be revised every five years, and the year 2010 was the time to formulate the third plan. The birth of the DPJ government in the previous year created a favorable environment in which the Third Basic Plan for Gender Equality could contain ambitious goals. Under the encouragement of Yoshito Sengoku, the then-Chief Cabinet Secretary, the Third Basic Plan for Gender Equality required political parties to examine the possibility of implementing quotas. Based on the Third Basic Plan, since its formulation, the Minister of Gender Equality has customarily visited each party every year to demand the consideration of introducing quotas. Nakagawa was the first Minister of Gender Equality who actually visited each party and later became the leader of the quota movement on the side of the political elites.

The appearance of quotas in the Third Basic Plan for Gender Equality birthed the Association to Promote Gender Quotas, which is simply called *Q no kai* (Association Q). Ryōko Akamatsu, the president of WIN WIN (Women in New World-International Network) visited Minister Nakagawa in 2011 to congratulate him on the government's initiative and then decided to create a national organization that would encompass all the related organizations. The Association Q was formed in 2012 with eight executive organizations and thirty member organizations. Executive organizations include WIN WIN, AFER (Alliance of Feminist Representatives), BPW (National Federation of Business and Professional Women's Clubs in Japan), and the Japanese Association of International Women's Rights. Association Q soon embraced over sixty member organizations.

Not only did quotas draw attention in the women's movement but they also did so in academia. Being inspired by the adoption of the quota law in Poland, I organized a symposium on quotas at Sophia University on International Women's Day (March 8) in 2011, inviting leading speakers on the issue such as Miyoko Tsujimura and Ki-young Shin from academia and Yōko Komiyama and Mizuho Fukushima from Nagatachō.[8] The symposium eventually led to the publication of the first academic book on gender quotas in Japanese, *Gender Quotas in Comparative Perspectives: Understanding the Increase in Women Representatives* (*Jenda Kuota: Sekai no Josei Giin wa Naze Fuetaka*), co-edited by Mikiko Etō and myself in 2014.

Association Q has held several meetings at the Diet members' building to invite and lobby interested parliamentarians. In 2014, during such a meeting, Nakagawa proposed to create a parliamentary group to introduce quotas, which was created in 2015 with Seiko Noda as the general secretary and Kuniko Kōda as the executive director.

Association Q is a federation of the existing women's organizations, run mostly by senior feminists who are close to Ryōko Akamatsu. Its tactics concentrate on lobbying. Core members frequently visit parliamentarians' offices and hand in their demand for passing the Gender Parity Law. They also regularly hold events at the Diet members' building, taking advantage of such occasions as International Women's Day (March 8), Women's Suffrage Day (April 10), and usually the beginning and end of each parliamentary session. Association Q easily mobilized approximately two hundred participants, which is a good size for pressuring the MPs. It also holds a symposium every year during the three-day summer forum on gender equality at NWEC (National Women's Education Center), the biggest annual event in Japan, attracting activists and administrators who work on gender equality policy, in the largest conference auditorium and with a huge audience.

The formation of Association Q gave visible form to the agency of women's organizations calling for quotas; thus, its formation was a decisive factor in the formation of the parliamentary group led by Nakagawa. Simultaneously, the high frequency of attracting media attention to the quota movement was also crucial to sustain the commitment of key actors of the parliamentary group. Public events hosted by Association Q were not enough to sustain media attention. Journalists also needed to learn about quotas: their mechanism, rationale, and international trends. Academia made a great contribution toward disseminating the knowledge needed in Japanese society and raising social awareness of the necessity to increase women's representation.

Between March 2014 and May 2019, I was involved in fourteen public events that discussed quotas, parity democracy, or women's underrepresentation, either as an organizer or as an invited speaker. The biggest one was the celebration of the 70th anniversary of women's suffrage in

Japan in 2016 at Sophia University, with about four hundred participants. The Institute of Gender Studies at Ochanomizu University, owing to the efforts of Ki-young Shin, has organized several international symposia. The Science Council of Japan also hosted a public event in 2016, inviting both scholars and MPs to discuss the necessity of enacting the Gender Parity Law. Simultaneously, I launched a social media campaign with young activists to disseminate the idea of parity democracy, called "Parité Campaign" in 2015, which also hosted several public events. Nakagawa or other members of the parliamentary group participated in many of these public events and exchanged opinions through which the MPs deepened their commitment to the legislation. Mainstream media reported most of the events, which allowed the enactment of the Gender Parity Law to remain on the public agenda.

Social movements usually need to employ both insider and outsider strategies to achieve legal changes successfully.[9] Insider strategy refers to lobbying policymakers that often occurs behind the scenes, whereas outsider strategy refers to rallies, petitions, and campaigns that entail mass mobilization and the visual presence of stakeholders. Association Q concentrated on insider strategy, as the core activists were savvy, senior women who have been active on gender equality issues for many decades with extensive networks within and outside of the locus of policymaking. It should also be noted that the participation of three retired MPs gave valuable leverage to Association Q as they knew exactly when and where to talk to effectively pressure the legislators. The fact that Ryōko Akamatsu, a former Minister of Education and a mother of the Equal Employment Opportunity Law, was a founder gave it a special status so that even high-profile politicians could not turn down its requests easily. Her charisma was another factor that kept the organization active all way through, from the beginning to the enactment, which took seven years.

Japan's quota movement did not rely on the typical repertoire of outsider strategy such as rallies and petitions but carried out advocacy through public events, including public speeches and marching before the Diet building (2017), and the social media campaigns discussed above to raise social awareness. A de facto coalition of activists, scholars, journalists, and MPs was formed and, in retrospect, I played the role of a coordinator or sometimes a director because I have positioned myself at the crossroads of different organizations, as a scholar of gender and politics, academic advisor to the parliamentary group, advisor to Association Q, and founder of the Parité Campaign. A small, well-connected circle of those who were concerned about women's underrepresentation mobilized all the resources they possessed to pressure political elites.

Political Elites' Strategic Decisions

The revitalization of the quota movement was a necessary condition for the adoption of the Gender Parity Law, but it was the strategic decisions of political elites that turned social pressure into actual legislation. Nakagawa's leadership and parliamentary tactics were crucial for the enactment. Several key actors also played important roles to forge a consensus.

The parliamentary group drafted the bill in summer 2015, after which an internal review within each party began. In February 2016, the DPJ, which was frustrated by the slow pace of discussions within the LDP, made an official decision that it would propose the principle law in the Diet session. This act signaled to the LDP that the DPJ might even propose it alone. Since Prime Minister Abe had advocated the empowerment of women, the LDP did not want to give the voters the impression that his intentions were not sincere. The DPJ's decision pushed the LDP to accelerate its internal review, but the LDP did not agree on the words "the same number." It then proposed the term "balance" (*kinkō*) but opposition parties rejected it, as discussed above.

In May–June 2016, the ruling parties and the opposition squared off against each other as the Upper House election was scheduled in July. They were incentivized not to make an easy compromise so that they could appeal to their supporting base. To take credit, the opposition parties proposed the original bill using the term "the same number" to the Diet even though the bill was prepared by the all-partisan parliamentary group. The ruling parties did not hide their fury, condemning the opposition's move and saying that they had proposed the bill as if it was their own. Since the election was approaching in a month, both sides blamed each other. It took a few months for everything to calm down. Kōmeitō proposed an amendment, changing the wording from "the same number" to "parity in number" (*kintō*). In the fall of 2016, Noriko Miyagawa and Seiko Noda worked hard to get the LDP's approval on this term. In December 2016, during the prime minister's "question time" in the Diet, Renhō, the then president of the Democratic Party, asked Prime Minister Abe about the Gender Parity Law, which presumably hastened the LDP's decision. At the very end of the supplementary session in December, the LDP and Kōmeitō submitted their own bills.

The opposition parties prioritized the passage of the law and thus accepted the wording of the law submitted by the ruling parties. Eventually, the parliamentary group agreed that the chairperson of the Committee of Cabinet Affairs would propose the bill. Customarily, when a chairperson of a Diet committee proposes a bill, the deliberation process becomes simpler and the committee passes the bill on the same day they are introduced. Although the partisan agreement had already been concluded, the bill was not voted on in 2017. The ordinary session starts in January and lasts for 150 days if there is no extension. Customarily, private member's bills are deliberated only after all the government's bills are passed. If there is a controversial bill in a relevant committee, the committee is less likely to have time left for private member's bills. This was not the case in 2017, but the prime minister's office avoided parliamentary deliberations because Prime Minister Abe was embroiled in scandals alleging improper use of the power of his office to promote two educational institutions, Moritomo Gakuen and Kake Gakuin. Even though all the parties agreed on the Gender Parity Law and the chairperson of the Committee of Cabinet Affairs promised to propose the bill, he was not able to do so because the legislative session ended too soon.

The Diet finally voted in 2018. The parliamentary group tried to modify the custom that the Diet would deliberate private members' bills only after all the government's bills were deliberated, arguing that the Gender Parity Law was exceptional, as it was directly related to Diet members. Nakagawa joined the Cabinet Committee to directly negotiate the scheduling of the bill and, indeed, succeeded in moving the deliberation date ahead of the government's bills. On April 11, 2018, the chairperson of the Cabinet Committee proposed the bill and received unanimous support. The plenary session of the Lower House voted the next day. Then, in the Upper House, the Cabinet Committee passed it on May 15, 2018, and the plenary session on May 16, 2018. The law came into effect on May 23, 2018.

The passage of the law in 2018 owed much to the brilliant negotiation skills of Nakagawa as well as Kiyomi Tsujimoto (DP), the minority leader of parliamentary affairs in charge of scheduling bill deliberations. The timing of April 2018 was also conducive to the passage of women-friendly laws because the LDP needed to claim the credit for good lawmaking after a sexual harassment scandal by the administrative Vice-Minister of Finance.

The policymaking process of the Gender Parity Law indicates that the official commitment of the Abe administration to women's empowerment, no matter how superficial it was, compelled them to support the bill. It was already public knowledge that the LDP was not enthusiastic about the passage of the bill, and the media tried to hold the LDP accountable by questioning their attitude toward the bill. The rise of the quota movement was able to push through the resistance of the LDP because it became politically risky to delay the passage of the bill any longer.

Discursive Politics and Transnational Feminism

Third, the discursive turn from *quotas* to *parity* also played a critical role in forging a consensus. It is usual for quotas to be opposed because they often appear to discriminate against men and assist unqualified women to win. Public awareness of gendered hurdles to run for office is necessary for a society to embrace the idea of quotas. Such a condition did not exist in Japan as of 2015. Doubts surrounding the constitutionality of quotas had precluded the development of meaningful discussions. Once the working team of the parliamentary group gave up on drafting a legal quota, the idea of parity served as a glue to hold different perspectives together toward the enactment of the Gender Parity Law.

The idea of parity had power in itself. People usually denounce quotas because they have heard of the term but do not understand it. In contrast, no one has ever heard of parity or "parité," a Japanese term closer to the French pronunciation. The invention of a new word worked because it can subvert resistance without evoking clichéd counterarguments. The rationale of 50–50 representation can be intuitively understood and is difficult to refute. It is quite challenging to say that women should comprise 10 percent in decision-making bodies even though men and women roughly constitute 50–50 percent in society. Some would oppose parity from the standpoint that women's share should not be limited to 50 percent. To compensate for the long history of gender inequality, there are certain justifications to holding all-women's panels or a women's supermajority. However, such counterarguments were nonexistent in Japan. As women's organizations called for quotas, meaning the target of 30 percent, the idea of parity practically raised the bar and yet made consensus possible.

On the one hand, conservatives who uphold the value of gendered roles do not have trouble accepting parity representation, as they believe that men and women have different roles and perspectives. On the other hand, those who care for representative justice support parity because the systematic elimination of women is not democratic, regardless of the possibility that women representatives are more likely to advance women's interests. Therefore, the idea of parity appears as an overarching scheme in which people from different political ideologies and gender perspectives can agree.

As a scholar, I always present to Japanese audiences the difference between quotas and parity as that of means and goal. Quotas are a *means* to achieve gender equality, whereas parity is a democratic *principle* in itself. Such an explanation is derived from transnational feminism. In 1992, twenty women leaders at the European Summit of Women in Power issued and signed the Athens Declaration, which established a common ground for European discussions on parity democracy. In 2000, France passed the Parity Law, the first law in the world that required political parties to field candidates in parity. Later, in Latin America, seven countries transformed their quota law to parity law. At the United Nations, the Secretary-General is advocating for "Planet 50–50 by 2030," to achieve equal representation of men and women by 2030.

The collective effort of transnational feminism has shaped the idea of parity democracy. Japan is not immune from such a global trend. Every year, a certain number of activists, including the younger generations, participate in the Commission on the Status of Women (CSW) in New York and are inspired by new ideas and practices around the world. The availability of parity as a normative idea helped the Japanese activists to push through the resistance to achieve the adoption of the Gender Parity Law.

THE IMPACT OF THE GENDER PARITY LAW

In April 2019, consolidated local elections were conducted, followed by the Upper House election in July. The results of the two elections indicate that the Gender Parity Law has affected the behaviors of political parties, albeit to a varying degree.

Among the contesting candidates, women comprised 12.7 percent, 21.2 percent, 17.3 percent, 26.5 percent, and 12.1 percent in the elections to the prefectural assemblies, city councils of designated cities, city councils, ward councils of the Tokyo Metropolitan area, and town/village councils, respectively; all of these constituted record high numbers. The share of elected women officials were 10.4 percent, 20.8 percent, 18.4 percent, 31.0 percent, and 12.4 percent in the prefectural assemblies, city councils of designated cities, city councils, ward councils of the Tokyo Metropolitan area, and town/village councils, respectively. It can be said that the Gender Parity Law had some impact, although the pace of change is modest.

Table 7.1 shows the party-wise breakdown of the share of women among elected local officials at various levels. It clearly indicates that both the LDP and Kōmeitō were reluctant to elect women to the legislatures of the prefectures and designated cities. Among the candidates for prefectural assemblies, women made up only 4 percent of the LDP nominees and 8 percent of those from Kōmeitō, whereas they constituted 46 percent, 26 percent, 18 percent, and 12 percent of the candidates in the Japan Communist Party (JCP), the Constitutional Democratic Party (CDP), the Social Democratic Party (SDP),

Table 7.1. Share of Women in the Officials Elected through the Consolidated Local Elections (2019)

	LDP	*Komei*	*CDP*	*DPP*	*JCP*	*SDP*	*ISHIN*
Prefecture	3.5	8.4	24.6	14.5	51.5	18.2	12.5
Designated City	7.3	16.4	28.3	21.2	52.2	0	18.8
City	7.2	33.4	31.0	15.8	42.3	18.9	19.6
Tokyo Ward	14.6	27.3	41.7	16.7	45.6	42.9	18.2

and the Democratic Party for the People (DPP), respectively. The fact that the LDP, the largest party in all the assemblies and councils, did not comply with the Gender Parity Law, led to the modest improvement in women's representation.[10]

The results of the Upper House election presented a similar pattern. As many as 104 women ran for office; this resulted in females accounting for a record 28.1 percent of the total candidates. Of these, twenty-eight—the same number as in the previous election—were elected. Because the total number of seats in the Upper House had increased, the share of women elected decreased from 23.1 to 22.6 percent; the fifty-six women representatives (elections are held for half of the seats every three years) constitute 22.9 percent of the Upper House—a record high.

Figure 7.1 shows women's share among the candidates of the major parties and Figure 7.2 represents their share among elected officials. The low shares for women in the LDP and Kōmeitō had an impact on the overall trend.

The Gender Parity Law encourages parties to take measures to increase political participation by women; this includes setting up numerical targets. Indeed, the DPP set a target of selecting 30 percent women for all elections and the CDP had a target of choosing 40 percent women in the proportional representation list for the Upper House election. Both parties succeeded in achieving these targets. The actions of the opposition parties put pressure on the LDP, leading Prime Minister Abe to comment that "speaking about

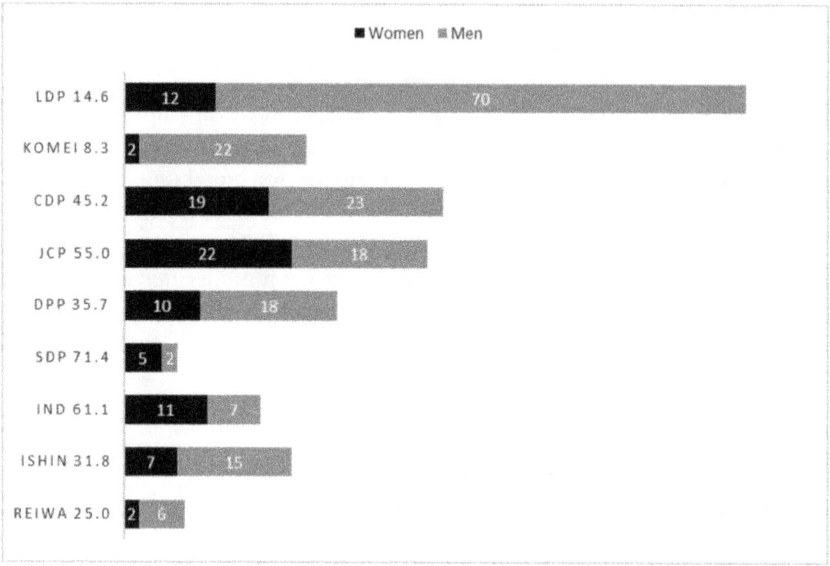

Figure 7.1. Women's Share among the Candidates
Created by the author.

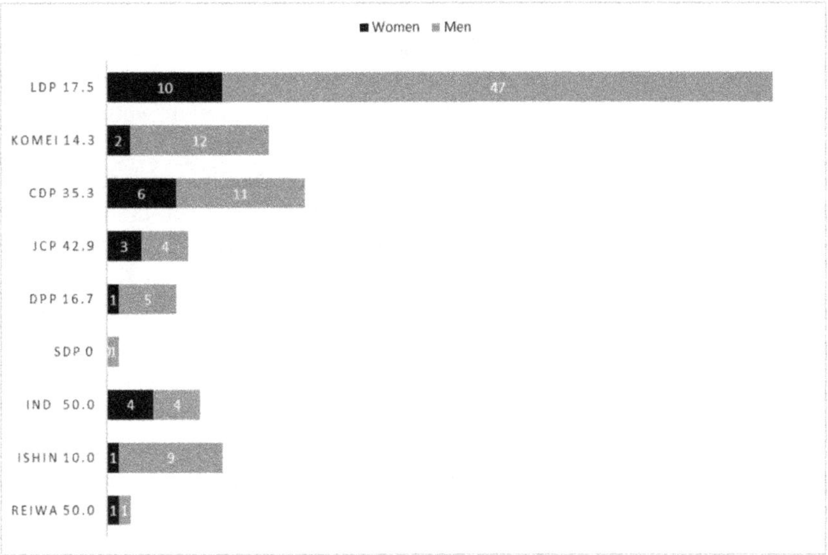

Figure 7.2. Women's Share among Elected Officials
Created by the author.

the next election is beyond my remit, but we would like to make an effort to increase women candidates to more than 20 percent."[11]

The media played an important role in monitoring the political parties and holding party leaders accountable. All the major newspapers compared the ratio of women among the different parties and highlighted the new female candidates who challenged the male-dominant politics. They also shed light on gender issues and compared parties' positions on separate family names and same-sex marriage. Media attention is crucial for the Gender Parity Law to have an impact by triggering a contagious effect. Parties on the Left have already committed to increasing female candidates. Their further electoral victory would put extra pressure on the LDP to modify its habitual way of recruiting candidates.[12]

The passage of the Gender Parity Law signals a change in the landscape surrounding women's activism. This chapter shows that significant changes took place in four dimensions that usually explain the adoption/non-adoption of quotas—the women's movement, political elites, normative discourse, and transnational feminism. In particular, the revitalization of the quota movement generated a political dynamism in which those who were concerned about women's underrepresentation mobilized all the resources, which had an negligible impact on strategic calculations of the political elites.

The passage of the Gender Parity Law also embodied women's engagement with constitutional democracy. Even though mainstream constitutional scholars did not academically back up the constitutionality of quotas, women activists believed that equal representation of men and women denote the spirit of the constitution that stipulates that there shall be no discrimination in political relations because of sex. The underrepresentation of women would violates the principle of gender equality that is granted as a constitutional right. Given that the ruling party (the LDP) was reluctant, if not hostile, to the idea of quotas, we should conclude that the adoption of the non-binding parity principle was indeed an achievement of women's activism.

The development of constitutional debate regarding quotas is necessary in order for Japan to adopt quotas in any form. There are a variety of quotas in the world, and their effectiveness in increasing women representation varies depending on the actual design. The introduction of a 50 percent quota for proportional representation in both the Houses is worth considering within the boundary of constitutionality. The quota movement—a de facto coalition of the women's movement, academia, journalism, and MPs—stimulated by transnational feminism will be the key to sustain and amplify the pressure on political elites, as has been always the case. The passage of the Gender Parity Law and its impact, especially on opposition parties, will keep the quota movement active for the foreseeable future.

NOTES

1. Law for the Promotion of Gender Parity in Politics (*Seiji bun'ya ni okeru danjo kyōdō sanga suishin hō*).
2. The IPU renews the world rankings every month. See IPU's ranking: http://archive.ipu.org/wmn-e/classif-arc.htm.
3. Pippa Norris and Joni Lovenduski, *Political Recruitment: Gender, Race and Class in the British Parliament* (Cambridge: Cambridge University Press, 1995); Mona Lena Krook, "Beyond Supply and Demand: A Feminist-Institutionalist Theory of Candidate Selection," *Political Research Quarterly* 63, no. 4 (2009): 707–20; Miki Caul Kittilson, *Challenging Parties, Challenging Parliaments: Women and Elected Office in Contemporary Western Europe* (Columbus: Ohio State University Press, 2006).
4. Jennifer L. Lawless and Richard L. Fox, *It Takes a Candidate: Why Women Don't Run for Office* (Cambridge: Cambridge University Press, 2001).
5. The Japan New Party, created by Morihiro Hosokawa in 1992, introduced a 20 percent quota for its party positions, but the party was disbanded two years later. The Social Democratic Party has stipulated quotas of minorities in its party rules since its birth in 1996, but it does not specify the number.
6. I explained the policymaking process in a detailed fashion. See "Interview with Mari Miura: The Gender Parity Law in Japan—The Potential to Change Women's Under-Representation," *Journal of Gender Studies* 21 (2018): 87–99.

7. *Koyō no bun'ya ni okeru danjo no kintō na kikai oyobi taigū no kakuho tō ni kansuru hōritsu sekō kisoku.*

8. Nagatachō is the area of Tokyo around the National Diet building, encompassing lawmakers' office buildings and related government facilities.

9. Mari Miura, "Minshutō Seikenka no Rengō: Seisaku Katsudō to Shakaiteki Rōdō Undō no Bundan wo Norikoete," in *Minshūhō Seiken no Chōsen to Zasetsu: Son no Keiken kara Naniwo Manabuka*, ed. Mitsutoshi Itō and Tarō Miyamoto (Tokyo: Nihon Keizai Hyōronsha, 2014).

10. Mari Miura, "Seijibun'ya ni okeru Danjo Kyōdō Sankaku Suishinhō sekōgo Ichinen: Tōitsu Jichitai Senkyo kara miete kita Kadai," *Jichiken* (July 2019).

11. Prime Minister Abe commented in the debate among the heads of major parties held by the Japan National Press Club on July 3, 2019.

12. Mari Miura, "Kōhosha Kintōhō no Kouka to Kadai: Jizoku-teki Kōka ni mukete," *Voters* 52 (2019).

REFERENCES

Gaunder, Alisa. "Quota Nonadoption in Japan: The Role of the Women's Movement and the Opposition," *Politics and Gender* 11, no. 1 (2015): 176–186.

Kenny, Meryl. *Gender and Political Recruitment: Theorizing Institutional Change*. New York: Palgrave Macmillan, 2013.

Kittilson, Miki Caul. *Challenging Parties, Challenging Parliaments: Women and Elected Office in Contemporary Western Europe*. Columbus: Ohio State University Press, 2006.

Krook, Mona Lena. "Electoral Systems and Women's Representation." In *The Oxford Handbook of Electoral Systems*, edited by Erik S. Herron, Robert Pekkanen, and Matthew Søberg Shugart, 175–192, New York: Oxford University Press, 2018.

———. *Quotas for Women in Politics: Gender and Candidate Selection Reform Worldwide*. New York: Oxford University Press, 2009a.

———. "Beyond Supply and Demand: A Feminist-Institutionalist Theory of Candidate Selection," *Political Research Quarterly* 63, no. 4 (2009): 707–720.

Lawless, Jennifer L. and Richard L. Fox. *It Takes a Candidate: Why Women Don't Run for Office*. Cambridge: Cambridge University Press, 2001.

Lovenduski, Joni. *Feminizing Politics*. Cambridge: Polity Press, 2005.

Matland, Richard E. and Donley T. Studlar. "The Contagion of Women Candidates in Single-Member District and Proportional Representation Electoral Systems: Canada and Norway," *Journal of Politics* 58, no.1 (1996): 707–733.

Miura, Mari. "Seijibun'ya ni okeru Danjo Kyōdō Sankaku Suishinhō sekōgo Ichinen: Tōitsu Jichitai Senkyo kara miete kita Kadai." *Jichiken* (July 2019): 10–15.

———. "Kōhosha Kintōhō no Kouka to Kadai: Jizoku-teki Kōka ni mukete." *Voters* 52 (2019): 7–9.

———. "Interview with Mari Miura: The Gender Parity Law in Japan—The Potential to Change Women's Under-Representation." *Journal of Gender Studies* 21 (2018): 87–99.

———. *Gender Quotas in Comparative Perspectives: Understanding the Increase in Women Representatives.* In Japanese. Tokyo: Akashi Shoten, 2014a.

———. "Minshutō Seikenka no Rengō: Seisaku Katsudō to Shakaiteki Rōdō Undō no Bundan wo Norikoete." In *Minshūhō Seiken no Chōsen to Zasetsu: Son no Keiken kara Naniwo Manabuka*, edited by Mitsutoshi Itō and Tarō Miyamoto. Tokyo: Nihon Keizai Hyōronsha, 2014.

Norris, Pippa. *Electoral Engineering*. Cambridge: Cambridge University Press, 2004.

Norris, Pippa and Joni Lovenduski. *Political Recruitment: Gender, Race and Class in the British Parliament*. Cambridge: Cambridge University Press, 1995.

Chapter Eight

Soka Gakkai's Impact on Constitutional Revision Attempts

Levi McLaughlin

KOMEITO'S SHIFTING LANDSCAPE

During the campaign for the July 21, 2019, House of Councillors (Upper House) election, Prime Minister Shinzō Abe emphasized his cherished objective of constitutional revision.[1] Despite the fact that the governing coalition failed to gain the supermajority of two-thirds of the Upper House seat total required by Article 94 of the 1947 Constitution to proceed with a national referendum on a proposed revision, Abe took the election results as confirmation of his personal mandate. "I take it as my mission (*shimei*)," Abe stated on election night, "so I of course wish to press forward with constitutional revision during the remainder of my term in office."[2] He went on to discuss the possibility of working across the aisle with the Democratic for the People Party (Kokumin Minshūtō) to acquire the numbers necessary to overcome the 2/3 seat margin.[3]

Abe did not mention working with his Liberal Democratic Party's coalition partner Komeito to realize his amendment goal. This was not surprising, as Komeito, in coalition with the Liberal Democratic Party (LDP) at the national level since 1999, has routinely defined its role as a "brake" (*hadome*) against what it and its support organization Soka Gakkai regard as LDP intransigence.[4] Historically, this has meant standing in the way of LDP plans to amend Article Nine, guaranteeing that the original wording of the Constitution's famed peace clause remains unaltered. As Abe looked to the opposition, he must have been aware that Komeito would comprise the coalition's swing vote in the Upper House and that LDP politicians in the Lower and Upper Houses still relied on voter mobilization by Soka Gakkai members to keep their seats. It therefore appeared as if the July 2019 election reinforced what has become Japan's political status quo: a would-be revisionist LDP forced to concede to its Komeito ally to ensure its continued political domination. The coalition appeared to be holding.

However, as Komeito solidified its coalition hold, new challenges to the party emerged within Soka Gakkai, the religion from which Komeito emerged. Komeito leader Natsuo Yamaguchi was boldly opposed in his district by Yoshimasa Nohara, a fifty-nine-year-old teacher and Gakkai member who traveled from Okinawa to Tokyo to run as a candidate for Reiwa Shinsengumi, a small, recently formed, socially progressive party. Nohara was motivated by his own sense of mission, having been roused to political action when he sided with other Gakkai protesters who aided the successful campaign in September 2018 against the LDP/Komeito-endorsed gubernatorial candidate to elect Denny Tamaki on a platform opposing the national government's planned relocation within Okinawa of the U.S. airbase to Henoko; the base relocation was proceeding, with Komeito support, in spite of outcry against the U.S. military presence by Okinawan residents. In his Upper House campaign speeches, Nohara castigated his religion and its affiliated party for having been led astray by administrators who compromised foundational pacifism to retain political power. At a July 5, 2019, address to supporters outside Shinbashi station in central Tokyo, Nohara appealed to those who had been forced from their local Gakkai communities for opposing Komeito's policy shifts: "If Soka Gakkai people are here, especially if there are Married Women's Division members here . . . those of you who have been expelled, been ostracized (*mura hachibu*), would you step forward?"[5] On July 21, Nohara garnered 214,438 votes, well below the 815,445 votes that ensured Yamaguchi's reelection.[6] In spite of this, Nohara characterized his campaign as a success, as his principal intent had been to illuminate what he considered rot at the center of Komeito and Soka Gakkai. Unless the Gakkai undergoes comprehensive administrative reform, Nohara warned on election night, "Japan has no future."[7]

The July 2019 election results presented us with opposing pictures of Komeito and Soka Gakkai. One picture affirmed that Soka Gakkai continued as Japan's most powerful and most reliable voting bloc. Komeito increased its total from 25 to 28 House of Councillors seats, adding to its 29 seats in the House of Representatives (Lower House), and it remained the coalition's casting vote on constitutional matters. However, while it gained seats, Komeito's popular vote number dropped to 6,536,336, markedly below the 6,977,712 proportional representation (PR) votes for Komeito in the 2017 general election.[8] Seat gains notwithstanding, the number of party supporters is dropping at a significant rate. And Nohara's campaign to repudiate the party's leadership is symptomatic of fissures that are widening within Komeito's support base. The axiom that Soka Gakkai functions as Japan's most reliable vote-gathering machine cannot remain valid, because Komeito faces an uncertain future.

As the ground shifts under Komeito, deliberations on constitutional interpretation and revision become unsettled. Given the influence Soka Gakkai wields on the ability of Komeito and LDP politicians alike to keep their seats, it is important to understand Gakkai voters' actions and motivations. Concerns about Article Nine propel a growing conflict between Soka Gakkai members on justifications for political engagement. Their concerns grow out of decades-long engagements with Buddhist and humanist teachings. To understand members' conflicting claims, we must look at how Soka Gakkai and Komeito emerged from Buddhist enlightenment and modern Enlightenment aspirations.

KOMEITO'S TWIN LEGACIES

Soka Gakkai (the "Value Creation Study Association) is conventionally referred to as a lay Buddhist association following Nichiren (1222–1282).[9] Nichiren was a Japanese Buddhist reformer who broke from the temple-based traditions of his day to propagate the belief that only exclusive faith in the *Lotus Sūtra*, the putative final teachings of the historical Buddha Śākyamuṇi, serves as an effective means of salvation. Soka Gakkai maintains Nichiren Buddhist liturgies, such as chanting sections of the *Lotus* and repeatedly invoking its seven-syllable title, *namu-myōhō-renge-kyō*, and members rely on Nichiren's writings as their Buddhist scriptural base. However, as the name "Value Creation Study Association" indicates, lay Buddhist practice is only one of the group's constitutive elements. It began as an educational reform movement, first called Sōka Kyōiku Gakkai (Value Creation Education Study Association), that marks its founding on November 18, 1930. The Gakkai's first president was Tsunesaburō Makiguchi (1871–1944), a schoolteacher and intellectual whose early writings evoke neo-Kantian thought and the educational philosophy of John Dewey. In 1928, Makiguchi, along with his fellow teacher Jōsei Toda (1900–1958), converted to lay affiliation under Nichiren Shōshū, a small temple-based sect following a minority Nichiren lineage. Throughout the 1930s, Makiguchi and Toda's Nichiren Buddhist convictions hardened, and Sōka Kyōiku Gakkai became primarily dedicated to Nichiren Buddhist practices, including *shakubuku*, a conversion tactic Nichiren prescribed for lands, such as Japan, that slander the *Lotus Sūtra*. Pursuing *shakubuku* led the Gakkai to run afoul of the wartime Japanese state, as did the government's requirement that all religious groups enshrine *kamifuda* (deity talismans) from the Grand Shrine at Ise. Makiguchi and Toda were some of very few adherents to uphold Nichiren's strict rejection of heterodox teachings. They refused to enshrine the Shinto talismans, and they were arrested in July 1943 for violating the terms of the 1925 Peace Preservation Law. Both were imprisoned, and Makiguchi died of malnutrition on November 18, 1944, on the Gakkai's founding anniversary.

Released weeks before the end of the Pacific War in 1945, Toda reformed the group as Soka Gakkai and focused the organization on a particularly hard-sell version of *shakubuku*. By the time of Toda's death in April 1958, Soka Gakkai had expanded to over one million adherent households. Converts were largely poor and socially atomized women and men who moved from the countryside into Japan's rapidly growing cities. They were attracted by the Gakkai's promise of material and soteriological benefits, as well as by its charismatic leadership, tight-knit social networks, and inspiring institutional goals. While the Gakkai's aggressive proselytizing produced a massive surge in membership, it also created a negative public image. The most important reason why Soka Gakkai gained a negative image, and a major reason why it remains stigmatized in the present, however, was its move into electoral politics.

Komeito today must be characterized as a "normal" political party, in the sense that it, like other parties, gathers votes by promoting policies that appeal to its constituents. Komeito's normalcy is confirmed by that fact that, despite the policy influence it has wielded in coalition with the LDP since 1999, there is no evidence that it seeks to enact a religious agenda.[10] Komeito nonetheless grew out of a campaign to satisfy an eschatological Nichiren Buddhist objective: the construction of a *honmon no kaidan*, or "true ordination platform." This was to be a temple facility constructed at the Nichiren Shōshū sect headquarters at Taisekiji, near Mount Fuji, at which the sect's (and then Soka Gakkai's) principal object of worship was to be enshrined. This enshrinement would celebrate the conversion of the populace to exclusive worship of the *Lotus Sūtra*. Following Nichiren's dictates, a governmental decree ordering the ordination platform—referred to by Toda Jōsei as the *kokuritsu kaidan*, or "national ordination platform"—was required.[11] In postwar Japan, this required a decree from the Japanese Diet. As Soka Gakkai grew by leaps and bounds from the early 1950s, Toda inspired members to begin working toward the lofty *kaidan* goal by sending them into politics. The group first fielded independent candidates for local elections in 1955, in 1956 three Gakkai administrators were elected to the Upper House, and other electoral victories soon followed. Driven as they were by the conviction that political mobilization enabled religious conversion, members in early Gakkai campaigns transgressed against elections law. In July 1957, Daisaku Ikeda, then a Young Men's Division leader, was arrested alongside other young leaders for violating the legal prohibition against house-to-house campaigning. Soka Gakkai came to eulogize Ikeda's legal tribulations as the "Osaka Incident," an episode they treat as their future Honorary President's *hōnan*, or "persecution [for defending] the dharma." He was ultimately cleared of all charges in 1962.

By this time, Daisaku Ikeda was third president of Soka Gakkai, having taken the mantle on May 3, 1960. Both Toda and Ikeda ascended to the Gakkai presidency on the third of May, the same day that the 1947 Constitution was promulgated. The day that serves as Japan's Constitutional Memorial Day serves as the anniversary for numerous important Gakkai events, including its "President's Day," its "Mother's Day," and Ikeda and his wife Kaneko's wedding anniversary. Under Ikeda's leadership, the Gakkai's political engagement increased dramatically, keeping pace with the lay sect's explosive membership growth and institutional expansion into education, publishing, the market economy, and other components of the nation-state. Between 1960 and 1970, Soka Gakkai in Japan grew from just over one million to over seven million households, and the organization gained significant numbers of followers in countries overseas—first under Nichiren Shōshū, and from 1975 as Soka Gakkai International. In November 1961, Gakkai politicians in the Diet organized as Kōmei Seiji Renmei (or Kōseiren), reported in English as "The League for Just and Fair Politics."[12] On May 3, 1964, Ikeda declared that henceforth Soka Gakkai would be a purely religious organization and that politics would be left to Kōmei politicians. This declaration, falling as it did on Constitutional Memorial Day, resonates with the Constitution's separation of religion and government. On November 17,1964, the day before Soka Gakkai's founding anniversary, Ikeda announced the dissolution of Kōseiren and the establishment of Kōmeitō, or the "Clean Government Party."

Initially, Komeito did not separate religious and political objectives. Just as Soka Gakkai is heir to the twin legacies of medieval Nichiren Buddhism and modern humanism, eschatological Nichiren-inspired aims and a utopian modern ideal of world peace through democratic rule merge in Komeito's official founding statement. It reads (in part):

> We hold the firm conviction that it is only through the singular path of the Buddhist philosophy of absolute pacifism—that is, the superior path of a harmonious fusion of government and Buddhism (*ōbutsu myōgō*)—that the world will attain salvation from the horror of war. The Clean Government Party, through the founding ideals of a harmonious fusion of government and Buddhism and Buddhist democracy (*buppō minshūshugi*), will fundamentally cleanse Japan's political world, confirm the basis of government by parliamentary democracy, put down deep roots in the masses, and realize the well-being of the common people. Furthermore, from the broad position of world nationalism (*wārudo nashonarizumu*), we solemnly pledge to the people of the nation that it is our ultimate ambition to fight bravely to establish an institution for eternal peace in the world.[13]

From August 1, 1956, Jōsei Toda had issued an essay titled *Ōbutsu myōgōron* (On the Harmonious Union of Kingship and Buddhism) in which he stated that "the only purpose of our going into politics is to erect the *kokuritsu kaidan.*"[14] Ikeda's use of *ōbutsu myōgō* in Komeito's founding statement reaffirmed Toda's goal, and members continued to be inspired by this millenarian aim as they worked for Komeito campaigns. From 1964, Komeito fielded candidates in both the Lower and Upper Houses, and it expanded its presence in local legislatures across Japan. By June 1969, Komeito had 2,088 members in local government, and it was the third-largest party in the National Diet. On May 3, 1970, following a scandal the previous year surrounding a failed attempt to quash the publication of a book titled *I Denounce Soka Gakkai*, Ikeda announced a formal institutional separation between Soka Gakkai and Komeito. The religion renounced its "ordination platform" plans, and Komeito eliminated its references to Buddhism and replaced them with a pledge to uphold the Constitution.

Ikeda's Pacifism and Komeito's Political Pragmatism

Except for a diminishing number of elderly pioneers who converted under Toda, members who power Komeito's campaigns today came of age entirely under Daisaku Ikeda's leadership. From early in his presidency, Soka Gakkai began to transform from an organization run *by* Ikeda into a group dedicated *to* Ikeda, and after the lay sect split from Nichiren Shōshū in November 1991, member reverence for Ikeda, Honorary President since 1979, grew ever more intense. Having left behind the Nichiren Buddhist ordination platform objective, Soka Gakkai increasingly focused on cultivating Ikeda's profile as an international statesman who reached across religious and cultural lines to advance peace. During Ikeda's most vigorous decades, from the 1960s into the early 2000s, members were shaped by a heady mix of peace-promoting activities. The group became famous for its "world peace culture festivals" (*sekai heiwa bunkasai*) in which thousands of costumed members swirled through stadiums in complex dance numbers as marching bands blasted out Gakkai songs and attendees in the stands held up placards bearing peace messages. The Gakkai's Youth Division organized a Peace Conference in 1979, and from 1980 the Married Women's Division led member efforts through its Peace Committee. Adherents took their cue from Ikeda, who engaged in hundreds of high-profile dialogues, beginning with his conversations in 1973 with historian Arnold J. Toynbee, to promote world peace. From January 1983, Ikeda began issuing annual *Peace Proposals*, treatises with detailed recommendations for multilateral action in the interest of resolving global conflicts. Nichiren Buddhism's status inversed, shifting from being Gakkai's guiding framework into one component woven into the group's declared "three pillars": peace, culture, and education.

As Ikeda promoted world peace, Komeito compromised on pacifism. No longer justified after 1970 as a means of realizing the national ordination platform, Komeito at first emphasized absolute pacifism; it initially hewed to an orthodox reading of Article Nine, advocating that Japan should maintain neutrality and not participate in any kind of military treaty.[15] From 1978, however, the party acknowledged the legality of the 1960 U.S.-Japan Security Treaty and the Japan Self-Defense Forces. Komeito's next significant shift came in 1992, when the party supported the LDP decision to include a limited number of JSDF troops in UN peacekeeping operations. More significant changes came when Komeito, in the governing coalition with the LDP, went along with decisions made by the Cabinet of Prime Minister Jun'ichirō Koizumi to send troops to the Persian Gulf (2002) and Iraq (2004).[16] This inspired some of the first protests by Soka Gakkai members.[17] On January 21, 2004, a group of adherents calling themselves the "Society for Preserving the Peace Constitution Opposed to the Iraq Troop Dispatch" (Irakku Hahei ni Hantai Shi Heiwa Kenpō o Mamoru Kai) submitted a petition with 1,800 signatures to Komeito headquarters.[18]

In exchange for acquiescing to successive LDP-led reinterpretations of Article Nine, Komeito points to a high *seisekiritsu*, or "success ratio," in passing legislation. The party's policies are geared in particular toward Soka Gakkai's Married Women's Division, the religion's subgroup that serves as its primary vote-gatherer. Ensuring a lower consumption tax rate on household necessities, providing funds for childcare, ensuring comprehensive healthcare, and pushing for affordable education all come before discussion of defense or constitutional issues in recent Komeito election manifestos.[19] When it comes to constitutional revision, Komeito dissembles. Party manifestos for the 2014 and 2017 general elections, for example, included short discussions in their final sections that allowed for *kaken*, or "adding to" Article Nine by including a third clause that acknowledged the legality of the JSDF, should this be supported by a majority of Japanese voters. In the 2019 manifesto, however, the only mention of the Constitution appears in a short appendix on the final page and simply states that revision "should be discussed carefully from now on."[20]

The party is now reluctant to meet constitutional debates head-on, but recent analysis confirms Komeito's historical success as a brake against LDP revision attempts. Adam Liff and Ko Maeda compared the LDP's 2012 draft to comprehensively amend the Constitution to proposals Abe made on May 3, 2017.[21] When it came to Article Nine, Abe capitulated to a written proposal Komeito put forward in 2004: instead of pursuing the 2012 LDP amendment strategy of *kaiken* (wholesale revision), Abe's 2017 proposal hewed to the Komeito *kaken* (adding as needed) principle, sticking to a modest plan to potentially add a third clause to Article Nine while leaving the first two clauses unchanged. As Liff and Maeda put it, "the LDP's seemingly impressive Diet seat totals mask significant electoral weakness." They demonstrated that without 80% Komeito voter support for LDP politicians, particularly those running in single-member districts, the LDP would probably have only gained 47.1% of the Lower House—below a simple majority, and far from two-thirds of the House. The LDP has been left with no choice but to defer, when necessary, to Soka Gakkai.

CONSTITUTIONAL CONCERNS IN SOKA GAKKAI'S ERA OF LIMINAL LEADERSHIP

Daisaku Ikeda last appeared before members at a Soka Gakkai General Headquarters Meeting on May 13, 2010. Since then, the Gakkai leadership has asserted that he is alive and dedicating himself to writing.[22] Annual *Peace Proposals* have continued to appear under Ikeda's name, along with numerous other publications. There are even recent interviews. In an April 2019 interview conducted via email with Ikeda by International Press Syndicate, for example, Ikeda hearkens back to his conversations with Mikhail Gorbachev as he urges global nuclear disarmament and cautions against the rise of AI-driven autonomous weapons systems.[23] The remarkable technical detail the Gakkai's Honorary President brings to bear in this interview underlines an unavoidable impression: even if their mentor is still alive, Gakkai administrators are speaking for him.

A decade-long absence of unambiguous intervention by Ikeda himself has seen a disaggregation of members' political commitments. Their disaggregation has kept pace with Komeito policy shifts. In September 2015, Komeito Diet politicians voted alongside their LDP coalition allies to pass eleven new laws collectively referred to as the *anpo hōsei*, or "security legislation." These laws put into effect a July 1, 2014, Abe Cabinet decision that allowed for "the right of collective self-defense" (*shūdanteki jieiken*), a reinterpretation of Article Nine to allow the JSDF to come to the aid of the United States and other Japanese military allies under armed attack. In the lead-up to the September 19, 2015, Upper House vote, thousands of protesters gathered in front of the National Diet and at hundreds of other locations across Japan. Observers were surprised to note the presence of Soka Gakkai members among the demonstrators. Their messages included harsh condemnation of Natsuo Yamaguchi as having accrued *butsubachi*, or "Buddhist demerit," and a sign that read "Komeito Diet members: reread *The Human Revolution*!" that called on their elected officials, and fellow Gakkai adherents, to revisit the novelized history of their religion that begins with the sentence "There is nothing so miserable as war."[24]

The anti–security law movement gave rise to numerous local-level member initiatives. One was the Osaka-based "Gathering of Soka Gakkai Members to Study Japan's National Constitution" (Nihonkoku Kenpō o Benkyō Suru Sōka Gakkai'in no Tsudoi), led by Taichi Asayama, a Soka University graduate and author of the remarkably dispassionate "Soka Gakkai and Komeito

Seen from Within" (*Uchigawa kara miru Sōka gakkai to Kōmeitō*).[25] In Aichi Prefecture, a member named Tatsushi Amano gained national recognition when he gathered 9,177 signatures through Twitter and Facebook for a petition calling for the withdrawal of the bills; he attempted to submit a printed version at Komeito's national headquarters the week before the September 2015 vote, where he was rebuffed. At the same time, a collective of Soka University alumni opposed to the new legislation issued a manifesto recalling Tsunesaburō Makiguchi's death in prison and Daisaku Ikeda's human rights struggles in the vein of Mahatma Gandhi and Martin Luther King Jr. It declared that the bills' opponents confirmed their vow to uphold the ideal Ikeda promulgated when he founded Soka University: "Be a fortress for the peace of mankind."[26]

While the LDP-Komeito coalition retained power in the 2017 general election, Komeito lost five Lower House seats and received its lowest-ever vote count. This drop may be attributable in part to sympathy for messages spread by Gakkai protesters, who continued to build on anti–security law activism. They were further propelled by Komeito's support for subsequent LDP measures they regarded as chipping away at constitutional guarantees. Critics pointed in particular to Komeito voting in June 2017 in favor of a controversial anti-conspiracy law that criminalized the plotting and committing of 277 acts. They argued that the law could be used to target government critics for surveillance and was in effect a recapitulation of the 1925 Public Security Preservation Law that was used to imprison and martyr their founding president, Tsunesaburō Makiguchi. During his campaign speeches in July 2019, Yoshimasa Nohara was flanked by a large banner that featured Makiguchi's photo under the words *kyōbōzai wa iranai!*: "We don't need the anti-conspiracy law!"[27]

Even among members who number themselves among Komeito's vanguard, support is diluted with resentment. Without the unifying power of Ikeda's direct presence, lifelong supporters are increasingly apt to voice their opposition to Komeito policy reversals. On August 14, 2018, I interviewed several Men's Division members, all second- or third-generation adherents who graduated from Soka University, and all veterans of a Young Men's Division symphony orchestra.[28] I had spent countless hours over twenty years with these adherents as a non-member participant in rituals, rehearsals, and other activities, but I had never before heard the sentiments they expressed to me that night. "I don't think Soka Gakkai will exist in twenty years," Mr. Takazawa stated. "I'll always have this circle," he gestured to his colleagues around the table, "but I think Soka Gakkai will scatter." An unapologetic Komeito supporter, even at the time of this conversation, Takazawa told me of his dismay at the collective self-defense legislation. "I wrote a complaint letter and sent it up the Soka Gakkai administration. I know it was received at the Chapter level. Then it disappeared, somewhere at the [regional] Head-quarter or Zone level." He continues to vote for Komeito, and to electioneer, but he remains opposed to the direction the party has taken. "I think it would be better if Komeito returned to the opposition," he stated. This is an opinion that members routinely express to me as they simultaneously confirm their continuing Komeito support; in opposition, the party may have been relatively powerless, but it could maintain an ideological purity it lost in government. Hamasaki and Tsukamoto, two others present at the orchestra alumni meeting, took me aside to tell me they saw no future for Komeito and that Tsukamoto had ceased to practice *f-tori*: "friend-getting," or convincing nonmembers to vote for Komeito. "Soka Gakkai in Japan needs to be reformed," Hamasaki asserted. Just as Japan was rebuilt by the United States after the Pacific War, they told me, Soka Gakkai needs leadership from outside the country to overhaul its governance; perhaps, like Japan itself, leadership from the U.S. This would have the effect of radically re-contextualizing Japan within the Gakkai world. Hamasaki even referred to Soka Gakkai in Japan as "SGI-J," demoting it from its headquarters status and placing it in a horizontal relationship with SGI-USA and all 191 other countries within Soka Gakkai International. Hamasaki and Tsukamoto affirmed their feeling that Japanese dominance of Soka Gakkai's component institutions has come to an end and that any future for them lies in salvation from outside. "I don't recommend Komeito anymore," Tsukamoto admitted. "I can't."

"I think that Komeito will probably undergo natural extinction (*shizen shōmetsu*) within ten years," said Mr. Matsuoka, a former Soka Gakkai administrator.[29] Matsuoka spent thirteen years at the Gakkai's main headquarters, writing doctrinal study materials. After he was forced from his position, having run into conflicts with his superiors over interpretation of Nichiren's writings, he was further ostracized when he was asked to stop attending local Gakkai meetings. Advocating from his experience as a well-informed insider, Matsuoka is an active critic on social media, connecting with Taichi Asayama and other exiled Gakkai members who call for institutional reform. "The reason why Komeito will go extinct is because the number of Gakkai members is radically decreasing. It won't take ten years. Komeito won't be able to retain its seats. The LDP also, because it wins elections thanks to Gakkai members' support, in the immediate future will suffer [defeats]. I think that what happened in Okinawa will come to happen across the country." That is, that candidates put forward by the LDP-Komeito coalition will rely on a declining voter base, making it possible for opposition candidates to defeat them. He considered how the LDP will respond to a loss of member support: "It will part ways with Soka Gakkai. And after a split from the LDP, Komeito on its own will not have the influence to continue. It will dwindle in size below even that of the Japanese Communist Party. Once it splits from the LDP, I think there will be a decision to break up Komeito."

KOMEITO'S UNCERTAIN FUTURE

Matsuoka's predictions contrast starkly with evidence for what looks like robust Gakkai support for the party. On the afternoon of June 5, 2019, I observed thousands upon thousands of Komeito supporters, the vast majority women, pouring out of Tokyo Dome. They filled the staircases surrounding the stadium, overwhelmed the surrounding restaurants, and flowed into the streets as they filed into Suidōbashi station. They had just attended "Kōmei Forum 2019," the first of two identical 50,000-strong rallies organized one month before the Upper House election campaign began. According to Gakkai sources, the two rallies marked the first time Tokyo Dome held the same event twice on the same day. Both rallies were closed to the vernacular press (and to non-member observers, I discovered), and neither appeared on the Dome's official schedule. The party's newspaper *Kōmei shinbun* reported that Natsuo Yamaguchi emphasized staple party policies, such as support for childcare and education, and revved up voters by appealing to Komeito's role as the brake—as well as the accelerator and the steering wheel—that guides the government. Yamaguchi's appeal was supported by idols singing inspiring songs and speeches by other Komeito candidates running in districts across Japan.[30]

The sheer number of people pouring out of Tokyo Dome was certainly impressive, but I could not help noticing that they were mostly elderly—perhaps in their late sixties, on average. Matching this gathering with Matsuoka's prediction that Komeito will undergo "natural extinction," and aligning his prediction with the party's dropping vote count, brings demographic inevitability to the fore. Add to this admissions from members whose Komeito advocacy mingles with ambivalence and resentment, and the Dome rallies must be regarded with circumspection.

There is no doubt that Komeito support remains a mainstay for Gakkai members. And that it remains heavily gendered. "My parents always tell me that Komeito is the voice of the people (*minshū no koe*)," says Morita, a twenty-one-year-old Soka University student.[31] She continues to electioneer "because even my voice can be heard [in the party], however faintly." But other Gakkai youth have turned away. "I vote secretly for the Constitutional Democratic Party of Japan," admits Shimoyama, a male student of the same age. "I can't tell anyone at Soka University, of course."[32] The children of the members I know from my orchestra days follow their parents' example, in most cases, either drumming up Komeito votes or drifting away from the party. They are comparatively few in number, in keeping with Japan's overall demographic collapse.

On top of the group's demographic shift is a Gakkai-specific dilemma: fundamental change awaits Soka Gakkai and Komeito, and therefore the

LDP, when Daisaku Ikeda's death is officially announced. Up to the present, adherents have been able to justify their continued Komeito support because, however attenuated or affective their belief in Ikeda's approval, they could justify electioneering as what Ikeda *wants*. After Ikeda's death, Komeito must appeal to Gakkai voters as the party their deceased mentor *would have wanted* them to support. This will be an opinion expressed by administrators rather than a wish expressed by Ikeda himself. As such, it is a claim that will be challenged, particularly in light of Komeito's departure from Buddhist and pacifist ideals. Having long ago abandoned the Nichiren Buddhist justification that drove its founding, and having turned away from staunch peace advocacy, particularly in the years after Ikeda's public departure, Komeito has lost ideological justifications that motivated generations of Gakkai adherents. Rival claims by adherents who seek to return to what they regard as Ikeda's true intent promise to undermine Komeito electioneering after his death.

Soka Gakkai's demographic and ideological shifts will pull in opposite directions on the Liberal Democratic Party. Komeito's dropping vote count and a loss of Diet seats will mean that it loses its power to mitigate against LDP revision efforts. At the same time, dwindling Gakkai voter support for LDP candidates may give organized opposition parties that seek to preserve Article Nine a chance to oust the coalition from national government. At least in the immediate future, however, how Soka Gakkai voters proceed after Daisaku Ikeda's death will fundamentally shape revision strategies, and understanding Gakkai member political activism will remain a key academic undertaking.

NOTES

1. *Japan Times*, July 4, 2019.
2. *Asahi shinbun*, July 22, 2019.
3. Also aligning with Nippon Ishin no Kai, the other opposition party that supports revision, would have still left the LDP-Komeito coalition four seats short of a two-thirds majority. See *The Asahi Shinbun*, July 22, 2019.
4. Axel Klein and Levi McLaughlin, "Kōmeitō 2017: New Complications," in *Japan Decides 2017*, edited by Robert J. Pekkanen, Ethan Scheiner, and Steven R. Reed (New York: Palgrave MacMillan, 2018).
5. Footage of this speech circulated on Twitter: https://twitter.com/kamotetsu/status/1147059741870264320. Elections data from Japan's Ministry of Internal Affairs and Communications: http://www.soumu.go.jp/senkyo/. Yamaguchi's vote count went up incrementally from his last election in 2013, and 83% of Komeito supporters voted for him in the district, indicating steady Gakkai support for the party leader.

7. https://twitter.com/TOYOsanshin/status/1153225741795905536.
8. Klein and McLaughlin, "Kōmeitō 2017." The 2017 general election marked the first time after the party joined the LDP in coalition in 1999 that Komeito's popular vote count dipped below seven million votes.
9. For detailed discussion of Soka Gakkai, see Levi McLaughlin, *Soka Gakkai's Human Revolution: The Rise of a Mimetic Nation in Modern Japan* (Honolulu: University of Hawai`i Press, 2019). For Komeito's history, see George Ehrhardt et al., eds., *Kōmeitō: Politics and Religion in Japan* (Berkeley, CA: Institute for East Asian Studies, 2014).
10. This point is emphasized in Ehrhardt et al., eds., *Kōmeitō.*
11. For a history of the push for a "national ordination platform" in politically active Nichiren Buddhist circles, see Eiichi Ōtani, *Nichirenshugi to wa nan datta no ka: kindai Nihon no shisō suimyaku* (Tokyo: Kōdansha, 2019).
12. *New York Times,* May 13, 1964.
13. Kōmeitō, Transcript of founding declaration, 1964. See also Ehrhardt et al., eds., *Kōmeitō*, 67–68.
14. Jōsei Toda, *Kantōgenshū* (Tokyo: Sōka Gakkai, 1956), 204.
15. Kōmeitō, *Kōmeitō handobukku* (Tokyo: Kōmeitō, 1973), 44–45.
16. See Petter Lindgren, "Kōmeitō's Security Ideals and Collective Self-Defense: Betwixt Pacifism and Compromises," *East Asia* 33 (2016): 233–54, for a chronicle of Kōmeitō, Manifesto, http://www.komei.or.jp/campaign/sanin2019/_assets/pdf/manifesto2019.pdf.
17. Jun Nakano, *Sōka gakkai/Kōmeitō no kenkyū: jiko renritsu seiken no naizai ronri* (Tokyo: Iwanami Shoten, 2016), 68–69.
18. *Asahi shinbun,* January 21, 2004; Nakano, *Sōka gakkai/Kōmeitō no kenkyū,* 2016, 67–69.
19. Axel Klein, "Kōmeitō—Rock 'n' Roll the Coalition Boat," in *Japan Decides 2014*, edited by Robert J. Pekkanen, Ethan Scheiner, and Steven R. Reed (New York: Palgrave MacMillan, 2016); Klein and McLaughlin, "Kōmeitō 2017."
20. Kōmeitō, Manifesto, http://www.komei.or.jp/campaign/sanin2019/_assets/pdf/manifesto2019.pdf.
21. Adam Liff and Ko Maeda, "Electoral Incentives, Policy Compromise, and Coalition Durability: Japan's LDP-Komeito Government in a Mixed Electoral System," *Japanese Journal of Political Science* 20 (2019): 53–73.
22. Interview with sixth Soka Gakkai president Harada Minoru in *Asahi shinbun,* September 22, 2016.
23. https://www.indepthnews.net/index.php/opinion/2633-eminent-buddhist-leader-urges-halt-to-nuclear-weapons-and-killer-robots.
24. Coverage of Komeito's Soka Gakkai protesters and defenders appears in Levi McLaughlin, "Komeito's Soka Gakkai Protestors and Supporters: Religious Motivations for Political Activism in Contemporary Japan," *Asia-Pacific Journal: Japan Focus* 13, iIssue 41, no. 1 (2015).
25. Taichi Asayama, Uchigawa kara miru *Sōka gakkai to Kōmeitō* (Tokyo: Discovery Twenty-One, 2017).
26. http://sokauniv-nowar.mystrikingly.com/.

27. *Ryūkyū shinpō*, July 23, 2019.
28. All members interviewed here appear under pseudonyms.
29. Interview, November 1, 2018.
30. *Kōmei shinbun*, June 6, 2019.
31. Interview, December 17, 2018.
32. Interview, November 7, 2018.

REFERENCES

Asayama, Taichi. *Uchigawa kara miru Sōka gakkai to Kōmeitō*. Tokyo: Discovery Twenty-One, 2017.

Ehrhardt, George, Axel Klein, Levi McLaughlin, and Steven R. Reed, eds. *Kōmeitō: Politics and Religion in Japan*. Berkeley, CA: Institute for East Asian Studies, 2014.

Klein, Axel. "Kōmeitō—Rock 'n' Roll the Coalition Boat." In *Japan Decides 2014*, edited by Robert J. Pekkanen, Ethan Scheiner, and Steven R. Reed, 72–78. New York: Palgrave MacMillan, 2016.

Klein, Axel and Levi McLaughlin. "Kōmeitō 2017: New Complications." In *Japan Decides 2017*, edited by Robert J. Pekkanen, Ethan Scheiner, and Steven R. Reed, 53–76. New York: Palgrave Macmillan, 2018.

Kōmeitō. Transcript of founding declaration, 1964.

———. *Kōmeitō handobukku*. Tokyo: Kōmeitō, 1973.

———. Manifesto. 2019. http://www.komei.or.jp/campaign/sanin2019/_assets/pdf /manifesto2019.pdf.

Liff, Adam and Ko Maeda. "Electoral Incentives, Policy Compromise, and Coalition Durability: Japan's LDP-Komeito Government in a Mixed Electoral System." *Japanese Journal of Political Science* 20 (2019): 53–73.

Lindgren, Petter. "Kōmeitō's Security Ideals and Collective Self-Defense: Betwixt Pacifism and Compromises." *East Asia* 33 (2016): 233–254.

McLaughlin, Levi. "Komeito's Soka Gakkai Protestors and Supporters: Religious Motivations for Political Activism in Contemporary Japan." *Asia-Pacific Journal: Japan Focus* 13, issue 41, no. 1 (2015).

———. *Soka Gakkai's Human Revolution: The Rise of a Mimetic Nation in Modern Japan*. Honolulu: University of Hawai'i Press, 2019.

Nakano, Jun. *Sōka gakkai/Kōmeitō no kenkyū: jiko renritsu seiken no naizai ronri*. Tokyo: Iwanami Shoten, 2016.

Ōtani, Eiichi. *Nichirenshugi to wa nan datta no ka: kindai Nihon no shisō suimyaku*. Tokyo: Kōdansha, 2019.

Toda, Jōsei. *Kantōgenshū*. Tokyo: Sōka Gakkai, 1956.

Chapter Nine

Nippon Kaigi Working for Constitutional Revision

Helen Hardacre

Established in 1997, Nippon Kaigi is a group of politically engaged conservatives who devote themselves to changing Japan in a highly conservative direction. It is one of Japan's largest civil society organizations promoting constitutional revision. It has gained nationwide attention through mass meetings, petition campaigns, and lobbying among legislators. Nippon Kaigi attracts traditionalists who respect the monarchy, regard the educational system as too liberal, believe that Japan should strengthen its military defense, and hold that greater equality for women threatens family stability. Its sustained activism and relations with the Liberal Democratic Party (LDP) are shaping Japanese democracy. How strong is Nippon Kaigi, and what is the extent of its political influence? This essay examines Nippon Kaigi activism, emphasizing its ties with the Association of Shinto Shrines (Jinja Honchō), to understand its goals and assess its strength.

As of 2016, Nippon Kaigi had 38,000 members, including 280 MPs, roughly 1,700 local assembly members, and branch offices in every prefecture.[1] As of 2019, this organization had secured constitutional revision resolutions from 36 out of 47 prefectural assemblies, and from 59 municipal assemblies.[2] While Nippon Kaigi activism has been producing results like these at least since 2012, both journalistic and academic research have lagged behind. As late as 2014, newspapers generally did not cover Nippon Kaigi–sponsored events.[3] Beginning in 2016 with Tamotsu Sugano's *Research on Nippon Kaigi* (*Nippon Kaigi no kenkyū*), journalists and a few academics began researching the group, producing a number of popular books. These publications share a perspective warning against Nippon Kaigi as a dangerous "right-wing" organization, identifying its support for constitutional revision as proof of the characterization. Recent publications also see Nippon Kaigi as an icon of Japan's "rightward leaning tendency" (*ukei-ka*) and claim that it seeks to return Japan to its pre-surrender past.[4] Because the "right-wing" label is both pervasive and vague, it is important to clarify whether and in what sense Nippon Kaigi exemplifies Japan's right wing. Perhaps because Nippon Kaigi drew press attention only after it had already become a nationwide organization and had won significant support, writings tend to assume that there is something hidden and possibly sinister about it.

In an influential study of the right wing in postwar Japan, Yukio Hori described Nippon Kaigi as representing the vanguard of "the new right wing." Whereas the "old right wing" had largely been defined by its opposition to communism, with the fall of the Soviet Union and the subsequent hollowing out of communism as an actual form of government in the Soviet Union and the People's Republic of China, the right lost a major plank in its rationale. The new right wing emerged subsequently, differing from the old in a diminished anti-communism and adopting a diffuse and shifting list of conservative and traditionalist causes, closely allying with the LDP. Hori writes that the new right wing has not necessarily eschewed violence, but instead has adopted a more presentable appearance, wearing suits and appearing to be "softer" than its predecessors.[5]

Nippon Kaigi's stances on constitutional revision and other issues fall unquestionably on the far right of the political spectrum—and its spokespeople do wear suits—but the organization is not linked to criminal organizations, has not been charged with crimes, and remains aloof from rougher elements of the right wing, such as the Zaitokukai and its open promotion of hate speech against Koreans. While Nippon Kaigi has utilized the courts to dispute the claims made by Sugano Tamotsu in his book mentioned above, filing a lawsuit is a right enjoyed by anyone in a democracy. Though Nippon Kaigi may have rightist views, it is mistaken to associate it with the violent tactics and domestic terrorism utilized by some elements in the right wing.

Nevertheless, it is undeniable that Nippon Kaigi is widely perceived as a powerful right-wing group. A short report on a recent Nippon Kaigi event shows that the organization adopts various guises to attract participants who might react negatively if they knew that Nippon Kaigi was the sponsor. Nippon Kaigi's website announced a *mikoshi* parade to celebrate Emperor Akihito's thirty years on the throne, to be held in Yokohama on March 17, 2019, co-sponsored by a Shinto youth group associated with the Association of Shinto Shrines, the Shintō Seinen Kai. Neither sponsor's name was used in the event's announcements or signage, but a sound truck at the head of the parade instead explained that eight *mikoshi* clubs were staging the event. In other words, no one casually encountering this parade would have understood its connection with Nippon Kaigi or the shrine association.

Mikoshi are the portable shrines used in shrine festival processions.[6] *Mikoshi* clubs are volunteer hobby associations composed of people who enjoy parading the portable shrines, displaying their personal strength and panache. However, *mikoshi* clubs may have no ongoing relation to the shrines whose *mikoshi* they carry, simply arriving for the occasion and departing at the end. Those carrying the *mikoshi*, and the grandparents looking after their children, waving mini national flags and drawing up the tail of the parade, may also have been unaware that they would be counted as participants in a Nippon Kaigi event. At the opening ceremony, an organizer announced that some 3,900 people had registered, though observation and films suggested that no more than half that number were actually present. Later, the event was reported in Nippon Kaigi's monthly magazine *Nihon no Ibuki* as having drawn 5,000 people.[7] As this anecdote suggests, Nippon Kaigi has developed techniques that paradoxically can both understate and exaggerate its actual presence.

While the event organizer's manual specified the division of labor between Nippon Kaigi and the Association of Shinto Shrines, it seems odd that the organizers did not use the occasion to make their sponsorship known. The reason lies in this fact: if a person can name two organizations in Japan today that can be called "right wing" (*uyoku*), those two groups will be Nippon Kaigi and the Association of Shinto Shrines. The description "right wing" carries strong negative associations in society at large. Widespread public perception of Nippon Kaigi and the Association of Shinto Shrines as "right wing" has a reality and a significance in itself, quite apart from the policies and actual conduct of either organization.

NIPPON KAIGI'S POSITION ON THE CONSTITUTION

In 1992, the group issued a statement titled "Outline for a New Constitution" (revised 2001), proposing its preferred wording for articles on the emperor, defense, rights and duties of citizens, and emergency powers for the prime minister. In a significant departure from the current constitution, the draft names the emperor head of state (*genshu*), while also retaining "symbol of the unity of the people" as in the existing document. The draft also proposes that the emperor's ritual duties be further enumerated in the constitution and that respect for the emperor be codified. In place of Article 9, Nippon Kaigi's statement calls for a "national military" (*kokugun*) under the command of the prime minister. No restrictions regarding its deployment are mentioned. No substantial changes to the current constitution's positions on religious freedom or separation of religion from state are proposed in the draft. The statement instead calls on the state to respect, protect, and nurture the family as the basis of society.[8]

In addition to its public statements on the constitution, Nippon Kaigi has published more than twenty books, pamphlets, and DVDs on constitutional revision. Nippon Kaigi also advocates the 1890 *Imperial Rescript on Education* and reverence for the imperial family. It opposes allowing a woman to be named emperor, married women's use of their maiden names, and critical views of Japan's modern history prior to 1945.[9]

While this account of Nippon Kaigi's "Outline for a New Constitution," might suggest that its position on constitutional revision is clear, the "Outline" merely states the talking points on which all pro-revision organizations would more or less agree. Rather than pushing for adoption of its "Outline," Nippon Kaigi seems to accept the LDP's changing formulations about constitutional revision, sponsoring lectures by a variety of revisionists, each of whom is free to present a perspective within the general framework of revisionism. Perhaps to counter the perception that the leadership is composed mainly of men over seventy, the organization frequently features women lecturers. The organization and its prefectural branches also cooperate with auxiliary women's groups to sponsor lectures and other activities attuned to married women's interests. Lectures are presented in public forums across Japan, later uploaded to the Internet, or made available for sale as DVDs. A Nippon Kaigi forum in Tokyo on Constitution Day, 2019, illustrates the meeting style. First, the forum opened with a pre-recorded video message from Prime Minister Shinzō Abe, praising and encouraging the group. Then followed a keynote speech delivered by journalist Yoshiko Sakurai. A strong advocate of constitutional revision, Sakurai emphasized the suffering of the Japanese after "the late war" (*saki no taisen*) as the Allied Occupation schemed, she claimed, to crush the Japanese spirit, destroy the imperial system, and root out all pride in Japan's history and traditions. The constitution, she asserted, is the embodiment of this Occupation plot, yet not one word has been changed in the seven decades since its establishment. "Without constitutional revision, there can be no true rebirth of our country," she proclaimed.[10] As this summary suggests, Sakurai's remarks advocated no specific revision.

THE ORIGINS OF NIPPON KAIGI

Nippon Kaigi was formed by men who first became politically active within Seichō no Ie, a new religious movement founded in 1930 by Masaharu Taniguchi (1893–1985). Up to the time of the founder's death in 1985, Seichō no Ie had successfully supported its members standing for political office as

LDP candidates, promoted constitutional revision, lobbied to establish the Law on Reign Names (*Gengō Hō*; see below), and campaigned to criminalize abortion. In his 1972 book, *The Present Constitution: Source of All Evil* (*Shoaku no in, Gen kenpō*), Taniguchi had written that the Occupation drafters of the constitution planned to destroy Japan by weakening patriotism, undermining the family, and corrupting morality. This opinion was absorbed by activists in Seichō no Ie's Student Association (Seigakuren; from 1969 called Zenkoku Gakusei Jichitai Renraku Kyōgikai). After Taniguchi's death, however, Seichō no Ie withdrew from politics.[11]

Rightists who emerged from Seichō no Ie are among the most prominent people linked to Nippon Kaigi today. They include Yūzō Kabashima (b. 1945), Secretary-General of Nippon Kaigi; Kunio Suzuki (b. 1943), supreme advisor of the right-wing group Issuikai (founded 1972); Tetsuo Itō (b. 1947), Director of the Japan Policy Institute (Nihon Seisaku Kenkyū Sentā, founded 1984), a think tank that provides policy advice to the current LDP administration; and Shirō Takahashi (b. 1950), Professor at Meisei University and former vice-president of the Association to Create New History Textbooks.[12]

Kabashima pioneered a mobilization strategy that was to become a hallmark in Nippon Kaigi, the "Caravan Corps," drawing on religious groups to lobby politicians to give legal status to reign names. Using affiliates of the Association of Shinto Shrines and a variety of new religious movements as lobbyists, Nippon Kaigi secured resolutions in favor of a law on reign names from forty-six of the forty-seven prefectural assemblies and 1,632 city or town assemblies.[13] Since the public generally favored reign names and opposition was nil, the Caravan Campaign strategy chalked up a success in its first foray into national politics. Many like-minded groups, including right-leaning religious organizations, rallied around Kabashima.[14] When the People's Council to Protect Japan (Nihon o Mamoru Kokumin Kaigi) was founded in 1981, Kabashima was chosen as its Secretary-General, later becoming head of Nippon Kaigi in 1997.[15]

NIPPON KAIGI AND THE LIBERAL DEMOCRATIC PARTY

Nippon Kaigi aligns itself closely with the LDP, and it cultivates close ties with the prime minister. If the prime minister, who also holds the position of party president, were constrained by disparate views within his party, he might not be able to patronize a polarizing group like Nippon Kaigi, but current LDP prime ministers face no such constraint. Changes to election laws in 1994, combined with enhancement of the prime minister's powers in 2001, effectively nullified the influence of the intraparty factions that previously determined policy. Factions once acted to restrain the prime minister in power, because they included a variety of positions, which the party president/prime minister had to accommodate. Now largely freed of that limitation, however, the party president and the secretary-general exercise such power over selection of electoral candidates that politicians must fear that dissent could result in punishment or even expulsion. Thus, LDP politicians rarely express opposition to the premier's position on constitutional revision.[16]

Nippon Kaigi and former Prime Minister Abe are united in their determination to root out elements they find incompatible with Japanese "tradition." Both call for constitutional revision as a means to "restore" national pride rather than as a means to improve the quality of government, and both are resolved to draw a line between undefined Japanese "traditions" and universal standards, even if it means jettisoning the latter.[17] For Nippon Kaigi, constitutional revision symbolizes a vision of Japan as a nation anchored by the imperial house, rather than based on principles like human rights, pacifism, or popular sovereignty. Within that vision, the emperor's role is religious. He should perform ritual on behalf of the people rather than exercise governing powers over them (see below).

While the LDP and Nippon Kaigi are closely aligned, however, Nippon Kaigi occasionally criticizes the party. For example, Nippon Kaigi found it inappropriate that the LDP announced the new reign name, Reiwa, before enthronement ceremonial began, based on Shinto tradition holding that the reign name must not be revealed until a new emperor has been enthroned. Likewise, Nippon Kaigi criticizes government "dithering" in the face of armed attacks on Japanese tankers in the Persian Gulf, urging that Japan join the U.S.-led coalition to defend maritime security, Operation Sentinel.[18]

Personal contacts bridged the Abe administration and Nippon Kaigi. This is exemplified particularly well by Seiichi Etō (b. 1947), Minister for Okinawa and the Northern Territories, previously Special Advisor to the prime minister (*naikaku sōri daijin hosakan*). Reputed to be one of Abe's closest confidants, Etō is also the head of Nippon Kaigi's Diet members' study group on the imperial house (see below). He has lectured at Nippon Kaigi events for over a decade, encouraging its grass-roots activists to promote constitutional revision.[19] To have among its strongest allies a cabinet minister so close to the prime minister is undoubtedly a factor in Nippon Kaigi's ongoing ties to the LDP, but not all of those connections depend so directly on personal relationships.

Nippon Kaigi's regular interactions with the LDP take place on two levels: consultations with national-level legislators and bureaucrats, on the one hand, and organizing representatives in sub-national administrations to work for the organization's signature issues, on the other. In order to establish credibility at the national level, Nippon Kaigi has named recognized persons to its executive. For example, Tōru Miyoshi, former Chief Justice of the Supreme Court is Honorary Chairman. Former Prime Minister Abe is a "special advisor," and the head of the Association of Shinto Shrines, Korekiyo Tanaka, is a vice president.

Nippon Kaigi has created a group of affiliated MPs, most of whom belong to or generally support the LDP, called the Nippon Kaigi Diet Members' Association (Nippon Kaigi Kokkai Giin Kondankai). While the membership is not publicized, it was believed in 2016 to have about 280 members. This group hosts intra-Diet committees on constitutional revision, the emperor (headed by Etō Seiichi), the revision of textbooks to reflect Nippon Kaigi's preferred views on imperial Japan, the Yasukuni Shrine, the disputed islands, and other issues. According to Nippon Kaigi's website, the Diet members' association has held numerous meetings since 2013 on these and other rightist causes. Participation in these apparently ideologically neutral "study groups" allows Nippon Kaigi to establish ongoing consultations with the goverment, for example, by dispatching lecturers such as Hidetsugu Yagi [20] or Shirō Takahashi[21] to address a study group on a particular topic. Participating Diet members do not have to reveal their affiliation with Nippon Kaigi, and therefore can participate without alienating their constituents. These niche subgroups of Diet members help Nippon Kaigi to spread far-right views of the topic at hand, gain a kind of insider status with the government, and are seen as possessing significant expertise.[22]

Nippon Kaigi shapes the work of legislators in sub-national administrations through its League for Local Legislators (Chihō Giin Renmei), founded in 2007. As of 2016, this group had around 1,700 members. According to an interview with Yoshiko Matsuura, an assembly member for Suginami Ward in Tokyo, the league hosts an annual meeting to discuss the year's goal, attended by around 100 people. Each local branch subsequently receives monthly instructions. For example, Matsuura's job was to ensure that all members of the Ward Assembly signed a petition in favor of constitutional revision. Subgroups meet four or five times per year, and Suginami Ward's 100 members meet monthly. Matsuura reports that she receives some electioneering assistance from the league, but no funding.[23]

The LDP has recognized Nippon Kaigi for expertise on its signature issues, and that recognition has enhanced Nippon Kaigi's national prominence. The imperial abdication issue is a case in point. On August 8, 2016, Emperor Akihito took the unprecedented step of broadcasting a video message to the Japanese people, explaining his wish to abdicate in view of his advanced age and his heavy duties. With that, a political process began that resulted in the passage of a law allowing him to abdicate.[24] Prime Minister Abe convened a cabinet committee to compile a report making recommendations.[25] This committee was expected to endorse abdication, since it is unthinkable that the LDP would contravene imperial will. After "hearings" in which sixteen speakers chosen by the government presented their views, the committee report endorsed abdication for Akihito only, and that led to passage of the law on May 19, 2017, permitting the abdication.[26]

Sixteen "experts," fifteen men and one woman, with an average age of 74, were chosen to give testimony. Six of them, or 37 percent of the total, have been associated with Nippon Kaigi: Sukehiro Hirakawa, Akira Momochi, Shōichi Watanabe, Yasuo Ōhara, Hidetsugi Yagi, and Yoshiko Sakurai. Collectively, they told the committee that the emperor should remain in the palace and pray on behalf of the nation, and that abdication should be prohibited.

Hirakawa and Watanabe stoutly opposed abdication and suggested appointing a regent. As the emperor is Shinto's principal "successor" (*kōkeisha*), his role in praying for the country has higher priority than any other activities he may choose to undertake.[27] The emperor's job is to pray on behalf of the people; his principal duty is ritual, and if he finds this burden too onerous, the Crown Prince should be appointed regent.[28]

Momochi is one of the closest advisors to former Prime Minister Abe.[29] He is a frequent speaker for Nippon Kaigi, having entered that group via Seichō no Ie, as well as an officer in the Society to Answer the War Dead (Eirei ni Kotaeru Kai), which favors state support for the Yasukuni Shrine.[30] Momochi stressed the importance of imperial ritual, also calling on the emperor to act in a way that truly unifies the people, suggesting that Akihito's manner of enacting the symbol monarchy was divisive.[31]

Ōhara is a linchpin linking Nippon Kaigi and the Association of Shinto Shrines. He is best known for his 1993 book providing line-by-line analysis of all five drafts of the 1945 Shinto Directive, an Occupation order that ended state support of Shinto shrines, which has been the object of undying hatred among Shinto activists ever since.[32] Ōhara stressed the urgent need to overcome the mistaken view that palace ritual is a private matter of the imperial family and does not belong to the emperor's official public duties (*kōmu*).

Yagi described the emperor as the "Supreme Commander" of the nation, whose principal significance lies in his continued existence and performance of ritual. If abdication is permitted, what is to prevent future emperors from being *pressured* to abdicate?[33]

It is no exaggeration to describe Sakurai as Nippon Kaigi's most prominent female representative.[34] She is well known for her opposition to feminism in any form, her keen desire to upgrade the Self-Defense Force to a full-scale military, her support for nuclear power no matter what the safety concerns, and advocacy for constitutional revision.[35] Like the others above, Sakurai stressed the primacy of palace rites above any other activity, speaking of the emperor as the country's center and its "great ritual master" (*Nihon no chūshin ni dai saishu*). All he need do is continue to exist as ritual master. There is no reason for him to do anything else. The constitution and the Imperial Household Code must be revised to make clear that ritual is the emperor's highest duty, coming before anything else.

The Abe administration's decision to choose so many Nippon Kaigi affiliates to give expert testimony handed Nippon Kaigi a plum soapbox and boosted its influence. If in the future a referendum on constitutional revision is held, a similar setup of "experts" testifying before a blue-ribbon Cabinet committee will be part of the scenario, and Nippon Kaigi spokespeople would likely be chosen again and given another premier opportunity to influence national discourse.

NIPPON KAIGI AND THE ASSOCIATION OF SHINTO SHRINES

From the beginning of the twentieth century, organizations of shrine priests, shrine stewards,[36] corporate sponsors, and ordinary people drawn from shrine communities have organized and lobbied for shrine-related causes. Before 1945, the National Association of Shrine Priests (Zenkoku Shinshoku Kai) cultivated Diet members by visiting their offices, hosting them at fancy restaurants, and lobbying them to pass resolutions calling for greater funding for shrines, funds to promote priests' professional development, and creation of a special branch of government for shrine administration. The shrine priests' association frequently sent friendly politicians on lecture tours of regional shrines, where they would praise the association, promote its causes, and become informed on the actual needs of shrine priests and their communities. When shrine-related issues were to be disussed in the Diet, the friendly politicians would arrange for the association's leadership to be invited to give expert testimony. Beginning in the 1930s, the association also cultivated ties with business and the military, inviting high-ranking figures to lecture, and donating funds for the purchase of military aircraft. Meanwhile, the association received donations from such firms (or their foundations) as Mitsui, Mitsubishi, and the Yasuda *zaibatsu*.[37]

This tradition of activism continued when the shrine priests reconstituted after the war as the Association of Shinto Shrines, enjoying success in influencing the Allied Occupation's land reform as it affected shrines, the Law on Reign Names, and the establishment of Foundation Day. The Association was deeply committed to re-establishing state support for the Yasukuni Shrine, but in spite of energetic campaigning, that effort failed. Through this experience, the Association gained important experience for its future dealings with the LDP, concluding that the LDP had cynically used the Yasukuni issue to energize its most conservative supporters but had not been willing to expend political capital sufficient to push the bill through the Diet.

In 1969, the shrine association created its own group of MPs who supported its positions, called Shinto Seiji Renmei, or Association of Spiritual Leadership [their preferred translation], "Shinseiren" for short. As of 2016, there were 304 MPs in this group, 223 in the Lower House and 81 in the Upper House, making it larger than Nippon Kaigi's Diet Members' Association, though there is significant member overlap.

If we compare Nippon Kaigi and the Assocation of Shinto Shrines, the shrine group is older, larger, and more cohesive. It differs from Nippon Kaigi in that its membership is rooted in attachment to shrines as symbols of home, family, honor, and nation, all bundled together as "Japanese tradition." Strong religious and patriotic sentiments pervade membership in this organization, and its activists are deeply committed. While some priests may question why their association spends so much time and resources on politics, few express dissent openly. Its activists have decades of experience transcending the organization's links with Nippon Kaigi.

Examining their approaches to a shared issue reveals parallel activism between Nippon Kaigi and the Association of Shinto Shrines, employing some of the same spokespeople and talking points. Both organizations began to attack the Basic Law on Gender Equality (*Danjo kyōdō sanga kihon hō*) soon after its enactment in 1999. Nippon Kaigi's opposition took on new intensity in 2002, when Tōru Miyoshi became the head of the organization. Nippon Kaigi used its monthly publication *Nihon no Ibuki* to publish such articles as "Spouses Using Separate Surnames Destroys Childrearing." This was followed in May by an "emergency meeting" on the issue. The October, November, and December issues each carried articles attacking the gender equality law.[38]

Meanwhile, the newspaper of the Association of Shinto Shrines, *Jinja Shinpō*, began an all-out attack in November 2002, reporting on a lecture by Shirō Takahashi, who told a meeting of the Japan Women's Group (Nihon Josei no Kai) held at the Meiji Shrine, that Japan's original culture (*koyū no bunka*) was being undermined by the notion that women can choose whether or not to bear children. In February 2003, *Jinja Shinpō* again covered Takahashi's ideas, titling the article "Gender Equality Running Wild." Takahashi took aim at educational policies promoting gender equality in Chiba Prefecture, whose governor at the time was female.[39] In May 2003, Nippon Kaigi's

Nihon no Ibuki interviewed Takahashi, titling the article "The Time Bomb Set to Destroy Motherhood." In each issue for the remainder of the year, *Nihon no Ibuki* carried articles aiming to undermine the gender equality law, promoting "traditional" ideas of masculinity and femininity as central to the development of the infant brain, and also criticizing day care as a danger to young children. Several symposia were held, one of them titled "The Gender Equality Law Will Lead to Women's Unhappiness," featuring Eriko Yamatani, a female rightist MP and frequent speaker for the Association of Shinto Shrines.[40] Other ideologues shared by the two organizations include Michiyoshi Hayashi, purveyor of "junk science," claiming for the Association of Shinto Shrines that the infant brain cannot develop without firm distinctions between male and female, while promoting the view for Nippon Kaigi that the constitution will destroy the family.

The effects of this parallel activism are to create multiple outlets for opposition to gender equality, lend credibility to rightist ideologues, and make opposition to gender equality appear widespread. Examination of the sources reveals, however, that a small number of figures making the same arguments is simply being recycled. A central purpose behind both organizations' push for constitutional revision is to undermine the postwar progressive gains that women have achieved.

Involving the shrine association makes it possible for Nippon Kaigi to ask large, wealthy shrines for monetary support, and not just the shrines but their governing boards, where larger shrines typically have significant corporate representation. A more detailed understanding of this relationship emerges through an interview with Masato Ishikawa, Head Priest (*Gūji*) of Moro-oka Kumamo Jinja (*Moro-oka Kumano Jinja*) in Yokohama, and head of the Kanagawa Prefectural branch of Shinseiren. Like Kabashima and Etō, he first became involved in politics as a student, angered by leftists who had hurled Molotov cocktails at the Kokugakuin University shrine used by young priests-in-training like himself. Yasuo Ōhara became the faculty spokesperson for this issue.[41]

Nippon Kaigi is currently campaigning to collect ten million signatures in favor of constitutional revision, with cooperation from the prefectural branches of the Association of Shinto Shrines. Kanagawa Prefecture's share is 400,000, and as of 2016, Ishikawa and his colleagues had collected 280,000 (almost 80 percent). There are around 80,000 shrines in Japan, but less than 10 percent of them set out the petition signature forms for constitutional revision, Ishikawa said. The plan is to use those forms (which ask for the signer's name and telephone number) as a call list if a national referendum on constitutional revision is ever held. Head Priest Ishikawa estimated that perhaps 15 to 20 percent of Kanagawa priests are relatively active in Nippon

Kaigi. We cannot know for certain whether his estimate is accurate, but if it is, and if we use it to calculate how many activist shrine priests there might be nationwide, based on a total of 25,295 shrine priests, we can "guesstimate" that there may be as many as 2,530 to 3,794 activist priests in the country as a whole.[42] These numbers may, however, be significantly inflated. Recalling the *mikoshi* parade anecdote near the beginning of this essay, Head Priest Ishikawa was the person who claimed a number in attendance that was probably twice the actual participants.

Head Priest Ishikawa is confident that if the Association of Shinto Shrines were asked to assemble ten thousand to twenty thousand people to attend some Nippon Kaigi meeting, it would have no problem meeting the goal, mobilizing not only priests but also shrine stewards and other shrine supporters. The local prefectural shrine association would be asked to produce a number proportional to the prefecture's population, and the prefectural Shinseiren would contribute 30 to 40 percent of the cost of renting a hall. Any money that the Association of Shinto Shrines or its prefectural branches can collect, however, comes from the largest and richest shrines. At the national level, that includes such shrines as the Meiji Shrine or the Ise Grand Shrines, while each prefecture has its own hierarchy of shrines that could be asked for contributions on a smaller scale. Donations may also come from shrine stewards (some of whom are businessmen), but not the priests, and donations cannot be drawn directly from a shrine's operating budget.

Ishikawa denied that Nippon Kaigi or the Association of Shinto Shrines seeks to "return to prewar Japan." Virtually no shrine priest today has any personal memory of prewar or wartime Japan, nor would they willingly submit to the level of government supervision imposed on shrines before the surrender. Shrine priests' concerns today are largely economic. Some large proportion of Japan's smaller, rural shrines are barely surviving, and their priests have neither time nor disposable income to devote to political activism. Because shrine communities encompass people across the spectrum of political opinion, priests have to avoid alienating their affiliates by aligning with a polarizing issue or organization, and as Ishikawa pointed out, only a small minority of shrine priests are drawn to political activism.

There are Nation-Protecting Shrines (*gokoku jinja*) in every prefecture except Kanagawa, and as the places where the war dead from the prefecture are enshrined, they have a special connection to the Yasukuni Shrine, the national shrine for the war dead. Nippon Kaigi jointly hosts events honoring the war dead with some Nation-Protecting Shrines, timed to coincide with Yasukuni Shrine's spring and autumn festivals for those spirits, and especially on August 15, the anniversary of Japan's World War II surrender. Nippon Kaigi is particularly active in Okayama Prefecture and has ten branch organizations there. The branch in Okayama City maintains close connections with the prefecture's Nation-Protecting Shrine (Okayama-ken Gokoku Jinja), crossposting each other's events on their websites. Nippon Kaigi sends its officials to shrine ceremonies, where they may give short addresses and greetings, alongside prefectural representatives to the Diet, prefectural assembly, and city council. Placing Nippon Kaigi representatives in the lineup of politicians normalizes the connection with the shrine and presents an image of Nippon Kaigi as playing a constructive role in shrine ceremonial, local politics, and society.

Nippon Kaigi's 33rd Annual Memorial for the War Dead at Yasukuni Shrine (*Senbotsusha tsuitō chūō kokumin shūkai*), held on August 15, 2019, illustrates how the pattern seen in Okayama operates at the national level. Nippon Kaigi President Tadae Takubo and Yoshiko Sakurai both spoke, appealing to the audience of 1,500 to support constitutional revision. Takubo sounded an alarm, saying that Japan is at a great turning point, because "America has changed," citing Donald Trump's criticism of the U.S.-Japan Security Treaty, to the effect that if the U.S. were attacked, the Japanese would "stay home watching their Sony TVs." Trump's remark, Takubo said, gets at the heart of the greatest defect of the treaty, its lack of reciprocity. Takubo went on to say that the Abe government's indecision on joining a coalition to defend shipping in the Strait of Hormuz is a great disgrace—even the Koreans have joined up, drawing applause when he asked the audience if they weren't ashamed to hear that. He concluded by saying that the constitution is an obstacle to the rightful defense of Japan and should speedily be revised. Following Takubo, Sakurai called on the audience to vow to work for constitutional revision and to build a peaceful, "courageous country" (*yūki aru kuni*).[43] As is typically the case with Nippon Kaigi speakers, neither Takubo nor Sakurai called for any specific revision to the constitution, emphasizing instead the urgency of the need for revision in some form.

Nippon Kaigi activism is proceeding at local, municipal, prefectural, and national levels, capped by resolutions for constitutional revision. Nippon Kaigi has built a nationwide network, in which shrines act as nodes, communicating Nippon Kaigi's message to the local level.

While relations with shrines are very important to Nippon Kaigi, however, one should not exaggerate the connection. Surveying reports of 100 Nippon Kaigi events in 2019, only eleven took place in shrines or were co-sponsored by shrine organizations. On the other hand, *Nihon no Ibuki* recently published seasonal greetings from 235 affiliated groups and individuals. Of them, 105 (45 percent) came from shrine personnel or shrine-related groups.[44]

Constitutional revision activism aimed at women is a major part of Nippon Kaigi's grassroots organizing. To cite a single example combining women's activism with shrine connections, a female shrine priest founded the organization's Iwate Prefecture women's group, called Nihon Josei no Kai, Iwate. Head Priest Akiko Suzuki is also the vice president of the prefectural women shrine priests' association. She holds meetings in her shrine, Ōmiya Jinja, where women gather to discuss constitutional revision "from a mother's perspective."[45] By such means, Nippon Kaigi objectives may come to be seen as overlapping with Shinto.

While Nippon Kaigi's current focus is constitutional revision, as we have seen, this issue is inseparable from the organization's vision for the monarchy and gender relations. Nippon Kaigi activists are committed to the long haul, and they have made great headway, thanks to their interactions with government. The organization has been rewarded by the LDP, which recognizes Nippon Kaigi spokespersons as experts on topics of national significance. That recognition is transmitted to each political forum where the group is active, and through shrines to the local level of society across the country. In this way, Nippon Kaigi is weaving itself into the fabric of Japanese society and politics and becoming a powerful force shaping Japanese democracy.

NOTES

1. Osamu Aoki, *Nippon Kaigi no shōtai* (Tokyo: Heibonsha, 2016), 31, 46, 51.
2. Nippon Kaigi, *Pride of Japan*, accessed August 20, 2019, http://prideofjapan.blog10.fc2.com/.
3. Kei Satō, "Heito supīchi, goku-u seijika Nippon Kaigi—tokuhōbu no genba kara," in *Nihon no ukeika: Nani ga doko made susunde iru no ka?*, ed. Hotaka Tsukada (Tokyo: Chikuma shobō, 2017), 63.
4. Tamotsu Sugano, *Nippon Kaigi no kenkyū* (Tokyo: Fusōsha, 2016). The major book-length publications on Nippon Kaigi are usefully discussed in Saitō Masami, Nogawa Motokazu, and Hayakawa Tadanori, with an introduction by Sven Saaler, "Dissecting the Wave of Books on Nippon Kaigi, the Rightwing Mass Movement That Threatens Japan's Future," *The Asia-Pacific Journal, Japan Focus* 16, issue 19, no. 1 (October 2018): 1–33.
5. Yukio Hori, *Zōho sengo no uyoku seiryoku* (Tokyo: Keisōsho, 1983, 1994), 275.
6. For the initial announcement of the event, see http://www.nipponkaigi.org/event/archives/11528. For film of the event posted online, see http://www.youtube.com/watch?v=vhv5kTreLVU and http://www.youtube.com/watch?v=IxnNADvNHsM.
7. *Nihon no Ibuki* 378 (May 2019), 6.
8. "Shin kenpō taikō," *Nippon Kaigi*, revised February 11, 2001, http://www.nipponkaigi.org/opinion/archives/8502.
9. For extensive treatment of Nippon Kaigi's understanding of each of these issues, see Satoshi Uesugi, *Nippon Kaigi to wa nanika: Kenpōkaisei ni tsuki susumu karuto-shūdan* (Tokyo: *Gōdō shuppan*, 2016) and Yoshifumi Tawara, *Nippon Kaigi no zenbō. Shirurezaru kyodatsoshiki no jittai* (Tokyo: Kadensha, 2016).

10. "Sakurai Yoshiko-shi, 'Kenpō kaisei naku shite waga kuni no saisei wa nai,'" *Sankei shinbun*, May 3, 2019, http://www.sankei.com/politics/news/190503/plt 1905030027-n1.html. The event, including Abe's address, was covered in a video posted to YouTube, accessed May 9, 2019, no longer available.

11. Seichō no Ie's website suggests that environmental issues are its principal concern now: http://www.jp.seicho-no-ie.org/, accessed December 28, 2016.

12. Kōji Sonoda, "Nippon Kaigi and Grassroots Mobilization of Japan's Right Wing," *Program on US-Japan Relations Occasional Papers* (Harvard University, 2015). For biographical data on persons associated with Nippon Kaigi, see Yūki Endō, *Nippon Kaigi no jinmyaku*, Sansai mook, vol. 899 (Tokyo: Sansai Books, 2016).

13. Aoki, *Nippon Kaigi*, 164–66; Sonoda, "Nippon Kaigi and Grassroots Mobilization," 34

14. Aoki, *Nippon Kaigi*, 164–66.

15. Kabashima expresses his goals for Nippon Kaigi in a video posted on YouTube, accessed December 29, 2016, no longer available.

16. Arthur Stockwin and Kweku Ampiah, *Rethinking Japan: The Politics of Contested Nationalism* (Lanham, MD: Lexington Books/New Studies in Modern Japan, 2017), 76–84.

17. Stockwin and Ampiah, *Rethinking Japan*, 82–85.

18. Remarks by Nippon Kaigi President Tadae Takubo at Yasukuni Shrine, at the 33rd Annual People's Central Convocation to Honor the War Dead (*Senbotsusha tsuitō chūō kokumin shūkai*), accessed August 16, 2019, http://www.nipponkaigi.org /activity/archives/11088.

19. A recent example is Etō's address on Foundation Day, 2019, on "Building a Strong Japan" (*Tsuyoi Nihon o tsukuru tame ni*) at a Nippon Kaigi forum in Fukuyama City, Hiroshima Prefecture.

20. Past president of an association to reform history textbooks in order to promote pride in the Japanese empire, Yagi, who holds an appointment at Reitaku University, is a member of a working group on the civil code in the Ministry of Justice's legislative council and the Cabinet Secretary's Council on Implementing a Rebirth of Education (*Kyōiku Saisei Jikkō Kaigi*); see Saitō et al., "Dissecting the Wave of Books on Nippon Kaigi," 15. Yagi has also served as an expert witness for the prime minister's committee on the Heisei emperor's abdication. Yagi was opposed to abdication and is a frequent speaker for Nippon Kaigi.

21. Takahashi Shirō, of Meisei University, has twice been appointed to experts' conferences on gender equality in the Cabinet Office. Formerly associated with Seichō no Ie and as a strong opponent of abortion, Takahashi is a frequent speaker for both the Association of Shinto Shrines and Nippon Kaigi, specializing in their efforts to defeat law and social policy promoting gender equality; see Helen Hardacre, "After Aum: Religion and Civil Society in Japan," in *The State of Civil Society in Japan*, eds. Frank J. Schwartz and Susan J. Pharr (Cambridge, UK: Cambridge University Press, 2003), 242–43.

22. Yasmin Bottos, "Right-Wing Nationalist Groups in Japan: The Insider-Outsider Dichotomy" (Final Honours Thesis, University of Adelaide, 2015).

23. Aoki, *Nippon Kaigi*, 51–59.

24. See the poll by *Tokyo shinbun*, May 2, 2017. See also the most recent poll, which found 90 percent approving the abdication: "2017-nen 6-gatsu denwa zenkoku yoron chōsa shitsumon to kaitō," *Yomiuri shinbun*, June 19, 2017, https://www.yomiuri.co.jp/election/yoron-chosa/20190630-OYT1T50184/.

25. The committee's title was *Tennō no kōmu no futan keigen tō ni kansuru yūshikisha kaigi* (Council on Easing the Burdens of the Emperor's Public Duties). See this website for transcripts of each of its 14 meetings: "Tennō no kōmu no futan keigen tō ni kansuru yūshikisha kaigi," *Shushō Kantei*, http://www.kantei.go.jp/jp/singi/koumu_keigen/kaisai.html.

26. The special law regarding the Emperor's abdication was passed after the approval in the House of Councillors on June 9 and proclaimed on June 16. The original copy and detailed summary of the law are available on this government website: "Tennō no tai'i tō ni kansuru Kōshitsu Tenpan tokurei hō ni tsuite," updated March 9, 2018, http://www.kantei.go.jp/jp/headline/taii_tokurei.html.

27. This site provides a detailed summary of the views expressed by each of the sixteen speakers: "Yūshikisha hiaringu de hyōmei sareta iken ni tsuite," December 7, 2016, http://www.kantei.go.jp/jp/singi/koumu_keigen/dai6/sankou2.pdf. Hirakawa's views are summarized on page 1.

28. Watanabe's views are summarized at: "Yūshikisha hiaringu," 8.

29. "Nippon Kaigi kenkyū, kenpō-hen: Ka, Kazoku sonchō, jōbun meiki o shuchō," *Asahi shinbun* (March 25, 2016).

30. On Momochi's position in Eirei ni Kotaeru Kai, see http://eireinikotaerukai.com/concept/organization.html. For his activities in support of Nippon Kaigi, see the following sites: https://www.nipponkaigi.org/opinion/archives/3071, https://www.nipponkaigi.org/opinion/archives/5114, https://www.nipponkaigi.org/activity/archives/5983, https://www.nipponkaigi.org/activity/archives/4512, https://www.nipponkaigi.org/publication/book.

31. Momochi's testimony is summarized at: "Yūshikisha hiaringu," 17–18.

32. Yasuo Ōhara, *Shintō shirei no kenkyū* (Tokyo: Hara shobō, 1993). Ōhara's testimony is summarized at: "Yūshikisha hiaringu," 5.

33. Yagi's views are summarized at: "Yūshikisha hiaringu," 15–16.

34. Sakurai's testimony is summarized at "Yūshikisha hiaringu," 12.

35. See Sakurai's personal home page: http://yoshiko-sakurai.jp.

36. Shrine stewards (*ujiko sōdai*) are elected by a shrine's community (the *ujiko*) to assist the priest in the management and maintenance of a shrine. There are typically three to five stewards for small shrines, and a large shrine may have hundreds of them. Stewards generally make significant financial contributions to the shrine as well as commitments of time. A large shrine usually solicits representatives of local business to serve as stewards, as well as representatives of families who have provided stewards over generations.

37. Zenkoku Shinshoku Kai, *Zenkoku Shinshoku Kai Enkaku yō* (Tokyo: Zenkoku Shinshoku Kai, 1935), 77–141. See the timeline for the organization's history.

38. See the following articles published in *Nihon no Ibuki* during 2002: Michiko Hasegawa, "Fūfu bessei-sei wa kosodate o hakai suru" (February); Michiyoshi Hayashi, "Kenpō ga kazoku o hakai suru" (May); "Fūfu bessei dōnyū hantai kinkyū

shūkai repōto" (May); Hitoshi Nitta, "Danjo kyōdō sanga shakai, undō no shōtai-1" (October); Hitoshi Nitta, "Danjo kyōdō sanga shakai, undō no shōtai-2" (November); Hitoshi Nitta, "Danjo kyōdō sanga shakai, undō no shōtai-3" (December); "Danjo kyōdō sanga mondai de kokkai shitsugi, Naikakufu ga tsūchi" (December).

39. Shirō Takahashi, "Otokorashisha, onnarashisa: Nihon Josei no Kai setsuritsu isshū nen," *Jinja shinpō* 2670 (November 4, 2002). Shirō Takahashi, "Bōsō suru jendā-furii," *Jinja shinpō* 2683 (February 17, 2003).

40. Shirō Takahashi interview: "Shikakerareta bosei hōkai no jigen bakudan" *Nihon no Ibuki* (May 2003); Harumi Kimura, "Otokorashisa, onnarashisa no kachi," (June 2003); Toshiyuki Sawaguchi, "Yōji kyōiku ga nō o tsukuru" (August 2003); "Kyōiku shinpojyūmu: Ikuji no shakaika ga kodomo o kuzusu," (October 2003); "Shinpojyūmu: Josei o fukō ni suru Danjo Kyōdō Sanga Jōrei" (November 2003).

41. Aoki, *Nippon Kaigi*, 126–46.

42. Bunka-chō, *Shūkyō Nenkan*, 2018. This figure is current as of the end of 2017; of this total, 4,766 were women, and nine were non-Japanese.

43. Video coverage of the ceremony is available here: https://www.youtube.com/watch?v=GnWzwQ5yGCU uploaded August 16, 2019, accessed August 20, 2019.

44. *Nihon no Ibuki* 381 (August 2019), 38–46.

45. *Nihon no Ibuki* 377 (April 2019), 26–27.

REFERENCES

Aoki, Osamu. *Nippon Kaigi no shōtai*. Tokyo: Heibonsha, 2016.

Bottos, Yasmin. "Right-Wing Nationalist Groups in Japan: The Insider-Outsider Dichotomy." Final Honours Thesis, University of Adelaide, 2015.

Endō, Yūki, ed. *Nippon Kaigi no jinmyaku*. *Sansai mukku* 899. Tokyo: Sansai bukkusu, 2016.

Hardacre, Helen. "After Aum: Religion and Civil Society in Japan." In *The State of Civil Society in Japan*, edited by Frank J. Schwartz and Susan J. Pharr. Cambridge, UK: Cambridge University Press, 2003.

———. "Constitutional Revision and Japanese Religions." *Japanese Studies* 25, no. 3 (December 2005): 235–43.

———. *Shinto: A History*. New York: Oxford University Press, 2016.

Hori, Yukio. *Zōho Sengo no uyoku seiryoku*. Tokyo: Keisōsho, 1983, 1994.

Nihon no Ibuki 377 (April 2019): 26–27.

———. 378 (May 2019): 6.

———. 381 (August 2019): 38–46.

Ōhara, Yasuo. *Shintō shirei no kenkyū*. Tokyo: Hara shobō, 1993.

Saitō, Masami, Nogawa Motokazu, and Hayakawa Tadanori, with introduction by Sven Saaler. "Dissecting the Wave of Books on Nippon Kaigi, the Rightwing Mass Movement That Threatens Japan's Future." *The Asia-Pacific Journal, Japan Focus* 16, issue 19, no. 1 (October 2018): 1–33.

Satō, Kei. "Heito supīchi, goku-u seijika Nippon Kaigi—tokuhōbu no genba kara." In *Nihon no ukeika: Nani ga doko made susunde iru no ka?*, edited by Hotaka Tsukada. Tokyo: Chikuma shobō, 2017.

Sonoda, Kōji. "Nippon Kaigi and Grassroots Mobilization of Japan's Right Wing." *Program on US-Japan Relations Occasional Papers.* Harvard University, 2015.

Stockwin, Arthur and Kweku Ampiah. *Rethinking Japan: The Politics of Contested Nationalism*. Lanham, MD: Lexington Books/New Studies in Modern Japan, 2017.

Sugano, Tamotsu. *Nippon Kaigi no kenkyū*. Tokyo: Fusōsha, 2016.

Takahashi Shirō, "Bōsō suru jendā-furii," *Jinja shinpō* 2683 (February 17, 2003).

———. "Otokorashisha, onnarashisa: Nihon Josei no Kai setsuritsu isshū nen," *Jinja shinpō* 2670 (November 4, 2002).

Tawara, Yoshifumi. *Nippon Kaigi no zenbō: Shirarezaru kyodaisoshiki no jittai*. Tokyo: Kadensha, 2016.

Uesugi, Satoshi. *Nippon Kaigi to wa nanika: Kenpōkaisei ni tsuki susumu karuto-shūdan.* Tokyo: Gōdō shuppan, 2016.

Zenkoku Shinshoku Kai. *Zenkoku Shinshoku Kai Enkaku yō*. Tokyo: Zenkoku Shinshoku Kai, 1935.

Chapter Ten

Reflections on Part II

Helen Hardacre

These essays in Part II present a spectrum of civic activism supporting, opposing, or ambivalent about constitutional revision, mostly concentrating on the years 2012 to 2020, the second administration of Shinzō Abe.[1] Activism on the left has evolved from the orientation seen during the 1960s and 1970s that presupposed an unending struggle between conservative and progressive views of the good society. With the decline of organized labor, contemporary progressive activism now centers within student groups coalescing for intense, short-term counterculture demonstrations, dissolving once some proximate goal has been met or defeated (Ueda, Nakano, this volume). The exception is feminist activism aiming at gender equality in politics. Feminist activism has consistently focused on "the long haul," with activists prepared for sustained struggle to reform the electoral system (Miura). On the right, activists are likewise entrenched for the long durée, working toward achieving a constitution based on "Japanese values," free of the taint of military defeat and occupation. Umbrella organizations like SEALDs and Nippon Kaigi work with their affiliates in flexible constellations that may not articulate a clear guiding vision or require anyone to make long-term commitments.

The essays of Part II illustrate the centrality of religious organizations in civic activism around constitutional revision (McLaughlin, Hardacre). Nippon Kaigi's alliance with the Association of Shinto Shrines and numerous smaller new religious movements is crucial to Nippon Kaigi activism, enabling it to appear to be a mass movement, and undermining unpleasant associations with the right wing. Sōka Gakkai members, who had been a dependable electioneering force and source of block votes for the LDP/Kōmeitō coalition, are increasingly disaffected from Kōmeitō, with one maverick even running for election against the head of Kōmeitō. Other Sōka Gakkai members disappointed with Kōmeitō's toadying to the LDP on constitutional revision have defected to the new political party Reiwa Shinsengumi.

As Ueda points out, leadership of contemporary activist groups is acephalous, functioning through loose coalitions of the like-minded. Authoritative spokespeople play prominent roles but without necessarily assuming official positions. On the left, historians, constitutional law scholars, writers, and public intellectuals are magnets for recruitment and promotion. On the right, politicians from the LDP, a variety of conservative legal scholars, and media personalities play similar roles. Oddly, we find some activists who support revision by appearing regularly at Nippon Kaigi meetings, such as Yoshiko Sakurai, disavowing the group when politically expedient.

While groups involved in recent periods of intense activism such as the 2014–15 passage of new security laws appear from the outside to lack visible leadership, on both the left and right they are capable of highly effective organizing, turning out tens of thousands to demonstrate in front of the Diet building (opposing revision), to fill the seats of mass meetings (promoting revision), or to lobby successfully in virtually every prefectural assembly and many city councils for resolutions in favor of revision. On the left, organizing relies heavily on social media, while on the right, tight organization stems from the authoritarian character of leadership in the religious groups involved, a factor that also operates in Sōka Gakkai's electioneering for the LDP.

Activist groups differ in terms of the strength of their efforts to transmit their views to younger generations. Activists on the left include many educators, and short-term projects to educate the young on the importance of preserving the constitution in its present form are frequently carried out, especially at times of intense activism. However, outside feminist circles, ongoing programs of education and youth recruitment are few. On the right, we see a much more sustained commitment to recruit and indoctrinate the young. Shrine-based organizations and new religious movements affiliated with Nippon Kaigi will undoubtedly provide the activists of the next generation. These organizations promote their views to youth through sermons, public meetings, retreats, periodicals, books, *manga*, DVDs, websites, YouTube channels, and other forms of online media.

There are significant differences among activist organizations in terms of geographical coverage. SEALDs and other progressive groups are mainly located in the cities, while the Article 9 Association has branches in every prefecture, but with some decline in activity since 2014–15. Nippon Kaigi has branches in every prefecture (sometimes several), often with strong connections to shrines for the war dead (the prefectural *gokoku jinja*) and other shrine-based organizations. While the universities serve as nodes for progressive activism, shrine-based groups play an analogous role on the right.

Transnational connections are an important facet of progressive activism (Nakano, Miura, this volume), but such connections are absent on the right. Participation in international meetings over the postwar decades has connected Japanese feminists with international feminist networks. Miura shows that Japanese feminists' participation over the postwar decades in international summits, including but not limited to those sponsored by or related to the United Nations, has provided a wealth of experience, connections, and strategies that proved useful in the 2018 passage of Japan's Gender Parity Law. Student activists like SEALDs maintain connections with a variety of progressive movements outside Japan. By contrast, activist groups promoting constitutional revision are motivated by nativist sentiments that are not compatible with transnational cooperation. While many countries are revising their constitutions, with the exception of Russia, most are proceeding from progressive motives out of tune with the nativism at the base of pro-revision activism in Japan. Distaste for the U.S. role in the composition of the Japanese constitution remains strong and probably acts as an additional factor militating against transnational connections on the right.

A variety of groups have compiled drafts for a new constitution (Winkler, this volume), including the main organizations discussed in this Part: Kōmeitō, Nippon Kaigi, and the LDP.[2] For all concerned, however, the specific articles to be revised are less important than the victory that would be symbolized by (for revisionists) achieving *some* revision, or the defeat signaled by failure to prevent *any* revision (for opponents). After the LDP disavowed its 2012 draft, it substituted four points for revision, of which only one receives strong party support: inscribing the Self-Defense Force in Article 9, so that no future lawsuits can challenge the force's constitutionality. Kōmeitō continues to mention its idea of changing the constitution by adding new rights, but only as a brake to the LDP; Kōmeitō has not expended significant resources in order to actualize its stated goals for constitutional revision, leading observers to question the strength of its commitment to the plan.

Nippon Kaigi has a draft, which it virtually never promotes. Nippon Kaigi will support revision in any form that the LDP can achieve (Hardacre). As McLaughlin and others have pointed out, the LDP under Shinzō Abe has had the opportunity based on its numerical strength in the Diet to pass constitutional revision.[3] The fact that it does not push more aggressively to do so could mean either that it is not confident that a majority of the Japanese people would ratify a new draft (as required in Article 96), or that the party is reluctant to relinquish an issue that so reliably coalesces its support on the right, which might otherwise fracture or produce a rear-guard attack. Another possibility is that the LDP may calculate that if it steamrollered its proposals, it might lose the electioneering support of Sōka Gakkai, on which it depends to stay in office.

Gender occupies a paradoxical position in the debate on constitutional revision. On the left, outside of feminist activism, it seems to be assumed that although issues of gender equality will be negatively impacted if the right has its way, speeches and programs authored by progressive men regularly ignore gender, apparently assuming that it will be women's job to address equality of the sexes (Miura). Sōka Gakkai activists mainly adopt the position of the religion's powerful Women's Group, which favors the interests of married women not employed outside the home over the interests of working women. On the right, considerable attention and resources are devoted by Nippon Kaigi and the Association of Shinto Shrines to retaining and deepening women's acceptance of subordination to men, with numerous women's groups formed—and assembling frequently—in virtually every prefecture.

Although social inequality is arguably the greatest domestic issue that Japan confronts today, prior to 2019, activists did not link it to constitutional revision. Social inequality exposes divisions of interest along generational lines. Increasing numbers of elderly people must be supported by decreasing numbers in the younger generations due to a plummeting birth rate and the absence of significant immigration. The elderly see their social protections shrinking, while the young in non-regular employment face declining job security and lack the economic resources that would allow them to marry with confidence that they could support a family, even with two incomes. Social inequality has a strong gender dynamic because of women's concentration in non-regular employment and because of their economic precarity if divorced or raising children on a single income, especially if their income derives from non-regular employment. The first clause of Article 25 suggests how a connection to the issue of revision might be forged: "All people shall have the right to maintain the minimum standards of wholesome and cultured living." Indeed, in the July 2019 election for the Upper House, the new populist political party Reiwa Shinsengumi called for fresh attention to social inequality, opposing the LDP's approach to constitutional revision, saying that it would give government excessive powers (Ueda, this volume).

Even before the appearance of Reiwa Shinsengumi, however, debate within the opposition parties on the meanings of "constitutionalism" (*rikkenshugi*) shaped understandings of the proper ideological or philosophical basis for revising or preserving the constitution in its present form. Generally understood to imply that the constitution exists in order to limit the powers invested in government and to strengthen the rights of citizens, "constitutionalism" is a central concept in the debate (Ueda, Kuramochi, Horikawa). Hoping to enhance the power of the prime minister and stressing new external threats from China and North Korea, the LDP has proposed a variety of new powers that the executive could deploy in "emergency situations," covering natural disasters and military attack. While it is questionable how widely this debate is known and followed by society at large, the changing rhetoric filters into party platforms, becoming part of the guiding ideology with which civic activists engage. Future study of the debate's ideological basis could be advanced through studies of such activists as Akira Momochi and Yoshiko Sakurai (pro-constitutional revision); Kenzaburō Ōe and Chizuko Ueno (against revision); or Shiori Yamao, who is open to revisionism from a progressive stance.

NOTES

1. The full scope of activism over the postwar decades can be researched by consulting the website of the Reischauer Institute Constitutional Revision in Japan Research Project. The rhetoric, activists, and activism on both sides of the debate on constitutional revision have evolved over the postwar decades (Ueda).
2. These can be consulted and compared on the Reischauer Institute Constitutional Revision in Japan Research Project website.
3. Parties outside the governing coalition on the right could probably be persuaded to ally with the LDP on constitutional revision if provided with the various perks and legislative concessions they would demand at the time.

Part III

UNDERSTANDING JAPANESE CONSTITUTIONAL REVISION IN HISTORICAL AND COMPARATIVE PERSPECTIVES

Chapter Eleven

Interactions between Constitutionalism and Authoritarianism in Asian Democracies

A Japan-Taiwan Comparison

Weitseng Chen

INTRODUCTION

In the decades straddling the turn of the millennium, Taiwan and Japan both experienced political change that called for constitutional revision.[1] In Taiwan, this concerned the democratic transition in the 1990s and 2000s; in Japan, the political swing to the right resulted in a consequential reinterpretation of Article 9, the "peace clause." Both dealt with the legacies of one-party rule and state capitalism. The ruling parties, Taiwan's Nationalist Party (Kuomintang, or KMT) and Japan's Liberal Democratic Party (LDP), faced a similar set of challenges: an active general public scrutinizing the party's attempts to circumvent constitutional constraints in order to carry out their respective policy agendas, and pressure from the international community, whose support was vital for their legitimacy and/or performance. In response, both parties engineered their legitimacy against constitutionality, and such engineering reflected the legacies of authoritarian legality commonly seen in Asia.

Authoritarian states in the region have frequently borrowed legal institutions from their democratic counterparts for the purposes of nation-building and economic development, which altered the functions of such borrowed institutions. Various imported legal concepts have also often been conflated with home-grown ideas about the law, which are usually at odds with the original idea about the rule of law and constitutionalism. Constitutionality is only loosely tied to the legitimacy of the state, which is largely performance-based. Despite increasing legal consciousness amongst the general public, breaches of law could be perceived as justifiable if they had overall utility for society and/or better national performance (economically or politically). Unconstitutionality has not necessarily delegitimized the regime either. These traits represent shared patterns and dynamics among Asian democracies bent on achieving nation-building, modernization, rule of law, and democratic reforms within a very short period of time after World War II. Japan and Taiwan are two cases in point, even though both have since undergone democratic transitions.

And yet, constitutional revision followed different paths in the two countries. The KMT did not act unilaterally after four decades of authoritarian rule, but, under tremendous pressure, negotiated the proposed constitutional amendments with the relevant stakeholders. In contrast, the LDP government in Japan, which also ruled the country after World War II for decades, save for brief interruptions between 1993 and 1994 and from 2009 to 2012, ignored the alleged unconstitutionality of its proposed amendments altogether and made unilateral moves amid unprecedented protests. The Cabinet issued its reinterpretation of Article 9 of the Constitution, and new legislation quickly followed to crystallize the reinterpretation, thereby effectively amending the Constitution without following the statutory amendment procedure provided by the Constitution. In this regard, democratic Japan appeared to act in a more authoritarian fashion in the 2010s than authoritarian Taiwan did in the 1990s. Why?

This essay seeks to analyze how legality and constitutionalism operate in the two countries through the lens of authoritarian legality. It examines their respective socio-political structures that preserve the legacy of authoritarian legality post democratization. It also aims to identify the domestic and international factors that explain the subsequent divergence in the operation of constitutionalism in Japan and Taiwan.

CONSTITUTIONAL REVISION IN TAIWAN AND IN JAPAN

Constitutional revision occurred in Taiwan soon after democratization began when martial law was lifted in 1987. More than four decades of one-party rule by the KMT was shaken by the establishment of the Democratic Progressive Party (DPP), the main opposition party, as well as many other smaller parties. Notably, the 1947 Constitution of the Republic of China, ("1947 ROC Constitution") was passed in 1946 in Nanjing before the KMT relocated to Taiwan after being defeated by the Chinese Communist Party during the civil war. But it was never fully enforced, because martial law was announced when the KMT established its rule in 1949, thereby suspending the 1947 ROC Constitution. When it in fact came to life after martial law ceased in 1987, a practical need to make it functionable quickly emerged, especially the provisions regarding governmental structure and country-wide elections.

As a result, between 1991 and 2000, the KMT government amended the 1947 ROC Constitution six times, and the high frequency of revision gave rise to what scholars called "constitution-making in installments." The first amendment in 1991 authorized general elections for Congress. The 1992 amendment shortened the term of the President and the National Assembly and created a dual-track congress system, with the National Assembly mainly in charge of constitutional amendments and the Legislative Yuan in charge of legislative activities. The 1994 amendment subjected the presidency to direct general election every four years, whereas the 1997 amendment simplified the structure of government by eliminating the Taiwan provincial government, which largely overlapped geographically with the areas effectively governed by the central government in Taiwan. The 1999 amendment then paved the way for a single congressional system by ceasing direct general elections for members of the National Assembly. Finally, the sixth amendment in 2000 completed the structural reform of Congress and ended with a single Congress with members wholly and directly elected by the Taiwanese people every four years. In essence, this was a decade-long process of customizing and localizing the 1947 ROC Constitution.

This decade-long constitutional process was accompanied by fierce political confrontations, public protests, and student movements. Indeed, it began with the "Wild Lily Movement" in 1990, when approximately 6,000 students occupied the Chiang Kai-Shek Memorial Hall in the Taipei city center, demanding that the KMT government hold a national consultation meeting to discuss constitutional issues and formulate a timeline for political reforms. As in Japan, the narratives of both KMT supporters and opponents largely concerned issues regarding constitutional values, although the underlying causes of their disagreements and conflicts lay in economic inequality, social classes, ideology, and nationalism. Liberal constitutional law scholars and activist students led constitutional discourse in the media and through public events, challenging the constitutionality of the KMT-led process at every turn.

Nonetheless, this hardly compromised the KMT's political legitimacy. The party continued to dominate the political arena through this time. Protests by student organizations, opposition parties, and professional organizations such as the Taipei Bar Association eventually faded away, and politics returned to normal. In the new century, the general public and the political elites adapted to the new constitutional order and normalized the once hotly contested constitutional changes.

In Japan, the impetus for the LDP's constitutional revisionism mainly came from changing geopolitics in Asia, especially the rise of China. Two amendment drafts to Japan's Constitution ("1947 Japan Constitution") were announced in 2005 and 2012 respectively. LDP's electoral defeat in 2009 temporarily suspended this initiative, but Prime Minister Shinzō Abe's return to power in 2012 soon revived the agenda. Nonetheless, Abe's determination to amend the Constitution remained an uphill battle given the Japanese people's deeply pacifist belief system and the high threshold of the amendment procedure, which requires two-thirds of the vote in both Houses of the Diet followed by a simple majority vote in a public referendum. It required a new strategy by the Abe administration.

In 2014, based on a report concluded by the government's Advisory Panel on Reconstruction of the Legal Basis for Security, the Cabinet passed a resolution to unilaterally reinterpret the meaning of Article 9 to include the right to collective self-defense in case: 1) of an armed attack against a foreign country in close relationship with Japan; 2) "such attack threatens Japan's survival and poses a clear danger to fundamentally overturn the Japanese people's right to life, liberty and the pursuit of happiness"; 3) there are "no other appropriate means to repel the attack, ensure Japan's survival and protect its people"; and 4) the use of force is limited "to the minimum extent necessary" (Ministry of Foreign Affairs, 2014).

The following year, the National Diet, controlled by the LDP and its allies, passed the Legislation for Peace and Security, thereby effectively changing the 1947 Japan Constitution without an amendment. The Legislation also expanded the authority of the National Security Council, which allowed the Self-Defense Forces (SDF) to participate in international peacekeeping and asset-protection operations with foreign partners, and to provide a wider scope of logistics support in larger geographic areas (Ministry of Defense of Japan 2016). Thereafter, for example, in 2016 the Abe administration formally granted Japanese peacekeepers in South Sudan the ability to come to the aid of geographically separated persons or units (Bosack 2017).

Abe's informal approach to amending Article 9 triggered enormous outrage. Protests took place across the country and especially outside the National Diet in the summer of 2015 demanding the abolishment of the bills and the resignation of Prime Minister Abe. The Japan Federation of Bar Associations publicly stated that the security bills were in clear violation of the 1947 Japan Constitution, and scholars testifying in the House of Representatives, including LDP-recommended Professor Yasuo Hasebe, suggested that the bills were unconstitutional on the ground that the change in position represented a distinct break from pre-existing interpretations and therefore impermissibly strained the text of Article 9 (Hasebe 2017, 125). According to an *Asahi shinbun* survey, only two out of 209 constitutional scholars were willing to count the security bills as constitutional (*Asahi shinbun* 2015).

Japan's Asian neighbors also expressed dismay about what they saw as Japan's attempt to reassert its military presence in Asia. "South Korea will never tolerate any exercise of such a collective self-defense right without the Republic of Korea's request or consent on matters that can affect the security of the Korean Peninsula or national interests of the Republic of Korea," announced the Korean government.

Nonetheless, like the KMT in Taiwan, the LDP's constitutional maneuvers do not seem to have affected its political legitimacy. The Abe administration simply ignored the unprecedented massive student movements and the near-consensus among constitutional scholars about the unconstitutionality of the government's informal approach towards changing the Constitution, and the LDP won the subsequent parliamentary elections in 2016 and 2019.

AUTHORITARIAN LEGALITY IN ASIA

This apparent disconnect between a ruling party's political legitimacy and its honoring constitutionality is commonly seen in hybrid regimes in Asia, as many authoritarian states have borrowed institutional design from democratic countries. These countries have embraced the idea of the rule of law, elections, and constitutionalism for the sake of modernization. A case in point is Meiji Japan, where constitutionalism and the rule of law were introduced and made functional while the regime remained authoritarian (Ginsburg 2020). Pre-democratic Taiwan is another typical hybrid regime under which competitive elections were held regularly, and nascent constitutionalism and the rule of law slowly took root during the authoritarian era. Another example, although less authoritarian than the previous two examples, is Post–WWII Japan. The imposed democracy has gradually taken root over the course of more than six decades, but the LDP remains the dominant party in power, with civil society considered generally weak compared to other democracies.

Authoritarian legality refers to the reconfigured design and function of legal institutions in such hybrid regimes. In countries with functional authoritarian legality, there are formal rules and laws, which are enacted through a formal process, announced in advance and made public so as to create a certain level of predictability and certainty. The constitution institutionalizes power and thereby creates an institutional framework for various actors to interact. Accordingly, politics are to a large extent open to legal reasoning and legal disputing (Meierhenrich 2018, 237). Authoritarian legality is stable and self-enforcing on account of all parties accepting that they would be better off within than without this legal system (Chen and Fu 2020). It engenders a legal culture where legal consciousness is well-developed and embedded in the society (Meierhenrich 2018, 246). Although authoritarian legality can genuinely constrain the government and its policies to some extent, the commitment to legality remains instrumental in nature and vulnerable to the exercise of actual power.

In light of several constitutional amendments via informal channels in the context of the United States, Bruce Ackerman famously develops the concept of "constitutional dualism" to conceptualize those rare occasions in which *constitutional politics* led by committed private citizens emerge and move beyond the course of *normal politics* led by political elites. Such "constitutional moments" may eventually lead to constitutional amendments that appear prima facie illegitimate, but can nonetheless be validated by subsequent democratic elections or referendums, and further consolidated during everyday politics which practice such constitutional amendments (Ackerman 1991; 1998; 2014). At first glance, this view seems to be able to explain Taiwan's and Japan's constitutional politics and controversial amendments (Martin 2017).

However, the application of this view to post-transition, one-party dominant polity might overlook the legacies and continuity of authoritarian legality (Dixon and Baldwin 2019). The strategy of authoritarian legality, once adopted by the tiny cluster of Asian hybrid regimes such as Japan, Taiwan, and South Korea, seems successful as all these countries have established functional and largely satisfactory legal systems. However, legacy of authoritarianism still lingers after political reforms, with dominant parties able to maintain their status in the democratic system. Political elites are not shy in revealing their non-democratic, instrumental attitude towards constitutionalism when necessary. As such, constitutional moments do not necessarily represent a switch between *normal* and *constitutional* politics, but also one between *democratic* and *authoritarian* politics.

AUTHORITARIAN LEGACIES IN DEMOCRACIES

Although Japan and Taiwan are no longer considered hybrid regimes but rather democracies, the continuity of authoritarian legality may persist through the mindset of personnel and legal professionals, as well as the common trap of path dependency that could well determine the institutional design post-transition. In tracing the personnel foundation of Japan's judiciary, for example, Koichi Nakano indicates that the same group of judges and legal professionals dominated the judiciary before and after World War II, thereby giving rise to the conservative attitude of the Japanese Supreme Court that rarely checks the LDP-dominant executive branch (Nakano 2020). In his examination of judicial precedents, John Haley also points out that, in nearly every field of law, there exist long-standing precedents that continue to be followed, some of which can be traced back to the prewar era. Judges' reluctance to alter or overrule prior cases reflects the values and habits of common conservative inclinations, with emphasis on consistency, consensus, and an equally conservative deference to the contributions of their predecessors, judges of the past (Haley 2013, 500–501).

The function of judicial review could be reconfigured under the practice of authoritarian legality. To empower Asian developmental states in the process of nation-building and economic development, constitutional rights and mechanisms that check the executive branch are usually weakened. As a result, the judiciary is not expected to check but rather collaborate with the executive branch, identifying social issues and solving problems together (Thio 2014; Upham 2011, 251). There may also exist a shift in style of judgments, from terse to expository, forgiving of procedural flaws, and patient with immature constitutional argument (Thio 2014). As a result, judges often seek to maintain a realm of professional autonomy by not interfering with political authorities (Ginsburg 2004). Constitutional courts emphasize continuity instead of disruption of social cohesion. Consequently, no matter how capable the courts are, they are usually not proactive, but are instead reactive to social and political needs (Yeh and Chang 2014; Haley 2011; Yoon 1990).

It may well be that most Japanese judges view the Constitution as more of a source of political and moral principles than a source of law which they can cite in their decisions (Martin 2011; Matsui 2011; Law 2011). The 1947 Japan Constitution was neither borrowed nor transplanted, but rather imposed by the occupying forces (Hasebe 2003, 224). Although French, German, and American jurisprudence have been borrowed and studied for the purpose of understanding various concepts of this imposed Constitution, a substantial exploration of the idea of constitutionalism and its function in a democracy has been left out in the scholarly literature developed after World War II (Hasebe 2007, 296). As a result, legality plays a more important role in constraining the government than the Constitution does.

Such an understanding of the constitution naturally leads to the Japanese Supreme Court's passivity. Relying on a narrow understanding of the U.S. political question doctrine, the Supreme Court set the principle that the courts must defer to the judgment of the political branches and will not exercise judicial review of any legislation and governmental action in the realm of national security unless such legislation and action are "obviously unconstitutional" (Haley 2017; Seymour 1974, 421). As such, a resolution through judicial review of the dispute over the constitutionality of the revision made to Article 9 is therefore unlikely.

Legality and Legitimacy

In democracies, commitment to the rule of law and constitutionalism is normative rather than instrumental. As such, constitutionality, and more broadly, legality, are an integral part of the legitimacy of democratic government. In comparison, the practice of authoritarian legality and its legacies often render the commitment to legality and constitutionalism instrumental and strategic (Tushnet 2015, 73). Legality serves utilitarian goals, which are subject to the country's and rulers' preference at the time. For example, if the law is used for the pursuit of economic development, any breach of law can be justified if it helps achieve the desirable economic outcome. Consequently, legality and constitutionalism are not necessarily an integral part of maintaining the legitimacy of the government. Rather, the regime's legitimacy is more often performance-based, such as the delivery of wealth and nationalistic power or dignity.

Furthermore, legality and constitutionality are not tightly intertwined. Since the constitution of an authoritarian or non-liberal country is usually perceived as a mere political statement and/or a set of moral principles, it is not necessarily considered a source of justiciable law. Consequently, legality matters to the regime's legitimacy more than constitutionality does. Compared to the constitution, a law usually provides more details about how the government is expected to act; therefore, a breach of such requirements is easier for laypeople to observe and more difficult for the government to justify. This is especially true when legality, despite its authoritarian nature, has gradually given rise to legal consciousness among the general public.

In comparison, a government's failure to comply with the constitution would be considered as the postponement of a promise or a pragmatic approach to implementing long-term national objectives stated in the constitution, rather than its outright rejection. While rejections immediately put the regime's credibility at stake, postponed promises stimulate hope. To the extent that the general public perceives the constitutional promise as one being postponed rather than broken, the regime's legitimacy would not be jeopardized by the unconstitutionality of legislation or other governmental acts. As a result, a legally enacted but unconstitutional law could be commonly seen and even accepted.

In this regard, Abe's informal approach for amending Article 9 serves as a testing ground for the exercise of constitutionalism in Japan. Historically, any attempt by incumbent prime ministers to revise Article 9 would trigger a political backlash due to the general public's concern about the possibility of being dragged into an ally's war (Panton 2010, 133–134). Several prime ministers who tried to amend Article 9 became political victims of such public sentiment. In the most recent saga of the Article 9 amendment in 2015,

Japanese constitutional law scholars, student activists, and other opponents to amendment tried to appeal to the general public's commitment to pacifism. However, the government showed little interest in engaging in such a normative narrative. It responded with a realist narrative by emphasizing the practical purpose of the proposed constitutional amendments—to respond to the threat posed by the rise of China. As it turned out, the Abe government's realist narrative prevailed over the normative discourse that was based on universal values, and successfully avoided any significant backfire caused by its controversial move. The nearly unanimous view among constitutional law scholars on the unconstitutionality of the Abe government's revision came to nothing.

In retrospect, the pacifist narrative also reflects a realist understanding of the 1947 Japan Constitution. The persuasive power underlying the discourse of pacifism comes from the fear of Japan being dragged into the wars of the United States rather than constitutional principles of checks and balances on the executive branch that commands the military (Ryu 2018, 10). This fear explains, in part, the once considerable restraint shown by several rightist LDP-led administrations that wished to amend Article 9. In fact, it sometimes served the government's interest of warding off political pressure from the United States to take on greater international security obligations.

Today, declining American dominance in the region has led to a drastic change in the role and function of Article 9. And the public perception of China or North Korea posing an imminent threat to Japan's security finally made a strategic move towards reinterpreting Article 9 acceptable. If a strategic move due to a change in policy preference can appear so strongly that constitutionality can be ignored, it is a typical manifestation of authoritarian legality, or at least, its legacy.

JAPAN-TAIWAN COMPARISON

Despite such similarity in historical patterns, Japan's top-down approach to constitutional revision is a far cry from Taiwan's relatively stronger bottom-up constitutional amendment process, with key elites more willing to concede to popular will. Why did democratic Japan behave in a more authoritarian manner than the erstwhile authoritarian KMT government at the time? By comparing Japan with Taiwan, we may better understand the operation and development of constitutionalism on both sides. Three major dynamics informing their shared constitutional movement patterns offer clues to deviation in the evolution of their legacy of authoritarian legality.

Exogenous Democracy vis-à-vis Endogenous Democracy

While Japan's 1947 "peace constitution" and constitutional democracy were imposed after World War II, Taiwan's 1947 "ROC Constitution" was brought in by the KMT, with constitutional democracy serving no more than a token during the authoritarian era from 1949 to 1987. Their starting points appear to have largely determined the trajectory of the constitutional movement in both countries.

The 1947 Japan Constitution established the institutional foundation of a parliamentary democracy that appreciates accountability, rule of law, and human rights. Although recent revisionism can be seen as long-lingering attempts to overcome the "foreign-imposed" democracy, as conservatives in power saw it, Japan's starting point is much ahead of Taiwan's as far as democracy is concerned. The imposed democracy also created a much greater space for the judiciary to function as a dispute resolution institution to address the people's grief.

That being said, the authoritarian continuity also established the norm of limiting the function of the courts as a mechanism to check the executive branch (Upham 2011, 251). Politically sensitive cases were largely excluded from the courts' day-to-day operations; rather, the court system focused on delivering everyday justice. Such an institutional setting created an institutional equilibrium that lasted for decades without disruption.

In comparison, the quality of the judicial system in Taiwan under authoritarian rule was much more limited. The government was wary of an independent judicial system. Military personnel without formal legal education were allowed to sit on the bench. Martial law deprived the normal courts of their jurisdiction over politically sensitive cases as well as matters concerning the KMT's control over the media, social organizations, and education. More specifically, the ruling elite viewed the prosecutorial system as the most vital mechanism for controlling the judicial system in order to ensure that it would not challenge the party's own interests (Wang 2002, 531). These policies greatly constrained the development of the judicial system and the tensions therein accumulated over many years before they erupted in the 1990s. Paradoxically, compared to Japan, years of suppression appear to have led to a stronger commitment to constitutionalism during the post-transition era in Taiwan.

From the beginning, the KMT had to manage its position as a minority émigré regime led by an authoritarian and military party and dominating the majority of local Taiwanese. After 1949, the majority of local Taiwanese arguably made a social contract with the KMT, which promised economic goods in exchange for a degree of constraints on personal liberty and political rights. Its success in delivering rapid economic growth in turn produced a heightened consciousness of personal and constitutional rights and an increase in income disparity. This ultimately produced wide-ranging civil movements calling for laws that guaranteed political freedom, labor rights, consumer protection, judicial independence, freedom of assembly, academic freedom, etc. Universal values such as human rights and dignity were the focal point of public debates at the time.

As a result, constitutional discourse became the norm of politics in transition, and as something people fought for and gained after years of political struggles. Accordingly, the commitment to constitutionalism appears to be normative and does not vary according to the change in policy choices or preferences. Taiwan's Constitutional Court became one of the most active and progressive courts in Asia (Yeh and Chang 2011, 805). Governmental agencies take serious heed of the constitutionality of their acts and policies. For vital issues that have implications on politics, the unconstitutionality of an announced policy is considered as a political setback to the ruling party and its administration. In this regard, constitutionality is an integral part of the political legitimacy of the state.[2]

Homogeneous Society vis-à-vis Divided Society

Historically, very few states began an endogenous democratic transition with a high degree of nation-state homogeneity (Linz and Stephan 1996, 24–33). Taiwan is a case in point as such a homogeneity did not exist during authoritarian years. After 1949, the KMT kept tight control in a society that was deeply divided between a mainland immigrant community and the local population that had experienced fifty years of Japanese colonial assimilation.[3] But in the 1980s, local Taiwanese increasingly confronted mainlanders in the political arena. By then, four decades after the KMT's takeover, KMT party elites were themselves divided along similar ethnic lines, causing an internal party split in the early 1990s during the democratic transition (Chu 2000, 102–103).

Democratization appears to be tolerating, rather than eliminating, Taiwan's divisions. In contrast to a revolutionary transition, a gradual and peaceful transition often signals the legitimacy of the previous authoritarian government, which allows the party to survive the transition and transform itself into one that is well adapted to the new democratic climate. This is the case for the KMT, which returned to power eight years after it lost the presidential election in 2000 for the first time in more than fifty years. In response, weary of authoritarian legacies, dedicated democrats continued to keep civil activism vibrant and ran NGOs that monitored judicial reforms, anti-corruption, workers' rights, Taiwan-China relations, consumer protection, LGBT rights, and freedom of speech. The political distrusts and deep divisions between the two camps gave rise to a vibrant civil society.

Unlike Taiwan, divisions along the lines of national identity hardly exist in Japan in a comparable way. While Japan's democratic transformation after the war benefited from an active civil society as well, Japanese society looked very different decades later. In response to massive social activism in the 1960s, for example, the Japanese government managed civil society in a way similar to the KMT—by promising and delivering economic affluence to the middle class. From the 1970s onwards, however, civil organizations came to be less invested in political ideology and achieved more of their social aims through collaborative rather than confrontational relationships with the state (Garon 2003, 42–62). Organizations that engaged with policy making and public discourse were usually those with strong ties with government, or with vested business interests such as agricultural unions (Haddad 2007; Pekkanen 2003). Officials often sought to mobilize society through these organizations to carry out their agenda in relation to public governance (Garon 2010, 48).

With respect to critical issues such as national security or Article 9, sharp divisions reappeared; but it seemed challenging for Japan's fragmented and harmonious civil society to advocate a view that substantially deviated from the government's position. In 2013, the LDP-loyal *Sankei shinbun* called for the elimination of the second paragraph of Article 9 and suggested renaming the SDF a national military that could both defend Japan and participate in collective security operations. The Japan Association of Corporate Executives, Keizai Doyukai, in its earlier 2003 proposal, called for the replacement of Japan's "inactive" pacifism with an active role in international peace. The Japanese Business Federation also called for a relaxation of the requirements for constitutional revision (Council on Foreign Relations 2019). Most of their proposals resonated with the LDP's positions. And yet the majority of Japanese from the scholarly community to major social interest groups and the general public opposed revision. This public opinion motivated Abe, in an astonishing move, to threaten to revoke the broadcasting licenses of "overly critical networks" and appointed an ally to run Japan's national broadcaster NHK, which promised that "the network will not deviate too far from the government's views" (Panton 2010, 129). In short, the balance of power tilts significantly towards the state.

Opposite International Influence on Constitutional Amendments

Regional geopolitics also played a crucial role in constitutional politics in both countries, but they operated in opposite ways. In Japan, the threat of a rising China has turned out to be the most effective rhetoric to push through the effective amendment of Article 9 by circumventing constitutional procedure, thereby negatively affecting the supremacy of the Constitution. In contrast, China's increasing might in trade, diplomacy, national defense, media, and domestic politics is felt even more keenly and directly in Taiwan. Consequently, the response from the general public is to strengthen constitutionalism and the performance of democracy, which helps Taiwan to distinguish itself from authoritarian China and thereby earn international support. Constitutionalism and democracy have become the focal points of Taiwanese nationalism and patriotism that unite the people and serve as a defense mechanism in the face of China's rise (Chen 2018).

The "China factor" is further complicated by each country's respective alliance with the United States. In 2015, for the first time in nearly 20 years, the United States and Japan released the newly revised defense guidelines for their alliance, which Prime Minister Abe called "historic." The guidelines promised the intensification of deterrence and responsiveness to the new security environment in East Asia and other areas (Tiezzi 2015). Accordingly, the major objective of reinterpreting Article 9 is to implement Japan's strengthened commitments under its military alliance with the U.S., for which Japan expects to provide "greater contributions to international security initiatives wherever appropriate" (Lee 2015). However, the execution of two Japanese reporters by ISIS a few months earlier also made it clear to the public that internationalized constitutional amendment carried risks. And indeed, no proposed amendment regarding Article 9 has ever garnered a significant majority support, let alone the supermajority required by the Constitution to pass a referendum.

Faced with such a complex situation, with international pressure from various stakeholders, Abe's indirect approach for amending the 1947 Japan Constitution could be seen as a compromise. It achieves the LDP's diplomatic goal without touching the text of Article 9. In the election that followed, the LDP avoided making the amendments a focal point and yet reaped the electoral victory for such amendments by treating the election outcome as a positive referendum for the controversial, extra-constitutional changes. Subsequently, Prime Minister Abe continued to advocate for formal constitutional amendments, but in a much less urgent manner and with a softer tone. The new legislation may eventually be legitimized as normal practice accepted by the general public, with little challenge to its underlying unconstitutionality (Martin 2017).

U.S. influence on Taiwan's constitutional amendment is equally prominent, albeit with very different dynamics as far as the practice of constitutionalism is concerned. The U.S. position during Taiwan's constitutional movements is to support democratization but not constitutionalization of its de facto independence. Before the first party turnover happened in 2000, Taiwan's constitutional amendments aimed to carry out necessary changes to the 1947 ROC Constitution designed for the whole of mainland China in order to make it functional in post-democratization Taiwan. The United States supported such amendments for practical reasons, as long as all stakeholders could be accommodated under the new democratic framework, and accordingly, the KMT moved in line with the U.S.'s position. As a matter of fact, the KMT had been using "democratization" as diplomatic leverage to gain diplomatic support in the face of China's rising threat (deLisle 2008, 185). Therefore, the KMT's position is not new, as it became necessary once more to differentiate democratic Taiwan from authoritarian China. As the U.S. encouraged dialogue between the KMT and its rivals, KMT leaders were incentivized to engage in substantive negotiations with the opposition.

However, the U.S.'s position changed in the early 2000s after the DPP won the presidential election. Confronted with China's threats and intimidation over Taiwan's sovereignty, the pro-independence DPP government tried to legalize Taiwan's de facto independence by further amending the Constitution or, more controversially, writing a new constitution. The U.S. fiercely opposed such a provocative proposal, reminding Taiwan that U.S. military support must not be used to antagonize China (Kan 2014, 47). Clearly, any effort of democratic consolidation in Taiwan not conducive to U.S. interests and safety would be discouraged (U.S. Congressional Research Service 2015).

In short, the U.S. exerted strong and direct influence on constitutional movements in both Taiwan and Japan. While it encouraged Abe's revisionism, it ultimately discouraged Taiwan's beyond merely supporting constitutional dialogue among stakeholders for the sake of the promotion of democracy. Although the factor of international pressure played a key role in triggering constitutional moments in both Taiwan and Japan, it did so in a diametrically opposite fashion in terms of its impact on the operation of constitutionalism.

CONCLUSION

Both Japan and Taiwan are democracies with authoritarian legacies. Such legacies are preserved because of their host countries' peaceful and gradual transition towards democracy, and continue to exert influence through governmental personnel, institutional design, and pluralist politics. Consequently, authoritarian legality characterizes the operation of their legal system during not only pre- but also post-transition eras, and therefore makes the exercise of constitutionalism different from most Western democracies.

A case in point is Japan's arguably unconstitutional amendment of Article 9 in 2015 that paradoxically did not affect the legitimacy of the Abe administration. In other words, a normative commitment to constitutionalism does not seem to be an integral part of the government's legitimacy; rather, such a commitment could be instrumental and strategic when necessary. Furthermore, Japan and Taiwan are two rare examples in which the constitutional amendments have been "internationalized." The world, specifically the United States, has a clear stake in their constitutional movements as far as geopolitics is concerned, which has affected both countries' constitutional movements at home.

Interestingly, despite similar authoritarian legacies in both countries, recent constitutional revision has activated opposite dynamics. During respective constitutional movements, the KMT government in Taiwan substantially engaged and negotiated with the opposition, while the LDP government in Japan repeatedly ignored requests for dialogue with the opposition.

This essay has argued that the political and social structures of both countries have largely determined how various institutional actors and individuals reacted to authoritarian legacies through the practice of constitutionalism. While Taiwan's authoritarian era was characterized by a brutal and outright suppression of personal liberty and political rights, constitutionalism eventually did take root through a bottom-up process characterized by street protests, political struggles, and, finally, negotiations. Such an endogenous democracy gave rise to an active civil society that continues to check the executive branch. In comparison, Japan's imposed democracy was much more tolerant and pluralist than Taiwan's authoritarian rule at the time, but authoritarian continuity nonetheless existed and gave rise to the country's fragmented civil society, which is more cooperative and embedded in governmental networks. It is by no means as active as Taiwan's and therefore renders much less constraint on the Japanese government.

The U.S. alliances also played a key role for both countries albeit in opposite ways or to opposite effects. In Taiwan, the U.S. supported the constitutional movements if they made Taiwan more democratic, but it also bluntly leveraged its political clout to prevent such movements from destabilizing the region by provoking China. In contrast, U.S. interests in boosting Japan's military capacity to help maintain the American order in Asia compelled the Abe government to amend the Constitution informally by leveraging public concern about China's rise, and to do so by circumventing the formal amendment procedure. Although scholars vehemently criticized the constitutionality of the government's move, calling it "authoritarian constitutionalism," the LDP government has yet to face any significant challenge.

Authoritarian legacies have posed serious challenges to both democracies of Japan and Taiwan. Taiwan does not necessarily offer a better model to address such challenges, but in recent decades it has demonstrated a stronger commitment to constitutionalism than Japan due to various domestic factors. Nonetheless, as we have seen, authoritarian legacies not only coexist with democracy, but also quietly evolve behind the shadow of democracy, and affect the performance of democracies in complex ways.

NOTES

1. This essay benefited from comments by Hui-Wen Chen, Ming-Sung Kuo, Erik Mobrand, Yongwook Ryu, Franziska Seraphim and Frank Upham, as well as research assistance from Benjamin Heng. The author is also grateful for the financial support of NUS AcRF (R-241-000-163-115).

2. Problems of Taiwan's active constitutional politics nonetheless exist, such as excessive burden on the Constitutional Court. This essay does not intend to evaluate the state of constitutional politics in Taiwan. Rather, the point being stressed here is that the normative commitment to constitutionalism in Taiwan appears more prominent than that in Japan.

3. Although the division between mainlanders (15%) and native Taiwanese (85%) is not ethnic in nature, the characteristics of this split are very similar to the economic and political tensions that tend to emerge in ethnic divisions.

REFERENCES

Ackerman, Bruce. *We the People: Foundations*. Boston: Belknap Press of Harvard University Press, 1991.

———. *We the People: Transformations*. Boston: Belknap Press of Harvard University Press, 1998.

———. *We the People: The Civil Rights Revolution.* Boston: Belknap Press of Harvard University Press, 2014.

The Asahi shinbun. "Anpo hōan 'iken' 104 nin, 'goken' futari kenpō gakushara" (104 Constitutional Scholars Find the National Security Legislation Unconstitutional, Two Consider It As Constitutional), July 11, 2015, https://www.asahi.com/articles/ASH797JMJH79ULZU01W.html.

Bosack, Michael. "Japan's Security Legislation Turns Two," *Tokyo Review,* September 29, 2017, https://www.tokyoreview.net/2017/09/japan-peace-security-legislation.

Chen, Weitseng. "Student Activism and Authoritarian Legality Transition." In *Authoritarian Legality in Asia: Formation, Development and Transition*, edited by Chen Weitseng and Hualing Fu, 303–335. Cambridge, UK: Cambridge University Press, 2020.

———. "Twins of Opposites—Why China Will Not Follow Taiwan's Model of Rule of Law Transition toward Democracy," *American Journal of Comparative Law* 66 (2018): 481–535.

———, and Hualing Fu, eds. *Authoritarian Legality in Asia: Formation, Development and Transition.* Cambridge, UK: Cambridge University Press, 2020.

Chu, Yun-Han. "Taiwan's Unique Path to Democracy." In *Conference Prague 1999: Transitional Societies in Comparison: East Central Europe vs. Taiwan,* edited by National Science Council, Taipei, Bonn Office 89, 102–103. New York: Peter Lang Publishing, 2001.

Council on Foreign Relations. "Constitutional Changes in Japan: Evolving Proposal for Revisions," 2019, https://www.cfr.org/interactive/japan-constitution/politics-of-revision.

deLisle, Jacques. "International Pressures and Domestic Pushback." In *Political Change in China: Comparisons with Taiwan*, edited by Larry Diamond and Bruce Gilley, 185–214. Boulder, CO: Lynne Rienner Publishers, 2008.

Dixon, Rosalind, and Guy Baldwin. "Globalizing Constitutional Moments? A Reflection on Japanese Article 9 Debate," *American Journal of Comparative Law* 67 (2019): 145, 173–174.

The Economist. "A New Bill Reveals the Japanese Government's Authoritarian Streak," April 20, 2017, https://www.economist.com/asia/2017/04/20/a-new-bill-reveals-the-japanese-governments-authoritarian-streak.

Fackler, Martin. "Effort by Japan to Stifle News Media Is Working," *New York Times*, April 26, 2015, https://www.nytimes.com/2015/04/27/world/asia/in-japan-bid-to-stifle-media-is-working.html.

Garon, Sheldon. "From Meiji to Heisei: The State and Civil Society in Japan." In *The State of Civil Society in Japan*, edited by Frank J. Schwartz and Susan J. Pharr, 42–62. Cambridge, UK: Cambridge University Press, 2003.

Ginsburg, Tom. *Legal Reform in Korea*. Oxfordshire, UK: RoutledgeCurzon, 2004.

———. "Meiji Japan and Authoritarian Constitutionalism." In *Authoritarian Legality in Asia: Formation, Development and Transition*, edited by Weitseng Chen and Hualing Fu, 205–224. Cambridge, UK: Cambridge University Press, 2020.

Haddad, Mary Alice. *Politics and Volunteering in Japan: A Global Perspective*. Cambridge, UK: Cambridge University Press, 2007.

Haley, John. "Constitutional Adjudication in Japan: History and Social Context, Legislative Structures, and Judicial Values," *Washington University Law Review* 88, no. 6 (2011): 1467–1491.

———. "The Role of Courts in 'Making' Law in Japan: The Communitarian Conservatism of Japanese Judges," *Pacific Rim Law & Policy Journal* 22, no. 3 (2013): 491–503.

———. "Article 9 in the Post-Sunagawa World," *Washington International Law Journal* 26, no. 1 (2017): 1–16.

Hasebe, Yasuo. "Constitutional Borrowing and Political Theory," *International Journal of Constitutional Law* 1, no. 2 (2003): 224–243.

———. "The Supreme Court of Japan: Its Adjudication on Electoral Systems and Economic Freedoms," *International Journal of Constitutional Law* 5, no. 2 (2007): 296–307.

———. "The End of Constitutional Pacifism?" *Washington International Law Journal* 38 (2017): 125–135.

Kan, Shirley. "Major U.S. Arms Sales Since 1990," *Congressional Research Service*, August 29, 2014, https://fas.org/sgp/crs/weapons/RL30957.pdf.

Law, David S. "Why Has Judicial Review Failed in Japan?" *Washington University Law Review* 88, no. 6 (2011): 1425–1466.

Lee, Jaemin. "Collective Self-Defense or Collective Security: Japan's Reinterpretation of Article 9 of the Constitution," *Journal of East Asia and International Law* 8, no. 2 (2015): 373–392.

Li-ann Thio. "We Are Feeling Our Way Forward, Step by Step." In *Constitutionalism in Asia in the Early Twenty-First Century*, edited by Albert H.Y. Chen and Andrew Harding, 270–294. Cambridge, UK: Cambridge University Press, 2014.

Linz, Juan J., and Alfred Stephan. *Problems of Democratic Transition and Consolidation: Southern Europe, South America, and Post-Communist Europe*. Baltimore: Johns Hopkins University Press, 1996.

Martin, Craig. "The Japanese Constitution as Law and the Legitimacy of the Supreme Court's Constitutional Decisions: A Response to Matsui," *Washington University Law Review* 88, no. 6 (2011): 1527–1558.

———. "The Legitimacy of Informal Constitutional Amendment and the 'Reinterpretation' of Japan's War Powers," *Fordham International Law Journal* 40, no. 2 (2017): 427–522.

Matsui, Shigenori. "Why Is the Japanese Supreme Court So Conservative?" *Washington University Law Review* 88, no. 6 (2011): 1375–1423.

Meierhenrich, Jens. *The Remnants of the Rechtsstaat: An Ethnography of Nazi Law*. Oxford, UK: Oxford University Press, 2018.

Ministry of Defense of Japan. "Outline of the Legislation for Peace and Security," 2016, https://www.mod.go.jp/e/publ/w_paper/pdf/2016/DOJ2016_2-3-2_web.pdf.

Ministry of Foreign Affairs. "Cabinet Decision on Development of Seamless Security Legislation to Ensure Japan's Survival and Protect Its People, English Translation," July 1, 2014, https://www.mofa.go.jp/fp/nsp/page23e_000273.html.

Nakano, Koichi. "Neoliberal Turn of State Conservatism in Japan: From Bureaucratic to Corporatist Authoritarian Legality." In *Authoritarian Legality in Asia: Formation, Development and Transition*, edited by Weitseng Chen and Hualing Fu, 337–363. Cambridge, UK: Cambridge University Press, 2020.

Panton, Michael A. "Japan's Article 9: Rule of Law versus Flexible Interpretation," *Temple International and Comparable Law Journal* 24, no. 1 (2010): 129–171.

Peerenboom, Randall, and Weitseng Chen. "Developing the Rule of Law." In *Political Change in China: Comparisons with Taiwan*, edited by Larry Diamond and Bruce Gilley, 135–160. Boulder, CO: Lynne Rienner Publishers, 2008.

Rowland, Ashley, and Kyong Chang Yoo. "South Korea Tempers Response to Japan's Expanded Military Role," *Stars and Stripes*, July 7, 2014, https://www.stripes.com/news/south-korea-tempers-response-to-japan-s-expanded-military-role-1.292268.

Ryu, Yongwook. "To Revise or Not to Revise: The 'Peace Constitution,' Pro-Revision Movement, and Japan's National Identity," *Pacific Review* 31, no. 5 (2018): 655–672.

Seymour, Robert L. "Japan's Self-Defense: The Naganuma Case and its Implications," *Pacific Affairs* 47, no. 4 (1974): 421–436.

Tiezzi, Shannon. "A Closer Look at the New US-Japan Defense Guidelines," *The Diplomat,* May 1, 2015, https://thediplomat.com/2015/05/a-closer-look-at-the-new-us-japan-defense-guidelines.

Tushnet, Mark. "Authoritarian Constitutionalism," *Cornell Law Review* 100, no. 2 (2015): 391–462.

Upham, Frank. "Reflections on the Rule of Law in China," *National Taiwan University Law Review* 6, no. 1 (2011): 251–268.

U.S. Congressional Research Service. "China/Taiwan: Evolution of the 'One China' Policy—Key Statements from Washington, Beijing, and Taipei," March 12, 2001–January 5, 2015, https://www.everycrsreport.com/reports/RL30341.html.

Wang, Tay-Sheng. "The History of National Taiwan University College of Law 1928–2002," *Guoli Taiwan daxue falü xuen yuanshi 1928–2002*. Taipei: National Taiwan University.

———. "The Legal Development of Taiwan in the Twentieth Century: Toward a Liberal and Democratic Country," *Pacific Rim Law and Policy Journal* 11 (2002): 531–559.

Yeh, Jiunn-Rong. "Presidential Politics and Judicial Facilitation of Political Dialogue between Political Actors in New Asian Democracies: Comparing the South Korean and Taiwanese Experiences," *International Journal of Constitutional Law* 8, no. 4 (2011): 911–949.

Yeh, Jiunn-Rong and Wen-Chen Chang. "The Emergence of East Asian Constitutionalism," *American Journal of Comparative Law* 59, no. 3 (2011): 805–840.

———. *Asian Courts in Context*. Cambridge, UK: Cambridge University Press, 2014.

Yoon, Dae-Kuo. *Law and Political Authority in South Korea*. Boulder, CO: Westview Press, 1990.

Chapter Twelve

Peace, Land, and Bread

Constitutional Revolution in Postwar Japan and South Korea

Sung Ho Kim

INTRODUCTION

As[1] it appears now, Japan is going back to the future, while Korea is plunging into the unknown. To turn postwar Japan back to a "normal state,"[2] an avowed goal of the ruling Liberal Democratic Party since its inception, Article 9 was transformed via Abe Shinjo's Cabinet decision in the 2014 and 2015 Security Laws. Likewise, in 2018, the self-styled "revolutionary" government in Seoul unveiled a comprehensive constitutional draft by which to turn South Korea into a "nation hitherto never experienced," in the words of Moon Jae-in's inaugural vow.[3] Undoing the long-held status quo is what they both aspire to, and some form of constitutional revolution seems more imminent than ever. For all those aspirations, however, what is meant by those constitutional changes and how they can be implemented seem unclear in contemporary Japan and Korea.

The South Korean constitution has seen nine amendments since 1948, while the postwar constitution of Japan has not witnessed a single formal revision over the past seven decades. Even so, Japan's Article 9, the emblematic peace provision, has come to depart radically from its original meaning after the 1954 establishment of the Self-Defense Forces in a way that has far-reaching implications for the basic identity of the so-called "Peace Constitution." One might say that in South Korea, by contrast, the national aspiration towards a robust form of economic equality survived its many constitutional revisions, still underwriting one of the core constitutional identities of Korea. Arguably, fewer constitutional revolutions took place than meets the eye in Korea, while Japan experienced a more sweeping constitutional change despite no formal amendment. From this altered vantage point, a comparative-constitutional glimpse at Korea and Japan raises questions about the conventional way of explaining constitutional changes, especially, when constitutional identities are concerned.

Against this backdrop, my essay revisits the experiences of Japan and South Korea during the Cold War era and its aftermath in order to deepen our understanding of constitutional changes in general. This enhanced understanding will also help put the constitutional revolutions currently unfolding in those two countries in sharper analytic perspective. To this end, I will first turn to reflect briefly on what is called the constitutional revolution, unpacking my conceptual toolkit along the way.

ON CONSTITUTIONAL REVOLUTION

The[4] making of a constitution is predicated on a revolutionary political rupture. Following this conventional dogma in political and legal theories,[5] Miyazawa Toshiyoshi, the doyen of postwar Japanese constitutional scholarship, held that Japan's unprecedented defeat and unconditional surrender in 1945 demanded a conceptual status that was on a par in magnitude with the total revolution in political life. If a radically new constitution was made, then there had to be a political revolution prior to such a legal change. If none could be found, then a revolution had to be invented on paper, thus, the legal fiction called "August Revolution" [Hasebe 1997]. A fundamental political rupture, formal constitution-making and a substantive sea-change in the constitutional landscape seemed to entail each other by logical and historical necessity.

Drawn from the great democratic revolutions of the eighteenth century in Europe and North America, however, this dogma does not always do justice to the complex nature of the constitutional change in general. The New Deal constitutional revolution, for one, was a genuine case of abrupt and decisive change in American constitutional history. And yet, it was neither preceded by an illegal or extraordinary political event nor followed by constitutionalization of the New Deal achievements via formal amendment. Closer to our time, Egypt witnessed the so-called Jasmine Revolution in 2011 which was followed quickly by a democratic regime-change and new constitution-making. However, the new constitution thus made is often described as hardly a fundamental departure from the one it replaced [Lipin 2012]. In Egypt, both political and legal changes of a seemingly revolutionary nature took place but with little revolutionary consequence of constitutional importance, whereas in New Deal America, a profound and enduring constitutional change happened indeed but without any recourse to a political revolution or legal amendment. It seems to be the case that the method by which a constitution is made and revised (i.e., whether via legal, illegal, or extralegal routes) is not necessarily commensurate with the scope and magnitude of the substantive changes that a new or amended constitution is supposed to usher in with lasting consequences.

This complexity is the reason why an increasing number of comparative constitutional scholars (broadly following Bruce Ackerman's lead) are devising new concepts by which to theorize constitutional changes with more hues and shades. The latest examples would be "unconstitutional constitutional amendment" [Roznai 2017] and "constitutional dismemberment" [Albert 2018], which were devised to address the key discrepancy between form (method) and substance (contents) in constitutional change. In the same vein and with more clarity, the concept of "constitutional revolution" [Jacobsohn 2014; Jacobsohn and Roznai, 2020] foregrounds the problem of form (i.e., the process by which a constitution changes) and substance (i.e., the degree of substantive transformation in the way constitutionalism is experienced), thereby opening up four distinct conceptual possibilities. They are: 1) *classic* constitutional revolution, where the transformation is great, i.e., abrupt, decisive, and enduring, as a result of cataclysmic political disruption and/or official amendment; 2) *quiet* constitutional revolution, where the transformation is great even in the absence of such disruption and/or amendment; 3) *nominal* constitutional revolution, where there is little transformation even after such disruption and/or amendment; 4) *no* constitutional revolution, where neither great transformation in substance nor sharp rupture in the process takes place. According to this schema, of those haphazard examples of constitutional revolution cited above, the fictional August Revolution of Japan may be characterized as *classic*, America's New Deal revolution as *quiet*, and the Jasmin Revolution of Egypt as *nominal*. The lesson is that, depending on the way formal process and substantive changes are combined, a constitutional revolution may take various modalities.

Against this conceptual schema, I take "constitutional identity" to mean a loose constellation of aspirations and aversions as reflected in the constitution which underwrite a system of rights- and structure-provisions in the constitutional law. Generally, an inquiry into constitutional identity is about isolating attributes, predicated as they are upon the constituent people's sustained aspirations and commitments, that make one constitutional order recognizably different from another. As such, those collective desires sanctioned by a legal gestalt of institutionalized practices do not and can never exist in a wholesome harmony. The so-called "constitutional disharmony" [Jacobsohn 2010, 351] is about a cacophony that sounds out from within the constitution itself as it confronts the changes, or obstruction thereof, in its political, economic, and social surroundings. An all too well-known example is the disharmony that slavery had sown into the constitutional identity of antebellum America. As a result of the Civil War, the U.S. constitutional identity, "a republican form of government" in the Guaranty Clause of 1789, has come to mean something radically different from that which would inform the Amendment XIV in 1868. To draw from the quasi-Hegelian nomenclature of Ronald Dworkin, republic as an abstract "conception" is continuously overcome in reference to, even in confrontation with, republic as an empirical "concept" [Dworkin 1986, 70–72].

The point is that constitutional identities are less stable than meets the eye, more often than not caught in the ebbs and flows of the restless changes in the course of which a constitutional law itself changes. The most radical among those transformations is the constitutional revolution by which the way constitutionalism is experienced changes abruptly, decisively, and enduringly with ramifications for the core identity of a constitution. However, the way such a revolution in constitutional identities takes place also varies, as the form and substance of those revolutionary changes make different combinations in practice. In other words, not all constitutional revolutions, even the most dramatic changes in constitutional identities, take a classic modality, a lesson that enables us to understand different ways, such as nominal and quiet, in which constitutional identities are revolutionized.

LAND AND BREAD IN KOREA

South Korea's current constitution was promulgated in 1988 and is the tenth supreme law of the land since the country's independence in 1948. Five revisions may be described as revolutionary as each of them launched a new "republic" (as locals call a new constitutional regime à la French practice). The Founding Constitution of 1948 gave birth to the First Republic of Syngman Rhee and was replaced in 1960 by the Second Republic born out of the so-called 4.19 student revolution. This short democratic interlude was interrupted by the 5.16 military coup of 1961, which led to the Third Republic with its own constitution. Although this constitution would undergo a controversial amendment in 1969, it was not until 1972 that it was entirely replaced by the so-called "Yushin Constitution" as part of a palace coup staged to prolong Park Chung Hee's dictatorial presidency. His assassination brought an end to the authoritarian Fourth Republic; a brief yet widespread demand for democracy ensued, only to be violently suppressed by another military junta; and a new constitution was promulgated to usher in the Fifth Republic in 1980. This soft-authoritarian regime lasted seven years before it was brought down by civil protests, out of which the current constitution of

1988 emerged to codify the successful struggle for democracy. These wholesale revisions of 1960, 1962, 1972, 1980, and 1987 represent the substantive reorientations in the constitutional text, a fact which comprises, along with four other relatively minor amendments, a telling testimony to the soiled history of constitutional democracy in Korea.

According to this constitutional précis, then, Korea is a land of *classic* constitutional revolution par excellence. Since the 1948 founding, one extraordinary political disruption followed another, and each post-revolutionary status quo sought edification by a new constitution. The way in which constitutionalism was experienced as a whole changed dramatically as a result of these cataclysmic ruptures in the political process and substantive rewriting of the constitutional text itself. But the changes introduced by the formal revisions were unevenly felt across different parts and various provisions of the constitution. Some changes in the constitutional text were as dramatic as the revolution that triggered them; others were seemingly trivial in words yet consequential in deeds; still others turned out to be less significant than anticipated. As dramatic as these revolutionary changes appear, however, not all in fact fit the classic model of constitutional revolutions. A closer textual and historical scrutiny reveals that the Korean experience with constitutional change involves various modalities of *nominal* and *quiet* in addition to *classic* constitutional revolutions.

Nominal Constitutional Revolution

Some amendments were made with the intent to significantly reorient the constitution as a whole, but they turned out to have little substantial impact on the core values and principles of the amended provisions. The best example for this kind of *nominal* constitutional revolution is the endurance of the constitution's primary concern with economic well-being by guaranteeing the people basic economic rights such as property and labor, and, emanating from those rights, by mandating and enabling government policies on specific economic affairs. The designation of a separate "Economy Chapter," a feature of all Korean constitutions since 1948, is rarely found in other constitutions. Even the Weimar Constitution, renowned for its progressive socio-economic rights, that allegedly inspired Korea's Founding Constitution, did not have a separate chapter on the economy. This keen focus on the critical importance of the economy was at once the most realistic *and* most idealistic feature of the Founding Constitution. That is why its Economy Chapter turned out to be relatively "socialistic"[6] for a new nation born on the capitalist side of the Cold War's fault line.[7]

It is also for the same reason of constitutional realism combined with idealism that the original economic constitution underwent changes as the Cold War circumstances deepened after the Korean War. Postwar economic rehabilitation could be achieved only with the aid of the foreign investment sponsored by the United States, which necessitated a substantial amendment towards a more open, market-oriented economy. Under pressures from Washington, thus, constitutional revision in 1954 liberalized foreign trade and facilitated the privatization of the state-controlled economy [Park 2011]. By 1962, the economic order of Korea had been redefined "as based on respect for the freedom and creative initiatives of individuals in economic affairs" (Article 111) and the unusual mandate on the equal share of corporate profits (Article 18) removed to shift emphasis from the state's right of control to its obligation to foster foreign trade (Article 116). Article 111 was a dramatic, even revolutionary, departure from the "socialistic" spirit of the Founding Constitution and a continuation and culmination of those constitutional developments of the 1950s, including granting the state the power of intervention on the ground of "social justice and equitable economic development." Constitutional realism carried the day, now focused on national economic development rather than economic justice, and the export-led industrialization soon took off.[8]

Political authoritarianism in the 1960s and 1970s hardly stood in the way of Korea's transformation into a modern industrial nation within less than a generation. Conversely, successful economic development and the consolidation of the middle class contributed to the demise of the Yushin dictatorship and the semi-authoritarian Fifth Republic, and thereby paved the way to the democratic constitution of 1987. Where did this leave the Economy Chapter? On the one hand, the spirit of Article 111 took a business-friendly turn in that "enterprises" in addition to "individuals" were inserted as the proprietor of the "economic liberty and creative initiative." On the other hand, the state's powers increased remarkably:

> The State may regulate and coordinate economic affairs in order to maintain a balanced growth and stability of the national economy, to ensure proper distribution of income, to prevent the domination of the market and the abuse of economic power and *to democratize the economy* through harmony among the economic agents [italics added].

For sure, constitutionally authorizing an active role for government in economic affairs comported with Korea's entrenched experience of state-led development. No doubt constitutional realism of the Economy Chapter needed to be balanced out with a healthy dose of idealism that would sanction even stronger forms of state intervention in coping with the growing social ills that came with the rapid economic and social transformation of Korea. And yet, the way in which Article 119 spelled out this constitutional idealism was extraordinary as it set concrete policy goals with such attention to details. Also under the broad and general rubric of "democratization of the economy," the new Article 123 went so far as to mandate a "balanced development" for farming and fishing interests, small and medium businesses, and different regional provinces. Its fourth clause even obliged the state "to stabilize the prices of agricultural and fishery products by maintaining an equilibrium between the demand and supply of such products and improving their marketing and distribution systems."

Given such constitutional attention to what are basically policy matters, it is no wonder that the economic constitution of 1987 has been at the center of public controversies both in and out of the courtroom. Although the Constitutional Court has held consistently that the first clause (on economic liberty) declares the main foundation of Korea's economic order, while the second clause (on economic democratization) is a supplementary principle,[9] such a ruling has only intensified the controversy among justices, lawyers, and scholars over the nature of Korea's economic constitution. For example, even under the current constitution there is support for reintroducing the employee's right to an equal share of corporate profits, which was first established in the Founding Constitution but subsequently eliminated in the 1962 revision. The reason is mainly that economic liberty and economic democratization in Article 119 are better interpreted as constituting two principles of equal value and importance. This reading, a significant departure from the Court's, recognizes the questionable right to equal share of profit as one of the "rights of citizens [that] shall not be neglected on the grounds that they are not enumerated in the Constitution" (Article 37) [Hwang 2017, 88–89]. As such, this interpretation relies on a historical argument by asserting that giving equal weight to political liberty and economic equality is the original intent behind the economic constitution of 1948 and, as such, a guiding constitutional spirit that survived nine official revisions [Hwang 2017, 104]. According to such a quasi-Originalist interpretation of the economic constitution, which finds many a sympathetic ear in contemporary Korean society,[10] the constitutional revisions of 1954 and 1962 were merely instances of *nominal* constitutional revolution that introduced substantial changes in the black letter laws without enduring consequences for the constitutional identity of Korea.

In the light of these recent developments, it is not surprising that the government draft constitution of 2018 proposed to steer the Economy Chapter in the direction of more robust "economic democratization" [Korean Government 2018, 26–28]. Although this proposal failed to pass the National Diet, with the Supreme and Constitutional Court already reformed in the image of the present progressive government, it is possible that the established court ruling on economic constitution be turned over even before the next push for a constitutional revision resumes. The supporters of this direction of constitutional change, be that formal or informal, might as well argue that this is all for the restoration of the original intent and/or the re-edification of the unchanging identity of the economic constitution of Korea. As such, that constitutional soul shall be revered as having survived all those constitutional revolutions that prove to be merely *nominal* in their future retrospective.

Quiet Constitutional Revolution

The claim that the constitutional change in the Economy Chapter is less dramatic than meets the eye and better seen as an instance of nominal constitutional revolution does not mean that substantial constitutional transformation has not occurred in Korea. For instance, the constitutional protection of basic rights has waxed and waned subtly but significantly along with the political ups and downs. It just means that such a constitutional change does not always adopt the form of a classic constitutional revolution. Even in Korea, those revolutionary changes can take place without any formal revision of the black letter law of the constitution to effect what can be called a quiet constitutional revolution.

In this regard, a good place to start is the General Provisions, in which the fundamental political identity of the nation is declared along with the human and territorial boundaries of the nation. In particular, Article I (providing for the basic form of the polity and the ultimate locus of sovereignty) can be traced back to the 1919 Charter of the Provisional Government of Korea and other proto-constitutional documents that this organization of the exiled independence activists produced in China before 1945. Its Article 1 declares that the "Republic of Korea is a democratic republic" as all subsequent constitutional laws have done invariably since then. Naturally, this lofty declaration has come to mean different things to different people in different times even as the nomenclature remained unchanged for a century.

When the declaration made its first appearance in 1919, it was meant to signal a historic break from the defunct dynasty of Choson that was responsible for the colonization as well as a pointed rebuke to its perpetrator, the Empire of Japan, also ruled by a hereditary monarch [Park 2013]. The identical term was revived for the Founding Constitution in its Article 1 after the Japanese imperial rule collapsed and a return to the pre-annexation monarchy became a foregone conclusion in the postcolonial constitutional politics. This was mostly because the political semiotics had changed, and the "democratic republic" came to signify something altogether different. Now the main political *signifié* of this concept was the rivalry with North Korea, where a communist regime was emerging under Soviet occupation in the name of a "people's republic." If the pre-1945 usage meant indeed "people's republic" as a rejection of both the Choson monarchy and the *tennō*'s empire, the "democratic republic" of 1948 came to have a radically different connotation in a way that antagonized the "people's republic" of the North. For the drafters of the South Korean constitution, in other words, the "people's republic" was no longer a symbolic depository of national and popular sovereignty, but a code name for the Marx-Leninist dictatorship of the proletariat. In conscious contrast, the "democratic republic" of South Korea came to acquire a new constitutional connotation that went beyond popular sovereignty—it now had an added meaning of the *liberal* separation and balance of power as opposed to the *communist* concentration of power in the one-party state [Yu 1959, 19]. The term remained unchanged before and after 1945, but its connotation was radically transformed, even revolutionized, in the process of constitution-making in South Korea.

Thus revived against the dawning Cold War backdrop, Article 1 has been undergoing a *quiet* constitutional revolution triggered by the thawing of the Cold War. This transformation began, albeit in an unwitting way, with the making of Article 4 (mandating a unification with North Korea) in the 1980 constitution and further fueled by the United Nations admission of the two Koreas in 1991. These developments in constitutional and international law have complicated the interpretation of "democratic republic" in Article 1, now also involving that of Article 3 as well as Article 4. Never amended since 1948, Article 3 defines the territory as the "Korean peninsula and its adjacent islands" in total and purposeful disregard of the political reality that the northern half of the peninsula is under the effective territorial jurisdiction of the Democratic People's Republic of Korea. According to this provision, the North Korean government is merely a de facto entity, without a de jure status, in unlawful occupation of a part of South Korean territory. In mandating a "peaceful unification [with the North]," by contrast, Article 4 signals some kind of recognition of the North Korean government without saying as much, an interpretation that is reinforced by the two Koreas' simultaneous admission to the United Nations. This post–Cold War status quo has further strained the domestic constitutional dilemma regarding how to reconcile these new realities, mandates, and assumptions that pulled constitutional interpretation in different directions. Unsurprisingly, those new developments have prompted various attempts at legal-dogmatic legerdemain without clear consensus among justices, lawyers, and scholars in contemporary Korea.[11]

What is more, the international coexistence and national unification with North Korea posed particular challenges to Article 1, because the meaning of "democratic republic" needs to be substantively expanded to allow room for a mandated unification with the hostile communist regime in the North. In these changed circumstances, the Cold War anti-communist intent behind the making of Article 1 is in need of reexamination, if not elimination, lest the constitution sounds out an insufferable dissonance regarding its most foundational identity. Thus ensued one heated debate after another on the basic constitutional identity not only in the courtrooms (e.g., regarding the constitutionality of the anti-communist National Security Law), but also at the level of civil society (e.g., surrounding how to teach Korea's constitutional identity in school textbooks). The main question revolves largely around whether the "democratic republic" of Article 1 means *liberal democracy* in the narrow sense of the term or *democracy with no adjective* that may be elastic enough to accommodate the so-called "people's democracy" of the North *pace* the original intent of 1948. The current progressive government has vowed to make a total constitutional overhaul and already unveiled its revision draft in 2018 which was suspected to be underwritten largely by the latter understanding of democracy in Korea.[12] While the government draft failed to pass the National Diet, the "democratic republic" of Article 1, that most enduring and fundamental constitutional identity of South Korea, may be undergoing yet another *quiet* constitutional revolution presently.

WAR AND PEACE IN JAPAN

The relatively large number of constitutional revisions in Korea does not necessarily indicate that the constitutional revolution in the classic sense of the term happened with as much frequency. The way in which constitutionalism was experienced in Korea changed materially without formal revision in some cases, but not always so despite significant changes in the constitutional text. Likewise, a closer scrutiny might reveal that, even as postwar Japan witnessed no formal amendment to its constitutional law, its constitution, at least in some parts thereof, has undergone what may be described as a constitutional revolution. In other words, neither *classic* nor *nominal* constitutional revolution can be said to have taken place for the all too self-evident reason. Even so, this undeniable fact cannot warrant the conclusion that there was *no* constitutional revolution in postwar Japan.

Quiet Constitutional Revolution of 1954

Seen from a longer perspective, Japan is *not* without its own experience of constitutional revolution, and it followed quickly on the heels of the total defeat in 1945. The postwar constitution-making was as much about designing a new future as it was about negotiating its rupture with the immediate past. In an important sense, the postwar constitution was born in the penumbra of the prewar Imperial Constitution even as it was rejecting that "unmasterable past" [Maier 1997]. This predicament has drawn a long shadow over the way in which the meaning of such a dis/continuity was teased out by the Japanese government and the public at large under the U.S. military occupation. The conservative government made every effort during the deliberation process to ensure that, despite the unconditional surrender, the novel "symbol emperor system" was a continuation in essence of the sovereign emperorship of the prewar constitution—or, to use a prewar term, the *kokutai*.[13] If this impossible argument was to be believed, the constitutional revolution in postwar Japan was only *nominal* when it came to the emperor's sovereign status irrespective of the formal introduction of popular sovereignty.

For liberals, in contrast, the new democratic constitution represented a decisive departure from its imperial predecessor and a genuine constitutional revolution both in form and substance. As such, the postwar constitution-making is better understood as the legal edification of a political revolution that was posited as a matter of logic where none existed in fact. In other words, the total defeat in August 1945 became a proactive revolution, even if only on paper, because Japan's acceptance of the Potsdam Declaration had the effect of shifting the ultimate locus of sovereignty from the emperor to the people. According to this so-called "August Revolution" theory, then, the postwar constitution-making was an archetypical case of a *classic* constitutional revolution. In the beginning was the constitutional revolution, in short, although it remains unclear if it was nominal or classic in postwar Japan.

Even after this constitutional big bang, Japan cannot be said to have remained immune to revolutionary constitutional changes. And, of course, even more pertinent evidence for this kind of seemingly counterfactual claim can be found in what happened to Article 9 over the past seven decades, or in the changes that may be understood in terms of *quiet* constitutional revolutions.

Article 9 mandates in two terse clauses that Japan shall renounce war, prohibit armament, and surrender the right of belligerency. Extraordinary though it was for a workable constitution, the meaning of these mandates was curiously undebated during the deliberation process for a number of reasons. Although it was welcomed and genuinely embraced by the war-weary public, for realists in the government bureaucracy, it merely reflected a defeated Japan in which no military could be legally recognized after total demilitarization by the occupation authorities [Moore and Robinson 1998, RM058.1]. Governmental and parliamentary leaders shared a tacit acknowledgement that Article 9 was a Faustian bargain by which the military was given up to save the emperor.[14] The government's official position was to embrace this extraordinary pacifism to mean that no war, even for self-defense purposes, could be authorized since the absolute ban on armament prevented Japan from exercising any right of self-defense (even if such were permissible under Article 9) [Moore and Robinson 1998, RM319.PM.SP3.P3]. Ironically, only the Communist Party questioned this restrictive interpretation by the Cabinet Legislation Bureau (CLB), which denied Japan the universal right of sovereign nations as per the newly minted UN Charter.

Another irony was that this official interpretation, consistent with the GHQ's original intent,[15] served Prime Minister Yoshida Shigeru's diplomacy well in resisting Washington's pressure to rearm during and after the Korean War. Constitutionally, the consequence of this diplomatic maneuver against the American second imposition (rearmament) on account of its first (disarmament) was the deeper entrenchment of Article 9 in its most self-constraining guise [Hahm and Kim 2015, 92]. By the time the Self-Defense Forces (SDF), Japan's quasi-military, were created in 1954, the interpretation of Article 9 as prohibiting self-defense had become an established convention shared by both the government and the public at large. The contradiction that the establishment of the SDF created, however, meant that the official interpretation, if not Article 9 itself, had to be adjusted in a way that reversed Yoshida's previous diplomacy on how to square the demand for rearmament with the constitution's pacifism.

Obviously, the SDF fell out of Article 9's original purview, and the constitution's parameters had to be stretched to accommodate this de facto military establishment that was "legal but unconstitutional."[16] Having rejected Washington's suggestion for a wholesale revision, the Japanese government thus managed to negotiate the pivotal constitutional change via various cabinet reports to the Diet in 1954 as the SDF Law was enacted. In its essentials, this reinterpretation was predicated on the explicit affirmation of Japan's sovereign right of self-defense under international law, which justified the maintenance of a minimum of armed forces necessary for national security. The reasoning was the exact reversal of that of the original position held by the CLB in 1946, i.e., "if no military, then no meaningful right of self-defense," from which followed that a military ought to be recognized in one form or another in order for the right of self-defense to have any meaning at all. At the same time, the SDF was constrained in a way that other military establishments were not. The kind of permissible armament was limited to the minimum necessary level; more to the point, the scope of authorization was restricted as *not* all the rights of self-defense (à la UN Charter) were permitted—it affirmed only the right of individual, and not collective, self-defense. Enabling and disabling in one stroke, the new Article 9 of 1954 had it both ways as it recognized a de facto military establishment while constraining its organization and operation in a constitutionally binding way. This remarkable constitutional change by the CLB reinterpretation was subsequently endorsed by the voting public in the 1955 general election[17] and upheld by the Supreme Court in the *Sunagawa* case of 1959,[18] persisting with remarkable integrity and consistency until the end of the Cold War. It may be seen a great feat of *quiet* constitutional revolution indeed that combined no formal revision with enduring consequences for the way Article 9 was experienced in postwar Japan.

Dismemberment by Stealth in 2014

By comparison, it is not at all clear if the same label of quiet constitutional revolution can do justice to what the Japanese government under Abe's premiership has done to change Article 9 lately. First to be made clear is that Article 9 is no longer the primary goal of the constitutional revision pursued by Abe, the Liberal Democratic Party (LDP), and other conservative elements in the Japanese society. In this regard, Abe's own proposal of 2017 suggested merely adding a third clause to Article 9 to recognize the SDF explicitly, thereby purporting to end controversies about its constitutionality once and for all. In other words, the first and second clause, always loathed by the right-wing advocates of a return to the "normal state," were left intact in Abe's proposal. This seeming oversight does not indicate a change of mind but a reflection of the new status quo regarding constitutional pacifism. Article 9 had in fact already been reinterpreted in 2014 so as to endorse the right of collective self-defense in a pointed departure from the 1954 interpretation. Now fully equipped with both the rights of individual and collective self-defense, Japan has already become a de facto "normal state" that may wage a war as per the United Nations charter as well as a more equal partner in the military alliance with the United States (now that the military assistance can be mutual). To Abe and his right-wing supporters, gutting Article 9 as such must seem neither necessary nor politically prudent. For the conservative constitutional agenda has a long list of other provisions that need to be revised in the direction of "Japanization"—i.e., shifting the emphasis from individual freedom and universal human rights to duty and obligations, family and tradition, and country and the emperor.[19] Compared to these cumbersome issues, amending Article 9 seems to be a fait accompli [Goodman 2017, 19].

More to the point, that which distinguishes the 2014 reinterpretation from the one in 1954 is the unprecedented process itself, namely, by cabinet decision. Although the Japanese constitution vests the authority to interpret the constitution in the Supreme Court, in actuality it is the CLB that does this, as was the case in 1946 and 1954 regarding Article 9.[20] The CLB adhered to its own 1954 reinterpretation with remarkable steadfastness, resisting political pressure by asking the government to adhere to the constitutional process of amendment, which requires a two-third majority in a popular vote [Yamamoto 2017, 112]. But in 2014, after a decade and a half of unsuccessful campaigns for formal constitutional amendment under LDP governments, the Abe Cabinet effectively sidelined the CLB and announced a Cabinet decision on security issues and foreign policy matters on which the legitimacy of the right to collective self-defense in fact rested. It paid scant attention to the constitution itself; in addition to Article 9, perfunctory references were made only to Article 13 ("the right to life, liberty, and the pursuit of happiness") and the preamble ("the right to live in peace") which has no legal effect in the Japanese court of law.

This Cabinet decision was based on recommendations by an ad hoc Advisory Board created for the sole purpose of changing Article 9. Chaired by a political scientist from the University of Tokyo, this Advisory Board was curiously devoid of legal expertise as well as a clear constitutional ground. In addition to its questionable ground of authority, the Board's so-called constitutional interpretation was written mostly in extralegal terms so contingent and ambiguous that its conclusion became nearly non-judiciable in the strict legal sense. Thus, an expert commentator on the 2014 change of Article 9 concluded that an "interpretation that either renders the provision irrelevant or hopelessly ambiguous and vague . . . simply cannot be accepted as a normal interpretive development" [Martin 2017, 501–02]. What makes this 2014 decision truly unprecedented is the irregularity with which it was reached and justified, rendering Article 9 hardly enforceable in the end. The crux of the problem is that the Cabinet decision has undermined the viability of Article 9 as a living constitutional norm, thereby threatening the pacifist identity of the postwar constitution.

Arguably, this constitutional irregularity orchestrated by the Abe Cabinet may have to do with the more structural problems of Japanese democracy. In order for something like a quiet constitutional revolution to take place, a genuinely contestatory party politics, judicially vigilant courts, and the alert participatory citizenship are necessary lest those informal revisions be abused. For all its virtues, postwar democracy in Japan is not known for these cultural and institutional conditions that enable a wholesome constitutional politics [Dixon and Baldwin 2017]. This may, however, be an oversimplification or overgeneralization, for compelling counterevidence can be found in the 1954 constitutional revolution. Indeed, it was no small achievement for the then-budding constitutional democracy of postwar Japan in which institutions such as the CLB proved their sturdiness and the electoral party dynamics did compel a national referendum of sort that culminated in the "1955

System." Albeit with passivity, perhaps even meekness, the Supreme Court also went along to render an a posteori endorsement of this constitutional rearrangement. Overall, the outlook was that of a quiet constitutional revolution successfully executed with lasting consequences. Abe's 2014 reinterpretation of Article 9 has none of these features, a deficiency that cannot be blamed solely on the cultural and institutional peculiarities of Japanese constitutional democracy.

The Abe Cabinet's willy-nilly reinterpretation of Article 9 seems to suggest less a constitutional revolution of any sort than what may be called "constitutional dismemberment" [Albert 2018] or "constitutional amendment by stealth" [Albert 2015]. The former concept applies to a situation in which formal or informal constitutional change results in a radical and unauthorized reorientation in the fundamental core of a constitutional identity. The latter describes a constitutional change intended to circumvent the formal revision process and entrench the change as a binding constitutional convention. It is a method that is characterized by the lack of the rule of law requirements of transparency, accountability, and predictability. As such, the Abe Cabinet's decision looks like an affront to the postwar pacifist identity to such an extent that it resembles a dismemberment rather than a reinterpretation of the "Peace Constitution." The reinterpretation was accomplished in a way that falls perilously outside the open rule of law processes of democratic decision-making. While it is still premature to evaluate the durability of Abe's tampering with Article 9, albeit highly unlikely, the Supreme Court might abandon its long-held "political questions doctrine" and adopt a more activist posture at last. Also possible as a scenario is the political turn of fate in which a new Cabinet would unveil another decision to revert back to the Article 9 of 1954 now that a precedent has been made. For now, however, it seems more likely that the constitutional feat of 2014 will go down in history as a "dismemberment by stealth" which has shaken up the core constitutional identity of postwar Japan by a method constitutionally questionable, if not outright unconstitutional.

CONCLUDING REMARKS

Constitutional change is hard to define and harder to evaluate. A significant constitutional change can take place without formal amendment, whereas an official revision of the constitutional law may not amount to such a change. Postwar Japan and South Korea is a case in point.

The advent of the Cold War in East Asia quickly followed by the hot war on the Korean Peninsula stretched the limit of Korea's and Japan's respective constitutional frameworks, which had been designed only a few years earlier.

The new Cold War reality made Japan's peace provision vulnerable to the domestic allegation of unhinged idealism as well as to the subsequent pressure for rearmament from Washington. The same external pressure compelled changes in nationalistic and/or socialistic economic provisions as Korea struggled to rehabilitate its war-torn economy with the aid of foreign investment. It was not until the year 1954 when Japan established the Self-Defense Forces followed by a radically new interpretation of Article 9 that the dust settled, albeit neither permanently nor incontrovertibly, in and around the meaning of unarmed peace in postwar Japan. Likewise in Korea, 1954 also saw changes to the economic provisions in a way that could moderate the government's ownership of major industry and control over a free market. All in all, it seems fair to say that both Japan's and Korea's constitutional identities were readjusted to the political and economic reality immediately following their original making, before their original meanings could be discerned with a modicum of stability. The constituent moment in Korea and Japan is therefore better expanded to include these later developments culminating in the constitutional revolutions of 1954.

For all those similarities, the differences are also striking. The first is the blatant fact that Japan's creation of a de facto military, a feat of constitutional revolution by any measure, did nothing to affect the black-letter law of the constitution. In comparison, retuning the economic provisions in Korea took the posture of constitutional amendment, while leaving the constitutional essentials comprising the economic constitution intact except for provisions that have more narrow policy rather than constitutional ramifications. In other words, Korea seems to have experienced a "nominal constitutional revolution" in contrast to the Japanese case in which a "quiet" but genuine constitutional revolution took place.

This contrasting pattern of constitutional change is also borne out by the subsequent constitutional development in two countries. In the ensuing decades, Korea went through six more times of formal revision triggered in turn by a student revolt, military coups, and a democratization movement. In tandem with those amendments, the economic constitution also changed incrementally towards a more free market form of capitalism. Still, the basic identity of Korea's "economic constitution" survived them all and remains essentially unchanged in the present Article 119, the so-called "economic democratization" provision. It is no surprise, then, that the left-leaning government of Moon Jae-in presently wants to reinforce this constitutional identity via a comprehensive constitutional revision as well as judicial reinterpretations by the Supreme and Constitutional Courts.

The contrast to Japan could not be starker. In the quiet constitutional revolution of 1954, the authoritative Cabinet Legislation Bureau held in essence that maintaining a "minimum necessary force" and military alliance for "self-defensive" purposes was permissible, but exercising the right of "collective self-defense" as an armed ally or UN member was not. This long-held position was changed in 2014, however, when the Abe government announced a decision to stretch the penumbra of Article 9's meaning via reinterpretation. Japan may now exercise the right to engage in collective self-defensive actions abroad if faced with an "existential crisis" even when its own territory is not under direct attack. Arguably, one might characterize this decisive move as yet another instance of "quiet constitutional revolution" comparable to what transpired in 1954, and, to that extent, as conforming to the pattern of constitutional change established in postwar Japan. Were it merely a precursor to the wholesale constitutional revision as sworn by the resolute Abe Cabinet, the relatively minor constitutional revolution of 2014 would likely go down in history as a prequel to a greater revolution in the Japanese constitutional history not only in substance but also in the method of constitutional change. For it will mean that the postwar constitution of Japan would be "dismembered" through a legal process of amendment the outcome of which may be unconstitutional. The impact of such a constitutional dismemberment will be hard to fathom especially when it comes to the pacifist constitutional identity of postwar Japan.

NOTES

1. Note on styles: Japanese and Korean sources are used only when no English translation and/or alternative is available. All references to the contemporary constitutional texts of Japan and Korea follow the English translation as provided by the authoritative Constitute Project (www.constituteproject.org). Those to the past constitutions, especially in Korea, are not included in the Project, thus their translations are mine.
2. On this conservative rhetoric in contemporary Japan, see, e.g., Inoguchi (2005).
3. Korean Culture and Information Service/Ministry of Culture, Sports, and Tourism (2017), 7 [translation mine].
4. Due to editorial interventions, this section has come to contain a radically truncated version of the conceptual and theoretical reflections on constitutional revolution. Other sections have similar problems. For a fuller version of this chapter, please see my "Constitutional Revolution Redux: Postwar Japan and South Korea," *Yonsei Law Journal*.10, nos. 1–2 (2020).
5. E.g., Arendt (1965), 142. For a constitutional scholar's variation on this Arendtian theme, see Ackerman (1991), 203–12. For a sustained critique of this political-legal dogma, see Hahm and Kim (2015), 13–65.
6. See, e.g., "Chapter Six, entitled 'Economy,' ostensibly makes the Korean Republic a *socialistic* state." Dull (1948), 207.

7. This "socialistic" chapter began with the proclamation that the basic principle of Korea's economic order shall be to realize social justice, meet every citizen's basic demands, and develop an equitable economy whereas economic liberty of the individual citizens shall be protected only within the parameter set thereby (Article 84). In order to realize this goal, the chapter also provided for state-regulation of foreign trade and government management of most public utilities (Article 87) as well as state-ownership of most natural resources (Article 85). But even those private enterprises permitted under this chapter could be made state-owned or government-managed when necessary for *public welfare* as well as national security (Article 88). In other parts of the constitution, too, while the right of property was recognized, the constitution also made it clear that its exercise must "conform to the public welfare" (Article 15). The state had a duty to protect those unable to work due to old age, infirmity, or incapacity (Article 19). In addition to a general provision for labor rights, the constitution gave special protection for the labor of women and children (Article 17). Most unusual perhaps was the provision on so-called workers' rights to equal share in the profits of private enterprises (Article 18).

8. For more on these revisions, see Hahm and Kim (2015), 115–25.

9. For instance, see Constitutional Court of Korea, 1989.12.22.88HeonGa13 [on Land Use Law]; 1997.11.27.96HeonBa12 [on Door-to-Door Sales Act]; 2002.7.18.2001 HeonMa6052001HeonMa605 [on defining unfair monopoly in the Newspaper Act]; 2008.12.26.2005HeonBa34[on Restructuring of the Financial Industry Act].

10. E.g., one of the leading progressive politicians, Sim Sang-jung, publicly advocated the rejuvenation of this particular constitutional right during her presidential campaign in 2017. See, e.g., *The Joong-Ang Ilbo Daily*, April 12, 2017.

11. For an authoritative survey of this issue, see Korean Ministry of Government Legislation (2010), 118–37.

12. Both the Preamble and Article 4 make clear that a "free and democratic basic order" is the meaning of democracy in Korea. During the deliberation process, the report was made that the government draft would eliminate "free" from the Preamble and Article 4. Indeed, the government's commentary on the revised Preamble emphasized democracy and democratization only [see Government Draft Proposal 4]. Although this omission did not happen in the eventuality (thanks in part to this scandal), such a movement within the government fueled the conservative suspicion of the Moon government's ulterior motive, undermining its already slim chance of passing the National Diet where consent from two-thirds of the members are required.

13. Kanamori Tokujiro, the Yoshida Cabinet's Minister of State during Diet deliberations in charge of explaining the Government Draft to the lawmakers, was particularly instrumental in presenting this impossible argument. To the criticism that the new constitution would alter the *kokutai*, he responded that, although sovereignty now belongs to the entire people of Japan, also included among "the people" is the emperor. See Moore and Robinson (1998), RM325.PM.SP4.

14. In a sense, the sacrifice was a matter of course. The war had been fought against the militarism of imperial Japan, and its utter defeat was bound to demand that the "Emperor's Military" (*kōgun* 皇軍) should be broken up somehow. Faced with the prospect that the emperor (皇) and his military (軍) would no longer be allowed

to share the same fate, both SCAP and the Japanese government chose to sacrifice the military and save the emperor [Otake 2001, 50].

15. See the second item of the MacArthur Note of 1946, laying out the three basic principles for the GHQ draft, which reads: "War as a sovereign right of the nation is abolished. Japan renounces it as an instrumentality for settling its disputes and *even for preserving its own security*" [emphasis mine].

16. This paradoxical proposition holds that, on the one hand, Article 9 cannot be construed to sanction SFD in view of the original legislative intent as manifested during the Diet deliberation process in 1946. The procedural legality by which SFD was created in 1954, on the other, cannot be questioned and invalidated in the absence of clear judicial intervention. Kobayashi (1982), 149–54.

17. See, generally, Masumi (1985).

18. 13 Keishū 13, 3225, 3232 (Sup. Ct. Grand Bench, Dec. 16, 1959, summary of judgment in English available on http://www.courts.go.jp/app/hanrei_en/detail?id=13.

19. Thus, the LDP Q&A for its 2012 revision draft explains its overall policy as follows: "Rights are gradually generated from the history, tradition, and culture of the community. Accordingly, human rights provisions need to be based on the history, culture, and tradition of our country. There are some provisions in the current constitution that could be viewed as being derived from the European idea that human rights are granted by God. We believe that these provisions need to be revised" [as quoted in Matsui (2018), 74]. Never mind that the underwriting conservatism is also an European idea derived from Edmund Burke! Those provisions to be revised under this general philosophy are too numerous to list here. Even a random glance at the 2012 LDP draft shows that the current emphasis on the universal fundamental character of constitutional rights were toned down in Articles 11 and 97, even as those rights could be reserved by ordinary law on account of "public interest or public order," as in the prewar Imperial Constitution, in Articles 13 and 21 (freedom of expression). The state and public support for Shintoism could be permitted on account of "social ceremonies or customary practices" in Article 20, while the new Article 24 added family values to the rights regime in a way potentially prejudicial to women's status in Japanese society. For more, see Komamura (2017), especially, 84–92.

20. For CLB's role in the interpretation of Article 9, see Yamamoto (2017), 108–11. On the judicial passivism of the Supreme Court in general, see Matsui (2011).

REFERENCES

Books and Articles

Ackerman, Bruce (1991). *We the People: Foundations.* Cambridge, MA: Harvard University Press.

Albert, Richard (2015). "Constitutional Amendment by Stealth." *McGill Law Journal* 60: 673–736.

———. (2018). "Constitutional Amendment and Dismembermen." *Yale Journal of International Law* 43: 1–84.

Arendt, Hannah (1965). *On Revolution*. New York: Viking Press.

Dixon, Rosalind, and Guy Baldwin (2017). "Globalizing Constitutional Moments? A Reflection on the Japanese Article 9 Debate." *University of New South Wales Law Research Series* 74.

Dull, Paul S. (1948). "South Korean Constitution." *Far Eastern Survey* 17: 205–7.

Dworkin, Ronald (1986). *Law's Empire*. Cambridge, MA: Harvard University Press.

Goodman, Carl F. (2017). "Contemplated Amendments to Japan's 1947 Constitution: A Return to *Iye, Kokutai*, and the Meiji State." *Washington International Law Journal* 26: 17–74.

Hahm, Chaihark, and Sung Ho Kim (2015). *Making We the People: Democratic Constitutional Founding in Postwar Japan and South Korea*. New York: Cambridge University Press.

Hasebe, Yasuo (1997). "The August Revolution Thesis and the Making of the Constitution of Japan." *Rechtstheorie* 17: 335–42.

Hwang, Seung Heum (2017). "Kyŏngje Hŏnpŏp ŭi Byŏnchŏn" [Change of the Economic Constitution]. *Hyŏndaesa Kwangjang* [Contemporary History Forum] 9: 82–103.

Inoguchi, Takashi (2005). "Japan's Ambition for Normal Statehood," in *Between Compliance and Conflict: East Asia, Latin America and the "New" Pax Americana*, eds. Jorge I. Dominguez and Byung Kook Kim, 135–64. New York: Routledge.

Jacobsohn, Gary J. (2010). *Constitutional Identity*. Cambridge, MA: Harvard University Press.

———. (2014). "Theorizing the Constitutional Revolution," *Journal of Law and Courts* 2: 1–32.

———, and Yaniv Roznai (2020). *Constitutional Revolution*. New Haven, CT: Yale University Press.

Kim, Sung Ho (2020). "Constitutional Revolution Redux: Postwar Japan and South Korea." *Yonsei Law Journal* 19, nos. 1–2.

Kobayashi, Naoki (1982). *Kenpō Daikyūjō* [Constitution Article 9]. Tokyo: Iwanami Shinsho.

Komamura, Keigo (2017). "Constitution and Narrative in the Age of Crisis in Japanese Politics." *Washington International Law Journal* 26: 75–97.

Lipin, Michael (2012). "Egypt's New Constitution: How It Differs from the Old Version." https://www.voanews.com/africa/egypts-new-constitution-how-it-differs-old-version (accessed 9 January 2020).

Maier, Charles (1997). *The Unmasterable Past: History, Holocaust, and the German National Identity*. Cambridge, MA: Harvard University Press.

Martin, Craig (2017). "The Legitimacy of Informal Constitutional Amendment and the Reinterpretation of Japan's War Powers." *Fordham International Law Journal* 40: 427–521.

Masumi, Junnosuke (1985). *Postwar Politics in Japan, 1945–1955*, trans. E. Carlile. Berkeley: University of California Press.

Matsui, Shigenori (2011). "Why Is the Japanese Supreme Court So Conservative?" *Washington University Law Review* 88: 1375–423.

———. (2018). "Fundamental Human Rights and 'Traditional Japanese Values': Constitutional Amendment and Vision of the Japanese Society." *Asian Journal of Comparative Law* 13: 59–86.

Moore, Ray A., and Donald L. Robinson (1998). *The Japanese Constitution: A Documentary History of Its Framing and Adoption, 1945–1947.* Princeton, NJ: Princeton University Press. [Footnote entries that begin with "RMxxx" refer to the document number within this database]

Otake, Hideo (2001). "Two Contrasting Constitutions in the Postwar World: The Making of the Japanese and the West German Constitutions," in *Five Decades of Constitutionalism in Japanese Society,* ed. Yoichi Higuchi. Tokyo: University of Tokyo Press.

Park, Chan Seung (2013). *Taehan Min'guk-ŭn Minju Konghwaguk-ida* [The Republic of Korea Shall Be a Democratic Republic]. Seoul: Dolbegae.

Park, Myung Lim (2011). "Constitution, National Agenda, and Presidential Leadership: Focusing on a Comparison between the Articles on Economy in the 'National Founding Constitution' and the 'Post-Korean War Constitution.'" *Korean Social Science Review* 1: 263–302.

Roznai, Yaniv (2017). *Unconstitutional Constitutional Amendments: The Limits of Amendment Power*. Oxford: Oxford University Press.

Schmitt, Carl (2004). *Legality and Legitimacy,* trans./ed. Jeffrey Seitzer. Durham, NC: Duke University Press.

Yamamoto, Hajime (2017). "Interpretation of the Pacifist Article of the Constitution by the Bureau of Cabinet Legislation: A New Source of Constitutional Law?" *Washington International Law Journal* 26: 99–124.

Yu, Chin-o (1959) *Shin'go Hŏnpŏp Haeŭi* [Constitutional Law Explained, Revised Edition]. Seoul: Ilchogak.

Court Cases and Other Government Documents

Japanese Cabinet Legislation Bureau (1946). *Kenpō Kaisei Sōan ni kansuru Sōtei Mondai* [Expected Questions Regarding the Draft Revised Constitution], No. 118–52.

Japanese Supreme Court 13 Keishū 13, 3225, 3232 (Sup. Ct. Grand Bench, Dec. 16, 1959), summary of judgment in English available on http://www.courts.go.jp/app/hanrei_en/detail?id=13.

Korean Constitutional Court 88HeonGa13 [on Land Use Law Article 31-2-1 and 21-3]

———. 96HeonBa12 [on Door-to-Door Sales Act Article 18-1]

———. 2001HeonMa605 [on defining unfair monopoly in the Newspaper Act Article 3-1]

———. 2005HenonBa34 [on Act on the Restructuring of the Financial Industry Article 5]

Korean Culture and Information Service/Ministry of Culture, Sports, and Tourism, 2017 Inaugural Address of the 19th President. In *Selected Speeches of President*

Moon Jae-in of the Republic of Korea, May–July 2017. Seoul: Korean Culture and Information Service/Ministry of Culture, Sports, and Tourism.
Korean Government (2018) *Taehan Min'guk Hŏnpŏp Kaejŏngan* [Government Constitutional Revision Draft]. https://webcache.googleusercontent.com/search?q=cache:tqljNk5v_HUJ:https://www1.president.go.kr/dn/5ab3794c3da8d+&cd=4&hl=ko&ct=clnk&gl=kr (accessed 9 January 2020).
Korean Ministry of Government Legislation (2010) *Hŏnpŏp Jusŏksŏ* I [Constitutional Commentary I]. Seoul: Ministry of Government Legislation

Chapter Thirteen

Constitutional Revision Going Astray

Article Nine and Security Policy

Yoshihide Soeya

In September 2015, under the strong leadership of Prime Minister Shinzō Abe, the Japanese Diet (national assembly) passed the so-called "Legislation for Peace and Security" (hereafter, the 2015 Legislation) which consists of a new law commonly called the "International Peace Cooperation Law" and a set of revisions to ten existing laws. The legislation covers three areas of Japan's security policy: "international peace cooperation," "important influence situations," and "existential crisis." Of the three, the last one, "existential crisis," deserves our special attention in that it is at the center of efforts to dismantle the long-standing consensus in postwar Japanese security policy that while individual self-defense is constitutional under Article 9, collective self-defense is not. Under the 2015 Legislation, collective self-defense becomes constitutional *in the case of an "existential crisis"*; what that entails is thus of the utmost importance.

An "existential crisis" is defined in the new legislation as a situation in which "an armed attack against a foreign country that is in a close relationship with Japan occurs and as a result threatens Japan's survival and poses a clear danger to fundamentally overturn people's right to life, liberty and pursuit of happiness" (Cabinet Secretariat, 2014). This authorizes the prime minister of Japan to proactively deploy the Self-Defense Forces (SDF) outside Japanese territory to assist "a foreign country that is in a close relationship with Japan." In such an event, "use of force must be carried out while observing international law. In certain situations this is based on the right of collective self-defense under international law" (Government of Japan, 2016). The point in need of close examination is that the virtual exercise of the right of collective self-defense was made possible without actually changing Article 9 of the Japanese Constitution. A second long-standing consensus was thus overridden: that the use of force in exercising the right of collective self-defense required formal constitutional revision.

Shinzō Abe's original intention was very much to revise Article 9, which originated from his ideological aspiration to reform the legacies of the occupation and thus to depart from the "postwar regime," whose basic pillars are Article 9 and the U.S.-Japan Security Treaty. But this turned out to be difficult if not impossible, given the steep hurdle of a two-thirds majority in a popular referendum on constitutional revision. Abe therefore chose to realize the exercise of the right of collective self-defense within the confines of Article 9. Ironically, and counter to Abe's original motivation, this has resulted not in a dismantling but rather in a virtual confirmation of the "postwar regime."

To unpack this complex mix of norms, intent, and effect, we will first examine the logic of the constitutionality of collective self-defense in terms of the law as well as Japan's security needs in the current context to determine how much of a departure from earlier reinterpretations of Article 9 the 2015 Legislation represents. From these perspectives, the new interpretation evidences a number of inconsistencies and logical pitfalls. Second, we will analyze the political framework, consisting of Article 9 and the U.S.-Japan security relationship, that made the recent security legislation possible in comparison with two 1950s cases: (1) the establishment of the SDF in 1954 under the Ichirō Hatoyama administration, and (2) the 1960 revision of the U.S.-Japan Security Treaty by the Nobusuke Kishi administration. In 1954, as in 2015, what used to be understood as requiring the revision of Article 9 ended up being justified by the logic of Article 9. The 1960 case brings into relief intriguing similarities between Shinzō Abe and his grandfather Nobusuke Kishi: both politicians were driven by a strong ideological desire to overcome the constraints of the "postwar regime" sustained by Article 9 but instead ended up consolidating them.

These comparative points reveal two fundamental truths about postwar Japanese diplomacy and security/defense policies. One is the robustness of the postwar framework premised on Article 9 and the U.S.-Japan Security Treaty. The other is an enduring sense of unease about this robust framework, which does indeed constrain Japan's freedom of action and evokes periodic attacks on ideological and political grounds from both the liberal Left and conservative Right. Prime ministers have tried to exert leadership according to their ideological motivations, but policy outcomes have never truly challenged the "postwar regime" but instead tended to consolidate it even further. In this respect, the 2015 Legislation was no departure from postwar precedent.

CONTRADICTIONS IN THE 2015 LEGISLATION FOR PEACE AND SECURITY

The Logic of Collective Self-Defense

Up until the 2015 revision, the conditions for the use of force in the name of self-defense were: (1) when an armed attack against Japan occurs; (2) when there are no other appropriate means available to repel the attack and ensure Japan's survival and protect its people; (3) use of force should be limited to the minimum extent. The new legislation added to (1):

> [when an armed attack against Japan occurs] *or when an armed attack against a foreign country that is in a close relationship with Japan occurs and as a result threatens Japan's survival and poses a clear danger to fundamentally overturn people's right to life, liberty, and pursuit of happiness.* (Cabinet Secretariat, 2014)

Whereas the previous interpretation maintained that Japan as a sovereign state has the right of collective self-defense but the Constitution does not allow the exercise of that right, formalized in 1972 (Naikaku hōseikyoku, 1972) and refined in 1981 (Naikaku sōri-daijin Suzuki Zenkō, 1981), the 2015 Legislation justified the exercise of the right within the confines of Article 9 of the Constitution. How was that possible? The Cabinet decision of July 1, 2014, argued as follows:

> As a matter of course, Japan's "use of force" must be carried out while observing international law. At the same time, a legal basis in international law and constitutional interpretation need to be understood separately. In certain situations, the aforementioned "use of force" permitted under the Constitution is, under international law, based on the right of collective self-defense. Although this "use of force" includes those which are triggered by an armed attack occurring against a foreign country, they are permitted under the Constitution only when they are taken as measures for self-defense which are inevitable for ensuring Japan's survival and protecting its people, in other words for defending Japan. (Cabinet Secretariat, 2014)

This follows a roundabout logic that asserts the right of collective self-defense (applicable under international law) as in fact an integral element of self-defense (applicable under Article 9 of the Japanese Constitution). The insistence on nevertheless keeping the legal bases of international and national law separate serves to simultaneously justify the virtual exercise of the right of collective self-defense in the name of Article 9 and limit the situations in which it can occur. To that effect, Article 76 of the Self-Defense Law was revised to expand the prime minister's power (as supreme commander of the SDF) so that he can now order the deployment and dispatch of the SDF to assist a friendly country under attack, but only when the threat to the country causes Japan to face an "existential crisis" (Boeishō, 2015).

Internationalist Agenda vs. "Existential Crisis"

The revision of the first two regulations on "important influence situations" and "international peace cooperation" signify the steady advancement of Japanese regional and global security roles, which are internationalist in nature. The former expanded the "Guidelines of Defense Cooperation between Japan and the United States," initially agreed on in 1978 and revised in 1997, as well as the "Law Concerning Measures to Ensure the Peace and Security of Japan in Situations in Areas Surrounding Japan" enacted in May 1999. The role of the SDF expanded to include activities in support of American military objectives in cases that bear upon Japan's survival. In addition, the SDF is now able to provide those support activities not only to the United States but also to other foreign countries with whom Japan has close relations.

As for the specific measures that Japan can provide for the United States, the law prohibits "threat or use of force" and limits Japanese support activities to logistic support, search and rescue operations, and vessel inspection (Denshi seifu (a), 2016). An "important influence situation" is defined as "a situation that has an important influence on Japan's peace and security in that it could lead to a direct armed attack against Japan if left unattended." The nature of such danger is different from that of an "existential crisis," and therefore the law does not deal with any case relating to collective self-defense. More strikingly, the so-called "Law on Measures relating to Actions by the Militaries of the United States and Other Countries" includes the terms "armed attack" and "existential crisis" in its full title (Denshi seifu (b), 2016). But instead of giving specific instructions, it merely refers back to Clause 1 of Article 76 of the SDF Law, that is to say, the SDF can act only in case of an armed attack on Japan. In other words, the expansion of the two laws has little to do with the new interpretation concerning the right of collective self-defense.

Similarly, under "international peace cooperation," the range of use of force by the SDF in peacekeeping operations (PKO) has expanded to include, for example, the so-called "coming to the protection of individuals in response to urgent request" (*kaketsuke keigo*), and at the same time long-standing restrictions on the operations by the Japanese SDF are kept intact. Japanese participation in UN peacekeeping operations requires a prior ceasefire agreement, the explicit consent of the host country and all other parties to the conflict, must maintain strict impartiality, and may be suspended if guidelines are not met (Secretariat of the International Peace Cooperation Headquarters, 2015). In these ways, the 2015 Legislation represents steady progress of Japan's role in response to regional and global security needs. What courted controversy in domestic politics and among the Japanese public, however, concerned the right of collective self-defense, which was the most important agenda for Prime Minister Shinzō Abe and his allies.

Dual Logic as a Political Scheme

The two-fold logic of declaring the exercise of the right of collective self-defense constitutional looks legalistic but is in fact political. If the use of force outside Japan in a situation that throws Japan into an "existential crisis" is interpreted as part of self-defense and thereby constitutional, why was it necessary to add a second layer of logic justifying this as Japan's right of *collective self-defense*? For decades, all attempts to acquire the right to collective self-defense were understood to require the revision of Article 9 and therefore failed.

Abe staked his political agenda on the revision of Article 9 from the time he was first voted into the prime minister's in 2006. Voted in again in 2012, he changed tactics, focusing on changing Article 96 (which stipulates the procedure by which the Constitution may be amended) from the required two-thirds majority vote in both houses of the Diet to a simple majority vote before being put to a national referendum. This proved overwhelmingly unpopular. Since then, Abe has sought to legalize the exercise of the right to collective self-defense without changing Article 9, thereby preserving the very core of the "postwar regime" he had set out to unmake for ideological reasons. Now that the exercise of the right of collective defense has become de facto constitutional, the need for revising Article 9 for this purpose has dissipated. Instead, he then sought to add a third clause to Article 9 which would legitimize the SDF while leaving the present first and second clauses intact. This way, Abe argued in May 2017, the debate about whether or not the SDF is constitutional is resolved without any changes to Japan's defense and security policies (Abe Shinzō, 2017).

Contradiction as an Abe Agenda

There is, however, a serious pitfall in this proposal. The new interpretation under the 2015 Legislation justified the exercise of the right of collective self-defense only with respect to an "existential crisis," having substantial impact on Japan's survival. Article 51 of the UN Charter makes no distinction between individual and collective self-defense, but this is an internationalist right of the UN member states for the sake of international peace and security.[1] The Japanese interpretation of this right is only for the sake of the defense and security of Japan, and does not allow Japan to engage in military operations with the United States and other friendly nations if the case has no direct bearing on Japan's security. Legally, this incompleteness is because of Article 9: as long as the Japanese government has to justify the exercise of the right of collective self-defense within the confines of Article 9, this has to be justified in the name of self-defense. At the same time, however, many Japanese conservative advocates of the revision of Article 9, including Prime Minister Abe himself, appear content with the current interpretation achieved under the 2015 Legislation.

This suggests that the primary concern is Japan's own security, not increased willingness to contribute to the mission of international peace and security let alone that of collective security based on UN decisions. If Japan is to commit to the UN-led duties of maintaining international stability, then the next natural and logical step is the revision of Article 9, which would then allow the Japanese SDF to fully engage in international peace and security cooperation.[2] Prime Minister Abe, however, has not shown any interest or aspiration to move on to this phase, but instead reverted to his nationalist impulse to fight against Japanese pro–Article 9 liberals. Thus, the revision of Article 9 has become an end goal in itself, virtually a legacy issue for Prime Minister Abe.

Despite the legal changes justifying the exercise of the right of collective self-defense, an important question remains: Is Japan ready to use the right in real security contingencies? To say that the 2015 Legislation adds to deterrence, as the Japanese government often stresses, is one thing. Putting it into practice in actual contingencies is another. The most likely case in which Japan might actually consider invoking the right would be a Korean contingency, which would constitute an obvious "existential crisis" for Japan. But there have been no diplomatic efforts, either from Tokyo or Seoul, to create an environment conducive to substantial military cooperation between the two countries. In sum, the exercise of the right of collective self-defense has revealed itself as an issue of nationalism rather than internationalism, has remained within the confines of the postwar regime premised on Article 9 and the U.S.-Japan Security Treaty, and has no prospect of being put into practice even in a most obvious "existential crisis" on the Korean Peninsula. It is fair to conclude that the issue of the exercise of the right of collective self-defense was primarily an "Abe agenda," not necessarily an outcome of serious considerations of security policy.

THE ARTICLE 9 ALLIANCE (A9A) SCHEME

Japan's international security engagement is firmly grounded in its security relationship with the United States, anchored by the bilateral security treaty originally signed in the midst of the Korean War in 1951 by Shigeru Yoshida, and revised in 1960 under Nobusuke Kishi despite mass protests against it (and him) by the Japanese people. This security relationship is constrained by an earlier American invention, Article 9 of Japan's U.S.-written Constitution, which hails from the pre–Cold War years and the vision of a non-military Japan within a UN-centered global order. Soon, however, the Cold War engulfed Europe and then Asia as well. The tension between two visions that encapsulated the rapidly changing international relations in the first postwar decade has haunted Japan's place in the world ever since. But despite its contradictions, it consolidated in the 1970s into what I term the "A9A Scheme," or the Article 9-restricted U.S.-Japan Alliance (Soeya, 2017b) as the foundation of a pragmatic approach to Japanese defense and security policies that nonetheless belied its ideological tensions (Sadō, 2003).

The "A9A" scheme is fundamentally cracked, which in turn is reflected in the enduring divisions between the political Right and Left in Japan. From the 1950s through the 1970s, Japan's conservative nationalists focused on the revision of Article 9 as a condition for reducing dependence on the United States, while their liberal opponents argued for strategic neutrality amid the Cold War clash between the United States and the Soviet Union. Neutrality was a magic vision justifying both the anti-revision stance on Article 9 and the abrogation of the U.S.-Japan Security Treaty. But neutrality was as unrealistic as the quest for strategic independence sought after by conservative nationalists. As a result of the standstill in the political contest between conservative nationalists and progressive liberals, the "A9A" scheme became gradually entrenched in the "postwar regime" as a compromise not between political positions but by focusing on pragmatics instead of fighting out irreconcilable ideological differences (Soeya, 2005, 2017a).

Conservative nationalists arguing for revising Article 9 often criticize the legitimacy of the postwar Constitution's origin, which was drafted by young and inexperienced American legislators of the U.S.-led occupation in the time span of a week in 1946. Many see the occupation reforms as too progressive and tend to emphasize traditional values long tested since the Meiji period. Conversely, Japanese liberals support the occupation reforms as the foundation of postwar Japanese politics, and society as a negation of wartime colonialism and militarism. Thus, different views of the occupation reforms and the history of empire and war have become the fault line separating pro– and anti–Article 9 revisionists.

On an ideological level, the need for constitutional revision is bound up with a spiritual quest for "true independence" from the occupation and to overcome defeat. Shinzō Abe embodies this sentiment, and stated it clearly in a book he published shortly before becoming Prime Minister when he was Cabinet Secretary in the Junichirō Koizumi Cabinet:

> Japan recovered sovereignty in form by the conclusion of the 1951 San Francisco Peace Treaty. The framework of postwar Japan, however, was created during the occupation period, from, not to mention, the Constitution, to the Basic Law of Education, the basis of educational guidelines. . . .
>
> The foundation of the state has to be created from scratch by the hands of the Japanese people themselves. Only then, true independence can be regained. (Translation mine)[3]

If such emotional aspirations for independence are tantamount to a postwar revolution, the actual outcome of political moves initiated by them tend to fall squarely within the parameters of the "A9A" scheme. In this sense, the 2015 Legislation is almost a replay of what the three most nationalistic politicians attempted back in the 1950s, Prime Ministers Ichirō Hatoyama and Nobusuke Kishi, and their close ally, Foreign Minister Mamoru Shigemitsu.

DÉJÀ VU? THE CONSERVATIVE AGENDA IN THE 1950s COMPARED TO THE 2010s

Shigemitsu, Hatoyama, and Kishi, all prewar politicians purged under the occupation, held strong revisionist views in the early 1950s, when Shigeru Yoshida was prime minister and successfully resisted American pressure to rearm and instead gain space for economic development. Yoshida did agree to establish the National Police Reserve, consisting of 75,000 men equipped with light infantry weapons, which evolved into the National Safety Force of 110,000 men in October 1952 and the Self-Defense Forces two years later. This was a compromise both in international and domestic political relations. It partially satisfied Japan's obligations as per the 1951 Mutual Security Act to take on responsibility for its own national defense, and it was an astute political move to placate Yoshida's conservative rivals by creating a force to defend Japan without changing Article 9 and to pave the way for consolidating the main conservative parties into the LDP.

It fell to Hatoyama, who succeeded Yoshida as prime minister in late 1954, to justify the SDF in the name of Article 9, and against his personal belief. Director-General of the Defense Agency, Seiichi Ōmura, explained the government's reinterpretation of Article 9 as compatible with the right to self-defense in the Lower House:

> First, the Constitution does not deny the right of self-defense. For an independent country, the right of self-defense is a natural right. The Constitution does not deny this. Accordingly, it is quite obvious that Japan has the right of self-defense.
>
> Second, the Constitution renounced war but did not renounce a conflict for the sake of self-defense. 1. War and the use or threat of force are renounced "as means of settling international disputes." 2. It is self-defense itself to rebuff an armed attack itself in case of an armed attack by a foreign country, which is essentially different from a settlement of an international dispute. Therefore, it is not a violation of the Constitution to use force as a means to protect the homeland in case of an armed attack against Japan. (Translation mine; Kokkai kaigiroku, 1954)

The government's declaration of the SDF's constitutionality took the wind out of the sails of the pro-revisionists, at least for the moment. Public opinion was largely against the revision of the Constitution in general and that of Article 9 in particular, which contributed to the growing influence of the progressive opposition parties, most notably the Socialist Party of Japan. The sense of crisis felt by the two conservative parties, the Liberal Party and the Democratic Party, encouraged them to merge into the Liberal Democratic Party (LDP) in November 1955. This ushered in almost four decades of continuous governmental rule by the LDP with the JSP leading a permanent opposition, or what is known as the "1955 system."

During these long years, the LDP played both sides: while advocating constitutional revision to its ideologically conservative constituents as part of the party's platform, in practice it shelved the issue and adhered to Article 9 as the foundation of its foreign and defense/security policies. Not until Shinzō Abe became Prime Minister did the incumbent government embrace constitutional revision as a formal policy agenda. The outcome, however, felt like déjà vu: just as the SDF had been justified in the name of Article 9 in 1954, the exercise of the right of collective self-defense was deemed constitutional within the confines of Article 9.

One significant difference today is that Prime Minister Abe still continued to pursue the goal of revising Article 9 despite the reinterpretation, whereas in the 1950s the argument as well as political moves to revise Article 9 subsided significantly. While the leaders since the 1950s had complied with the basic premises of the "A9A" scheme, it appears that Shinzō Abe is still strongly motivated by his ideological aspiration when it comes to the issue of constitutional revision, perhaps as an issue of personal legacy as the longest serving Prime Minister of Japan since the Meiji period.

Even Abe's grandfather Nobusuke Kishi, a Cabinet member of the Hideki Tōjō administration in the early 1940s and prime minister from 1957–1960, was more realistic about the lack of prospect for constitutional revision. Upon realizing the difficulty of revising Article 9, Kishi began to contemplate a two-stage vision toward revising Article 9 and regaining "independence" from the occupation reforms (Sakamoto, 2000). Revision of the security treaty with the United States was the first step in his grand vision of regaining "independence" in the true sense of the term, and this is exactly why achieving an "equal partnership" with the United States was more than a slogan revealing the essence of Kishi's ambition.

Kishi's ideological aspiration was shared by his close ally Shigemitsu Mamoru, who had served as foreign minister of the wartime Cabinets of Hideki Tōjō and Kuniaki Koiso and became foreign minister again in the Ichirō Hatoyama Cabinet from 1954 to 1956. When Shigemitsu visited Washington, DC, in August 1955, he told John Foster Dulles, Secretary of State of the Dwight Eisenhower administration, that he was contemplating a plan to build a fully equipped army of 180,000 men, large enough to replace U.S. troops stationed in Japan in three years. Shigemitsu also suggested the replacement of the security treaty with "an alliance between equal partners on the basis of reciprocity" like that between the U.S. and the Republic of China, the U.S. and the Philippines, and the U.S. and the Republic of Korea (Gaimusho, 1955a).

In the second meeting with Dulles on August 30, Shigemitsu specified that a new security treaty was to declare that "each party should recognize that an armed attack against territories or areas under the administrative control of the other party poses a danger to its own peace and security, and take actions to cope with a common danger based on constitutional procedures (translation mine)" (Gaimusho, 1955b: 35). Shigemitsu basically proposed a new security relationship involving the exercise of the right to collective self-defense, which was a clear expression of his personal aspirations even if it was unrealistic given Japanese domestic politics and public opinion. The ultimate goal, however, was the complete withdrawal of U.S. troops from Japanese soil. In fact, these aspirations were shared by most conservative (and indeed left-liberal) nationalists in Japan at the time. And it was under Nobusuke Kishi's premiership that the U.S.-Japan Security Treaty was up for renewal in 1960.

The revised security treaty signed by Kishi and Eisenhower in January 1960 stated in its preamble that both parties "have the inherent right of individual or collective self-defense as affirmed in the Charter of the United Nations," and "a common concern in the maintenance of international peace and security in the Far East." The main elements of the security relationship were stated in Articles 5 and 6:

> Article V:
> Each Party recognizes that an armed attack against either Party in the territories under the administration of Japan would be dangerous to its own peace and safety and declares that it would act to meet the common danger in accordance with its constitutional provisions and processes.

> Any such armed attack and all measures taken as a result thereof shall be immediately reported to the Security Council of the United Nations in accordance with the provisions of Article 51 of the Charter. Such measures shall be terminated when the Security Council has taken the measures necessary to restore and maintain international peace and security.
>
> Article VI:
> For the purpose of contributing to the security of Japan and the maintenance of international peace and security in the Far East, the United States of America is granted the use by its land, air and naval forces of facilities and areas in Japan.
>
> The use of these facilities and areas as well as the status of United States armed forces in Japan shall be governed by a separate agreement, replacing the Administrative Agreement under Article III of the Security Treaty between Japan and the United States of America, signed at Tokyo on February 28, 1952, as amended, and by such other arrangements as may be agreed upon (Gaimusho, 1960).

Article 5 basically spells out Japan's obligations to engage in common defense, that is, collective self-defense. This point becomes obvious if one compares it to Article 4 of the ANZUS treaty of 1951 between the United States, Australia, and New Zealand. It states that "each Party recognizes that an armed attack in the Pacific Area on any of the Parties would be dangerous to its own peace and safety and declares that it would act to meet the common danger in accordance with its constitutional processes" (Department of External Affairs, Australia, 1951).

The single most substantive difference between Article 5 of the revised U.S.-Japan Security Treaty and Article 4 of the ANZUS treaty is that while the former designates a common danger for each party as "an armed attack against either Party in the territories under the administration of Japan," that for the latter is simply "an armed attack in the Pacific Area." That is to say, the area of joint defense of Japan and the United States is limited to "the territories under the administration of Japan," whereas Australia and New Zealand committed themselves to mutual defense "in the Pacific Area."[4] The Japanese limitation was of course due to Article 9, which was interpreted as justifying self-defense only. Since Japanese SDF would not be able to go beyond the Japanese territories to engage in an act of mutual defense, security situations beyond Japan would be taken care of by American forces stationed in Japan, as stipulated in Article 6. In the ANZUS treaty, where the parties are committed to act jointly in the Pacific area, the basing clause for the U.S. military does not exist.

Thus, it can reasonably be argued that an aspiration for an "equal partnership" had not been achieved by the revision of the treaty in 1960, let alone gaining "independence" from the United States. Rather, the original logic and setup of the 1951 treaty, i.e., Japan's dependence on the United States for its own security as well as that of the Far East, became firmly institutionalized. Kishi's vision was frustrated not only by the United States but also by unprecedented turmoil in Japanese politics and society against the treaty revision, and he was forced to resign. His successor Ikeda successfully re-directed people's energy away from the controversial agenda of constitutional revision and security policy and towards economic growth and joining the club of advanced economies in the world. The outcome was the consolidation and settlement of the "A9A" scheme, whose process continued into the 1970s, the 1980s, and even the post–Cold War 1990s.

As examined above, the striking trait of the new initiative by Shinzō Abe is that Abe has revitalized the old ideological aspirations to depart from the "postwar regime" after his grandfather failed in the endeavor fifty years ago, and indeed after a half-century process of consolidation of the "A9A" scheme. It is an impossible task, it seems, and Abe has struggled within the walls of the "postwar regime," causing unnecessary confusion and division in Japanese politics and society.

CONCLUDING REMARKS

An interesting development since legitimizing the exercise of the right of collective self-defense by the 2015 Legislation is that Prime Minister Shinzō Abe has stopped raising Article 9 as an obstacle to Japan's security policy. Abe now proposes to add a third clause to legitimize the existence of the SDF which would not change present defense/security policies. He also now makes occasional references to constitutional revision as a general issue, saying it needs to be debated nationally. This confirms the point that, with the 2015 Legislation, Abe has perhaps achieved what he wanted within the confines of Article 9. Still, this does not mean that the problem of the "postwar regime" as the conservative nationalists see it is thereby solved.

Japan's advancement into the domain of international security in the post–Cold War 1990s was made possible by strategically mobilizing the assets of what I have termed the "A9A" scheme. With Shinzō Abe as Japanese Prime Minister, however, some of the key assumptions of postwar Japanese diplomacy in general, and those of its defense/security policies specifically, have been reverted. Historical issues and territorial disputes on which LDP governments used to take a low-key stance have now become the subject of an assertive public diplomacy and foreign policy. Is this an impossible anachronism? Or will this be the beginning of a fundamental transformation of the "postwar regime"? This essay suggests the former. It is nonetheless clear that this point will be one of the most critical aspects of Japanese politics and foreign policy in the post-Abe era.

NOTES

1. Article 51 says, "Nothing in the present Charter shall impair the inherent right of individual or collective self-defense if an armed attack occurs against a Member of the United Nations, until the Security Council has taken measures necessary to maintain international peace and security."

2. This has long been my argument for the revision of Article 9 as part of Japan's middle-power strategy. See Soeya, 2005, 2011.

3. Shinzō Abe. *Utsukushii kuni e* (Tōkyō: Bunshun shinsho, 2006), 28-29.

4. In 1986 the U.S. suspended the treaty's applicability to New Zealand due to the latter's refusal to allow U.S. nuclear-powered ships to enter its waters.

REFERENCES

Abe, Shinzō. *Utsukushii kuni e*. Tōkyō: Bunshun shinsho, 2006.

Hatano, Sumio. *Rekishi toshite no Nichi-bei Anpo-jōyaku*. Tōkyō: Iwanami shoten, 2010.

Sadō, Akihiro. *Sengo Nihon no Bōei to seiji*. Tōkyō: Yoshikawa kōbunkan, 2003.

Sakamoto, Kazuya. *Nichibi domei no kizuna*. Tōkyō: Yuhikaku, 2000.

Soeya, Yoshihide. *Nihon no midoru pawā gaikō.* Tōkyō: Chinama shobō, 2005.

———. "A 'Normal' Middle Power: Interpreting Changes in Japanese Security Policy in the 1990s and After." In *Japan as a 'Normal Country'? A Country in Search of Its Place in the World*, edited by Yoshihide Soeya, Masayuki Tadokoro and David A. Welch, 72–97. Toronto: University of Toronto Press, 2011.

———. (a). *Nihon no gaikō: "Sengo" o yomitoku.* Tōkyō: Chikuma shobō, 2017.

———. (b). "The Case for an Alternative Strategy for Japan: Beyond the Article 9-Alliance Regime." In *Postwar Japan: Growth, Security and Uncertainty since 1945*, edited by Michael J. Green and Zack Cooper, 19–39. Washington, DC: Center for Strategic and International Studies, 2017.

PRIMARY SOURCES

Abe, Shinzō. "Kenpō kaisei ni kan suru shushō messēji zenbun," *Nihon Keizai Shinbun,* May 3, 2017, https://www.nikkei.com/article/DGXLASFK03H16_T00C17A5000000/.

Boeishō. "Jieitaihō, Article 76," revised on September 30, 2015, Ministry of Defense, https://elaws.e-gov.go.jp/document?lawid=329AC0000000165.

Cabinet Secretariat. "Cabinet Decision on Development of Seamless Security Legislation to Ensure Japan's Survival and Protect its People," July 1, 2014, https://www.cas.go.jp/jp/gaiyou/jimu/pdf/anpohosei_eng.pdf.

Denshi seifu (a). "Jūyō eikyō jitai ni kanshite waga kuni no heiwa oyobi anzen o kakuho suru tame no sochi ni kan suru hōritsu," March 29, 2016, https://elaws.e-gov.go.jp/search/elawsSearch/elaws_search/lsg0500/detail?lawId=411AC0000000060.

——— (b). "Buryoku kōgeki jitai tō oyobi sonritsu kiki jitai ni okeru Amerika gasshūkoku tō guntai no kōdō ni tomonai wagakuni ga jisshi suru sochi ni kan suru hōritsu," March 29, 2016. https://elaws.e-gov.go.jp/search/elawsSearch/elaws_search/lsg0500/detail?lawId=416AC0000000113.

Department of External Affairs, Australia. "Security Treaty between Australia, New Zealand and the United States of America [ANZUS], September 1, 1951, https://www.aph.gov.au/Parliamentary_Business/Committees/Joint/Completed_Inquiries/jfadt/usrelations/appendixb.

Gaimushō (a). "Gaimu daijin kokumu chōkan kaidan memo 1," August 29, 1955, https://www.mofa.go.jp/mofaj/annai/honsho/shiryo/shozo/pdfs/2019/02_03-1.pdf.

———. (b). "Gaimu daijin kokumu chōkan kaidan memo 2," August 30, 1955, https://www.mofa.go.jp/mofaj/annai/honsho/shiryo/shozo/pdfs/2019/02_03-1.pdf.

———. "Treaty of Mutual Cooperation and Security between Japan and the United States of America," January 19, 1960, https://www.mofa.go.jp/region/n-america/us/q&a/ref/1.html.

Government of Japan. "Japan's Legislation for Peace and Security: Seamless Responses for Peace and Security of Japan and the International Community," March 2016, https://www.mofa.go.jp/files/000143304.pdf.

Kokkai kaigiroku kensaku shisutemu. "Dai 21 kai kokkai shūgiin niakaku iinkai 2 gō," December 22, 1954, https://kokkai.ndl.go.jp/#/detail?minl=102105261X00219541222.

Naikaku hōsei kyoku. "Shūdanteki jieikan to kenpō no kankei ni tsuite," October 14, 1972. In *Boei Handbook 2012*, Tōkyō: Asagumo shinbun-sha, 2011: 665–666.

Naikaku sōri daijin Suzuki Zenkō. "Shūgiin giin Inaba Seiichi kun teishutsu 'kenpō, kokusaihō to shūdanteki jieitai' ni kan suru shitsumon ni tai suru tōbensho," May 29, 1981, http://www.shugiin.go.jp/internet/itdb_shitsumona.nsf/html/shitsumon/b094032.htm.

Secretariat of the International Peace Cooperation Headquarters. "Frequently Asked Questions," September 2015, http://www.pko.go.jp/pko_e/faq/faq.html.

Chapter Fourteen

Reflections on Part III

Comparative Perspectives

Franziska Seraphim

The essays in Part III widen the lens to place Japan's contemporary move towards revisionism in comparative perspectives. Each highlights a puzzle or paradox in Japanese revisionism seen against the longer postwar process of constitutionalism that comes into sharp relief by contrasting it with the constitutional trajectories in South Korea, in Taiwan, and in early postwar Japan. One puzzle is the relative meaninglessness of the very fact that Japan's Constitution has never been formally revised or amended in contrast to South Korea's nine formal revisions (Kim). Another is the comparatively authoritarian nature of democratic Japan's current constitutional revisionist efforts in contrast to Taiwan's successful democratic revision process following four decades of authoritarian rule based on martial law (Chen). A third is the counterintuitive outcome of ideologically driven revision efforts led by the nationalist right in Japan that—today as in the past—ended up entrenching the postwar pragmatics of subordinate independence that the nationalists have been keen on destroying (Soeya).

Rather than examining a common, broadly post–Cold War context of changing regional pressures or even global imperatives such as climate change measures that might impact the rethinking of early postwar constitutions, these three essays focus squarely on national processes over the seven postwar decades. Today, Japan, South Korea, and Taiwan simultaneously face the ghosts of their respective pasts, which intersect, as they always have, in particular but hardly novel ways. Insofar as outside imperatives dictated the original shape of their constitutions, the early postwar power dynamics remain at the center of contemporary constitutional questions. For Japan, this was the military alliance with the United States, which aimed to contain Communist China. For South Korea, postcolonial economic security and equity has always depended on its relationship with the United States while marking a systemic counterpart to North Korea. For Taiwan, the constitution—whether under authoritarianism or democracy—continued to be informed by its rivalry with Communist China. To that extent, Soeya's observation that the more things changed in the 2000s the more they stayed the same has validity across the three comparative cases.

Context, of course, does matter. Of particular interest in this regard is Kim's discussion of the parallel process of constitutional "congealing," without formal revision, in 1954. This modified the core identities of the original 1947/1948 Constitutions of Japan and South Korea, respectively, to produce what is today considered each country's founding document. The shared context was the changed Cold War situation after the end of the hot war on the Korean peninsula, which altered each country's relationship with the United States with parallel and equally important ramifications for the political (Japan) and economic (Korea) innovations at the core of each country's constitution: Article 9 (the "peace clause") in Japan and the Economic Chapter in Korea. Outside pressures thus enabled domestic critics to adjust Japan's "pacifist" and South Korea's "socialist" constitutional identities in crucial ways. In contrast, Chen points to divergent responses in Japan and Taiwan to the shared context of China's economic rise and increasingly aggressive military posturing in the South and East China Seas since the 2000s. As in the early Cold War context, outside pressures—the "China threat" and its impact on Japan's and Taiwan's alliances with the United States—boosted the political cloud of domestic proponents of constitutional revisionism, but to different ends. While revisionism in this context took the form of legitimating a top-down conservative agenda that further entrenched the status quo of Japan's subordination to U.S. military interests (Soeya), in Taiwan it helped catapult a liberal democratic agenda from the bottom up designed to set Taiwan further off from authoritarian China, against U.S. interests in the region (Chen). Both historical moments demonstrate, however, the importance of regional power relations to domestic constitutional reform, and the centrality of bilateral relations with the United States to the process.

Most importantly, the comparisons introduced here help us think about constitutional revisionism conceptually. First, considering Japan and South Korea side by side raises the fundamental question of what constitutes a "constitutional revolution" and whether formal black-letter revision is indeed needed for revolutionary change. Sung Ho Kim contends that Japan has paradoxically departed from the central spirit of its "peace constitution" more fundamentally than has Korea changed the original cornerstone of its "economic constitution" despite the fact that the Japanese Constitution has never been formally revised whereas Korea's has undergone nine official revisions. The discrepancy between form and substance in altering a constitution leads Kim to reflect on what attributes—meaning a historically specific constellation of aspirations, commitments, and aversions reflected in a body of law—give a constitution its unique "core identity" and how we are to assess the impact of different modalities of constitutional revolution on identities that turn out to be inherently unstable. With an eye to Japan's 2014 and South Korea's 2018 constitutional tampering, he finds Shinzō Abe's reinterpretation of Article 9 and 2015 Security Laws to amount to a "quiet dismemberment" of Japan's pacifist constitutional identity, whereas Jae-in Moon's 2018 revision proposal in fact reinforces Article 119's so-called economic democratization provision.

Second, reading Japan's and Taiwan's recent constitutional histories against each other directs attention to the role of "authoritarian legality," by which Weitseng Chen means the tendency of authoritarian regimes, even under democratic systems, to engineer their legitimacy via delivering public goods irrespective of constitutionality. Rather than examining "constitutional moments" of revolutionary change, Chen finds it more persuasive to unpack how authoritarian legacies affect the operation of constitutionalism in young democracies such as Japan and Taiwan, and how geopolitical interests abroad have influenced constitutional movements at home. The timeline here, of course, differs between Taiwan, whose democratic transformation in the late 1980s followed forty years of authoritarian constitutional rule under the KMT, and Japan, which during those same forty years had institutionalized its prewar authoritarian legacies under a democratic system. Chen points to institutional and legal personnel continuities that condition the function of judicial review as reconciling with rather than checking government policies, as well as a relatively non-confrontational civil society in constitutional matters. Japan's current top-down constitutional revisionism under Shinzō Abe exemplifies such entrenched authoritarian legacies. In contrast, Taiwan's bottom-up process of gradual but persistent constitutional change beginning with the Wild Lily Movement in 1990 sought to undo its long postwar history of authoritarianism, thereby exposing and deposing, rather than falling back on entrenched authoritarian legacies.

Third, understanding Japan's 2015 so-called "security laws" in light of the 1954 and 1960 reinterpretations of Article 9 makes visible an important pattern of nationalist constitutional revisionism, by which ideologically driven efforts to expunge the constitution's pacifist identity as a "foreign import" ironically serve to further entrench the Anpo-centered postwar security regime. Quite like his grandfather Nobusuke Kishi's aspirations in 1960, Shinzō Abe's 2015 push to legalize the exercise of the right of collective self-defense turned out to only confirm the parameters of the "postwar regime," namely the very real limits of "equal partnership" with the United States, precluding

Japan's independence. Yoshihide Soeya shows that if Kishi, and Hatoyama before him, employed a political scheme to try to institute legal and constitutional changes, Abe was using legal and even constitutional changes for his own political agenda, which was nationalist rather than internationalist in nature and should not be seen as the outcome of a substantive defense policy change. A careful reading of the 2015 legislation reveals a contradictory dual logic that results in the de facto constitutionality of the exercise of the right of collective self-defense in case of an "existential crisis," thereby capitalizing on current regional instabilities to realize a nationalist ideological agenda by way of positively responding to American military demands.

This "twisted logic" (Soeya) is admittedly not easy to follow. In my reading, however, it dovetails rather nicely with Chen's argument concerning "authoritarian legality." Both show how intricately intertwined domestic and international politics are in constitutional revisionist movements in East Asia, whether top-down as a government agenda or primarily bottom-up initiated by civic society as in Taiwan's Wild Lily Movement. Although none of the authors in this section is a historian, together they make a convincing case of constitutional revisionism's *historicity* in Japan as in South Korea and Taiwan. It is certainly true that the current focused engagement with constitutionalism operates in a shared context of regional and global geopolitical shifts that has so far precluded coherent domestic responses to the one clear vision for a future system that has appeared, namely, China's vision of its dominance. Instead, the constitutional struggles we are witnessing here seek to adjust the domestic systems that were created as part of the United States' vision of its global dominance in the ruins of the Japanese empire and developed distinct dynamics of their own in the decades since then. Those postwar histories played out very differently in South Korea, Taiwan, and Japan despite their respective authoritarian legacies and dependence on the United States' security framework. Accordingly, no congruence between form and substance of revising one's constitution has emerged among the three, and it is precisely this incongruence that reveals each unique process of creating and re-creating a constitutional identity. In this way, the conceptual contribution each of these authors makes helps to better understand the other cases. This is what comparative studies are all about.

Part IV

HUMAN RIGHTS AND ENVIRONMENTAL ISSUES IMPLICATED IN CONSTITUTIONAL REVISION DEBATES

Chapter Fifteen

Wartime Roots of Postwar Pacifism

Japanese Antiwar Activism in Occupied China

Erik Esselstrom

Confronted with evidence of terrible crimes committed against the Chinese people by Japanese military forces, foot soldier Mitsushige Maeda explained, "I saw that justice was with the Chinese side in the Japanese invasion, and I came to believe that I would be willing to die for China."[1] Maeda had been captured by the Chinese Communist forces in 1938 and taken to the Yan'an base area of the Chinese Communist Party (CCP) in Shaanxi province. In Yan'an, his captors put him through a program of reeducation that included face to face meetings with local Chinese residents who had been brutalized by the Japanese army. Maeda soon discovered that captured soldiers of the imperial army were not the only Japanese in Yan'an. Well-known Japanese communist and antiwar activist Sanzō Nosaka was there to assist in the POW reeducation programs, and Maeda ultimately became one of Nosaka's closest associates in China during the remainder of the war. Maeda's story of conversion, from loyal soldier of Japan's imperial army to devoted resister against that same military machine, is one of many that merit closer examination when reflecting on the history of antiwar activists in wartime Japan and their impact on constitutional pacifism in the postwar era.

Conservative advocates of unfettered remilitarization in Japan today often contend that the postwar Constitution's Article 9 is an outdated remnant of a time decades ago when a victorious occupying regime imposed irrational pacifism upon a defeated and desperate foe. The history of China-based Japanese resistance to the wartime imperial state, however, suggests that constitutional pacifism in Japan should not be casually dismissed as an onerous burden imposed by outsiders. Japanese antiwar activists who fled the home islands for Chinese treaty ports during the late 1930s offered the most ardent "domestic" opposition to Japan's imperial campaign on the continent. As they aided Chinese resistance to Japanese aggression by facilitating the reeducation of Japanese prisoners of war, many of these activists also crafted a vision of postwar pacifism infused with a language of universal human rights. By casting light on these native roots behind ideas central to the postwar constitution, this chapter provides valuable historical context for current debates on constitutional revision.

Antiwar activists during the wartime era were of two types: leftists who fled the homeland in the 1930s to escape police pressure, and soldiers who were captured in China and experienced "reeducation" while in custody of either Chinese communist or nationalist forces. Those of the second type are well known in Japan today. An organization of repatriated POWs known as Chūkiren (Chūgoku kikansha renrakukai), for example, played a significant part from the late 1950s until the early 2000s in bringing to light the crimes of Japanese soldiers in the field during the occupation of China. Conservative critics of such groups, however, have often dismissed the testimony of former soldiers who returned home after years in CCP captivity, claiming that because they had been brutalized and brainwashed by Chinese communists, their accounts cannot be taken at face value. Popular understanding of pacifist activism by former Japanese soldiers has thus been inextricably linked to broader Cold War political paradigms.

It is critical to remember, however, that the reeducation of Japanese soldiers began long before the empire's collapse in 1945. Moreover, fellow Japanese subjects, not Chinese communists, often delivered that reeducation while the war was still ongoing. Dismissing postwar pacifism as something imposed upon the Japanese people from the outside, and thus a restriction from which Japanese society must be freed in order to escape the legacies of the Occupation era, is to misrepresent the wartime past. Postwar pacifism can instead be better understood as a grassroots movement interpretively connected to the prewar and wartime years.

The story of antiwar resistance by Japanese activists in occupied China also illustrates the degree to which postwar pacifism derived from more than just regretful sorrow over Japanese suffering. Japanese activists in China perceived the suffering of Chinese under Japanese invasion as inseparable from the suffering of everyday Japanese under a fascist state. In their view, a genuine democratic future for all peoples of East Asia depended upon the liberation of China from Japanese aggression. They articulated a broader vision of antiwar activism that focused on fundamental rights of all people to be free from militarism and colonial violence. Some even articulated those ideas in the language of human rights discourse. In fact, the concept of *heiwateki seizonken* 平和的生存権 ("the right to a life of peace") that took shape in Japan during the late 1950s would have resonated strongly with Japanese activists in China during the wartime era.[2]

Japan's postwar discourse on human rights can be better understood as a product of both historical engagement with Chinese society as well as the legacies of U.S. Occupation. Prime Minister Shinzō Abe's proposed revisions to the 1947 Constitution included what amounted to the elimination of Japan's constitutional commitment to the notion of universal human rights.[3] The logic behind such a move rests on the assumption that universal truths of human experience are too often derived from Western models of philosophy that impose foreign ideas upon Japan's unique cultural traditions. Advocates of constitutional revision would have Japanese society reject the notion of universal human rights in order to nurture a stronger sense of national/cultural unity, which in turn can facilitate Japan's ability to compete with a more powerful PRC. As politically expedient as it might be to ascribe the human rights problem to the legacies of American neo-colonialism during the Occupation, human rights discourse in postwar Japanese society also derived at least in part from lessons learned during the invasion of China. Some Japanese rejected jingoistic nationalism when faced with the reality of mass violence perpetrated against the Chinese people, while others saw in the CCP's model of social revolution a vision of everyday life based on equality of all people without class distinctions. The fact that conditions within Chinese society did not always reflect these lofty ideological visions is largely irrelevant. For at least some wartime Japanese, China represented an attractive alternative to imperial Japanese fascism.

This chapter will look first at the experience of captured Japanese soldiers whose views on the war in China were transformed by their interactions with both Chinese communist forces and Japanese leftists who worked collaboratively with the Chinese side during World War II. After next examining the ideas of two such activists, Wataru Kaji and Teru Hasegawa, the chapter will finish with an overview of the postwar legacies of the Japanese antiwar movement in China. The aim is to explore how civic activism in Japan related to the protection of constitutional guarantees of fundamental human rights should be understood as more than simply a battle over whether to embrace or reject the neocolonial legacies of the U.S. Occupation. The struggle of everyday people in Japan to forge a relationship with their state within which basic rights to individual freedom and peaceful existence are protected is deeply connected to the entirety of Japan's twentieth-century historical experience.

THE JAPANESE ANTIWAR MOVEMENT IN OCCUPIED CHINA

During the war of resistance against Japan's imperial military machine, the Chinese Communist Party committed its Red Army forces to the struggle in several ways. The CCP organized and carried out small-scale guerrilla campaigns in occupied regions of the countryside, but it also participated in large-scale operations in coordination with the National Revolutionary Army of the Nationalist Party (Guomindang) under the leadership of Jiang Jieshi (Chiang Kai-shek). Communist forces in north China were known as the Eighth Route Army, while the New Fourth Army was comprised of communist soldiers fighting in central and south China. Despite the widespread belief, then and now, that Japanese soldiers routinely chose death over surrender, many Japanese did indeed lay down their arms and become prisoners of their Chinese enemies.

While violent retribution against Japanese prisoners for the terrible crimes they perpetrated against Chinese civilians did occur, the CCP officially followed a policy of non-violence against Japanese POWs. Not surprisingly, Japanese prisoners received instruction in Marxist theory related to capitalism and the nature of the Japanese war in China during their reeducation. However, more than ideology, according to historian Kōichirō Horii, what most inspired captured Japanese soldiers was the sincerity of Chinese communist soldiers as fellow human beings, a trait especially evident in their humanitarian treatment of prisoners. Moreover, humane treatment meant more than just obeying orders not to murder Japanese prisoners. Chinese officials running reeducation camps could even be disciplined for slapping Japanese POWs in their charge.[4] The slapping of rank-and-file soldiers by officers in the Japanese military was a routine occurrence, so it is easy to imagine the impact such humane treatment by their Chinese captors had on Japanese soldiers.

Beyond mere gratitude, Mitsushige Maeda's experiences as a POW also offer an example of how Japanese prisoners could provide frontline support to the Chinese by encouraging other Japanese to surrender. During a battle in October 1940, Maeda broadcast a plea by loudspeaker to Japanese fighters on the other side of the battlefront: "You are surrounded and in danger of utter annihilation, so give up on this fight. To die in this war is a useless death. Come over to the Eighth Route Army, where your lives will be guaranteed. I am a Japanese, so you can believe me."[5] Because Japanese soldiers had been so deeply ingrained with the notion that suicide was more honorable than capture, Maeda explained, assuring them that the Chinese communists would spare their lives was of utmost importance.

Many Japanese prisoners experienced a fundamental transformation in their perceptions of Chinese society and the Chinese people during their time spent in captivity. Maeda recalled that before shipping off to the front, he had firmly believed in such notions as "Manchuria is Japan's lifeline" and that the Japanese military was fighting to liberate the Chinese people from "Jiang Jieshi's repressive state." His experiences with the Eighth Route Army proved to him the opposite was true. "When I heard from Chinese families that their homes had been burned and loved ones murdered, I knew in my bones that this was no 'holy war'; it was a war of invasion."[6] Takashi Kagawa, who was captured by Chinese communist forces in August 1940, also saw his perceptions of China dramatically transformed. "When we were in the Japanese army, we only had the image of the Chinese people as a dirty, dull-witted and lazy race," Kagawa admitted. As he fought alongside soldiers of the Eighth Route Army, however, Kagawa noticed instead that "everyone was filled with energy and ambition, and what they spoke of was intellectually sophisticated; it was completely different from the impression we had before."[7]

More than just inspiring positive impressions of the Chinese society, POW encounters with the enemy could also open the eyes of some soldiers to the weaknesses of the Japanese side. Recounting his time with the Eighth Route Army, Takashi Kagawa explained:

> I had the strong sense that within the Eighth Route Army every person clearly understood the goals of the war and they fought battles with a scientific discipline and orderliness. Away from the battle, there was a harmony among them as equal comrades, not superiors and inferiors, a point of great difference with the Japanese army. . . . Japanese military officers were paper tigers, you know. They just used status and violence to bully their subordinates, and when it came to battlefield strategy, it was not scientific. If you can advance, then advance; retreat is not allowed . . . this is not rational.[8]

Significantly, these transformative interactions between Japanese prisoners and their Chinese captors were facilitated by left-wing Japanese activist intermediaries who worked closely with both Communist and Nationalist forces during the war. While Sanzō Nosaka is perhaps the most well-known leftist who spent the war years in China, assisting with POW reeducation near Yan'an, similar work was carried out by Wataru Kaji in central and south China. Kaji's prewar experiences in Japan were not unlike those of most leftist intellectuals, facing harassment by political police in the late 1920s and spending several stints in prison for violating prewar Japan's infamous Peace Preservation Law. After being released from jail in 1935, Kaji fled to Shanghai in early 1936 and found refuge within the leftist Japanese community until the Japanese military occupation of the city in the fall of 1937. After escaping to Hong Kong, by March 1938 Kaji reached Hankou, where he began to work for the Nationalist military in propaganda campaigns against Japanese soldiers in the field. In December 1939, Kaji formally established the so-called *Nihonjinmin hansen dōmei* ("Japanese People's Antiwar League") in Chongqing and through it he participated in frontline propaganda activities and Japanese POW reeducation programs.

The record of a conversation between Kaji and a Japanese prisoner sheds light on the mission behind his POW reeducation projects. A prisoner asked Kaji, "If you are full of such great ideas, why don't you return to your home country and take action there?" Many of his comrades were indeed battling on the home front, Kaji explained, and many had been murdered or arrested. "The struggle at home is important," he went on, "but it is also necessary to go overseas and join hands with our Chinese comrades for the fight against the same enemy." Kaji explained further that the fight was not a matter of the Japanese people alone. "If we look at nothing but Japan, we will not be able to help the Japanese people or the homeland . . . the struggle to build strong relations with outside countries is vital to Japan's future prosperity."[9] Kaji then asked the prisoner, "Are you not worried about the struggles of your family back home?" "They likely believe I've already died in battle, so I don't give any thought to going home," he replied. "The notion that death is like a falling cherry blossom is convenient for those who would turn the people into martyrs," Kaji said, and "it's ridiculous." "Can you not contribute to your country, to humanity, by living as long as possible? . . . This war is disgraceful. Now you understand your good fortune for not dying like a dog for it."[10]

In the guiding principles behind the southwest branch of the Japanese People's Antiwar League, Kaji laid out its central aims: 1. Stop the military invasion and see the repatriation of all expeditionary troops; 2. Overthrow the bureaucrats in government who are slaves to militaristic capitalists and military adventurers; 3. Establish civil rights and freedom of speech, assembly, education, and culture; 4. Revive the daily life of laborers and farmers who have suffered under the devastating conditions of war; 5. State guarantee for the livelihood of surviving soldiers and their families; 6. Establishment of popular government under conditions of genuine democracy to achieve the above aims.[11] Such proclamations make the primary motivation behind Kaji's wartime activism obvious. He sought the ultimate liberation of Japanese society from authoritarian political oppression and industrial capitalist exploitation, and the destruction of the imperial Japanese military machine in China was the first step in achieving that goal.

A close associate of Wataru Kaji during his years in Chongqing was Teru Hasegawa. Born in 1912, she was the second of three children. In the spring of 1929, at age seventeen, she graduated from high school and earned admission to the prestigious Nara Women's Teachers College (Nara Joshi Kōtō Shihan Gakkō), where she later developed an interest in Esperanto. With its focus on facilitating peaceful international relations through a universally intelligible language, Esperanto had gained popularity in East Asia by the 1920s, especially among Chinese intellectuals hoping to strengthen Republican China's ties to the international community. During the early 1930s,

Hasegawa's studies brought her into contact with Nara labor organizations and activist groups, and in a nationwide sweep of suspected leftists in 1932, police arrested Hasegawa on suspicion of socialist political activities. Returning to the Osaka area by early 1936, she performed in an Esperantist theatrical production in March of that year, meeting a young Chinese man named Liu Ren. Liu was an exchange student from the Japanese-controlled state of Manzhouguo in China's northeast, and by November 1936 Hasegawa and Liu secretly married against the wishes of her family. In January 1937, Liu left for Shanghai to join the burgeoning anti-Japanese resistance movement, and Hasegawa joined him in April. By June, she was participating in popular demonstrations and establishing connections with antiwar Japanese activists and Chinese nationalists.[12]

A few examples of Hasegawa's written work suggest both a transnational dimension to her commitment to pacifism, and her dedication to a broad, but distinct, conception of human rights. The first is a letter sent shortly after the war broke out to her Esperantist comrades in Tokyo, in which Hasegawa passionately argued that in China's victory and Japan's defeat, one could see a hopeful future for all of Asia. Entitled "Victory for China Is the Key to Tomorrow for All of Asia" this was one of Hasegawa's most eloquent statements on the war. "Friends, regardless of one's national identity," she began, "if one possesses a human heart and clear-headed reason, surely one will feel sympathy for China." In describing her role in the resistance movement as an Esperantist writer, she continued, "When I put a pen in my hand, in my heart my blood boils when I think of the rights that have been oppressed, and my anger towards our beastly enemy begins to burn like a flame. Then, I am able to remember with joy that I am one and the same with the Chinese people." Most striking is her articulation of a commitment to peace and mutual respect between the peoples of China and Japan that transcends their nation-state identities. She appeals to a fundamental sense of human compassion that will bind together all victims of oppression and violence regardless of their national background.

More than just transcending nationalism, however, Hasegawa also urged the active rejection of its destructive impulses. In one of her most often quoted passages from this letter, Hasegawa proudly claimed: "If I had my wish, it would be perfectly fine to call me a 'traitor' to my country. I do not fear that at all. Rather, I am far more ashamed to be of the same race as a nation that simply invades the lands of others and calmly brings down hell upon a completely innocent and powerless people. True patriotism can never be something that confronts the advancement of humanity."[13] Eschewing formulaic ideological affiliations and appealing instead to a belief in fundamental respect for human life, it is not surprising that Hasegawa's greatest supporters were often fellow East Asians suffering under the yoke of Japanese military aggression and colonial occupation. In the summer of 1941, for example, Chinese communist leader Zhou Enlai is to have said of Hasegawa: "The Japanese imperialists have called you a traitor, but in fact you are the most loyal daughter of the Japanese people, a true patriot."[14]

Teru Hasegawa believed in an abstract notion of fundamental human rights, defined as the inviolable right to freedom from exploitation and violence. In her view, the imperial Japanese state routinely violated these rights both at home and abroad. Her commitment to the Esperanto movement also reflected an internationalist tinge to her arguments that melded easily with a distinct brand of pan-Asian transnationalism rooted in both her sincere sympathy for the immediate sufferings of the Chinese people and Japanese society's long history of deep cultural ties to the continent. In short, Hasegawa sought to escape from a national identity she believed had been shamed by involvement in the brutal wartime invasion and occupation of China.

POSTWAR LEGACIES OF JAPANESE PACIFIST ACTIVISM IN CHINA

The "antiwar league" (hansen dōmei) of Japanese activists in wartime China changed its name to "liberation league" (kaihō dōmei) in 1944. The new nomenclature, Mitsushige Maeda explained, came about because "Japan had already lost the war. We changed the name because we had come to see our aim as joining with antiwar activists around the world, liberating Japan from militarism and the transforming it into a democracy."[15] What impact did the Japanese antiwar movement in occupied China have on the pursuit of that goal? Overseas activism did play at least some part in convincing the imperial state to surrender. Evidence suggests that state authorities on the home front saw the Japanese Antiwar League as a serious threat to the imperial system. A Justice Ministry document from June 1945 identified it as "the most dangerous organization of overseas communist elements . . . aiming to foment revolutionary action in Japan by advocating an immediate end to the war, the overthrow of military leadership, and the establishment of a democratic political system."[16] Perhaps even more significant is the link between the famous Konoe memorial to the throne of February 1945 and the Japanese Antiwar League in China. Prince Fumimaro Konoe urged Emperor Hirohito to seek an end to the war from fear that popular unrest could lead to communist revolution, and in that document Konoe cited the antiwar activism of Japanese leftists in China and their reeducation of Japanese POWs as a significant factor shaping wartime social movements. In this sense, one can say the Japanese antiwar movement in China had a direct influence on Hirohito's decision ultimately to accept the terms of surrender in August 1945.[17]

When members of the Japanese People's Antiwar League returned to Japan after the war, popular reaction to them varied widely. To some, rhetorically attacking their homeland and supporting the Chinese side against the Japanese military was a despicable path of cowardice. "The traitor Wataru Kaji! You sold out your country and now you've returned to it! Did you not know how much your countrymen in Japan were suffering when you broadcast your anti-Japanese propaganda from Chongqing?" exclaimed one critic. "You call yourself a warrior of the antiwar movement . . . why didn't you do something to help Japan before our devasting defeat?" asked another. "Don't you see that you didn't know anything about the suffering of the Japanese people at home while you were doing all that complaining from the Chinese interior?"[18]

To others, however, activists such as Sanzō Nosaka and Wataru Kaji were heroes who had kept alive the spirit of left-wing resistance to Japan's militaristic imperial regime when the police state on the home islands had all but snuffed out domestic dissent. Wartime experience in China also had a significant impact on the political views of activists such as Kaji and Nosaka. In an essay published shortly after his return from the continent, Kaji discussed a March 1946 meeting of Jiang Jieshi and Zhou Enlai, during which Jiang is said to have asked Zhou and the Communist Party for patience. Zhou agreed with Jiang's assessment that neither side was prepared to lead the country effectively at that moment. Kaji was deeply moved when he heard this story, particularly because of the harsh contrast between the Jiang-Zhou meeting and what Kaji believed was happening in Japan. He recalled reading news while still in Chongqing in March 1946 of conservative Japanese politicians claiming that the Japanese people were not suited for democracy, so that rushing through with dramatic reforms would lead to instability and chaos. While China's leadership was sincerely reflecting upon its current condition, Kaji explained, Japan's politicians were making utterly insincere arguments about Japanese society's incapacity for democracy.[19]

East Asian society at large in the autumn of 1946, Kaji continued, was facing a moment from which a new history could be forged. Kaji recalled a meeting he had in March 1938 with Nationalist General Chen Cheng during which Chen articulated his feeling about Nationalist cooperation with the Chinese Communist Party. "We are not only fighting Japanese militarism, we are fighting to liberate China and all of Asia from militaristic government," Chen explained. "It is in that spirit that we cooperate in the struggle." Reflecting upon these words, Kaji remarked sarcastically that Japanese militarists of that day would have made a similar argument about their own war in China as a war of liberation. In the Chinese case, however, that contention was filled with hope; for the Japanese it was nothing but a sham. While the spirit of Nationalist-Communist cooperation was far weaker in the autumn of 1946, Kaji conceded, he was still optimistic about China's future. If a popular movement against the civil war could be cultivated, he reasoned, China could finally move beyond the era of "our party comes first" to a new age of "the people come first."[20]

Kaji was less confident about conditions in Japan in the autumn of 1946. The Japanese people had not been oppressed by foreign invaders, he explained; their misery was the result of a reactionary dictatorship at home. The Japanese did not need a war of liberation from outside aggressors, but a struggle for liberation from domestic reactionaries. In Kaji's view, China by 1946 had thus made greater progress beyond the ranks of backward states, since its struggle was between nationalism and populism. Japanese society had yet to create a truly national consciousness, according to Kaji. A genuinely democratic society in postwar Japan, Kaji concluded, would only be possible once those internal contradictions were resolved.[21]

Teru Hasegawa lived to see the end of the war she so desperately opposed, but was never able to return to her native country. While living under the protection of the Chinese Communist Party in Manchuria after Japan's surrender, a botched surgery related to the birth of her second child led to an infection that took her life in 1947 at age thirty-five. Her memory, however, has continued to inspire progressive social activists throughout the postwar era, especially when the question of Japanese remilitarization is at stake.

In 1972, for example, the Tokyo feminist newspaper *Fujin minshu shinbun* published a passionate recounting of Teru Hasegawa's life story by well-known human rights advocate Yasuyo Kawada, founder of the Japanese branch of Amnesty International. In addition to providing the basic narrative of Hasegawa's wartime life, the feature praised her for having the courage to "tear off the mask of the Imperial Army's holy war" and expose it as the aggressive war of conquest it really was.[22] That Hasegawa's memory would be invoked by Japanese peace activists during the early 1970s is not surprising. Tokyo had seen widespread popular demonstrations against Japanese participation in the U.S. war against Vietnam because many of the high-altitude B-52 bombers that rained explosives down upon North Vietnam and Cambodia flew from U.S. bases on or near the Japanese archipelago. Kawada's article, however, was also timed explicitly to mark the 35th anniversary of the July 7, 1937, "China Incident" at the Marco Polo Bridge outside of Beijing that sparked Japan's full-scale invasion of China south of the Great Wall and thus the start of Japan's eight-year quagmire in the Second Sino-Japanese War of 1937–1945. Hasegawa's memory thus served Japanese leftists and human rights activists of the early 1970s as both a reminder of the tragedies that unrestricted militarism could unleash as well as a model of the individual bravery one must exhibit to resist such a reactionary slide.

Just as Japanese progressives employed the memory of Teru Hasegawa to articulate their anti–Vietnam War views during the 1970s, Japanese state support of U.S. wars in the Persian Gulf since the early 2000s has inspired contemporary leftists in Japan to look at Hasegawa's life as a model of resistance in the face of state efforts to silence opposition. Reflecting upon the support of the Japanese government for the U.S. war in Afghanistan in 2002, journalist Hiroshi Iwadare invoked the life of Teru Hasegawa in the pacifist journal *Agora*. "Is this not the time to embrace a spirit of internationalism, not petty nationalism?" he asked. "Should we not learn from those who lived to bring peace to the world?" In a clear reference to attempts by the ruling LDP regime and its then Prime Minister Jun'ichirō Koizumi to pave the way for constitutional revision, Iwadare continued: "Now the world is moving toward a new war and there is a growing trend to make Japan a nation that can wage war. Even in the face of being labeled a traitor by her country, Teru did not give up. The time to learn from that kind of courage has come."[23] Social Democratic Party figure Takako Doi, Japan's first female speaker of the Lower House, expressed similar sentiments concerning Hasegawa in the same journal two years later: "Our country has already taken the step of sending Self-Defense forces to participate in multinational military force in Iraq . . . But, even now it is not too late. Now our duty to the present and the future . . . is to return to the ideas of Prime Minister Shidehara who sat in power when article 9 was born and labored for the idea of abolishing war. That a special issue on Teru Hasegawa would once more appear at this moment has especially significant meaning."[24] Likewise, Kazuko Sawada of the Yuhigaoka women's history in Osaka group made a similar case for the significance of Hasegawa's legacy to contemporary peace activism in 2005. "Japan has become a world economic power," she wrote, "but it has forgotten the history of its invasion of Asia . . . and is now trying to change article 9. If Teru and her husband were alive today, how would they act?" Sawada pondered. "To protect article 9 of the constitution is to carry on the legacy of Teru and her husband, is it not? I have thought about what I should do as an individual Japanese. Perhaps my mission is to make Teru's way of life known to a great number of Japanese today."[25]

For an everyday Japanese high school social studies teacher during the 1990s, too, Hasegawa's life story provided a valuable classroom lesson in moral courage. After teaching his students about Hasegawa's wartime experiences, Hideaki Matsui asked them to write brief essays on their impressions of her writings and beliefs. The sentiment expressed by one student was common to many, according to Matsui. "If I had been there at that time, I think I likely would have criticized her. Not because I disagreed with her ideas, but rather because I would have been caught up in the current of those times. I don't think I would be able to step out from the dominant trend of the day. But she was able to do so, not during times like we know now, but during the time of the Japan-China war. That point resonates with me."[26] Indeed, Hasegawa's example of extraordinary individual resistance to a dominant social ideology she knew to be self-destructive is perhaps one of her most valuable legacies.

Advocates of constitutional revision, specifically the alteration (or even abolition) of Article 9, often characterize such change as a step toward the genuine democratization of Japan. By purging the document of its original sin of U.S. authorship, the argument goes, the Japanese Constitution becomes more authentic and legitimate. Viewing the struggle over Article 9 as an exclusively Japan-U.S. issue, however, oversimplifies the more complex historical processes that helped produce the ideas embodied in the Japanese Constitution. Reflecting on the history of Japan-China relations brings into focus many additional issues, including broader human rights–related themes, at work in the debate.

Indeed, looking at Japan's modern history through the lens of Japan-U.S. relations generates a distinctive narrative of twentieth-century Japanese society. In this narrative, late-nineteenth-century industrialization released progressive social forces and left-wing political energy, and during the 1920s democratic political and social movements battled against the conservative authoritarian nature of the Meiji imperial state. Tragically, domestic and international crises of the 1930s then enabled a state crackdown on progressive elements and the eventual dominance of ultranationalist militarism. During the Occupation, the United States imposed Article 9 to serve its own Cold War interests, and Occupation authorities simultaneously cultivated the rehabilitation of left-wing forces (as a weapon against Japanese militarism). Viewed in this way, primary agency behind Article 9 is assigned to the United States, and this facilitates the contemporary conservative viewpoint that constitutional limits on Japanese militarization are no longer reasonable in a post–Cold War world. The Constitution should be revised, the argument goes, to make it a truly democratic document that embodies Japan's national interests.

When that same historical trajectory is viewed from a Japan-China perspective, however, the narrative is altered. During the 1930s, while the domestic Left was suppressed, the overseas Left carried on the struggle, and their fight became closely intertwined with Chinese resistance to Japanese invasion. During the early Occupation era, popular support for the ideals embodied in Article 9 can be located in native antiwar movements, influenced significantly by Japanese leftists in China and Japanese soldiers reeducated by them, who renounced militarism and envisioned a democratic postwar society free of militaristic aggression. Constitutional pacifism, then, is not an imposition from beyond but rather the result of internal opposition to Japan's own misguided imperial wars. To abolish Article 9, seen from this perspective, is to betray Japanese democracy, not restore it. Ironically, viewing the debate from a more China-focused perspective serves to restore Japanese agency to the historical process that produced the constitution. This is not to say that the U.S. is irrelevant, but rather that the domination of U.S.-Japan relations over postwar historical imagination has left the function of China insufficiently understood.

Moreover, one could even go so far as to suggest that at least one current of Japan's postwar human rights discourse was initially inspired by the Chinese Communist Party. Japanese soldiers who became prisoners of the CCP noted with regularity their shock (a pleasant surprise, of course) at the Communist policy of non-violence against Japanese POWs. The party's intention behind that policy, of course, was to encourage surrender and also present itself as a humane and benevolent victor. But for Japanese soldiers indoctrinated with the notion of deep shame associated with battlefield surrender, to be treated with respect and generosity by Chinese captors left many of them deeply disillusioned with Japan's imperial ideology. Many POWs also noted the relative equality within Chinese Communist military forces between officers and everyday soldiers, something nearly unheard of in Japan's imperial army. The Chinese Communist Party's attack on traditional class divisions thus served as more than a rhetorical pillar of Marxist ideology. The rejection of class-based distinctions promoted a notion of fundamental egalitarian rights for all people.

The commitment of former Japanese soldiers to pacifism and fundamental human rights after the war is rooted not only in the sorrow and regret born from their own battlefield losses, but also in the lessons they learned from their CCP captors. The CCP regime under Mao during the postwar era, of course, is not typically praised for its commitment to human rights. The influence of the CCP during the wartime era, however, must be understood and evaluated within that specific historical context. Additionally, proponents of normalizing militarism in Japan today most often cite a continental threat to Japanese national security (either from the PRC or North Korea) as justification for significant revision to the 1947 Constitution. Fitting neatly within that conceptual framework is an historical narrative of that Constitution's creation in which contemporary Japan's inability to mount sufficient national defense is a structural weakness foisted upon the Japanese people without their democratic consent. In that interpretive light, it was issues in U.S.-Japan relations that gave rise to constitutional pacifism, while issues in China-Japan relations now demand its abandonment. The story of Japanese antiwar activists in occupied China laid out in this chapter, however, has offered a different and deeper historical context for the origins of Japanese pacifism.

NOTES

1. Mitsuyoshi Himeda, Kōichirō Horii, and Naoko Mizutani, "Nit-Chū sensō jiki, Chūgoku ni okeru Nihonjin no hansen katsudō: Hachirogun to shinshigun no naka de," *Sensō sekinin kenkyū* 21 (1998): 13.

2. Tomoyuki Sasaki, "Whose Peace? Anti-Military Litigation and the Right to Live in Peace in Postwar Japan," *Asia-Pacific Journal* 10, issue 29, no. 1 (July 16, 2012).

3. Lawrence Repeta, "Japan's Democracy at Risk: The LDP's Most Dangerous Proposals for Constitutional Change," *Asia-Pacific Journal* 11, issue 28, no. 3 (July 22, 2013).

4. Kōichirō Horii, "Nit-Chū sensōki, Ka-Chū ni okeru Nihonjin hansen katsudō: Shinshigun to no kanren o chūshin ni," *Rekishigaku kenkyū* 738 (2000): 8.

5. Mitsushige Maeda, Hirosumi Kobayashi, and Mitsuyoshi Himeda, "Konoe Fumimaro o shinkan saseta hansen yobigoe: Nihonjin hansen dōmei no tatakai," *Sekai* 768 (August 2007): 257.

6. Maeda, Kobayashi, and Himeda, "Konoe Fumimaro o shinkan saseta hansen," 256.

7. Takashi Kagawa, "Horyo kara hansen heishi e," *Kikan gendaishi* 4:4 (149) (1974): 69.

8. Kagawa, "Horyo kara hansen heishi e," 73.

9. Keiko Inoue, *Chūgoku de hansen heiwa katsudō o shita Nihonjin – Kaji Wataru no shisō to shōgai* (Tokyo: Yachiyo Shuppan, 2012), 83.

10. Inoue, *Chūgoku de hansen heiwa katsudō o shita Nihonjin*, 84.

11. Inoue, *Chūgoku de hansen heiwa katsudō o shita Nihonjin*, 98–99.

12. Teru Hasegawa, *Arashi no naka no sasayaki*, trans. Ichirō Takasugi (Tokyo: Shinhyōron, 1980), 203–4; Kōhei Nakamura, "Heiwa no hato: Veruda Maayo: Hansen ni shōgai o sasageta Esuperanchisuto Hasegawa Teru," *Kanagawa Daigaku jinbungaku kenkyūjohō* 37 (2004): 56–59; Lu Yuanming, *Chūgokugo de nokosareta Nihon bungaku: Nit-Chū sensō no naka de*, trans. Masaru Nishida (Tokyo: Hōsei Daigaku Shuppankyoku, 2001), 73, 75–79.

13. Hasegawa, *Arashi no naka no sasayaki*, 153–58; Masao Miyamoto, ed., *Hasegawa Teru sakuhinshū: hansen Esuperanchisuto* (Tokyo: Aki Shobō, 1979), 127–30; Ichirō Takasugi, *Chūgoku no midori no hoshi* (Tokyo: Asahi Shinbunsha, 1980), 80–85.

14. Nakamura, "Heiwa no hato," 62.

15. Mitsushige Maeda, "Senjika hansen wa naze kanō datta no ka? Hansen dōmeiin toshite no watashi no katsudō," *Chūkiren* 34 (2005), 13.

16. Maeda, Kobayashi, and Himeda, "Konoe Fumimaro o shinkan saseta hansen," 262.

17. Kōichirō Horii, "Nit-Chū sensōki, Ka-Chū ni okeru Nihonjin hansen katsudō," 13.

18. Inoue, *Chūgoku de hansen heiwa katsudō o shita Nihonjin*, 181.

19. Wataru Kaji, "Chūgoku no baai to Nihon no baai," *Shinseikatsu* (September 1946): 8.

20. Kaji, "Chūgoku no baai to Nihon no baai," 11.

21. Ibid.

22. Yasuyo Kawada, "Hansen Esuperanchisuto Hasegawa Teru no shōgai," *Fujin minshu shinbun*, July 14, 1972.

23. Hiroshi Iwadare, "Ima koso Hasegawa Teru no yūki ni manabō," *Agora* 80 (2002): 1.

24. Takako Doi, "Hisen heiwa no Teru ni omou," *Agora* 296 (2004): 1.

25. Kazuko Sawada, "Ima koso omoi okosō Hasegawa Teru no ikikata: Hansen Esuperanchisuto no yūki ni manabu," *Gunshuku mondai shiryō* 297 (August 2005): 71.

26. Hideaki Matsui, "Nit-Chū sensō ni hantai shita Nihon josei: Hasegawa Teru no kyōzaika," *Rekishi chiri kyōiku* 555 (1996): 55.

REFERENCES

Doi, Takako. "Hisen heiwa no Teru ni omou." *Agora* 296 (2004): 1.

Fujiwara, Akira, and Himeda Mitsuyoshi, eds. *Nit-Chū sensō ka Chūgoku ni okeru Nihonjin no hansen katsudō*. Tokyo: Aoki Shoten, 1999.

Hasegawa, Teru. *Arashi no naka no sasayaki*. Translated by Ichirō Takasugi. Tokyo: Shinhyōron, 1980.

Hasegawa Teru Henshū Iinkai, ed. *Hasegawa Teru: Nit-Chū sensōka de hansen hōsō o shita Nihon josei*. Tokyo: Seseragi Shuppan, 2007.

Himeda, Mitsuyoshi, Kōichirō Horii, and Naoko Mizutani. "Nit-Chū sensō jiki, Chūgoku ni okeru Nihonjin no hansen katsudō: Hachirogun to shinshigun no naka de." *Sensō sekinin kenkyū* 21 (1998): 2–36.

Horii, Kōichirō. "Nit-Chū sensōki, Ka-Chū ni okeru Nihonjin hansen katsudō: Shinshigun to no kanren o chūshin ni." *Rekishigaku kenkyū* 738 (2000): 1–16, 45.

Inoue, Keiko. *Chūgoku de hansen heiwa undō katsudō o shita Nihonjin: Kaji Wataru no shisō to shōgai*. Tokyo: Yachiyo Shuppan, 2012.

Iwadare, Hiroshi. "Ima koso Hasegawa Teru no yūki ni manabō." *Agora* 80 (2002): 1.

Kagawa, Takashi. "Horyo kara hansen heishi e." *Kikan gendaishi* 4:4 (149) (1974): 66–90.

Kaji, Wataru. "Chūgoku no baai to Nihon no baai." *Shinseikatsu* (September 1946): 8–11.

Kawada, Yasuyo. "Hansen Esuperanchisuto Hasegawa Teru no shōgai." *Fujin minshu shinbun*, July 14, 1972.

Lu Yuanming. *Chūgokugo de nokosareta Nihon bungaku: Nit-Chū sensō no naka de*. Translated by Masaru Nishida. Tokyo: Hōsei Daigaku Shuppankyoku, 2001.

Maeda, Mitsushige. "Senjika hansen wa naze kanō datta no ka? Hansen dōmeiin toshite no watashi no katsudō." *Chūkiren* 34 (2005): 3–13.

Maeda, Mitsushige, Hirosumi Kobayashi, and Mitsuyoshi Himeda. "Konoe Fumimaro o shinkan saseta hansen yobigoe: Nihonjin hansen dōmei no tatakai." *Sekai* 768 (August 2007): 253–63.

Matsui, Hideaki. "Nit-Chū sensō ni hantai shita Nihon josei: Hasegawa Teru no kyōzaika." *Rekishi chiri kyōiku* 555 (1996): 54–55.

Miyamoto, Masao, ed. *Hasegawa Teru sakuhinshū: Hansen Esuperanchisuto*. Tokyo: Aki Shobō, 1979.

Nakamura, Kōhei. "Heiwa no hato: Veruda Maayo: Hansen ni shōgai o sasageta Esuperanchisuto Hasegawa Teru." *Kanagawa Daigaku jinbungaku kenkyūjohō* 37 (2004): 55–66.

Repeta, Lawrence. "Japan's Democracy at Risk: The LDP's Most Dangerous Proposals for Constitutional Change." *Asia-Pacific Journal* 11, issue 28, no. 3 (July 22, 2013).

Sasaki, Tomoyuki. "Whose Peace? Anti-Military Litigation and the Right to Live in Peace in Postwar Japan." *Asia-Pacific Journal* 10, issue 29, no. 1 (July 16, 2012).

Sawada, Kazuko. "Ima koso omoi okosō Hasegawa Teru no ikikata: Hansen Esuperanchisuto no yūki ni manabu." *Gunshuku mondai shiryō* 297 (August 2005): 66–71.

Shinoda, Yūsuke. "Ritsumeikan daigaku kokusai heiwa myuujiamu Kaji Wataru kankei shiryō ni okeru gunji iinkai seijibu dai-san chō no tai-Nichi dentan ni tsuite." *Ritsumeikan heiwa kenkyū* 18 (2017): 86–96.

Takasugi, Ichirō. *Chūgoku no midori no hoshi*. Tokyo: Asahi Shinbunsha, 1980.

Chapter Sixteen

Do as Democracy Demands

The Irony of a Historic Preservation Movement and Its Relevance for Popular Sovereignty in Postwar Japan

Saburo Horikawa

A CART ON A SLOPE

Democracy is a cart on a slope. You have to keep loading things in it to make it useful. You also have to keep pushing to stay relevant. If you do not, the cart will roll back to where you started. It is only through the practice of pushing the cart up a slope that postwar democracy and the principle of popular sovereignty are given life. In other words, one cannot see the true state of postwar democracy just by looking at laws and institutions. Therefore, it is essential to observe how such practice is carried out, for the meaning of the Constitution is determined not only by whether or not it is amended, or how it is interpreted even without amendment (as in the case of what is permitted under Article 9). Equally important is how it is given life in actual practice, not only by government but especially by citizens, and this is not a one-time thing but a constant effort (pushing the cart up the hill).

A series of protest activities by students in the summer of 2012 (proceeding from TAZ—Temporary Autonomous Zone—to SASPL—Students Against Secret Protection Law—and then to SEALDs—Students Emergency Action for Liberal Democracy) made up one practical action aimed at pushing the cart up the hill. All were movements carried out primarily by students.[1]

An outstanding characteristic of SEALDs and other movements was their public speech style. An example is a speech by one member, Beniko Hashimoto, during a protest at the National Diet against the "War Bill" (June 12, 2015): "Before I came here today, I bought a swimsuit for summer, and I was troubling myself with questions such as when I should put on eyelash extensions."[2]

Why did she talk about a swimsuit in a speech against the War Bill? And the eyelash extensions, like the swimsuit, seem to have nothing to do with the protest. What is more, their elaborately designed T-shirts, flyers, and banners, as well as the popular music, rap-like slogans, and other features indicated the great care lavished on style and design. Where did all of this come from? Through these questions, this essay sketches the historical multilayered nature of practices meant to push that cart up the hill in postwar Japan.

DIFFERENTIATING THEMSELVES FROM THE 1960s: DÉJÀ VU?

SEALDs's emphasis on style and design, this insistence on their own style, is part of a strategy to divide (differentiate) themselves from past social movements.

In particular they attempted to differentiate themselves from the 1960s student movement. That movement was characterized by brooding faces, the shouting of slogans using arcane Marxist terms, doing battle by throwing Molotov cocktails and rocks, and ending with "dangerous" movements involving infighting and horrifying mutual killing. What SEALDs wanted to distance themselves from was this social memory of the 1960s student movement. In fact, one of SEALDs's main members, Aki Okuda, said, "In the history of postwar democracy, there's a traumatic feeling in Japan toward that radical student movement."[3] Another member, Masaaki Yamamoto, said, "The situation is that we planned the demonstration together, but to friends I couldn't say, 'We're gonna have a demonstration,' so I fudged it by saying, 'We're gonna have an event.' Saying 'event' sounds gentler."[4] Because the 1960s student movement was radical and off-putting, they had to say that their own movement had nothing to do with it.[5]

They used two strategies to differentiate themselves. One was self-presentation to show that they were "ordinary" people, not "thugs." The 1960s student movement, which became radical and degenerated into violent infighting, was alienated from society and in that sense existed *outside* of society. That is why SEALDs and other groups presented themselves as being *inside* society, as being ordinary neighbors who lived right next door.

The other strategy was a visual presentation in which looking cool showed that they were different from 1960s uncool. Through stylish design they assert themselves as *being a part of contemporary society*. They are not still dragging around baggage from the 1960s.

But there is déjà vu in this strategy and practice—in the nature of being within society and contemporary. Isn't this something that we have seen before? After the 1960s student movement subsided, a major theme of local movements all over Japan—which were often called resident movements or citizen movements—was, in a sense, differentiating themselves from student movements and "left-wing movements." Does this mean that the movement by SEALDs and others was just one stream in that current? Did it have no novelty or significance as a movement at all? Below, I would like to consider this in the context of a local movement in Otaru, Hokkaido, because both SEALDs and Otaru are examples of "progressives" working to preserve and protect the constitution as they understand it, in opposition to conservatives pushing for change. Such cases are just as illuminating of the life and meaning of the constitution as are the attempts to amend it.

THE RISE AND SPLIT OF THE OTARU CANAL PRESERVATION MOVEMENT

Since 1984 I have studied the movement to preserve the Otaru Canal in the city of Otaru, Hokkaido. The movement demanded local autonomy as a way for residents to control change.[6] I will briefly portray what happened up in Otaru, showing how people in Otaru have been pushing the cart up a slope and, therefore, how the principle of popular sovereignty has been given life.

The Otaru Canal is located in the center of the commercial port city of Otaru, northwest of Sapporo. The Port of Otaru has a good natural harbor, and since the city spreads out along the slopes of the nearby mountains, the port, the canal, and the rows of warehouses along the canal can be seen from throughout the city and naturally serve as Otaru's landmarks.

In 1869, Otaru was designated as an outport of Sapporo, and grew into one of the most important commercial cities in Hokkaido thanks to its use as a doorway for trade with Sakhalin and Europe. Otaru enjoyed enormous prosperity in its heyday. In 1921, nineteen major banks had branches in Otaru, and it came to be known as the "Wall Street of the North." Such prosperity brought further harbor development. The construction of the canal began in 1914 and was completed in 1923. It symbolized the prosperity of Otaru.

With time, however, World War II's system of controlled economy propelled wholesale markets to move to Sapporo, while the shift of energy from coal to oil reduced the importance of Otaru as a port for shipping.

A plan was drafted to construct six-lane highways by reclaiming the canal, in order to modernize the port facilities. In 1966, the Minister of Construction approved the plan and construction began. This road became the source of heated controversy dividing Otaru.

"Otaru will no longer be Otaru if the Canal is reclaimed." This was the battle cry of the residents who opposed the road plan. This marked the beginning of the Otaru Canal Preservation Movement lasting from 1973 to 1984. The city government supported the reclamation of the canal and the construction of highways to connect Otaru with Sapporo and other areas, and the preservation movement opposed this, saying that the community should be revitalized through the restoration of the canal.

The movement first appealed in vain to the Otaru residents' sentiments. Their catch phrases, such as "Otaru will no longer be Otaru," were quite powerless compared to the government slogans such as "economic boosts from road construction." The movement was hard-pressed to manage the contradictions between preservation and development. As a result, movement members began to argue that unregulated redevelopment based solely on economic factors was inexcusable. Limited changes were acceptable, but the existing historic townscape had to be integrated into the core of the town development plan as an asset to be utilized. Thus, the new goal of the movement was not to "freeze" the canal, but to make sure development centered on the lives of the residents around the canal. The movement envisioned the canal as a "tourist attraction" and worked to preserve it as a symbol of the community while simultaneously striving for city renewal (preservation as a strategy), instead of using an idealistic slogan such as "Just preserve the canal!" (preservation for the sake of preservation). They used the same term, "preservation," but its connotations and applications differed greatly.

The metamorphosis of the campaign's goals into "preservation as a strategy" during the later period of its history triggered active involvement from business circles and political parties. Major developers were motivated to join in the redevelopment of the canal area, whereas political parties saw the movement as an attractive power base because of its wide support. In 1982, the movement expanded to include people from a variety of backgrounds, with the establishment of the "Hundred Person Committee on Otaru Canal." This was a political intervention, dividing the movement internally and eventually collapsing it. In the summer of 1984, when the movement was about to obtain an agreement from the city to preserve the canal as it was, with no changes at all, by submitting a total of 98,000 signatures from pro-preservation supporters, local political parties suddenly began to aid some within the movement who were not part of the leading clique. These separatist members then declared the start of a new campaign for the local mayor's recall without a formal approval by the Hundred Person Committee. This estranged the conservatives within the movement, and wide support from local citizens faded. Now that there was no need to compromise further, the city quickly completed the construction of the road, which remains in use to this day.

SPACE, PLACE, AND PRESERVATION

As we have seen, Otaru administrative authorities regarded the canal as a "space," a three-dimensional area in which one thing and one use could be exchanged for another. To the residents, however, the canal was a "place" given a variety of meanings; it was an inconvertible "something," impossible to change into a mere land parcel of a certain size and length.

For example, in his little shop in Otaru, Mr. A. talked about the preservation movement he was deeply involved in:

> *Horikawa:* When Mr. Ohno at the Otaru Chamber of Commerce asked, "Why on earth do you want to preserve this canal?," how did you explain the reason?
>
> *Mr. A.:* I told him outright that "[the core of the canal problem] is not a matter of the length [of the reclaimed area]."[7]

If it was "not a matter of the length," what were they aiming for? Mrs. B., a former leader in the movement, explains:

> *Horikawa*: What did canal preservation mean to you after all?
>
> *Mrs. B.:* It was not a matter of the length [of the canal reclamation area], which was just 600 meters. It definitely meant to *live in the community*, you know.[8]

As is obvious from their explicit wording, preservation as envisioned by the movement was not a matter of width or length. While it was true that the canal was subject to preservation and its reclamation was at issue, the motive for preservation was to "live in the community," as Mrs. B. says here.

That community she refers to was lived in through its physical form (*katachi*). If the form is altered, the community will be altered, too. If the form is lost, the community will be lost, too. In order to "live in the community," the physical form has to be preserved and, therefore, to preserve the physical form is to preserve the form of the society.

In Otaru the movement sought to promote changes in which the residents' "place" would continue to be theirs. It rejected the city government's monopoly of power over city planning, and the idea that a "place" belonging to the residents should be seen as a mere "space" for road construction. The movement demanded local autonomy as a means for residents to control change. Forbidding every change was not their intention; rather, "the power to control changes in the way, and rate, that they wanted" was their goal. This is evident in one of the statements of the movement: "What matters is new lively contents in old containers."[9] The word "preservation," therefore, means not the *prevention* but the *control* of growth and development. Preservation allows and even promotes change.

DO AS DEMOCRACY DEMANDS

It is important to note that those preservationists were not "building huggers"; they demanded local autonomy in order to control change by themselves. While of course they love Otaru, where they were born and grew up, active involvement for more than ten years in the preservation movement was in fact regarded as *civil action*. Mr. C., one of the most influential leaders of the movement, says:

> There's nothing wrong with change itself; what's important is how primary actors are involved, and how they bring about changes. . . . But do people really have a philosophy when they proceed with change? In other words, . . . do people proceed with change based on each individual's future vision for the town? I think it's good to have passionate discussions about this . . . I'm not a historic building nut, or a fanatic about old ruins; I just wanted a city where generations of people raised in that area could keep living active and energetic lives. The key to that is not just the canal or tourism, but for each citizen to have his or her own vision for the future of their city. That means each citizen has to hold on to his or her own right to make decisions about their city, and not leave it up to politicians and business. In other words, self government by citizens begins when there are citizens like that, and things aren't just left up to government, or left up to business. So the movement started with doubts about whether there really was a "civil society" in Japan.[10]

Note that he raises such fundamental questions as "whether there really was a 'civil society' in Japan." This question offered incisive criticism of postwar politics, wondering if the civil society promised by postwar democracy has really come about, while at the same time showing enthusiasm for trying to establish a civil society in Otaru. And indeed the expressions "having a philosophy," "primary actors," and "what's important is how they bring about changes" straightforwardly express the essence of what postwar democracy is supposed to be. This movement in Otaru was not just another local movement but a movement with a much wider and longer scope and significance. Both SEALDs and Otaru are examples of citizens' struggles giving life and meaning to the constitution in this way.

Core members of the preservation movement were educated in the early 1960s when the principles of popular sovereignty and postwar democracy were taught with zeal and hope. Movement leaders such as Mr. C. demanded that redevelopment of downtown Otaru be done according to the principles of postwar democracy. The preservation movement was radical in a sense we cannot imagine today: it demanded the preservation of old buildings and canals, when the entire nation believed anything old was bad, obsolete, and conservative, while anything new was thought to be better, brighter, and progressive. Therefore even if people argued that old buildings should be preserved, they appeared "red" to others, i.e., they gave the same negative impression as the radical student movement, and so they were ignored or suppressed. One of the movement's leaders, Mr. A., explained:

> If it's called a "citizen movement," everybody says that "[those people] are red." In other words, "They're with the Communist Party." . . . I don't have anything to do with them. [You young people] probably don't know this, but if I do something like [get involved in a movement], people say I'm with the Communist Party. I hate the Communist Party, and the Communist Party hates me. . . So I have to say something the Communist Party wouldn't say.[11]

Not being called "red," or Communist—that is, differentiation from "red" —was an important strategy. It was the same strategy that SEALDs and other movements adopted later.

That is why the preservation movement stuck to a self-presentation style. In July 1987 participants planned and held not a preservation movement festival, but a "Port Festival in Otaru" as a festival for local young people. High school and college students did everything from planning to collecting donations, site setup, security, and cleanup, all without pay. In all respects, it was a young people's "hand-made" festival. Of great interest is the organizational principle of the "Port Festival," which ultimately brought in as many as 100,000 visitors.

The Port Festival staff members all spoke of something one might call "pure amateurism." "It isn't about calling for canal preservation. . . . What links us with one another is the desire to have the Port Festival. Jobs also have nothing to do with it, and neither does financial interest."[12] "Even if people are in business, they never bring it here, and there's no financial interest at all, so it's purely a matter of people associating with each other."[13]

Important here is the apolitical character of their "pure amateurism." The statement that Mr. D. led with, "It isn't about calling for canal preservation," meant that superficially the Port Festival was not a festival for the preservation movement. To the leaders who planned it, it was indeed a preservation movement festival, but in a bid to organize many young people, they strictly defined it as a festival for young people, who could come to enjoy rock music against the backdrop of the broad canal. It was precisely this "apolitical character" which was the style used to differentiate themselves from the appearance of being "red." While at first glance the plan looked like just an event for local young people, it attempted to show straightforwardly—while giving citizens a first-hand view of the canal at issue—that people can gather in the canal district, and that therefore it is a perfect venue for relaxation and business, and has new possibilities. The festival used neither crude leftist logic, nor experts' arguments about "scarcity"; rather, it used a clear mental image to convince ordinary citizens of the significance and possibilities of preservation. It was also a new style for Mr. C., Mr. A., and the other people who started the Port Festival—a style derived from the experience of their bitter defeat in the student movement. Their earlier experiences of anti-Anpo and other student protests in the 1960s, and their desire to avoid repeating earlier mistakes, prompted them to develop new strategies for saving the canal. This enabled the preservation movement to evolve in new ways. The past experiences of participants are thus not mere prehistory, but vital strands woven into the fabric of their activism and its evolution.

Here one can identify the layered nature of Japan's postwar social activism, in which the experiences of previous movements have shaped—both consciously and unconsciously—the development of subsequent movements. A seemingly straightforward regional youth event was thus shaped by the organizers' rejection of the tactics employed by the student movement of the 1960s and early 1970s, and by their refusal to become enmeshed in ideological confrontations or party politics.[14]

PROGRESSIVE CITIZENS AND CONSERVATIVE WORDS

The irony here is that the most *progressive* citizen activism that embodied the ideal of postwar Japanese democracy used the most *conservative* words.

In Otaru it was the word "preservation." As we have seen, preservation was about control of change. The movement demanded local autonomy, just as the principle of postwar democracy demands. When the community environment was about to undergo a major modification against the citizens' will, a movement arose on democratic principles. The citizens contended that they were sovereign. "Protect the canal that we the sovereign people love" was a defense of democratic principles.

Meanwhile, in SEALDs and other movements, people chanted slogans such as "Stop making fools of the citizens!" and "Defend the Constitution!" Inattention to what the sovereign people had to say was perceived as a crisis of postwar democracy and constitutionalism. That is why calls to abide by principles were directed at government administrations which did not adhere to democratic principles. This coincides with the analysis by Nakano in this volume: "The general focus of the movement has inevitably been to defend postwar democracy and the constitution that served as its foundation."[15]

Common to both is the sense that the ideals of postwar democracy were betrayed. Mr. C.'s "whether there really was a 'civil society' in Japan" and the SEALDs slogan "Stop making fools of the citizens!" share anger at betrayal and a demand that authorities abide by "what's right." SEALDs's Aki Okuda said that constitutionalism, which is the basis of postwar democracy, "is the premise shared by everyone regardless of personal stances, so there isn't any left or right . . . This is truly the 'what's right' coming before ideology."[16] Whether Left or Right, do "what's right," which is the "shared premise," is the reason why liberal people used the most conservative term, and why they had to.

CONCLUSION

This essay has examined the rise and fall of the preservation movement in Otaru, comparing the rhetoric of the movement participants with those of SEALDs. Although they are different and many years apart, their pattern and style of rhetoric are strikingly similar. What is important in their rhetoric is to portray themselves as not "dangerous" or "red" ("*aka*"). This is mostly because the attacks on the left, or progressives, by the conservative faction (e.g., LDP) during the 1960s were extremely successful, and those who questioned the status quo had to distance themselves from "the reds" by deploying a seemingly conservative rhetorical style. Many of the techniques and patterns followed by SEALDs were not new, but previously used in Otaru and in other cases as well, such as Minamata and Beheiren.[17] These include defining the movement as independent of the established "radical" parties with which many people would hesitate to be involved, and having a loose and not very hierarchical organizational structure.

The fact that two movements from two different eras had to use the same rhetoric for strategic purposes means that they were struggling with the same challenges to citizen sovereignty in postwar democracy. Their struggles unfolded in the wake of the 1960s student movement's achievements and failures and its negative image. Today's movements cannot be seen in isolation from the thick stratum of experience accumulated by the 1960s movement; indeed, they are deeply informed by it, both consciously and unconsciously. The *absent presence* of the student campus protests of the 1960s still haunts us.

The differentiation they adopted was to secure a space to carry out their own movements, but while that strategy achieved differentiation, it was not a break with the 1960s because, having secured their own space, "they were trying to connect" the "movement from the 1960s" with "the social movements since March 11 [2011]."[18] The movements attempting to give postwar democracy substance stand on that accumulated stratum and intend to link it to the present. In that sense, there is an unbroken connection to the present. SEALDs's slogans "Tell me what democracy looks like!" "This is what democracy looks like!" and "If democracy has ended we're gonna start it!" were indeed the first steps toward starting to call out forward-looking phrases. Do as democracy demands: today, too, citizens are pushing the cart up the hill, even while the way they push it is determined by the achievements and soul-searching of the previous era.

NOTES

1. SEALDs, ed., *Minshushugi tte kore da!* (Tokyo: Ōtsuki Shoten, 2015); Gen'ichirō Takahashi and SEALDs, *Minshushugi tte nan da?* (Tokyo: Kawade Shobō Shinsha, 2015); Eiji Oguma, Misao Redwolf, and Aki Okuda, "'Kantei mae' kara 'kokkai mae' e," *Gendai Shisō* 44 (7) (2016): 30–55.
2. SEALDs, ed., *Minshushugi tte kore da*, 13.
3. "Okuda Aki-san (sono 2) 'Demo wa kakko ii' tte iu, shakai no kūkikan o tsukureba ii," *Magazine Kyūjō*, 2014 (Accessed August 22, 2019, http://www.magazine9.jp/article/realpeace/16102/).
4. SEALDs, ed., *Minshushugi tte kore da*, 46.
5. See Kōichi Nakano, "Crisis of Constitutional Democracy and the New Civic Activism in Japan: From SEALDs to Civil Alliance," in *Japanese Constitutional Revisionism and Civic Activism*, ed. Helen Hardacre et al. (Lanham, MD: Lexington Books, 2021).
6. Saburō Horikawa, *Machinami hozon undō no ronri to kiketsu: Otaru unga mondai no shakaigakuteki bunseki* (Tokyo: Tokyo Daigaku Shuppankai, 2018); Saburō Horikawa, *Why Place Matters: A Sociological Study of the Historic Preservation Movement in Otaru, Japan, 1965–2017* (Cham, Switzerland: Springer Nature, 2021).
7. Mr. A., interview by Saburō Horikawa in Otaru, December 11, 1994. Information in brackets has been added by the author.
8. Mrs. B., interview by Saburō Horikawa in Otaru, December 27, 1994. Emphasis in original. Information in brackets has been added by the author.
9. Horikawa, *Machinami hozon undō no ronri to kiketsu*, 188.
10. Mr. C., interview by Saburō Horikawa in Otaru, September 12, 2011.
11. Mr. A., interview by Saburō Horikawa in Otaru, September 4, 1998. Information in brackets has been added by the author.
12. Mr. D., interview by Saburō Horikawa in Otaru, September 9, 2007.
13. Mr. E., interview by Saburō Horikawa in Otaru, September 10, 2011.
14. Horikawa, *Why Place Matters*.

15. Nakano, "Crisis of Constitutional Democracy and the New Civic Activism in Japan," 48.

16. Aki Okuda, Rintarō Kuramochi, and Tetsurō Fukuyama, *2015 Anpo, kokkai no uchi to soto de: Minshushugi o yarinaosu* (Tokyo: Iwanami Shoten, 2015), 22–23.

17. Timothy S. George, *Minamata: Pollution and the Struggle for Democracy in Postwar Japan* (Cambridge, MA: Harvard University Asia Center, 2001), 173–74, 196, 211.

18. Oguma, Redwolf, and Okuda, "'Kantei mae' kara 'kokkai mae' e," 55.

REFERENCES

George, Timothy S. *Minamata: Pollution and the Struggle for Democracy in Postwar Japan.* Cambridge, MA: Harvard University Asia Center, 2001.

Horikawa, Saburō. *Machinami hozon undō no ronri to kiketsu: Otaru unga mondai no shakaigakuteki bunseki*. Tokyo: Tokyo Daigaku Shuppankai, 2018.

———. *Why Place Matters: A Sociological Study of the Historic Preservation Movement in Otaru, Japan, 1965-2017.* Cham, Switzerland: Springer Nature, 2021.

Mr. A. Interview by Saburō Horikawa in Otaru, December 11, 1994.

———. Interview by Saburō Horikawa in Otaru, September 4, 1998.

Mr. C. Interview by Saburō Horikawa in Otaru, September 12, 2011.

Mr. D. Interview by Saburō Horikawa in Otaru, September 9, 2007.

Mr. E. Interview by Saburō Horikawa in Otaru, September 10, 2011.

Mrs. B. Interview by Saburō Horikawa in Otaru, December 27, 1994.

Nakano, Kōichi. "Crisis of Constitutional Democracy and the New Civic Activism in Japan: From SEALDs to Civil Alliance." In *Japanese Constitutional Revisionism and Civic Activism*, edited by Helen Hardacre, Timothy S. George, Keigo Komamura, and Franziska Seraphim, 39–60. Lanham, MD: Lexington Books, 2021.

Oguma, Eiji. *Shakai o kaeruniwa*. Tokyo: Kōdansha, 2012.

———. *Shushō kantei no mae de*. Tokyo: Kōdansha International, 2017.

Oguma, Eiji, Misao Redwolf, and Aki Okuda. "'Kantei mae' kara 'kokkai mae' e." *Gendai Shisō* 44 (7) (2016): 30–55.

Okuda, Aki, Rintarō Kuramochi, and Tetsurō Fukuyama. *2015 Anpo, kokkai no uchi to soto de: Minshushugi o yarinaosu*. Tokyo: Iwanami Shoten, 2015.

"Okuda Aki-san (sono 2) 'Demo wa kakko ii' tte iu, shakai no kūkikan o tsukureba ii." *Magazine Kyūjō*, 2014. Accessed August 22, 2019. http://www.magazine9.jp/article/realpeace/16102/.

SEALDs, ed. *Minshushugi tte kore da!*. Tokyo: Ōtsuki Shoten, 2015.

Takahashi, Gen'ichirō, and SEALDs. *Minshushugi tte nan da?* Tokyo: Kawade Shobō Shinsha, 2015.

Chapter Seventeen

Everything's Going to Be Alright?

An Analysis of Rights in Constitutional Amendment Proposals

Christian G. Winkler

The Constitution of Japan (COJ) is a unique document in a number of ways. While many constitutions have been bestowed upon countries by what Rousseau called a foreign law giver,[1] the COJ has the distinction of being the oldest unamended constitution in the (democratic) world. Furthermore, its fiercest critics are conservatives, the very people one would expect to be the guardians of the status quo. In contrast, elsewhere conservatives attack their political enemies on the left for threatening the constitutional status quo.[2] The curiosities do not stop there. Especially by the standards of 1947, the COJ is a very progressive document, enumerating an impressive list of rights.[3] Japanese conservatives, critical of liberal individualism, seek to curb those rights. However, at the same time, they propose the inclusion of new rights, making for a puzzle. This essay seeks to disentangle this puzzle by tracing the long history of constitutional amendment proposals in Japan. The main focus is the treatment of fundamental human rights therein. This essay will address the following questions: Has the treatment of human rights in the amendment proposals changed over time? How did authors view human rights? What was their reasoning for omitting or adding rights from their proposals?

In their authoritative study on the birth and death of constitutions, Elkins, Ginsburg, and Melton noted "more flexible constitutions that include a wide range of social actors and provide some amount of detail seem to endure longer than those that do not."[4] The COJ is an impressive example of longevity, surviving unamended for over seven decades. This staying power is particularly remarkable, seeing how the Constitution has been at the center of one of the main ideological battles in postwar Japan. As McElwain and Winkler[5] and Komamura and Machidori[6] have argued, the main reason for the Japanese constitution's longevity has been its flexibility. This has allowed the ruling Liberal Democratic Party (LDP) to shape institutions such as electoral systems and central-local government relations to its advantage, thus reducing the need for formal amendment. Despite the Constitution giving nominally conservative LDP governments much freedom to shape postwar Japan as they see fit, parts of the LDP and right-wing intellectuals and media have long pushed to amend Japan's supreme law.

A VERY BRIEF HISTORY OF AMENDMENT PROPOSALS

Since its controversial birth during the Occupation, the Constitution has withstood numerous concerted attempts to revise it. In the 1950s, purged politicians and bureaucrats such as Ichirō Hatoyama and Nobusuke Kishi returned to politics after the end of the Occupation and pushed for an amendment during the years of the reverse course.[7] However, this initial push came to an abrupt end after Kishi resigned after ramming through the revision of the Mutual Security Assistance treaty ("Anpo") with the U.S. amidst massive protests (*anpo tōsō*). Kishi's successors, most of them supporters of former Prime Minister Yoshida, either pragmatically acknowledged the difficulty[8] of an amendment or endorsed and supported the COJ.[9] It would take two decades before the issue briefly resurfaced in the late 1970s and 1980s. By then, public support for the Constitution, in particular Article 9, had grown.[10] In 1982 Yasuhiro Nakasone, a staunch proponent of amendment since the 1950s, became prime minister. Nakasone quickly realized that amendment would be a long-term rather than a short-term goal.[11]

This line of thinking changed radically with the end of the Cold War and the domestic and international criticism of Japan's refusal to send military transport planes during the First Gulf War. Unlike in the 1970s, however, the LDP was unable to take the initiative, as it was busy trying to reclaim the government. Instead, media outlets like the daily *Yomiuri Shimbun*, newly founded center-right opposition parties, and individual LDP politicians began publishing amendment proposals. It would take until 2005 for the LDP to unveil its own draft proposal.[12] After temporarily fading from the spotlight between 2008 and 2011, the amendment debate resumed after the LDP tried to shore up its conservative credentials as an opposition party in 2012. After one of the biggest proponents of revision, Shinzō Abe, reclaimed the prime ministership later that year, the race was back on. Abe, whose term as party leader was slated to run until 2021, stated his intention to realize an amendment during his term in office.[13]

One manifestation of this debate surrounding the Constitution, which is almost as old as the document itself, is the number of amendment proposals put forth by elites. Political parties, politicians, intellectuals, and media outlets have published dozens of drafts since the 1950s. The focal point has always been Article 9, but changes to Chapter 3: Rights and Duties of the People have also been high on the priority lists of would-be reformers.

As mentioned above, the COJ is very specific in enumerating the people's rights, particularly for a constitution drafted in 1946. In contrast, Chapter 3 mentions only three duties (to work, pay taxes, and have one's children receive compulsory education). This deliberate inclusion of many rights has been a key reason for the progressive support of the COJ,[14] but what about conservatives? It is impossible to delve deeply into the definition of conservatism here, but one could assume it involves support for the status quo based on a strong preference for individual rights and responsibilities as expressed by Hayek, Reagan, or Thatcher, or an attempt to curtail rights based on a more authoritarian interpretation of conservatism.[15]

Furthermore, we may also assume that the content of amendment proposals has changed over time. For instance, the period of the reverse course during the late 1940s and 1950s saw a partial rollback of rights; the same can hardly be said for the 1980s and 1990s. Thus, we might expect to find a greater emphasis on curtailing rights during the earlier period. To test these hypotheses, we shall examine 44 amendment proposals published by conservative elites since the end of the Occupation in 1952.[16] We will measure how many rights-related stipulations each proposal includes and note any identifiable trends.[17]

The battery of 35 rights-related provisions is part of the Comparative Constitutions Project (CCP),[18] the largest cross-national constitution database. Using this reference point allows for both time series and cross-national comparability. A list of the 35 indicators is provided in table 17.1.

Figure 17.1 shows the number of references to rights over time. In the COJ we find 77% of those stipulations. Thirty-four out of 44 proposals feature more rights than the COJ. There is significant change over time, as we can identify two clusters in figure 17.1. Amendment proposals published since 1990 include an average of 27.7 out of 35 rights-related stipulations (79%); in contrast, the average for proposals published before 1989 is 25 out of 35 or 71%. This is the result of around half the proposals published during the 1950s and 1960s including fewer references to rights than the COJ does, whereas 86% of the proposals released after 1990 feature a higher percentage of rights.

The amendment debate reflects political realities such as the attempts of the early LDP to roll back some liberal democratic reforms initiated by GHQ early in the Occupation. In this sense, the amendment proposals reflect various visions of postwar Japan, as Winkler has pointed out.[19] On average they have become literally more *conservative* over time, as the acceptance of the COJ has grown even among conservative elites.[20] The irony of this is that for at least several decades, the leadership of the nominally conservative LDP, a

Table 17.1. List of rights-related codes

Item	*Equality before the Law*	*Protection from Discrimination (Gender)*	*Nationality*	*Race*	*Religion*	*Sexual Orientation*	*Disabled (Mentally or Physically)*
CCP Code	EQUAL	EQUALGR_1	EQUALGR_2	EQUALGR_4	EQUALGR_6	EQUALGR_7	EQUALGR_9
COJ Article	Article 14	Article 14	N/A	Article 14	Article 14	N/A	N/A
Item	*Social Status*	*View Gov Files*	*Freedom of Religion*	*Right to Unionize*	*Right to Strike*	*Standard of Living*	*Consumer Rights*
CCP Code	EQUALGR_12	INFOACC	FREEREL	JOINTRDE	STRIKE	STANDLIV	CONRIGHT
COJ Article	Article 14	Article 14	Article 20	Article 28	Article 28	Article 25	N/A
Item	*Property Rights*	*Choose Occupation*	*Right to Marriage*	*Same Sex Marriage*	*Matrimonial equality*	*Child Rights*	*Right to Life*
CCP Code	PROPRGHT	OCCUPATE	MARRIAGE	SAMESEXM	MATEQUAL	CHILDPRO	LIFE
COJ Article	Article 29	Article 22	Article 24	N/A	Article 24	Articles 26, 27	Articles 13,25
Item	*Prohibition of slavery, servitude, forced labor*	*Prohibition of Torture*	*Prohibition of cruel, inhuman, degrading behavior*	*Right to Privacy*	*Right to free movement*	*Freedom of Opinion*	*Freedom of Expression*
CCP Code	SLAVE	TORTURE	CRUELTY	PRIVACY	FREEMOVE	OPINION	EXPRESS
COJ Article	Article 18	Article 36	Article 36	N/A	Article 22	Article 19	Article 21
Item	*Prohibition of Censorship*	*Freedom of Press*	*Freedom of Assembly*	*Inalienable Rights*	*Individual right to self determination*	*Environmental protection Reference*	*Academic Freedom*
CCP Code	CENSOR	PRESS	ASSEM	INALRGHT	DEVLPERS	ENV	ACFREE
COJ Article	Article 21	Article 21	Article 21	Articles 11,97	Article 13	N/A	Article 23

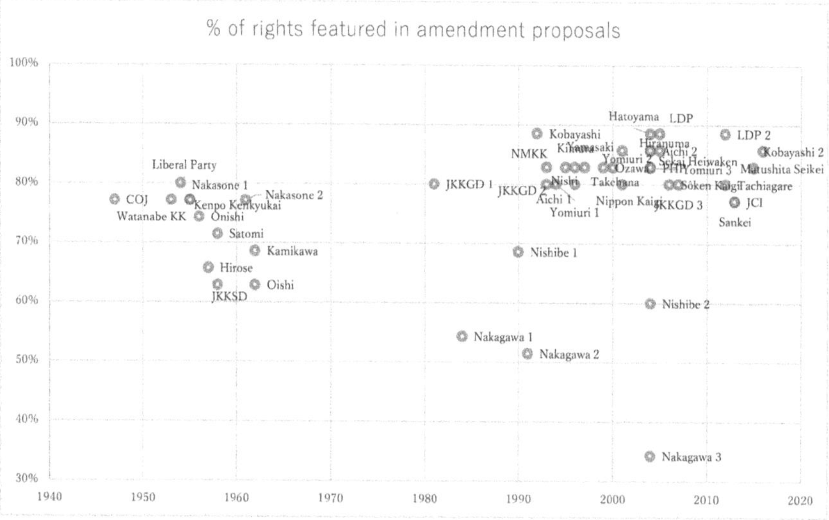

Figure 17.1. % of rights featured in amendment proposals.
Created by the author.

party whose initial goal was revision of the constitution, has upheld this rather liberal document.[21]

The biggest difference between earlier and more recent proposals is the addition of three so-called "new rights" (*atarashii kenri*): the right to know, i.e., access to (government) information; a right to privacy; and environmental rights. The inclusion of these rights was first proposed in the 1980s and early 1990s.[22] Since 1990, environmental rights (84%), privacy rights (77%) and the right to know (71%) have found their way into an absolute majority of proposals.

Authors cite demands of the present age, such as the arrival of the "information society"[23] and the challenges of environmental destruction as a side effect of the "unlimited pursuit of scientific progress"[24] as main reasons for these additions. Access to information or a safe environment had become needs that were too important to be left exclusively to interpretation.[25]

That being said, the numbers above tell only one part of the story. As noted, Chapter 3 of the COJ is entitled "the people's rights *and* duties." What about changes to the second part, duties? We have already noted that the COJ enumerates three duties. Returning to our previous hypotheses and our analysis above, we could expect an increase in duties at least during the earlier period.

As figure 17.2 shows, however, there has been a robust increase in duties across all decades, with some proposals adding up to five new duties. The proposals analyzed here add an average of two duties (for an average of 5.2). In addition to the existing three duties, 68% of proposals stipulate that

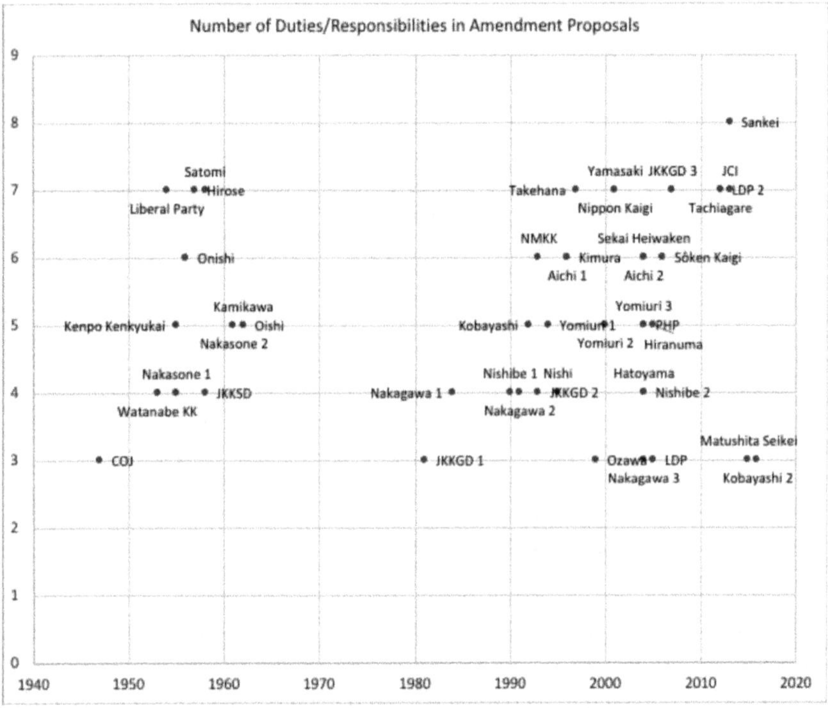

Figure 17.2. Numbers of Duties/Responsibilities in Amendment proposals.
Created by the author.

the people have to uphold the law and/or obey the Constitution. The same number feature provisions on the people's duty to defend the nation. Other duties include the duty to protect the environment (45%), the duty to respect or preserve Japanese culture and traditions (16%), responsibility to the community (16%), loyalty to the nation (11%), and respecting the national flag and anthem (5%). The duty to uphold the law is found in seven out of ten proposals. Meanwhile, the duty to be loyal to the nation is found only in proposals drafted in the 1950s and 1960s, which again is a clear reflection of the reverse course. References to the duty to protect the environment, in contrast, are found only in later proposals, because they always come paired with the right to enjoy a decent environment. Duties to preserve or respect culture and traditions and show respect to the flag and anthem also are fairly recent, first appearing in 1997 and 2012, respectively.

In summary, newer amendment proposals are more likely to add new rights, while the addition of new duties, albeit with some variety, is a more consistent feature dating back to the 1950s. Of course, the idea that rights should be balanced by duties and responsibilities is hardly exclusive to conservatives' discourse on postwar Japan.[26] That being said, it is of particular importance to understanding conservative elite discourse on the COJ. The fact that on average amendment proposals have come to include more rights suggests that earlier reactionary tendencies may be a thing of the past; at the same time, however, a closer look at the commentaries accompanying the proposals reveals significant continuities, dating back to the 1950s, in the underlying critique of the COJ in general and Chapter 3 in particular.

The conservative critique of the COJ in general and Chapter 3's rights stipulations in particular can be summarized in the following points: 1) an imbalance between rights and duties have bred egocentrism, irresponsibility, an unhealthy egalitarianism, and disregard for nation and nature; and 2) the claim of ignorance of and incompatibility with international standards.

This inevitably leads us to the question of how to reconcile this critique with the support for new rights. The answer is that numbers tell only one part of the story. In fact, most amendment proposals take a "yes, but . . ." approach to rights; specifically, rights are guaranteed, but often can be restricted. These restrictions together with new duties are the solution proposed by most authors to the alleged defects of Chapter 3 and their negative influences on postwar society.

Many would-be reformers are critical of why and how the COJ came into being. The U.S.-led drafting process was not only "unjust"[27] and undemocratic,[28] they say, but also guided by an ulterior motive: its intention was the systematic destruction of the very institutions (the *ie* system or the prewar education system) that had supposedly made the Japanese Empire so formidable. A classic example of this critique is the following passage in a document the LDP published at its foundation in 1955: "The democracy and liberalism imposed by the Occupation should be respected and upheld as leading principles of the new Japan, but because the Occupation's policies were oriented principally toward weakening Japan, many of the reforms of our education system and other institutions, beginning with the Constitution, wrongly suppressed respect for the state and patriotism and unduly fragmented and weakened the power of the state."[29]

Similar critiques can be found in many commentaries from the 1950s, including by the Liberal Party[30] and the Kenpō Kenkyūkai.[31] While the wording may be less aggressive, this discourse has continued to the present,[32] so it is hardly limited to the days of the reverse course.

In the 1950s and early 1960s, amendment proposals sought to remedy "wrongly suppressed respect for the state" by arguing that the people had to be loyal to the nation. As noted, this type of amendment has fallen out of favor since the 1980s, but the underlying critique about the COJ's definition of the relations between government and people has remained consistent.

Many would-be reformers have argued that the COJ's "excessive" protection of fundamental human rights and lack of duties were the result of an outdated understanding of constitutionalism. For instance, Kunitoshi Ōnishi, a scholar of comparative constitutional law and member of the constitutional research committee of the 1950s and 1960s[33] and his student, former vice president of Komazawa University Mitsunori Takehana,[34] criticized this understanding as a relic of the "eighteenth or nineteenth century," incompatible with twentieth- or twenty-first-century democracy. Some drafters readily admit that the contentious relationship and power imbalance between kings and people in Europe at that time necessitated strong protection of the people's rights.[35] However, with the universal acceptance of the democratic model, things had changed, as governments derived their authority from the free will of the sovereign people.[36] In the commentary accompanying its 2013 proposal, the *Sankei Shimbun* explains that the understanding of constitutions as limiting state power was "one-sided," because both the state and the people were also working together in creating a better nation.[37] Conservatives are quick to remind their readership that without state involvement, rights are not worth the paper they are printed on. After all, social rights require state involvement;[38] similarly, particularly in the age of global terrorism, guaranteeing fundamental human rights without the state protecting national security and public safety is impossible.[39] Most commentaries include similar critiques of the liberal view of constitutionalism in one form or another.

The attack on the COJ's alleged failings goes beyond questioning the "outdated" understanding of rights, though. Authors also allege that the COJ was responsible for the undesirable outcomes produced by the excessive emphasis on rights, or as one of the most reactionary proposal authors of the 1950s, Kishio Satomi, put it, "unlimited liberty, evil liberty, liberty of a ruined country."[40] As figure 17.1 shows, Satomi, an influential intellectual of the prewar years, and his draft are hardly representative, yet a majority of authors do reject unlimited rights. An excessive emphasis on rights would lead to "irresponsibility"[41] or worse, the collapse of democracy.[42] In their commentary on the Nippon Kaigi's 2001 proposal, Ōhara and Momochi argue that the "abuse of human rights supremacy" was based on the misconception of rights as claims based on "unruly biological desires."[43] In the United States this was no problem, because Christian morals and ethics exerted sufficient restraint over individual claims. The vast majority of Japanese, however, had never been introduced to these Christian values and thus misunderstood the concept of rights.[44] Other proposals resort to far less bold language to make their case for more duties and restrictions on fundamental human rights, arguing simply that the addition of such stipulations would "curb individualism and egoism and lead to the realization of a cooperative society."[45]

Conservatives have long dismissed the existing public welfare clause in the COJ as inadequate, at least as it is presently interpreted.[46] Even the authors of the relatively moderate third *Yomiuri Shimbun* proposal blame the "chaotic" conditions on all levels of Japanese society, from the state down to the family, on this "vague" term. As a result of this ambiguity, no public spirit could develop.[47] Given this damning criticism, it is logical that most amendment proposals do away with the much maligned phrase. However, once again there is a clear dichotomy between older and more recent proposals. While only half of the proposals published since 1990 retain the controversial phrase, 91% of drafts published in the 1950s and 1960s include it.

The reason for this shift can be found in the term's changing interpretation. During the early postwar years, i.e., during the first wave of amendment proposals, the courts interpreted public welfare as a tool to restrict fundamental human rights. Thus, early would-be reformers saw little need to tinker with it. However, critics saw this usage as reminiscent of the Meiji Constitution, which had allowed for the restriction of fundamental human rights through laws.[48] Thus, over time, public welfare became a tool to navigate inevitable clashes of individuals' rights, as the Courts adopted so-called ad-hoc balancing.[49] As mentioned above, conservatives have had little sympathy for this trend. They felt a different kind of rebalancing was in order. Thus, post-1990 proposal authors have added new specific restrictions of fundamental human rights, most prominently upholding public or constitutional order (55% of proposals published since 1990), others' rights (39%), national safety (32%) and public interest (32%). These figures have increased during the last two decades; since 2010 66% of proposals have made the restriction of rights permissible on the grounds of upholding public or constitutional order and the public interest.

Conservatives are quick to point out that their cause is not a reactionary one;[50] rather, they were trying to align the COJ with international standards. For instance, the aforementioned restrictions on fundamental human rights are often based on the International Covenant on Civil and Political Rights.[51] The Covenant's Article 19 states that "the exercise of . . . rights . . . carries with it special duties and responsibilities. It may therefore be subject to certain restrictions, but these shall only be such as are provided by law and are necessary: (a) For respect of the rights or reputations of others; (b) For the protection of national security or of public order . . . , or of public health or morals."[52]

Similarly, the addition of new rights is framed in the context of international developments in constitutional law.[53] And indeed, a quick look at the CCP database reveals that more rights have been added to constitutions over time.[54]

DISCUSSION: MORE RIGHTS AND MORE DUTIES

As mentioned above, conservatives have taken a "yes, but . . . " approach to more rights. The addition of new rights since the 1990s has been complemented by an increasing number of restrictions and duties. Considering the strongly worded criticism of the allegedly sorry state of postwar society as dominated by egocentrism, the addition of more duties and restrictions is no surprise.

Here the conservative nature of the amendment proposals reveals itself most prominently. If we accept that conservatism is skeptical of liberal individualism, then the need for further restrictions becomes obvious, especially in light of the damage that Chapter 3's stipulations had purportedly already done to all levels of Japanese society, including intermediate organizations such as the family. Conservatives since Edmund Burke have argued that a healthy society depends on "religion and family as forms of collective wisdom" against "extreme individualism that refuses to acknowledge the indispensable part played by social membership in the exercise of free rational choice."[55] Of course, the Christian element is missing from Japan and with the traditional Japanese morality allegedly in horrible shape, laws, e.g., new duties and restrictions on fundamental human rights, were necessary to keep egocentrism in check and prevent democracy from descending into mob rule.[56]

What to make of the addition of new rights then? Critics have argued that their inclusion in the amendment proposals was to sweeten the bitter pill of revising Article 9.[57] After all, for instance, the right to enjoy a decent environment has already been construed based on interpretations of Article 13 and/or 25.[58] At the same time, conservatives are right about international trends. As Elkins et al. put it, "the scope of constitutional rights has expanded from the eighteenth century conception of negative rights to include a panoply of positive rights and so-called third generation rights that belong to groups."[59] As a result, 77% of constitutions worldwide currently include stipulations pertaining to environmental protection, and 85% include privacy rights.[60] This is one manifestation of the transition from a minimalist ("night watchman") state to the more proactive states of the present.[61]

The same is true for the restriction of rights. Unlike with Article 9 and questions about the constitutionality of collective self-defense, almost all scholarly interpretations of the COJ's public welfare clauses acknowledge the possibility of restricting rights to some extent.[62] Internationally too, many constitutions include rights restrictions. Those restrictions are often more specific than the COJ's "public welfare" clause (see, e.g., Article 1 of Canadian Constitution Act of 1982 or Chapter 1, especially Article 19, of the German Basic Law).

In this sense, conservatives are following international trends in calling for clearer restrictions. Yet whether amendment proposal authors really wish to align the COJ with international trends is questionable. In contrast to conservative complaints about the horrid state of Japanese society as a result of unchecked individualism, the Japanese government has for decades faced criticism from the United Nations Commission on Human Rights about concerns over "public welfare" being (ab)used to enable "unlimited" restrictions of rights.[63] In fact, the theory of "inherent, inviolate and universal" rights has not prevented their violation in practice, be it in the case of the victims of industrial pollution (most prominently in the Big Four pollution cases in the 1960s/1970s), leprosy patients suffering from decades of isolation and rights violations, or thousands of women having been subjected to forced abortions based on the old Eugenic Protection Law.[64]

In all those cases, victims found that redress has been hard to come by. Ad hoc balancing may have become more prevalent in Supreme Court rulings, yet its adoption did not result in the Supreme Court striking down more government-imposed rights restrictions:[65] Japan's highest court has voided only nine government acts in its seventy-four years of existence.[66] As Matsui put it, "the Supreme Court has developed a very conservative jurisprudence, which upholds almost every kind of restriction on fundamental human rights."[67] In other words, despite the "vague" public welfare stipulation in the COJ, governments have had little trouble restricting individuals' fundamental human rights. Against this backdrop, there has been a considerable debate among scholars over the means and ends of those restrictions.[68]

Therefore, conservatives may need to be careful what they are wishing for: aligning the COJ with international trends may result in more specific rights restrictions. However, at the same time new, more concrete stipulations in an amended COJ might make it more difficult for the government to actually restrict rights based on those restrictions. Considering the harsh conservative critique of an egocentric, atomized postwar society where restrictions and duties were supposedly MIA, following international trends may not yield the desired results.

NOTES

1. Chaihark Hahm and Sung Ho Kim, *Making We the People: Democratic Constitutional Founding in Postwar Japan and South Korea* (Cambridge: Cambridge University Press, 2015), 67.

2. See e.g., Roger Scruton, *The Meaning of Conservatism* (Basingstoke, UK, and New York: Palgrave Macmillan, 2001), 38–39.

3. Kenneth Mori McElwain and Christian G. Winkler, "What's Unique about the Japanese Constitution? A Comparative and Historical Analysis," *Journal of Japanese Studies* 41 (2) (2015): 249–80.

4. Zachary Elkins, Tom Ginsburg, and James Melton, *The Endurance of National Constitutions* (New York: Cambridge University Press, 2009), 10.

5. McElwain and Winkler, "What's Unique about the Japanese Constitution?"

6. Keigo Komamura and Satoshi Machidori, *Kenpō kaisei no hikaku seijigaku* (Tokyo: Kōbundō, 2016).

7. The reverse course began during the Occupation, as the Cold War heated up and tensions between the center-right government of Yoshida Shigeru backed by GHQ and the left-wing opposition intensified. While some studies primarily treat the reverse course as a reversal of GHQ's policies and objectives—following Ishikawa and Yamaguchi (2010, 61)—we treat the reverse course as a longer series of events. In fact, it intensified after the end of the Occupation (examples include the establishment of the Public Security Intelligence Agency and the passing of the Subversive Activities Prevention Act) and continued until the end of the Kishi administration in 1960. Masumi Ishikawa and Jirō Yamaguchi, *Sengo Nihon seijishi* (Tokyo: Iwanami Shoten, 2010), 61; Christian G. Winkler, "The Evolution of the Conservative Mainstream in Japan," *Japan Forum* 24 (1) (2012): 63–69.

8. In 1954, Hatoyama failed to win support for his electoral reforms, leaving the opposition parties with at least one-third of the seats in both houses of Parliament. As a successful revision requires two-thirds majorities in both houses, the opposition could easily vote down any amendment bill.

9. Winkler, "The Evolution of the Conservative Mainstream in Japan," 61.

10. Shirō Sakaiya, *Kenpō to yoron: Sengo Nihonjin wa kenpō o dō mukiatte kita no ka* (Tokyo: Chikuma Shobō, 2017), 112–13, 123–24.

11. Christian G. Winkler, *The Quest for Japan's New Constitution: An Analysis of Visions and Constitutional Reform Proposals, 1980–2009* (Abingdon, UK: Routledge, 2011), 12.

12. Winkler, *The Quest for Japan's New Constitution*, 14–19, 125.

13. Mainichi Shimbun, "Close-Up 2018: Jimintō sōsai 3 sen (sono 2-shi)," September 21, 2018, Tokyo morning edition, p. 2.

14. McElwain and Winkler, "What's Unique about the Japanese Constitution?," 267.

15. Michael Freeden, *Ideologies and Political Theory* (Oxford: Oxford University Press, 1996), 317–414.

16. This list of amendment proposals is based on Winkler, *The Quest for Japan's New Constitution*, but also includes amendment proposals published since 2010.

17. If an amendment proposal makes no reference to a particular stipulation, and does not explicitly state that the article or paragraph in question should be deleted, I assume that the provision remains unchanged.

18. See Elkins, Ginsburg, and Melton, *The Endurance of National Constitutions*.

19. Winkler, *The Quest for Japan's New Constitution.*

20. Winkler, *The Quest for Japan's New Constitution*, 192.

21. For a detailed discussion see Winkler, "The Evolution of the Conservative Mainstream in Japan."

22. See Osamu Watanabe, *Kenpō "kaisei" no sōten: Shiryō de yomu kaikenron no rekishi* (Tokyo: Junpōsha, 2002), 722; and Winkler, *The Quest for Japan's New Constitution*, 71.

23. Mitsunori Takehana, quoted in Watanabe, *Kenpō "kaisei" no sōten*, 731–32.

24. Setsu Kobayashi, *Kenpō mamotte kuni horobu: Watashitachi no kenpō o naze kaisei shite wa ikenai no ka* (Tokyo: KK Bestsellers, 1992), 140.

25. Mitsunori Takehana, quoted in Watanabe, *Kenpō "kaisei" no sōten*, 732; Kobayashi, *Kenpō mamotte kuni horobu*, 141.

26. Roger Scruton, *Conservatism: An Invitation to the Great Tradition* (New York: All Points Books, 2017), 153.

27. Kenpō Chōsakai, *Kenpō Chōsakai ni okeru kakuiin no iken* (Tokyo; Kenpō Chōsakai Jimukyoku, 1964), 657.

28. Tachiagare Nippon, *Jishu kenpō taikō 'an,'* April 24, 2012, 1.

29. LDP, *Tō no shimei*, November 15, 1955, https://www.jimin.jp/aboutus/declaration/#sec01 (accessed on March 15, 2019).

30. Quoted in Watanabe, *Kenpō "kaisei" no sōten*, 511–12.

31. Quoted in Kenpō Chōsakai, *Kenpō chōsakai shiryō sō 39: Nihonkoku kenpō kaisei shoan* (Tokyo: Kenpō Chōsakai Jimukyoku, 1959), 218.

32. See e.g., Sankei Shimbun, *Kokumin no kenpō* (Tokyo: Sankei Shimbun Shuppansha, 2013), 148.

33. Kunitoshi Ōnishi, quoted in Kenpō Chōsakai, *Kenpō chōsakai shiryō sō 39*, 356.

34. Mitsunori Takehana, *Kenpō kaisei e no shōtai* (Tokyo: Seibundō, 1997), 90.

35. Hisatada Hirose, quoted in Kenpō Chōsakai, *Kenpō Chōsakai ni okeru kakuiin no iken*, 475–76.

36. Ibid.

37. Sankei Shimbun, *Kokumin no kenpō*, 108.

38. Sōken Kaigi, *Shin kenpō sōan: Kuni o tsukuru kenpō o tsukuru* (Tokyo: Ichigeisha, 2006), 36.

39. Yomiuri Shimbunsha, *Kenpō kaisei Yomiuri shian 2004 nen* (Tokyo: Chūō Kōron Shinsha, 2004), 107.

40. Kenpō Chōsakai, *Kenpō chōsakai shiryō sō 39*, 608.

41. Kenpō Kenkyūkai, quoted in Kenpō Chōsakai, *Kenpō chōsakai shiryō sō 39*, 223.

42. Ōnishi in Kenpō Chōsakai, *Kenpō chōsakai shiryō sō 39*, 404.

43. Yasuo Ōhara and Akira Momochi, *Shin kenpō no susume: Nihon saisei no tame ni* (Tokyo: Meiseisha, 2001), 77.

44. Ibid.

45. JCI, *Nihonkoku kenpō sōan*, 2012, http://www.jaycee.or.jp/2018/org/kenpoukaisei/wp-content/uploads/2017/12/日本国憲法草案2012年版.pdf (accessed on March 19, 2019), 3.

46. Winkler, *The Quest for Japan's New Constitution*, 158–60.

47. Yomiuri Shimbunsha, *Kenpō kaisei Yomiuri shian 2004 nen*, 100.

48. Shigenori Matsui, *The Constitution of Japan: A Contextual Analysis* (Oxford and Portland, OR: Hart Publishing, 2011), 30.

49. Matsui, *The Constitution of Japan*, 168–71; Kōichi Aoyagi, "Jinken to kōkyō no Fukushi," in *Kenpō no sōten*, ed. Makoto Ōishi and Kenji Ishikawa (Tokyo: Yūhikaku, 2008), 68–69.

50. See e.g., Liberal Party, quoted in Watanabe, *Kenpō "kaisei" no sōten*, 512.

51. See e.g., Taku Yamasaki, *Kenpō kaisei: Dōgi kokka o Mezashite* (Tokyo: Seisansei Shuppan, 2001), 99; Winkler, *The Quest for Japan's New Constitution*, 159.

52. OHCHR, "International Covenant on Civil and Political Rights," 1976, https://www.ohchr.org/en/professionalinterest/pages/ccpr.aspx.

53. Osamu Nishi, *Yoku wakaru Heisei kenpō kōza* (Tokyo: TBS Britannica, 1995), 202–6.

54. Elkins, Ginsburg, and Melton, *The Endurance of National Constitutions*, 86; McElwain and Winkler, "What's Unique about the Japanese Constitution?," 264.

55. Scruton, *Conservatism*, 45.

56. See e.g., Ōnishi, in Kenpō Chōsakai, *Kenpō chōsakai shiryō sō 39*, 404.

57. E.g., Watanabe, *Kenpō "kaisei" no sōten*, quoted in Winkler, *The Quest for Japan's New Constitution*, 168.

58. Makoto Itō, *Kenpō*, 3rd ed. (Tokyo: Kōbundō, 2007), 387.

59. Elkins, Ginsburg, and Melton, *The Endurance of National Constitutions*, 86.

60. Christian G. Winkler, "The Amendment Debate through Public Eyes" (Presentation at the Conference "Debating Japan's Constitution: On the Streets, in Parliament, and in the Region," Harvard University, November 2017).

61. See e.g., Toshifumi Sowa, "Kenri no hen'yō to kōhōgaku no Kadai," *Kōhō Kenkyū* 78 (2016): 25–46.

62. Kazuhiko Matsumoto, "Kōkyō no Fukushi," *Kōhō Kenkyū* 67 (2005): 136–47.

63. Makoto Kubo, "Naze, Nihonkoku kenpō 'kōkyō no fukushi' gainen ga kokuren jinken kikan de mondai to sareru no ka," *Osaka Sangyō Daigaku keizai ronshū* 18 (1) (2016): 1–27.

64. See e.g., Kubo, "Naze, Nihonkoku kenpō 'kōkyō no fukushi' gainen ga kokuren jinken kikan de mondai to sareru no ka."

65. Matsui, *The Constitution of Japan*, 169.

66. Nobutoshi Ashibe and Kazuyuki Takahashi, *Kenpō*, 7th ed. (Tokyo: Iwanami Shoten, 2019), 399.

67. Matsui, *The Constitution of Japan*, 229.

68. For a detailed account, see Matsumoto, "Kōkyō no Fukushi."

REFERENCES

Aoyagi, Kōichi. "Jinken to kōkyō no fukushi." In *Kenpō no sōten*, edited by Makoto Ōishi and Kenji Ishikawa, 68–69. Tokyo: Yūhikaku, 2008.

Ashibe, Nobutoshi, and Kazuyuki Takahashi. *Kenpō*. 7th ed. Tokyo: Iwanami Shoten, 2019.

Elkins, Zachary, Tom Ginsburg, and James Melton. *The Endurance of National Constitutions*. New York: Cambridge University Press, 2009.

Freeden, Michael. *Ideologies and Political Theory*. Oxford: Oxford University Press, 1996.

Hahm, Chaihark, and Sung Ho Kim. *Making We the People: Democratic Constitutional Founding in Postwar Japan and South Korea*. Cambridge: Cambridge University Press, 2015.

Ishikawa, Masumi, and Jirō Yamaguchi. *Sengo Nihon seijishi*. Tokyo: Iwanami Shoten, 2010.

Itō, Makoto. *Kenpō*. 3rd edition. Tokyo: Kōbundō, 2007.

JCI. *Nihonkoku kenpō sōan*. 2012. http://www.jaycee.or.jp/2018/org/kenpoukaisei/wp-content/uploads/2017/12/日本国憲法草案2012年版.pdf (accessed on March 19, 2019).

Kenpō Chōsakai. *Kenpō chōsakai shiryō sō 39: Nihonkoku kenpō kaisei shoan*. Tokyo: Kenpō Chōsakai Jimukyoku, 1959.

Kenpō Chōsakai. *Kenpo¯Chōsakai ni okeru kakuiin no iken*. Tokyo: Kenpō Chōsakai Jimukyoku, 1964.

Kobayashi, Setsu. *Kenpō mamotte kuni horobu: Watashitachi no kenpō o naze kaisei shite wa ikenai no ka*. Tokyo: KK Bestsellers, 1992.

Komamura, Keigo, and Satoshi Machidori. *Kenpō kaisei no hikaku seijigaku*. Tokyo: Kōbundō, 2016.

Kubo, Makoto. "Naze, Nihonkoku kenpō 'kōkyō no fukushi' gainen ga kokuren jinken kikan de mondai to sareru no ka." *Osaka Sangyō Daigaku keizai ronshū* 18 (1) (2016): 1–27.

LDP. *Tō no shimei*. November 15, 1955. https://www.jimin.jp/aboutus/declaration/#sec01 (accessed on March 15, 2019).

Mainichi Shimbun. "Close-Up 2018: Jimintō sōsai 3 sen (sono 2-shi)." September 21, 2018. Tokyo morning edition, p. 2.

Matsui, Shigenori. *The Constitution of Japan: A Contextual Analysis*. Oxford and Portland, OR: Hart Publishing, 2011.

Matsumoto, Kazuhiko. "Kōkyō no Fukushi." *Kōhō Kenkyū* 67 (2005): 136–47.

McElwain, Kenneth Mori, and Christian G. Winkler. "What's Unique about the Japanese Constitution? A Comparative and Historical Analysis." *Journal of Japanese Studies* 41 (2) (2015): 249–80.

Moore, Ray A., and Donald L. Robinson. *Partners for Democracy: Crafting the New Japanese State under MacArthur*. New York: Oxford University Press. 2002.

Nishi, Osamu. *Yoku wakaru Heisei kenpō kōza*. Tokyo: TBS Britannica, 1995.

Ōhara, Yasuo, and Akira Momochi. *Shin kenpō no susume: Nihon saisei no tame ni*. Tokyo: Meiseisha, 2001.

OHCHR. "International Covenant on Civil and Political Rights," 1976, https://www.ohchr.org/en/professionalinterest/pages/ccpr.aspx.

Sakaiya, Shirō. *Kenpō to yoron: Sengo Nihonjin wa kenpō o dō mukiatte kita no ka*. Tokyo: Chikuma Shobō, 2017.

Sankei Shimbun. *Kokumin no kenpō*. Tokyo: Sankei Shimbun Shuppansha, 2013.

Scruton, Roger. *The Meaning of Conservatism*. Basingstoke, UK, and New York: Palgrave Macmillan, 2001.

Scruton, Roger. *Conservatism: An Invitation to the Great Tradition*. New York: All Points Books, 2017.

Sōken Kaigi. *Shin kenpō sōan: Kuni o tsukuru kenpō o tsukuru*. Tokyo: Ichigeisha, 2006.

Sowa, Toshifumi. "Kenri no hen'yō to kōhōgaku no Kadai." *Kōhō Kenkyū* 78 (2016): 25–46.

Tachiagare, Nippon. *Jishu kenpō taikō 'an'*. April 24, 2012.

Takehana, Mitsunori. *Kenpō kaisei e no shōtai*. Tokyo: Seibundō, 1997.

Watanabe, Osamu. *Kenpō "kaisei" no sōten: Shiryō de yomu kaikenron no rekishi*. Tokyo: Junpōsha, 2002.

Winkler, Christian G. *The Quest for Japan's New Constitution: An Analysis of Visions and Constitutional Reform Proposals, 1980–2009*. Abingdon, UK: Routledge, 2011.

———. "The Evolution of the Conservative Mainstream in Japan," *Japan Forum* 24 (1) (2012): 51–73.

———. "The Amendment Debate through Public Eyes." Presentation at the Conference "Debating Japan's Constitution: On the Streets, in Parliament, and in the Region," Harvard University, November 2017.

Yamasaki, Taku. *Kenpō kaisei: Dōgi kokka o mezashite*. Tokyo: Seisansei Shuppan, 2001.

Yomiuri Shimbunsha. *Kenpō kaisei Yomiuri shian 2004 nen*. Tokyo: Chūō Kōron Shinsha, 2004.

Chapter Eighteen

Reflections on Part IV

Timothy S. George

The three defining characteristics of the Constitution of Japan are the principles of popular sovereignty, popular or human rights, and pacifism. When the new Constitution took effect on May 3, 1947, Article 1 transformed the Japanese people from subjects to citizens "with whom resides sovereign power" and made the formerly sovereign emperor a mere "symbol." At the same time, under Article 9 "the Japanese people forever renounce[d] war as a sovereign right of the nation." These dramatic changes imposed by the occupying Americans were intended to be explicit renunciations of Japan's recent history, and to prevent its recurrence. Neither principle, however, was entirely without precedent in Japan's modern political marketplace of ideas, but neither could be given life or meaning except through ongoing definition and redefinition through practice.

Debates have swirled around these principles since before the Constitution was ratified by the Diet on November 3, 1946. Conservatives have criticized it as having a foreign or American "smell" and abandoning traditional values, and pushed for strengthening the role of the emperor and amending Article 9.[1] Progressives, as well as drafters of the Constitution including Beate Sirota Gordon, have insisted that it gave the Japanese people what they had long wanted but had never been able to force the elites to grant them.[2] They point to the fact that the pathology that the Occupation designed the new Constitution to cure had only dominated during the "Dark Valley," the 15 years when the government was dominated by the military.

They note periods of cooperative, internationalist diplomacy earlier in the twentieth century, particularly the "Shidehara diplomacy" while Kijūrō Shidehara, known for his opposition to intervention in China, served as foreign minister (1924–27, 1929–31). Prior to the "Dark Valley," Japan was a founding member of the League of Nations (1920), agreed to naval arms limitations in the Washington Conference (1921–1922), signed the Kellog-Briand Pact renouncing war as a means of settling international disputes (1928), and accepted further naval arms limitations in the London Naval Treaty (1930).

They also point to examples suggesting demand for, and real possibilities of, expanded political rights for subjects, including the Freedom and Popular Rights Movement in the 1870s and 1880s and the period of "Taishō Democracy" from about 1905 to 1932.[3] For most of the period from 1918 to 1932, party leaders served as prime ministers, and the two leading parties alternated in power, suggesting that a British-style constitutional monarchy might be possible under the Meiji Constitution.

These trends in foreign and domestic affairs were reversed, however, by the Manchurian Incident of September 1931 and Japan's subsequent conquest of Manchuria, and by the May 1932 assassination of Tsuyoshi Inukai, the last party leader to serve as premier. Although regular elections continued to be held and martial law was never declared, the military dominated. Repression of dissent was stepped up under the Peace Preservation Law, and foreign policy turned fully unilateralist and aggressive, resulting in disaster and millions of deaths in East and Southeast Asia and the Pacific.

Erik Esselstrom's essay describes how under those conditions, while Japan brutally occupied much of China, some Japanese progressive antiwar activists, along with some soldiers captured by Chinese Communist troops, found in China both refuge and inspiration. The internationalism and pacifism they advocated during and after the war were core principles of Japan's postwar constitution. Esselstrom makes two very important contributions to the debates over the Constitution by taking the focus away from its drafting by Americans. First, he shows us the links between the domestic struggle during the "Dark Valley" for political rights by leftists and progressives, and the articulation of concepts of international human rights that were not alien "Western values" but were inspired by what those activists saw and learned in China. This is evidence that the Constitution of Japan did in fact reflect values that Japanese had demanded, and not only in the context of the Freedom and Peoples Rights Movement or Taishō Democracy. Second, this story brings China into the constitutional debate as an inspiration for internationalism and pacifism. This is an important reminder that China has not always been seen as it is today by many, as a potential military threat justifying arguments for amending Article 9.

After May 3, 1947—or certainly after April 28, 1952, when the Occupation ended and national sovereignty was regained—it was an open question whether the Japanese people would retain the Constitution, make it their own, and use their rights and freedoms to make themselves truly sovereign. Laws can change in a day, transforming subjects into citizens overnight. But what would define and redefine the meaning and extent of democracy and popular sovereignty for most Japanese over the coming decades was their own thought and behavior. In the early postwar period, Masao Maruyama emphasized the need for citizens to internalize democratic values by developing and acting with democratic "subjectivity," and not leaving politics to the politicians.[4]

Saburo Horikawa's essay on the historic canal preservation movement in Otaru offers a case study of such democratic activism, and he notes similar strategies in the protests by SEALDs (Students Emergency Action for Liberal Democracy) in 2012. The Otaru activists were defending a historic canal and the buildings lining it, while the SEALDs activists portrayed themselves as defending the Constitution and democracy itself. Yet in both cases they claimed to be defending something that belonged to them as citizens, not to politicians and bureaucrats. And both, like many citizens groups in environmental and other movements since the 1960s, were careful to avoid hierarchical structures and any connection with the Socialist and especially Communist parties. They portrayed themselves as groups composed of average citizens, groups which anyone could and should join if they shared their goals. Both might be said to have followed Maruyama's dictum of not leaving politics to professional politicians. Neither illustrates a steady trend toward increasingly well-established popular sovereignty. Yet they do suggest that citizen action can at times make a difference, and has left a creative legacy on which citizens can and do continue to draw.

In the 1950s Japan's conservative leaders were able to roll back some Occupation reforms, in what Christian Winkler's essay describes as a continuation of the Occupation-era "reverse course." They partly recentralized the education and police systems and established the Japan Self-Defense Forces. Yet they never had the two-thirds majority in both houses of the Diet required to initiate an amendment to the Constitution, so they were unable to revise Article 9 or strengthen the role of the emperor. Article 9 in particular has been the main target of conservative proposals to amend Japan's progressive constitution and has been the focus of most analysis of those proposals.[5]

Winkler's essay complements such studies by looking at amendment proposals involving rights. One might expect the LDP and other conservative groups to wish to take steps back toward the Meiji Constitution by adding restrictions on rights and specifying duties of citizens. Winkler's careful study shows that they did push such proposals, but less so over time, and interestingly he also shows that they have proposed a number of "new rights" in recent decades. One might wonder if proposals to add new rights such as privacy or environmental rights could be intended to serve as Trojan horses, persuading progressives to accept the idea of amending the Constitution in order to help clear the way for amendments affecting the role of the military or the emperor. Only time will tell.

NOTES

1. See Helen Hardacre's essay in this volume.

2. See Beate Sirota Gordon, *The Only Woman in the Room: A Memoir* (Tokyo: Kodansha, 1997).

3. See Irokawa Daikichi, *The Culture of the Meiji Period*, translation edited by Marius B. Jansen (Princeton, NJ: Princeton University Press, 1985); and Andrew Gordon, *Labor and Imperial Democracy in Prewar Japan* (Berkeley: University of California Press, 1991).

4. See Andrew E. Barshay, "Imagining Democracy in Postwar Japan: Reflections on Maruyama Masao and Modernism," *Journal of Japanese Studies* 18.2 (Summer 1992): 365–406.

5. See the essays by Keigo Komamura, Tatsuhiko Yamamoto, and Yoshihide Soeya in this volume.

Conclusion

Timothy S. George and Franziska Seraphim

As this book goes to press, we are a year into the Covid-19 pandemic, and Prime Minister Shinzō Abe unexpectedly announced his resignation four days after he broke the record as the longest-sitting Prime Minister in Japan's modern history. 2020 was the year on which Abe had staked his political legacy: to accomplish the first revision of the Constitution since its promulgation in 1947 and simultaneously demonstrate Japan's resilience and strength to the world by hosting the 32nd Olympic Summer Games. But along came a tiny virus that proved resistant to his ambitions and strong enough to threaten millions of lives, sink already vulnerable economies, and play football with carefully planned events worldwide, big and small. Abe dodged the most immediate bullet by having the Games postponed until summer 2021 rather than canceling them. And while he may have hoped against hope that the year he gained might be enough time to gain the required two-thirds majority vote in each house of the Diet before putting constitutional amendment to a national referendum, illness forced him to leave that task to his successors.

Ever since Prime Minister Jun'ichirō Koizumi put constitutional revision back near the top of the governmental agenda in 2001, the issue has waxed and waned in the public media, repeatedly outcompeted by publicly perceived crises that demanded full attention. But even when overshadowed by more immediate issues, it has persisted as an actively pursued political goal of rightist LDP administrations and Shinzō Abe in particular. The current pandemic and its related economic and civil rights threats are dire enough to displace public attention from the legal and political morass of constitutional revision. But even so, Abe continued chipping away at constraints to the national security framework without a move to change Article 9, stressing the need for proactive defense against military, economic, and public health threats.

In June 2020, the Cabinet ministers of the National Security Council announced a decision to withdraw from the U.S.-developed land-based Aegis Ashore interceptor missile system, citing spiraling costs and the safety of local host communities. In fact, this will be the first rewriting of Japan's National Security Strategy, signaling greater independence from the American military umbrella by augmenting Japan's own ballistic missile defense system and its readiness to attack enemy military bases instead of depending on the U.S. military to assure Japan's security. It also looks toward a post-corona world in which national security includes "strengthening the supply chain for medical care products and equipment as well as measures to handle future pandemics, including restrictions on entry into Japan," according to the *Asahi shinbun*.[1]

In Japan, as in many other countries, people are rightfully suspicious about government legislation rammed through quickly under the mantle of a coronavirus-induced national emergency. The student protest movement against the dismantling of Hong Kong's constitutional sovereignty and Beijing's doubling-down via the National Security Law of June 2020 kept the fate of civic activism against constitutional revision frighteningly in the public limelight. In Japan meanwhile, the government's border restrictions to curb the spread of Covid-19 singled out foreign residents and placed them on a strict reentry ban irrespective of testing to an extent hardly seen elsewhere. Foreign resident professionals, especially those employed in academia, led an international petition movement protesting this selective ban, and the Japanese government eventually responded by loosening the restrictions.

Rights-based activism affects all areas of political life, and the Constitution demarcates the rights of citizens and the duties of the state. Perhaps most fundamentally, then, it is "revisionism" itself—the idea that newly relevant interpretations and new demands in political life ought to be tackled by changing the constitution itself—that is at stake for the nationalist administration, even if precisely this option seems least likely to succeed. Opinion polls have consistently shown a healthy majority of voters mostly content to leave the Constitution as it is, or at least not ranking its amendment high on their list of immediate concerns. This conundrum raises questions that place debates and civic activism at the center of the historical, transdisciplinary, and comparative inquiry offered here. The contributors to this collection tell us a great deal about Japan's "constitution" in the broadest sense of the word, and the ways in which it has been a driver of political life since the end of World War II, from party politics to the roles of citizens, and of Japan's place in Asia and the world. In this book we have endeavored to describe, historicize, and analyze this political landscape.

We are not futurologists, and none of the contributors to this collection tells us how, when, or whether the debates over constitutional revision will be resolved in the future. All can, however, suggest some things to which we should pay attention. Will courts continue to refuse to judge controversial questions such as the constitutionality of Article 9? Will more far-reaching changes be realized through passing laws such as those dealing with religion, gender parity, or education, or through reinterpretation such as has been done with Article 9, without actually amending the Constitution? If the near future is anything like the recent past, constitutional revision will remain a goal, or a political tool, of nationalist politicians, quite possibly aided by provocations from China or North Korea.

Still, the majority of citizens will likely remain unpersuaded that revision is urgently needed. Activists arguably have even more tools at their disposal, and those tools are continuously evolving. They will continue to draw on past patterns of protest while finding innovative ways to use social media, as did SEALDs and the Otaru activists. Their organizational connections will unfold at different scales, from local to global. Contextual frameworks will certainly change, as we have seen with the pandemic, offering up new arguments for whether or how to revise the Constitution. Yet so far, even with such changes, the overall power constellation in the debates about amendment has remained impressively stable.

NOTES

1. "Japan to Revise Security Strategy with Halt to Aegis Ashore System," *Asahi shinbun*, June 20, 2020. http://www.asahi.com/ajw/articles/13474622.

Appendix

THE ANPO STRUGGLE (FOR CHAPTER 1)

The Anpo is a Japanese abbreviation of *Nichibei anzen hoshō jōyaku* (the U.S.-Japan Security Treaty). The Anpo struggle is the generic name for a series of protests against the revision of the Treaty, in particular, against the forcible tactics by Prime Minister Kishi Nobusuke of pushing the revision through the Diet. The 1960 Anpo struggle (1959–1960) is widely recognized as the largest civic anti-government/anti-America protests in postwar Japan, where college students and labor unions played a main role and more than 4.5 million people in total participated and mobilized. After the streamrolling of the bill of the Treaty's renewal followed by Kishi's resignation, the struggle steadly began to quiet down, and the protest on campuses or in the streets receded in the mid-1970s onward. On the other hand, the student sects increasingly became radical and even violent as they became isolated from public opinion.

FIRST-PAST-THE-POST SYSTEM (FOR CHAPTER 2)

Also known as the Single-Member District system, or as the "Small District" system in Japanese, the First-Past-the-Post (FPTP) system replaced the "Medium District" system, commonly known as the Multi-Member District system, to elect the members of the Japanese House of Representatives (Lower House) in 1994 and was put to use for the first time in the 1996 election. The revision of the electoral system brought about an important transformation in the dynamics of party politics in Japan. For one, the FPTP system has had the effect of centralizing power in the hands of the leader of the ruling Liberal

Democratic Party (LDP), who is also often the Prime Minister of Japan. Previously, under the Multi-Member District system, the LDP typically fielded multiple candidates in the same electoral district, each backed by different intra-party factions, in order to secure an overall majority of seats as a party. While this resulted in rampant factionalism, it also allowed for a greater degree of pluralism in the ruling party. For another, the adoption of the FPTP system has enabled the LDP (and once the Democratic Party of Japan in 2009) to win a large majority of seats without a majority of the votes cast. The disproportionality between the votes and seats is significantly greater in the FPTP system than in the Multi-Member District system. The voter turnout fell sharply in 1993, and it has on average remained significantly lower since.

Index

Page numbers of figures and tables are italicized.

About the Editors

Helen Hardacre is the founder of the Constitutional Revision in Japan Research Program of the Edwin O. Reischauer Institute of Japanese Studies, Harvard University, and, along with Professor Keigo Komamura (Keio University), co-director of a joint research project, *The 'Constitution' of Postwar Japan*. Her publications include *The Religion of Japan's Korean Minority* (1984), *Lay Buddhism in Contemporary Japan: Reiyukai Kyodan* (1984), *Kurozumikyo and the New Religions of Japan* (1986), *Shinto and the State, 1868–1988* (1989), *Marketing the Menacing Fetus in Japan* (1997), and *Shinto, A History* (2016).

Timothy S. George is professor of History at the University of Rhode Island. His research interests include Japan's environmental and local history. His publications include *Minamata: Pollution and the Struggle for Democracy in Postwar Japan* (2001), "Tanaka Shōzō's Vision of an Alternative Constitutional Modernity for Japan" (in *Public Spheres, Private Lives in Modern Japan, 1600–1950*, 2005), "Toroku: Mountain Dreams, Chemical Nightmares" (in *Japan at Nature's Edge*, 2013), *Japanese History and Culture from Ancient to Modern Times: Seven Basic Bibliographies* (co-authored with John W. Dower, second ed., 1995), and *Japan since 1945: From Postwar to Post-Bubble* (co-edited with Christopher Gerteis, 2013).

Keigo Komamura is a Professor of Law and Vice President of Keio University. He earned his BA in Law, LLM, and SJD from Keio University. His fields of study include constitutional law, free speech and law of journalism, human rights theory, and Japan's contemporary debate over constitutional revision. His recent works include *Kenpososho no Gendaiteki Tenkai* [Contemporary Turn of Constitutional Law Litigation] (2013), *Tekusuto tositeno*

Hanketsu [Reading the Opinions of the Court as a Text] (with Taro Kogayu et al.) (2016), and "Constitution and Narrative in the Age of Crisis in Japanese Politics," *Washington International Law Journal* 26, no. 1 (2017). From 2009 to 2010, he was affiliated with the Weatherhead Center Program on U.S.-Japan Relations and the Reischauer Institute at Harvard University, and he is currently a member of the Advisory Council for the Constitutional Revision Research Project at the Reischauer Institute.

Franziska Seraphim is Associate Professor of modern Japanese history at Boston College and director of the Asian Studies Program. She is the author of *War Memory and Social Politics in Japan, 1945–2005* (Harvard Asia Center Press, 2006) and a member of the working group on constitutional revision in Japan at Harvard University's Reischauer Institute for Japanese Studies directed by Helen Hardacre since its beginning. Her current book project is a comparative legal geography of Japanese and German war criminals convicted in Allied courts across Asia, Europe, and Eurasia from the 1940s to the 1960s. Most recently she held fellowships at the Davis Center at Princeton University and the National Humanities Center. She received her PhD in Japanese history at Columbia University.

About the Contributors

Weitseng Chen is Associate Professor at the National University of Singapore (NUS) Faculty of Law and specializes in comparative Chinese law in Greater China, with an emphasis on law and development. He holds degrees from National Taiwan University College of Law and a JSD from Yale Law School and was a Hewlett Fellow at Stanford University before joining NUS. His recently published books include *The Beijing Consensus? How China has Changed Western Ideas of Law and Economic Development* (2017) and *"Authoritarian Legality in Asia: Formation, Development, and Transition"* (2020).

Erik Esselstrom is Professor of Japanese and Chinese history at the University of Vermont. He is the author of *Crossing Empire's Edge: Foreign Ministry Police and Japanese Expansionism in Northeast Asia* (2008) and *That Distant Country Next Door: Popular Japanese Perceptions of Mao's China* (2019). He has worked collaboratively with Japanese, Chinese, and Korean scholars at both Waseda University and Kyoto University in Japan, and also taught and conducted research as a visiting faculty member in the Graduate School of Law at Hitotsubashi University near Tokyo.

Saburo Horikawa is Professor of Sociology at Hōsei University in Tokyo. He received his PhD in sociology from Keio University. In 2018, his thirty-three years of fieldwork in Otaru, Japan, culminated in the publication of *Machinami hozon undō no ronri to kiketsu* from the University of Tokyo Press. This book has gone on to win three major academic awards in Japan, and the English version (*Why Place Matters*) is published by Springer Nature. He was previously a Visiting Scholar at the Edwin O. Reischauer Institute of Japanese Studies at Harvard University.

Sung Ho Kim teaches political and constitutional theory in the Department of Political Science, Yonsei University, Seoul, Korea. He was Special Guest Professor of Law at Keio University, Kim Koo Visiting Professor of Government at Harvard University, and Visiting Scholar at the Harvard-Yenching Institute. He is the author of *Max Weber's Politics of Civil Society* and (with Chaihark Hahm) *Making We the People: Democratic Constitutional Founding in Postwar Japan and South Korea* (both published by Cambridge University Press). His articles have appeared in, among others, *History of Political Thought, I·CON: International Journal of Constitutional Law, Journal of Democracy, Max Weber Studies, Political Theory, Review of Politics*, and *Stanford Encyclopedia of Philosophy*. He received his PhD in political science from the University of Chicago and the Leo Strauss Award of the American Political Science Association.

Rintaro Kuramochi is a lawyer who received his bachelor's degree in legal studies from Keio University and his JD from Chuo University Law School. He specializes in constitutional law issues for the Japan Federation of Bar Associations and is a partner of the Tokyo-based law firm, Next. His specialties also include, legal support for start-up businesses, general business law, and labor law issues such as work-life balance reform. Mr. Kuramochi was an expert witness at the public hearing for the Special Committee on the National Security Legislation in the House of Representatives of Japan in 2015, a speaker for the World Forum for Democracy in 2015, and participated in the U.S. State Department's International Visitor Leadership Program in 2017. Currently he is a regular columnist for the *Asahi Shimbun* column "Ronza," and a policy advisor for some members of the Diet of Japan. He has published various articles and books, such as *2015 nen Anpo: Kokkai no Uchi to Soto de* [The 2015 National Security Legislation: Inside/Outside of the Diet] (Iwanami Shoten, 2015), *Gō-sen Kenpō Dōjō* [Gō-sen Constitution Dojo] (Mainichi Shimbun Publishing, 2018), and *Liberal-no-teki-ha-liberal-ni-ari* [Liberal's Opponents are Liberal] (Chikuma shobō, 2020).

Levi McLaughlin is Associate Professor at the Department of Philosophy and Religious Studies at North Carolina State University. He received his PhD from Princeton University after previous study at the University of Tokyo, and he holds a BA and MA in East Asian Studies from the University of Toronto. Levi is co-author and co-editor of *Kōmeitō: Politics and Religion in Japan* (2014) and co-editor of the special issue "Salvage and Salvation: Religion and Disaster Relief in Asia" (*Asian Ethnology*, June 2016). He is author of *Soka Gakkai's Human Revolution: The Rise of a Mimetic Nation in Modern Japan* (2019).

Mari Miura is Professor of Political Science, Faculty of Law, Sophia University, with a PhD from University of California, Berkeley. She is the author of *Welfare Through Work: Conservative Ideas, Partisan Dynamics, and Social Protection in Japan* (2012), editor of *Japan's Women Representatives* (in Japanese, 2016), and co-editor of *Gender Quotas in Comparative Perspectives: Understanding the Increase in Women Representatives* (in Japanese, 2014). Co-founder of the "Academy for Gender Parity," which provides training programs for young women to run for office, she received the Wilma Rule Award (IPSA Award for the Best Research on Gender and Politics) in 2018.

Koichi Nakano is Dean and Professor of Political Science at the Faculty of Liberal Arts, Sophia University. He received a BA in philosophy (Tokyo), BA in philosophy and politics (Oxford), and MA and PhD in politics (Princeton). He specializes in the comparative politics of advanced industrial democracies, particularly Japan and Europe, and in political theory. In English, he has published articles in the *Journal of Japanese Studies*, *Asian Survey*, the *Pacific Review*, *West European Politics*, and *Governance*; a single-authored book entitled *Party Politics and Decentralization in Japan and France: When the Opposition Governs* (Routledge, 2010); and two co-edited volumes, *Disasters and Social Crisis in Contemporary Japan: Political, Religious, and Sociocultural Responses*, with Mark R. Mullins (2015) and *The Democratic Party of Japan: Challenges and Failures*, with Yoichi Funabashi (2016). In Japanese, his publications include *Ukeikasuru Nihon Seiji* [Rightward Shift of Japanese Politics] (2015), *Sengo Nihon no Kokka Hoshushugi: Naimu/Jichi Kanryo no Kiseki* [Postwar State Conservatism in Japan: A Study of the Bureaucrats of the Ministry of Home Affairs] (2013).

Yoshihide Soeya is Professor Emeritus of Keio University, where he taught political science and international relations at the Faculty of Law for 32 years and served as the Director of the Institute of East Asian Studies and of its Center for Contemporary Korean Studies. He also served on advisory committees in Japan's Prime Minister's Office, the Ministry of Defense, and the Ministry of Foreign Affairs between 1999 and 2013. He received his PhD at the University of Michigan. Recent publications in English include book chapters on the rise of China in Asia, the evolution of Japan's public diplomacy, and a co-edited book (with Masayuki Tadokoro and David A. Welch), *Japan as a "Normal Country"? A Country in Search of its Place in the World* (2011).

Makiko Ueda is a research assistant working on the Constitutional Revision in Japan Research Project at the Edwin O. Reischauer Institute of Japanese Studies, Harvard University, and a fellow at Japan MOT (Management of Technology) Association. Her publications include "An Idea of Postwar Japan: Hitoshi Ashida and Japanese Liberalism" (2011, translated by Rikki Kersten) and *Chitsujo Hendō to Nihon Gaikō: Kakudai to Shūshuku no 70-nen* [International Order Change and Japanese Diplomacy: 70 Years of Expansion and Contraction] (2016, coauthored).

Christian G. Winkler is Associate Professor in the Faculty of Law at Seinan Gakuin University in Fukuoka. His main research interest is postwar political thought and its influences on modern Japanese society and politics, especially the debates about amendment of the Constitution of Japan. He is the author of *The Quest for Japan's New Constitution: An Analysis of Visions and Constitutional Reform Proposals, 1980–2009* (2011).

Tatsuhiko Yamamoto is Professor of Law at Keio University and Deputy Director of the Keio University Global Research Institute (KGRI). He earned his BA in law, LLM, and PhD (law) from Keio University. Professor Yamamoto's fields of study include constitutional law, privacy law, and the theory of popular sovereignty. He has written extensively on Japanese constitutional law and information privacy law, including *Kenpougaku no Yukue* [The Future of the Constitutional Theory] (co-editor with George Shishido and Masahiro Sogabe, 2016); *Privacy no Kenri wo Kangaeru* [The Right to Privacy in Japan] (2017); *AI to Kenpō* [AI and the Constitution] (editor, Nihon Keizai Shinbun Sha, 2018). In English, he has published "Restricting Profiling: Current Regulations in the United States, Europe, and Japan," *USJI Voice* 40 (2019); "The Constitution and Constitutional Education in Japan," in *How Public Law Is Taught in Asian Universities* (KEIGLAD, 2020). He has been working for several government committees, including the Conference toward AI Network Society organized by the Ministry of Internal Affairs and Communications, Japan.

www.ingramcontent.com/pod-product-compliance
Lightning Source LLC
Chambersburg PA
CBHW022259280326
41932CB00010B/919